THE LIFE

OF

LOUIS KOSSUTH

L. Kossuth
GOVERNOR OF HUNGARY

THE LIFE

OF

LOUIS KOSSUTH,

GOVERNOR OF HUNGARY,

INCLUDING NOTICES OF THE MEN AND SCENES
OF THE HUNGARIAN REVOLUTION;

TO WHICH IS ADDED AN APPENDIX CONTAINING HIS

PRINCIPAL SPEECHES, &c.

WITH AN INTRODUCTION, BY HORACE GREELEY.

BY PHINEAS C. HEADLEY

BOOKS FOR LIBRARIES PRESS
FREEPORT, NEW YORK

First Published 1852
Reprinted 1971

DB937
H43

INTERNATIONAL STANDARD BOOK NUMBER:
0-8369-5768-7

LIBRARY OF CONGRESS CATALOG CARD NUMBER:
78-154152

PRINTED IN THE UNITED STATES OF AMERICA

TO

COUNT FRANCIS PULSZKY,

THE HUNGARIAN HERO AND STATESMAN,

WHOSE DEVOTION TO HIS COUNTRY

HAS MADE HIM A FIT COMPANION FOR

The Immortal Kossuth,

THIS VOLUME,

AS A TRIFLING TOKEN OF THE HIGHEST RESPECT AND REGARD,

IS GRATEFULLY INSCRIBED BY

THE AUTHOR.

PREFACE.

THE advent of Kossuth in the United States, and the intense interest universally felt in the cause which he represents, create a demand for an American biography of the distinguished man, and a condensed history of the struggle that summoned him to the council-chamber of State, and to the field of battle. Notices of both have appeared, and excellent books on Hungary are accessible to all. But many current sketches of the Magyar Chief, and the scenes through which he passed, are incorrect. Besides, the people have neither time nor inclination to study the annals of any nation, in detached fragments, or elaborate detail; a comprehensive view of great events and men, is the more popular and useful narrative. The volume now offered to the reader is designed to meet this want. Not only were a number of foreign works consulted, among which the interesting Memoirs of Count

Pulszky and his Lady, and the Annals of Klapka, may be particularly mentioned; but other important facts were furnished by the Count, and by permission the volume is dedicated to him, though it was not possible to submit the pages to his eye for correction.

The brief Introduction by Mr. Greeley is a spirited glance at the mission of gifted leaders in revolutionary times. A large part of the Appendix was compiled from sources approved by the noble Hungarian to whom allusion has been made.

This volume is therefore added to the records of a singular and brave people, whose pantings after freedom have an impersonation in LOUIS KOSSUTH, with the hope that while it is not devoid of interest, it may elevate the aims of youth, and teach again the lesson that *goodness* alone can confer immortality—that *moral excellence* embalms the memory of even humble benefactors of a struggling race.

INTRODUCTION.

GREAT men, if not made, are at least proved by great occasions. But for the latter, we might possess but could not certainly recognize and assuredly distinguish the former. How many a " mute, inglorious Milton" has gone down to the grave unheard of beyond the narrow area of his village or neighborhood, for want of those opportunities which proclaim the Patriot and Hero, we may not know; but we may judge approximately from the fact that a spirit of popular resistance to tyranny has very rarely been crushed for want of a fit and competent leader of the aroused, determined masses. The names of Leonidas, of Arminius, of Tell, Washington, Kosciusko, Hofer, Palafox and hundreds of others are inseparably blended with the great struggles whereof they were severally the chiefs, and they serve as a cheering assurance to oppressed nations throughout all time that the arms of a stout-hearted and despot-hating people, when nerved by bold and virtuous hearts to strike for Liberty, will never be paralyzed by the want of a competent head to direct their efforts.

Of the many popular leaders who were upheaved by the great convulsions of 1848 into the full sunlight of European celebrity and American popular regard, the world has already definitively assigned the first rank to LOUIS KOSSUTH, Advocate, Deputy, Finance Minister, and finally Governor of Hungary. Though not originally of the dominant or Magyar race, he became of that proud, gallant and able race the fervently loved and thoroughly trusted leader and champion. Though by birth and education of the middle class, he was freely, unanimously chosen the chief of a Constitutional State, wherein aristocracy had held almost boundless sway for centuries, and wherein the aristocratic element, though no longer fortified by exclusive privileges under the law, was still essentially formidable. In a tremendous struggle which rocked ancient monarchies to their foundations, which was irradiated by genius, daring, heroism, and the noblest spirit of self-sacrifice

INTRODUCTION.

—wherein almost every day was marked by some memorable event and hundreds developed qualities which would have honored any nation— the name of Kossuth towered throughout peerless and alone. To him, far more than to that Carnot of whom it was originally affirmed, belongs the credit of having "organized victory." Against a dynasty whom they had been trained for three centuries to honor and obey— against the whole power of one of the greatest military empires of our age—against a most sanguinary and formidable insurrection into which the perfidious arts of Austria drew nearly half the population of Hungary itself—Kossuth had few resources to oppose but those found in the justice of his cause and he thrilling might of his eloquence. With these he created armies, mu itions, money, credit and supplies, by virtue of which the Austrian legions were hurled from the heart of Hungary back across the frontier to the vicinity of their own capital, tracking their flight by the lavish effusion of their blood. Never was a revolutionary government more promptly or more formidably subjected to the stern ordeal of the sword, and never was one more completely successful. Unlike nearly ever other nation revolting against Usurpation, Perfidy and Despotism, Hungary, when she first formally declared her independence, had already proved her ability to maintain it. She had proved her self-sufficiency a fact before she asserted it as a right. And the subsequent interposition of the Russian Autocrat, at the solicitation of the Austrian Court, to crush beneath his colossal weight the liberties of Hungary, so far from disproving the independence of the latter, is a striking confirmation of its intrinsic justice and verity. When an Empire so formidable as the Austrian confesses, by soliciting foreign aid, that it is unable to govern a neighboring State, it plainly admits that its right to do so, if it ever had any, has ceased to exist.

The life of Louis Kossuth, truly portrayed, has for us many impressive lessons; among them that of "the uses of Adversity." When the patriotic young advocate and editor was suddenly snatched from his friends and his labors, and hurried to the dungeons of Buda, the captive and victim of a gigantic, irresistible despotism, he may well have regarded that arrest as the termination of his efforts for his country, the death-blow to his hopes of her emancipation. Yet a few years sufficed to develop the truth that the stern ordeal of the malefactor's dungeon, without limitation of sentence or rational hope of deliverance, was an essential preparation for the memorable part which he was destined in the order of Providence to play in the not distant drama of Hungary's liberation. But for that ordeal, he might have been a leading Liberal

INTRODUCTION.

orator in the Diet, but would not have been called by the nation's undivided voice to be the chief, the champion, the embodiment, the animating soul of her heroic struggle for Independence. And, thus instructed and strengthened by the past, we may rationally, confidently trust that his more recent prostration and exile are but preludes to a still more triumphant restoration to a place in the government corresponding to that which he has never forfeited nor ceased to hold in the hearts of his countrymen.

Nor can we over-value the lesson taught us by Kossuth of the essential oneness of humanity, the unity of interests, and the consequent atrocity and madness of all wars waged for glory, for conquest, or the base phantom misnamed national honor. It has been the fashion of our Fourth-of-July orators for two generations to boast of ours as the only land in which *true* liberty is understood and appreciated—in which the golden mean between anarchy and despotism has been attained—in which men could submit to be governed without ceasing to be free. But at the very height of our self-complacency, a voice from the far Pannonia of Roman history breaks upon our ears, which even our self-conceit cannot mistake for aught but a true and living utterance from the great heart of humanity. With the eloquence of Demosthenes and the sublime fervor of Isaiah, it utters burning words which call men of diverse creeds and races to the battle-field in which the rights of all are to be asserted, the usurpations of the crafty few, however entrenched and hoary, are to be overborne and stricken down. At first we pause to wonder how this dweller by the far Danube, this Hun, this almost Asiatic, had learned those great truths which we have supposed discoveries of Jefferson and the special property of our own Republic; but, pausing, we discover that this child of Atilla has not merely imitated our fathers in their immortal declaration, but that what with them were figures of rhetoric, or at least barren abstractions, are with him living and practical verities. They *declared* all men rightfully born free and equal, but left one million of their own countrymen in slavery, in part to their individual selves; he grappled boldly with serfdom and abolished it; they *declared* all men by nature entitled to "life, liberty and the pursuit of happiness;" he apportioned lands without charge to the emancipated serfs, so as to insure them the means of supporting life, enjoying liberty, and pursuing happiness in the homes of their childhood. Who can rationally deny, therefore, that the great principle of equal rights was better understood and more faithfully regarded in Hungary in 1848, than it was in America in 1776 ? And how could the sincere lovers of human rights among us refuse to

INTRODUCTION.

accord to Kossuth a welcome as hearty and as imposing as that paid, a quarter of a century earlier, to the great and good La Fayette? How could they hesitate to hang upon his eloquent words and catch inspiration for new struggles for freedom and humanity from the light of his kindling eye, the sound of his trumpet voice?

Yes, KOSSUTH has visited our shores—even as I write, his presence hallows and ennobles this chief city of the western world. He is here, though unconsciously, to rebuke the degeneracy and factiousness of our partisan squabbles, the hollowness of our boasted love of liberty, if we turn a deaf ear to the cry of the oppressed in either hemisphere, the sordidness of our common life and the meanness of its aims. He is here to arouse us to a consciousness of the majesty of our national position and the responsibilities it involves; to show us that we cannot safely sleep while despots are forging chains for the yet unfettered nations, as well as to bind more securely their present victims; that, even if we have no regard for others' rights, we must assume an attitude of resistance to the expanding dominion of the Autocrat if only to secure our own. That "God hath made of one blood all the nations that dwell on the face of the earth,"—that we should "do to others as we would have them do to us,"—that we have no right to repel solicitude as to the fate of tyranny's victims, by the callous question, "Am I my brother's keeper?"—that the free nations of earth cannot afford, even were they base enough to wish, to leave each other to be assailed in succession by the banded might of despotism, and so overwhelmed and crushed—these are solemn truths which Governor Kossuth is among us to proclaim and enforce with the earnestness of a martyr's conviction and an exiled patriot's zeal.

God grant that he may leave our soil nerved and armed for the great work before him—strengthened not by words of cheer only, but by substantial and bounteous aid. The American people are spending at least one hundred millions of dollars annually for the gratification of vicious appetites and as much more in the indulgence of sumptuous tastes and ostentatious display—why should the hope that they will give or lend a few millions to free Hungary, and thereby insure the speedy emancipation of all Europe, be deemed chimerical? Ten millions would be but one dollar to each adult free person in the Union; is that too much to expect for such a cause? All Europe south of the Niemen is to-day a smothered volcano—only a signal is needed to insure its bursting into a magnificent eruption. This explosion cannot be delayed beyond the middle of 1852: the practical question for to-day is, Shall the republicans of Europe be armed, organized, prepared

INTRODUCTION.   xi

and united, as with means they may and will be, or shall they be divided, crippled, destitute, isolated, and so cut off in detail as they were in 1849?—There can be no question as to the leadership of the general movement—the finger of history (may we not venture to say of Providence?) points unerringly to LOUIS KOSSUTH as marked out for that position. The prayers of millions are with him; the hopes of hundreds of millions rest upon him. His success will lift the crushing weight of despotism from off the breast of prostrate humanity, and bid her rise and walk forth erect, redeemed and disenthralled. Who cannot give *something* in aid of such a cause? Who can hesitate to pray and labor and hope for its success?

But, even if, in the inscrutable Providence of God, the upheaval for which the millions are now preparing be destined to temporary miscarriage and discomfiture, the great Hungarian will not, cannot fail. "*His* fame at least is secure." His character has stood the ordeals of poverty, of sudden eminence, of courtly temptation, of bondage, of exaltation, of unbounded sway, of triumph, of deepest calamity, of exile, of strangers' adulation and of reviving hope, and has nobly overcome them all. He may be called to die in a palace or a dungeon, in his prime or in decrepitude, amid tears or execrations, but his place in history is already fixed and cannot be changed. Among orators, patriots, statesmen, exiles, he has, living or dead, no superior. His throne is in the heart, and he can only be discrowned by tearing that heart from the breast of humanity. Or, rather, let me close with the noble tribute of LOWELL, Bard of Freedom, and, after him, say—

"A RACE of nobles may die out,
   A royal line may leave no heir;
Wise Nature sets no guards about
   Her pewter plate and wooden ware.

"But they fail not, the kinglier breed,
   Who starry diadems attain;
To dungeon, axe and stake succeed
   Heirs of the old heroic strain.

"The zeal of nature never cools,
   Nor is she thwarted of her ends;
When gapped and dulled her cheaper tools,
   Then she a saint and prophet spends.

"Land of the Magyars! though it be
 The tyrant may relink his chain,
Already thine the victory,
 As the just Future measures gain.

"Thou hast succeeded; thou hast won
 The deathly travail's amplest worth;
A nation's duty thou hast done,
 Giving a hero to our earth.

"And he, let come what will of woe,
 Has saved the land he strove to save;
No Cossack hordes, no traitor's blow,
 Can quench the voice shall haunt his grave.

"'I Kossuth am; O Future, thou
 That clear'st the just and blott'st the vile,
O'er this small dust in reverence bow,
 Remembering what I was erewhile.

"'I was the chosen trump wherethrough
 Our God sent forth awakening breath;
Came chains? Came death? The strain He blew
 Sounds on, outliving chains and death.'"

H. G

NEW YORK. February, 1852.

CONTENTS.

INTRODUCTORY . . . . PAGE 7

CHAPTER I.

Birth of Louis Kossuth—Early Life—Enters the Profession of Law—Youthful Aspirations for Freedom—His Philanthropy during the Ravages of the Cholera in 1831—Is appointed Representative by Proxy in the Diet of 1832—Position and General Features of Hungary—Early History and Races—Primitive Polity—Written Constitution—Development of the Idea of Freedom—Hungary's Great Mistake—The House of Hapsburg—Condition of Hungary under its Sway—Rights and Wrongs—Diet of 1832—Wesselenyi 17

CHAPTER II.

Kossuth in the Diet of 1832—He publishes the Reports of the Diet—Opposition of the Government—He is arrested—Imprisoned—Is brought to Trial—Sentenced to Four Years' Confinement in the Fortress of Buda—He studies the English Language in Prison—Sympathy of the Masses—Austria is compelled to release the Captive—Kossuth is again an Editor—Influence—Is removed—Continues the untiring Advocate of Reform 40

CHAPTER III.

Count Batthyanyi—Kossuth is elected to the Diet of 1847—Measures for Reform—Austrian Slanders—Kossuth in Debate—The French Revolution—Kossuth's Speech—Address to the Throne

—Outbreak in Vienna—Action of the Diet—Deputation to the Emperor—New Ministry formed—Dark Pictures—The War of Races—Causes—Description of the Races in Hungary—Laws passed by the Diet—Testimony of Distinguished Writers . 55

CHAPTER IV.

Special Privileges granted to Croatia—Perfidy of Austria—Jellachich appointed Ban of Croatia—His Movements—Sclavic Union and Empire—Servian Revolt—Horrid Cruelties—Kossuth sends an Army to quell the Insurrection—Result—Tokens of a hastening Storm—Kossuth's Discernment—Jellachich proposes to invade Hungary—Remonstrance of the Ministry—Duplicity of the King—Royal Manifesto . . . 77

CHAPTER V.

Efforts of Jellachich—Opening of the New Hungarian Diet—Speech of the Palatine—Kossuth's Speech—The King withdraws his Denunciation of Jellachich—Surprise of the Hungarians—Deputation to the King—Evasive Answer—the Signal of Conflict . 69

CHAPTER VI.

Jellachich crosses the Drave—War Inevitable—The Hungarian Ministry resign except Szemere—Kossuth joins him—A New Cabinet demanded—Archduke Stephen called to the Command of the Army—Last Attempts at Conciliation—The Archduke resigns—Kossuth's Speech—Volunteers hasten to the Capital—Murder of Count Lamberg—Batthyanyi resigns—Battle of September 29th—The Ban's Retreat and Promotion—Insurrection at Vienna 109

CHAPTER VII.

The Progress of the Struggle—Gain and Loss of the Insurrection—Bem's Arrival—Kossuth marches to Pressburg—Siege of Vienna—The Hungarians advance towards the Austrian Frontier—Battle of Schwechat—Last Appeal by the Catholic Bishops—Executions—Condition of the two Armies—Abdication of Ferdinand 127

CHAPTER VIII.

Skirmishes with the Austrian Army—Kossuth and Count Pulszky—The Conflict opens—A Deputation despatched to Prince Windischgratz with Proposals of Peace, and are detained Prisoners—Transfer of the Government to Debreczen—Council of War—Plan of Defence—Gorgey's March—Storming of the Defiles of Brandiezko—Progress of the Armies—Battle of Kapolna—Kossuth's Prayer—Bem—Perczel—Hungarians advance towards Godollo—March of the Hungarians towards Pesth—Battle of Tapiolieske—Battle of Isaszeg—Rendezvous at Godollo—Battle of Waitzen—Declaration of Independence—Joy of the People . 145

CHAPTER IX.

Battle of Nagy Sarlo—Position of Affairs in Hungary—Rejoicings at Pesth—Kossuth at Debreczen—Message to the Army—Russian Intervention—Storming of Buda—Gorgey—Hungarian Army—Wallachian Insurrection—Government removed to Pesth—Military Movements—The Palatinal Hussars . . 166

CHAPTER X.

Gorgey retains Command—Csanyi's Interview with Klapka—Gorgey's Ambition—Kossuth—Battle of Comorn—Klapka at the Fortress—Battle of Herkaly—Kossuth's Resignation in Favor of Gorgey—Surrender at Villagos—Scenes at Pesth and Comorn—Capitulation of the Fortress—Executions—Kossuth's Flight—His Farewell to Hungary—Residence and Scenes at Widdin—He refuses to renounce his Protestant Faith—Letter to Lord Palmerston—Bem's Character and Death—Kossuth removed to Kutahia—Madame Kossuth joins him—Embarkation on board Mississippi—Difficulties at Marseilles—Sails for England . . 196

CHAPTER XI.

Reception in England—Enthusiasm—Banquets at Winchester and Southampton—Magnificent Welcome in London—Visits Birmingham—Embarkation for America—Arrival at Staten Island—The Pageant in New York—Banquets—Visit to Philadelphia—Banquets and Speeches—Visit to Washington 232

CHAPTER XII.

Kossuth's Mission—Character and Eloquence 291

APPENDIX.

Letter to the People of the United States 315
Speech at Winchester 330
Speech at Southampton 344
Speech at London 349
Speech at Manchester 361
Speech at Birmingham 375
Speech before the Corporation of New York 397
Speech to the Press of New York 421
Speech to the Bar of New York 436
Speech to the Ladies of New York 446
Speech at Washington 453

LIFE OF LOUIS KOSSUTH.

CHAPTER I.

BIRTH OF LOUIS KOSSUTH—EARLY LIFE—ENTERS THE PROFESSION OF LAW—YOUTHFUL ASPIRATIONS FOR FREEDOM—HIS PHILANTHROPY DURING THE RAVAGES OF THE CHOLERA IN 1831—IS APPOINTED REPRESENTATIVE BY PROXY IN THE DIET OF 1832—POSITION AND GENERAL FEATURES OF HUNGARY—EARLY HISTORY AND RACES—PRIMITIVE POLITY—WRITTEN CONSTITUTION—DEVELOPMENT OF THE IDEA OF FREEDOM—HUNGARY'S GREAT MISTAKE—THE HOUSE OF HAPSBURG—CONDITION OF HUNGARY UNDER ITS SWAY—RIGHTS AND WRONGS—DIET OF 1832—WESSELENYI.

LOUIS KOSSUTH, Governor of Hungary, was born on the 27th of April, 1802, at Monok, in the County of Zemplin, situated in the northern part of the kingdom. His father, Andreas Kossuth, was descended from an ancient family who originally lived in the County of Turoczer, and were among those who early defended the cause of nationality, and suffered in the struggle. His mother's maiden name was Caroline Weber, a woman of good mind and Protestant faith, who still survives to mingle with her tears of mourning for Hungary, and the exile, those of rejoicing over his spotless fame, and cheering prospects of redeeming his fatherland.* Ludwig, or Louis in our tongue, was an only son, and gave early indications of genius. Though not favored with the inheritance of wealth, he had the more precious blessing of parental piety. He was a Protestant by education, and afterward, to use his own words, "also by *conviction.*" He succeeded in making the necessary preparations for entering the Calvinist College of Patak, while yet a boy.

Amid the routine of recitations, and healthful exercise, he began to feel those promptings of a free spirit, which he many years after, called "*something nameless,*" in his breast. He graduated with the highest honors of the Institution, giving to young men of all lands an example of victory over discouragements in the pursuit of knowledge, and illustrating his own motto since,—"There is no difficulty to him that wills."

At the age of seventeen, he commenced the study of law, and attended sessions of the District Court at Eperies, in the County of Zips, a fortified city, and the seat of a Lutheran College. He also went to the delightful town of Pesth, on the eastern bank of the majestic Danube, whose fortress is the stronghold of Buda on the opposite shore. Here the royal Courts were held, and Kossuth attended its sittings, to finish his legal studies. Having completed his course, he returned to Monok in 1822, then but twenty years

---

* Since the first edition of this work was issued, intelligence of her death has been received.

old, and was appointed Honorary Attorney to the County; an office similar to that of District Attorney in this country.

He was passionately fond of manly sports, and gave more time to these than his profession. He was unconsciously preparing his frame, in the Magyar discipline, for the endurance of captivity, the self-denial of the battle-field, and the astonishing expenditure of energy in addressing popular assemblies, which has thrilled and delighted millions. Nor was he forgetful of his country. With indignation he met the tyrannical claims of Austria, and his youthful ardor was often expressed in burning speech and glowing eye, when the hand of the Hapsburg was laid afresh on some national right, and the invading claim approached more boldly a cherished Constitution.

While thus quietly employed in his native county, in 1831, the Asiatic Cholera broke out in Hungary. It was a strange and awful visitant, and its havoc was like the resistless march of the plague.— The peasant sickened in the field and hovel, and suddenly lay down to die. The nature of the terrible pestilence was unknown; and there seemed no cause in the customary tranquillity and apparent purity of the elements, for its mysterious work of death. It touched the strong man and the child, and they fell gasping "*water! water!*" to quench the thirst that attends this fatal disease. During the fearful panic which prevailed, the idea seized the peasantry that the higher classes had poisoned the fountains. They rose simultaneously upon the clergy, landlords, and Jews, and commenced the work of slaughter. Murder and pestilence then walked together along the streets, until terror and wailing spread over the land. This dark tragedy brought Kossuth from his comparative obscurity. He became the angel of mercy amid the horrors of those scenes. He sought the hamlets where the cholera was the most deadly, and lived under the outspread wing of the Destroyer, almost without repose. Measures of relief were suggested by him and urged with success; while his eloquent voice, dispelling the delusion which superstition and oppression naturally awakened, reached the frantic masses. And when a calm succeeded the excitement, and the grass was green above the buried victims, Kossuth was no longer an humble citizen. He was distinguished in the cottage of the poor, and the palace of the peer. And when the opportunity was presented, he was nominated to fill, according to an old custom, the place of an absent Magnate in the Diet of 1832. Several women of the nobility were the first to mention his name; and he took his seat. "But the laws then gave no influence to this kind of substitute;" to HIM the dawn of a resplendent day!

Having brought Kossuth upon the arena of his country's political strife, it is proper and necessary to pause here in his career, and describe the land of his birth, and the remote causes of that conflict between the people of Hungary and the House of Austria, of which from this date he became the guiding spirit on the side of national honor and ancient liberties.

GENERAL FEATURES OF HUNGARY.

Hungary will be found on the map of Europe, lying between the forty-second and forty-ninth degrees of north latitude, and the sixteenth and twenty-fourth degrees of east longitude. It is bounded on the north by Moravia, Prussia, and Gallicia; east by Gallicia and Transylvania; south by Wallachia, Turkey and Sclavonia, and west by Austria proper. There is a distinction to be made between the Kingdom of Hungary and Hungary proper, or Provincial Hungary, as it is commonly called. The former comprises not only Hungary proper, but also Croatia and Sclavonia; the three forming a united Kingdom, with the same Constitution and Diet or Legislative Assembly.

Hungary proper has an area of eighty thousand nine hundred and forty square miles, being in extent about the size of the six New England States, with the addition of Delaware and Maryland. The western, which is the more level part of the country, is commonly called Lower Hungary, and the eastern, which is the more mountainous part, is generally designated as Upper Hungary.

There is no part of Europe more richly adorned with the gifts of nature, than Hungary proper. It has all the advantages of a healthy, and in some portions an exceedingly pure and genial climate, whose serene sky, and refreshing breezes, are hardly surpassed by those of Italy. The appearance of the country, with its endless diversity of hill and valley, fruitful fields and luxuriant forest, is one of great beauty. The Danube rolls its tide of wealth through its plains, and receives at short intervals numerous tributaries, from the Carpathian mountains on the north and east, and the Alps on the south and west, alone giving exhaustless fertility, sublime scenery, and picturesqueness to the lands through which it passes. The productions are, therefore, varied and exuberant. The same crops are annually repeated on the unfailing soil; the surface is only once turned up to receive the seed, and a fallow is unknown; manure is not used, but is thrown away as injurious; "and yet," says a traveller in 1835, "with the greatest care and labor in other places, I never saw such abundant produce as ill-treated, unaided nature here bestows upon her children. Except the olive and orange, there is scarcely a product of Europe which does not thrive in the Banat.* I do not know that I can enumerate all the kinds of crops raised, but, among others, are wheat, barley, oats, rye, rice, maize, flax, hemp, rape, sunflowers, (for oil,) tobacco of different kinds, wine, and silk, nay, even cotton, tried as an experiment, is said to have succeeded." In addition to these harvests, the extensive forests, with which Hungary is shaded, furnish an unlimited supply of the finest timber and fuel. It has mines of gold, silver, copper, lead, iron, and rock salt, and all varieties of valuable minerals. The stock of cattle, sheep, and horses is very considerable. In 1847, there were numbered five millions head of cattle, seventeen

---

* "The Banat," says Paget, from whom the above extract is taken, "is a district in the south-east corner of Hungary, lying between the Sheiss Maros, and Danube, and containing the three counties of Thorontal, Temesvar, and Krass."

HISTORY AND RACES OF HUNGARY. 23

millions of sheep, and one million of horses. The rivers abound in fish, and also afford great advantages for intercourse and trade.*

We should naturally expect to find that a country blessed with so many physical advantages would present a marked history in the annals of nations. In this we are not disappointed. The history of Hungary is full of bold outlines, whose strong features are as conspicuous as the landmarks on her ancient soil, and in whose strange records we find a theme of unfailing interest upon which we would willingly linger, were we not at present summoned to the accomplishment of a more specific purpose. Yet so intimately is Hungary and her history connected with the life of her NOBLEST SON, that we cannot clearly treat of the latter, till we shall have given a cursory glance at the general features of the former. HUNGARY and KOSSUTH cannot be separated. Their histories are woven together in the same great web of destiny.

The annals of Hungary can be traced back till they become lost in the Cimmerian darkness with which they were early shrouded by Greek and Latin fable. It is, however, no part of our design to grope our way amid the dim shadows which veil those primitive records, and cluster around the races who inhabited the land. Our work belongs to a later period, and commences toward the close of the ninth century,

---

* For a more minute description of the country, see **Malte Brun**, Vol. 4.

when the Magyar* race left its home on the borders of the Caspian Sea, crossed the Carpathian mountains, and after a short but severe struggle, in which their name became synonymous with martial courage and bravery, drove out the inhabitants and made themselves undisputed masters of Hungary.

The original character of the race they have preserved to this day. It was bold and courageous, full of energy and activity, generous, high-spirited and impulsive, and marked, from the first, by an enthusiastic love of liberty, which has in its recent developments startled Europe, and baptized the banks of the Danube with the blood of martyrdom. It is a remarkable fact in confirmation of this, that when encircling nations lay groaning in vassalage, the Magyars possessed a written Constitution, distinctly propounding some of those fundamental principles of civil freedom which other nations were subsequently forced to wrest from their reluctant sovereigns on the battle-field. When they first invaded Hungary they were Pagans, and remained without any innovation upon

---

* There has been much dispute respecting the position which should be assigned the Magyars, in a classification of the family of nations. Our own opinion, after a careful investigation, is as follows: The Caucasian Race should be divided into the Indo-Germanic, Armenian, Iberian, Illyrian, Thracian, Etruscan, Semitic, Finnish, Turkish, Caucasian group, and North African stocks. To the Finnish stock, in this division, we assign the MAGYARS, and the Finns, as its two branches. The ancient Huns, whom the Magyars supplanted in Hungary, belong not to the Finnish, but to the Turkish stock, in the above division. Dr. Tefft has fallen into an error in giving to the Huns and the Magyars a closer affinity than this.

their old religion, until the beginning of the eleventh century, when the Duke* of the nation, the renowned St. Stephen, was converted to Christianity. His reign forms an era in Hungarian history. Imbued with the power of his new faith, he immediately applied its sublime teachings to the temporal and spiritual welfare of his people. He has been called the Solon of his nation. With views far beyond his age, he gave to the Hungarians a Constitution which made them then the freest people in Europe. So far as could be in a barbarous age, the laws seem to have been framed and administered upon equitable principles. Justice was sacredly regarded and enforced in simple yet satisfactory forms. The interests of the people were cared for, and to a good degree made the subject of an enlightened policy. A National Assembly was formed, composed of the three orders of the nobility, who in connection with the Monarch were to have the general oversight of the nation, enacting legal codes, and establishing provisions, as the common weal required. Many of the statutes passed, and the modes of their administration were, of course, extremely rude; but as a whole they present a surprising advance beyond the position of any other realm on the continent.

The Constitution, defining individual rights and duties, shows the great superiority of the Magyar

---

* This was the title of the Hungarian leader in the primitive Constitution. Stephen was the first one who assumed the regal name.

race, and the far-reaching wisdom of their lawgiver While we contemplate the semi-barbarous condition of Europe when it was promulgated, and the vague apprehension everywhere visible, concerning civil and social relations, we pause with wonder and admire the bright anomaly. In the Hungarian Constitution, we see the first faint flashes of glory, heralding the sun of freedom, as the tints of morning betoken the coming day.

In tracing the subsequent development of the civil polity, we are impressed with several prominent facts, to which we shall briefly advert. The first is, that for a number of generations succeeding St. Stephen, there is a clearly marked progression. The laws were more distinctly defined, and justice was more promptly and effectually administered: the interests of the common people were considered with increasing care, while the National Assembly, the great bulwark of Hungarian liberty, became more prominent in the State, and effective in its provisions for the general good. The power of this body in controlling the nation continually augmented, while the prerogatives of the king, if they did not diminish, were yet better understood, and more closely guarded. To the king belonged the power of summoning and dispersing the National Assembly at his will, the sole command of the army, and the privilege of nominating all the chief officers of the kingdom. He was the executor of the laws when made, but had no right to create statutes upon his own authority. He could propose them to the Assembly, but until there approved they

THE IDEA OF FREEDOM. 27

had no force whatever. The general duties and objects of this Assembly are thus specified by Fessler:

"To maintain the old Magyar Constitution; to support it by constitutional laws; to assert and secure the rights, liberties, and ancient customs of the nation; to frame laws for particular cases; to grant supplies and to fix the manner of their collection; to provide means for securing the independence of the nation, its safety from foreign influence, and its deliverance from all enemies; to examine and encourage public undertakings and establishments of general utility; to superintend the mint; to confer on foreigners the privileges of nobility, together with the permission to colonize the country, and to enjoy the rights of Hungarians, are the important functions of the Hungarian Diet."

This plain and just limitation of kingly authority, and exposition of legislative power, was a result not attained in a day. It followed from a long and slow development of THE IDEA OF CIVIL FREEDOM, which is a germ from the tree of life, sown in the bosom of humanity, and destined to toss its own branches wide and high in the sunlight of universal peace and well-being.

IDEAS GROW, and there is in history no more striking exhibition of this truth, than the annals of Hungary afford. Though sometimes there seemed a retrogression, when the great principles which were finally established were forgotten amid the divisions and anarchy prevailing in the public councils; when the crown rested upon the brow of a tyrannical or imbecile king; when civil wars reigned through the State, and every right sentiment appeared perverted; yet has there never been the hour when those immutable principles have positively ceased to progress.

The hand of the Almighty, which guides nations, as well as the stars in their courses, is seen through Hungarian history, bringing them forth even from political chaos, and pointing onward to their glorious issue. Yes, behind the clouds which despotism has rolled over the Magyar land, they are working in muffled but mighty energy, and soon shall shake ancient crowns to earth, like autumn leaves, when the storm succeeds the blight of the nightly frost.

We do not doubt it. Truths never die. Principles are immortal. And the great Idea of Liberty is penetrating the masses, and their day is only that of preparation for decisive conflict and abiding victory.

> "HUNGARY,
> Ermined and crowned, shall sit in her own seat
> In peaceful state and sober majesty,
> And ITALY, unloosening her bonds,
> By her strong will shall be at last the home
> Of broadly based and virtuous liberty."

The great calamity of Hungary, over which she mourns in the dust, was the transfer of the crown of St. Stephen to the reigning family of Austria. By intermarriage, the previous Hungarian dynasty had become so closely connected with the House of Hapsburg, that upon the death of Louis II., in 1526, Ferdinand, Archduke of Austria, claimed the throne. This claim was at once rejected by the nation. Hungary refused to acknowledge his right, and the Diet unanimously elected another to wear the crown. A war followed, in which Ferdinand sustained his ambitious usurpation with the sword, and vanquishing his rival, by fair promises he subdued opposition and was enthroned, upon taking the oath to support and preserve the Constitution, the 3d of February, 1527.

At this date commences a career of perfidy and unblushing crime, which saddens the indignant spirit of him who reads the record, and blackens the memory of a royal line. The House of Hapsburg from the time that we first discover it in the "Hawk's Nest,"* on the Alps, down through successive generations, has pursued a course of lawless ambition and fraud. Proud, narrow-minded—in public life continually breaking pledge and promise, trampling on every obligation, and regarding their most solemn oaths as made to be violated, they have, like the House of the Hebrew Ahab, transmitted with deepening stains of treachery and blood, the robes of royalty. They have sat upon the throne forgetful of the Sovereign before whose righteous tribunal even kings must stand in judgment. By an artful policy, Ferdinand, the first Hungarian king of his line, was able to secure the election of his son to the throne, and in the following century the crown was made hereditary in the House of Hapsburg, while the condition was at the same time expressly made and agreed to, that the ancient Constitution should not be disturbed.

The Emperor of Austria, absolute and irresponsible in his legitimate domain, was simply Constitutional King in Hungary. He was sovereign by the consent of the governed, and took a solemn oath to maintain

---

* Der Habichtsburg.

the Constitution and the Statutes of the realm. He was pledged to protect the rights of the people, and his own acts subject to review by the Legislature. His edicts were void of force until approved by the Municipal bodies; and his plans were limited by the popular will. This freedom of the Magyars was the occasion of their ruin. It was light blazing on the oppressor, and must be extinguished, or the masses under the night of his sway would discern their degradation and their rights. Before this spreading intelligence, the haughty encroachments of absolutism would cease, and lie on the path of the people like the cross beneath the feet of the scornful Greek. The House of Hapsburg understood perfectly the issue, and began, with undeviating purpose, the work of subverting, by slow and uncertain invasion, the constitution of St. Stephen.

When violence was impolitic, deception and fraud were employed. The plot was to narrow down the provisions and import of the ancient Instrument, until the genius of liberty was banished from its form, and the name of distinct national existence, an appendage to royalty. And for centuries the dark, deliberate conspiracy was prosecuted against the proud Magyars, sending at intervals a gifted orator or dangerous noble to the scaffold.

Leopold, Maria Theresa, and Ferdinand, are conspicuous among the heartless and sanguinary guardians of despotic principles. Upon the subversion of constitutional rights, followed a limitation of religious freedom, and an intermeddling with provincial language, and modes of dress, to prevent the contagion of converse and recognition among the suffering victims of tyranny

Joseph II. assumed the imperial purple, and refused to take the coronation oath of Hungary, affirming that the crown was his by hereditary descent. He laid his daring hand upon the elective franchise of the people, and unnecessarily provoked their indignation, to gratify his malignant lust of power.

Rudolph II. succeeded him, and thirsting for Protestant blood, he plotted their extermination. He enforced papal claims, closed the churches of the heretics, and with inquisitorial zeal and cruelty, he arraigned innocent peasants, and helpless women, and marched them to the gallows upon bare suspicion of religious or civil unrest.

The laws, literature, and conversation were commanded to be in the oppressor's tongue. "The ancient songs of the people were no more heard in their cornfields, the story-teller was silent by his native hearth, the workman was dumb at his bench, and a hideous paralysis, as of nightmare, froze up the very currents of the soul. Manners and customs, too, as well as civilization and the laws, whatever might remind the Magyar of his former freedom and independence, whatever cherished within him the seeds of nationality and the hope of its resurrection, whatever endeared him to his brother and stood in the way of his total amalgamation with the race of his conqueror—all were washed away, as with a sponge, but a sponge wet and reeking with his own heart's blood."

With an utter contempt for moral sanctions, the

Hapsburgs devoted their energies to carry out the principle expressed by one of their number; that having first reduced Hungary to beggary, he would next make it a German, and afterwards a Catholic nation. "*Faciam Hungariam prius mendicam, dein Germanum, postea Catholicam.*" To this the Hungarians could not quietly submit. They would not lie sullenly down, with the heel of the oppressor upon their neck, and the chains on their limbs. They battled long and well against both the insidious and the open inroads of the invader. They made gigantic efforts to throw off the manacles, and performed heroic deeds, illuminating their historic page with devotion and energy, and courage; but the dragon, whose deadly folds were about the nation, was too strong for their brave resistance. The feelings of the nation were those of universal mourning. They are shadowed forth in the following affecting extract, from a decree made by one of their own Diets, and passed under Rodolph II., 1602.

" Sorely grieved and vexed at heart, the faithful magnates and estates feel impelled—as formerly, so now—to complain to God and the king, that all their entreaties, remonstrances, and representations have never helped them to obtain even the slightest mitigation of their sufferings, horrors and miseries, but that the same have gone on increasing from day to day, and from year to year. When we are told that the Hungarians are in the habit of coming into Parliament with tears and all kinds of wailings and woful lament, and that when weary of sighs and of words, they proceed to business, we will not, indeed, deny that such is the case. But who is there that will command the tears of the lacerated and wounded? Who will stop the wailings of children when they submit their sufferings to their parents?

RIGHTS AND WRONGS. 33

"Nor are the grievances of Upper Hungary, Sclavonia, and other parts of the kingdom, less, or more endurable. In these provinces the soldiers take possession of the cities, market-towns, villages, houses and noble *curias*, as if they had come to them in due course of inheritance. They divide the same, and treat the natives of the soil, in their own homes, not as proprietors, but a vagrants or bondsmen. In many places, the foreign soldiers at tack and plunder the cottages of the peasantry, and the seats and possessions of the noblemen. They, by main force, open churches and graves, rob the corpses and bones of the departed of their funeral dresses, and flagellate, wound and kill the fathers of families. By force and violence, they bear away wives from their husbands, children from their parents, infant daughters from their mothers, chaste virgins from their parental home, and abduct them to the haunts of infamy and vice, where—may God pity the bitter sufferings of the Hungarian people!—they are sacrificed to beastly violence, and afterwards brought back if ransomed with large sums of money!

"Large numbers of dwellers within these realms, scions of old and honored families, once happy in befitting affluence—now expelled from all their possessions—wander about, naked, hungry and forlorn, praying for bread at every door!

"Such is the lamentable condition of the rest of the Hungarian people—a condition which even hearts of stone must pity. That people was once eminent in martial honors, wealth and merit; but, at this present time, we are bent with severe affliction, not on account of the tolerable dominion of the Turks and Tartars, but on account of the unrestrained misdeeds of foreign soldiers."

The Hungarians submitted, but did not yield. It was not in the power of despots utterly to crush the hopes, or break the will of such a people. They bore their wrongs for that dreary century; they saw their name blotted out of the book of nations; they saw their institutions, their laws, their popular privileges, their literature, their commerce invaded and prostrate; but they were still Magyars and men, and believed in the justice of God. But, alas! the aged fathers were laid in their graves before the triumph of justice had come.

It will not be considered a digression, if in this place we ask the reader to think for a moment *by what right* it was, that Austria laid thus her withering grasp upon this fair land. Let it be distinctly understood that the compact by which the crown of St. Stephen had been surrendered to the House of Hapsburg, this latter party had repeatedly broken. In numberless instances, Austria had violated the express stipulations by which alone she could claim Hungary as a part of her Empire. The compact, therefore, which, from its very nature could remain only so long as both parties should fulfil its conditions, was no longer binding upon Hungary. Still farther, when considering the question of right, we do not hesitate to make the assertion, that no king has a right to rule any people against their will. If they do not choose to accept him as their sovereign, his authority over them is a nullity; without foundation. This principle should be distinctly understood; for it not only lies at the basis of every correct notion of civil freedom, but is indispensable to the just apprehension of events which have echoed round the globe, and are the precursors of greater ones at hand. If it be doubted, we point in illustration to that history, where God Himself, has distinctly recognized it. We refer to

PRINCIPLES OF DIVINE GOVERNMENT 35

the Jewish Theocracy. God by His own administration, places the supreme civil power in the people. He does not assume the right to legislate *as a National Ruler*, and arbitrarily compel submission, without the free consent of the governed. In the very nature of the case, He, as Creator, and infinitely perfect, is the *moral* Governor of all intelligent beings, but is not a *civil* Ruler to any people. He has never sustained this relation but to one Kingdom, and in this he did not take upon himself the reins of authority until the people had promptly and cordially accepted him as their King.

This is a prominent and remarkable feature in the Hebrew State. God, thus early in the world's history, while the thick gloom of Despotism wrapped an idolatrous globe, stamped the Divine impress of his own sanction upon the fundamental principles of free government. The doctrine of the divine right of kings, finds no support from His example.

God affirmed that He gave the Hebrews "a King in his wrath," while he would not himself govern them without their consent. We might farther notice here, that even after Jehovah had been elected civil Monarch, he did not arbitrarily impose upon them a constitution and code of laws; but submitted these to the people for their adoption. Enough has been indicated for illustration of the point at issue. In the light of this fact, and from what has previously been said, it will fully appear that Austria had *no right* to control Hungary; and that in attempting to do so, she pursued a course of flagrant iniquity, which if indulged by one man towards another, would be adjudged felony in every human court. As though the God of heaven could wink at injustice, any more in nations than in individuals! —Impossible.

Such, then, were the old relations between Hungary and Austria, with their ancient rights and wrongs; and this the inheritance which either party had left to its successors.

With the present century began a new order of things. The Magyars, though wronged and oppressed, yielded to the despotism they could not successfully resist, and became the dependence of Austria, in the long and wasting wars that attended the French Revolution. They were impetuous and fearless soldiers, and often turned the tide of victory, when the battalions of the Hapsburg alone, would have been swept from the field.

The reward of the monarch and his court, was a continual pressure upon the helpless and sensitive spirit of the Hungarians; excepting an occasional interlude of mercy, to mature their despotic designs, during the hours of hope and thanksgiving among the people. But progress was made in the campaigns under Austrian colors. Magyars learned their value and strength; and the baptism of blood roused the ancient energies of the race, and revived the purpose of demanding a restoration of rights, rudely and cruelly seized by perjured Kings.

" When, therefore, in 1832, just after the second revolution in France had driven Charles the Xth from

DIET OF 1832.

his throne, and animated the popular heart of Europe with aspirations for change—when, we say, the National Diet was convoked in 1832, it was found to be a diet which not only opposed Austria, but which cherished plans of internal reform. Although, by the Constitution, it was the source of all law to Hungary, it had not been assembled for full seven years before. When it did convene, the purposes of good which had been fermenting all over the land, in the secluded nook no less than in the magnate's parlor, were brought to a head. Its first proposal, though it was composed mainly of landholders, (to their glory be it said,) was the emancipation of the peasants,—peasants, as we have seen, who had been originally in a tolerably good condition, but who had been reduced to a state of almost serfdom. Its next proposal was, to make every inhabitant of mature age a voter, thus placing the liberties of the nation on the most liberal and sure foundation. It then ordered the restoration of the native language of the people by new and strong enactments. It incorporated a college for the revival of the native literature. It stimulated industry by commencing a system of internal improvements, and thus for four years went on in the same wise and generous spirit, to recover the lost prerogatives and enlarge the freedom of the whole people."

Such exhibitions of the democratic principle, or foreshadowings of national independence, the Austrians did not brook.

Beholding in the success of these measures the inevitable downfall of absolutism, no means were unregarded which might prevent their dreaded consummation.

The leaders in the new reforms were singled out as the special objects of her vengeance. The first blow fell upon a venerable Magyar noble—the Baron Wesselenyi,* who had ventured to stand up in the House of Magnates, and boldly speak his sentiments against the despots, "Whose policy," he said to his fellow-nobles, "has been from the beginning to oppose your good deeds, and convert your land into a slavish province." He was at once arrested, and after a mock trial for treason, in which every principle of justice, and every form of law was arbitrarily set aside, he was adjudged guilty, and sentenced to three years' confinement in a dungeon. The civil law was expressly suspended, that the case might fall under military rule.

---

* Paget relates an anecdote of this nobleman which is worth preserving. The incident occurred previously to the circumstances above recorded, but at a time when Wesselenyi was already distinguished as a Liberal leader. Says Paget: "One time, when the Baron was attending a levee of the Emperor at Presburg, the sovereign, in making his round of the circle, stopped opposite him, and shaking his head very ominously said: 'Take care, Baron Wesselenyi, take care what you are about. Recollect that many of your family have been unfortunate!' (His father was confined for seven years in the Kuffstein.) 'Unfortunate, your majesty, they have been, but ever undeserving of their misfortunes!' was Wesselenyi's bold and honest answer. It is only those who know the habitual stiffness and decorum of an Austrian court that can conceive the consternation into which the whole crowd was thrown by this unexpected boldness. Explanations were offered to Wesselenyi to soften down the harshness of the royal reproof, in hopes of bringing him to beg pardon; but he could not apologize for having defended the honor of his family, even when attacked by his sovereign."

IMPRISONMENT OF PATRIOTS. 39

This inquisitorial cruelty had no other occasion than the utterance of solemn convictions in open parliament, upon a subject legitimately up for discussion before the body of which he was a member. At the same time, and by the same tribunal, several younger men, charged with *having held a political meeting*, were also doomed to breathe the dungeon air. A statute of the land positively forbade imprisonment for acts fearful to heartless tyrants; but might makes right with them.

And so the noble patriots went into the chill and polluted air that spreads the poisonous mould upon walls, which, were they less than rock, would long ago have crumbled before the sighs of innocence, and the prayers of breaking hearts.

CHAPTER II.

KOSSUTH IN THE DIET OF 1832—HE PUBLISHES THE REPORTS OF THE DIET—OPPOSITION OF THE GOVERNMENT—HE IS ARRESTED—IMPRISONED—IS BROUGHT TO TRIAL—SENTENCED TO FOUR YEARS' CONFINEMENT IN THE FORTRESS OF BUDA—HE STUDIES THE ENGLISH LANGUAGE IN PRISON—SYMPATHY OF THE MASSES—AUSTRIA IS COMPELLED TO RELEASE THE CAPTIVE—KOSSUTH IS AGAIN AN EDITOR—INFLUENCE—IS REMOVED—CONTINUES THE UNTIRING ADVOCATE OF REFORM.

THE vial of royal vengeance was not exhausted. There was one more object upon which its fury must fall. The man ordained by God to breast the angry waves of encroaching despotism, and like another Washington, unite the freemen of a hemisphere in the approaching struggle for rights, now attracted the notice of those that watched around a throne, whose deepening shadow concealed the elements of retributive power.

It was soon apparent in the Diet of 1832, that no ordinary citizen was present in the modest representative of Zemplin, who had not yet passed the youthful period of manhood. His enthusiasm, and ruling love for his country, his sympathy with the oppressed peasants, and advocacy of every measure of reform, made him conspicuous, and drew around him in imperishable friendship, the lords who introduced and supported liberal principles before the Diet. With Wesselenyi he was especially intimate. Kossuth occupied his time most successfully for the cause of freedom in a new direction.

The people were ignorant of the proceedings of the Diet. He, resolved to remedy this fatal want of general intelligence, applied himself to the art of stenography, that he might give to the nation a full and authentic record of the transactions of their representatives. This he attempted to publish, but was opposed by the Palatine,* who disentombed an old Austrian law, which forbade the "printing and publishing" of these reports. To evade the statute and secure his object, he *lithographed* his reports, with a press constructed at his own expense, and in this form they were scattered widely over the kingdom. The people seized them with earnest haste. They

---

* The dignity of Palatine is as old as the Hungarian Constitution itself, and cannot be compared with any of the dignities established in the other countries. The Palatine is elected by the Diet for life. He is the President of the House of Peers, Captain General of the Country, President of the King's Bench, and of the Home Office, Count and Captain of the Jazygs and Cumans, and Lord Lieutenant of the county of Pesth. If a difference arose between the King and the Realm, the Palatine was to be the mediator. If the King was a minor, the Palatine was his guardian. If the King failed to convoke the Diet, it was the Palatine's duty to do it. In a word the Palatine was to be the Warden of the Hungarian Constitution.

Though elected by the Diet, he must be nominated by the King, and the House of Hapsburg have usually contrived, either to have the office unfilled, or to fill it with one of their own tools.

read to each other, and in their homes, the liberal and reformatory speeches of members who uttered the wrongs of the masses, and demanded redress. Suddenly, Kossuth found himself stopped in the midst of his work, by a positive interdict from the Austrian Government. Despots, like every other class of evil-doers, hate the light; and the House of Hapsburg beholding *its deeds reproved*, and its sceptre shaken by the truth, was compelled to prohibit the publication, if it would hide its shame and preserve its power. But the ardor of the young patriot was not cooled by the iron hand of oppression, laid so rudely upon his maiden efforts for captive liberty.

Hiring a number of secretaries, he had the reports carefully *written out*, and scattered them in manuscript over the country, wherever his paper had gone. No law could be found on the rusting tables of tyrants, or framed by them, to prohibit these sheets, which would not essentially destroy the freedom of every kind of correspondence. But though the government could not forbid the circulation of letters, it could *intercept* them. Mercenaries of the court, were in every post-office in the land, and had the entire oversight of all the mail service of the nation. Kossuth soon found that his reports, which were directed to every part of the land, did not reach their destination. Determined to succeed, he resolutely established a post of his own. The writers of the letters, who had become imbued with his spirit, were their carriers. By this system of private expresses, he defied the malignity and machinations of the court, and succeeded in transmitting his messages to every town, and village, and hamlet of the kingdom. So great was the demand for them, that an edition of *ten thousand copies* was circulated, *every line of which had been carefully written out* by scribes employed by this silent herald of freedom's footsteps. The energy which he manifested in carrying forward this experiment was amazing. Men looked on with wonder, while purer and bolder than Junius, this young and almost unknown champion of the people, pitted himself against Metternich and the Austrian Cabinet. His mind, during the whole of this period, was intensely active. Besides reporting and superintending both the copying and circulation of the debates, he attended all the meetings of the Diet, and the conferences of the deputies, read the new publications on political economy, and studied French that he might be familiar with the proceedings of the Chambers. He allowed himself but three hours' sleep during the twenty-four. His mind seemed to need no rest, and its busy energies at this period were a presage of activity afterwards displayed; which has no parallel, unless in the mighty workings of Napoleon's genius. All this was but rendering him a more distinguished mark for the javelins of a modern Saul. It could not be that Austria would be foiled without making an attempt to crush the author of so great mischief, and increasing danger. She had broken up his press—placed an interdict upon his paper—refused to deliver his letters; but had not prevented his spreading the counsels of the Diet before the nation. The only possible way to stay the tide of redeeming influence, was to remove the hated fountain. Kossuth saw that the next blow must reach his brow, but he continued his labors. It does not appear in his history that fear of personal danger ever daunted his spirit trusting in God, or defeated any plan upon which his heart was fixed. At this time, he was once found by a friend walking in solemn revery along the pavement within the fortress of Buda; and when asked the subject of his meditations, said, "I was looking at the casemates, for I fear I shall soon be quartered there." But with this fate so probably awaiting him, he addressed himself with increased energy to his mission. His patriotic endeavors had made the opposition to the Government more determined; and after the close of the Diet he removed to Pesth, a central and beautiful city, where he could wield more widely his resources of reform.

Here he reported and circulated as before, the doings of the County Assemblies, but no longer confining himself to a bare record of the proceedings, he added to these political remarks of the keenest satire and most bitter denunciation. His pen was barbed with sharpest invective, and eloquent reproach. This exasperated his haughty foe. Wesselenyi and his companions had fallen, but Kossuth was an enemy more dreaded than all other enemies of royal usurpation.

On the evening of the 4th of May, 1837, the patriot was walking out for lonely and quiet contemplation in the vicinity of the fortress, where he had before been surprised in his reveries. The Danube was rolling in all its rushing freedom near his feet— —the stars were flashing in their unfettered and solemn march above him—the sighing yet soothing breeze came on free wing to his feverish temples— but his native land was in chains! His expanding and quickened mind wandered indignantly away to the palace whence went abroad the blighting curse upon the fairest handiwork of God. He *felt*, in the deep solitude, that Jehovah, after his own image, had made man free to think, to will and to do; and his whole being rose in rebellion against the arrogant and blasphemous claim, that would mar the divine impress upon the human soul. It was the unutterable yearning of his heart, that every one oppressed, or in unjust bondage, should throw off the shackles, and standing upon eternal justice, appeal from him who made him a slave, to Him who made him a man. In the midst of these reveries, the Austrian myrmidons found him, and before he was aware of their approach, they had seized him; in another moment he was blindfolded and hurried away to the fortress. Without explanation, with no crime charged upon him, and no reason assigned for the lawless violence, he was thrown into a loathsome dungeon, "there to consider," says the Austrian partisan, "in darkness and solitude, how dangerous it is to defy a powerful government, and to swerve from the path of law and prudence!" But the daring outrage was too bold a stride even for a despot.

The news of this arrest and imprisonment went like a thunder-peal over Hungary, awakening popular indignation, as widely as was known the name of KOSSUTH, and the voice of the nation rose spontaneously against the cowardly and cruel seizure. The Hungarian people were not apprised of the prisoner's condition, and this only increased the earnestness of their remonstrance.

It was enough to know that he was in the hands of Austria. The government was compelled, at the expiration of a year to bring him forth to trial. With sad thoughts for his country, he made the brief transit from his cell to the tribunal of Austrian justice. The judges were on the bench, sternly waiting for the *forms* of legal process; the prisoner was already condemned. Kossuth, yet in early manhood, of medium height, attractive person, and pale from confinement, stood before the coldly calm and frowning arbiters of his fate. His forehead was broad and high, his hair of a dark and beautiful brown, flowing in natural ringlets around it, and his large, light blue eyes, shone with a two-fold expression of amiability and intellectual energy. All his features were in harmony, and stamped with penetrating mind and grandeur of character. His bearing was dignified and imposing. A man of feeling, his self-command was perfect, and he tranquilly looked upon his foes. Around that hall of justice, an excited multitude had gathered. The captive's name was in their homes and on their hearts, and they pressed like tumultuous waves around the walls that confined him.

They anxiously awaited the issue of trial. A lawyer of profound research, and glowing oratory, he was permitted to defend himself. But on that hour hung mightier interests than life. The youthful patriot was to speak for Hungary; with his past career was identified the freedom of thought and speech. The concourse without, understood the questions pending, and these absorbed the interest of the prisoner at the bar. He opened his untrembling lips, and eloquence flowed as never before in that forum. He thrilled the spectators, while glancing along his struggle for ancient rights, and spread paleness on the cheeks of his astonished judges. It was a strange and sublime scene in the history of an empire. Around the fearless form, were gathered the hopes of millions; and the world's future was connected in his doom. He ceased, and in the interlude of silence, the murmur of suppressed emotion was heard. The pause was short; the startled and troubled expounders of law, were in the meshes of their monarch. The noble, the gifted, the surpassingly eloquent advocate, had not changed the decree which was made before he confronted the heartless parasites of a corrupt government. He was condemned to four years' incarceration in the strong-hold of Buda for treason.

The throng sorrowfully dispersed, and Kossuth was borne toward the dark and lonely towers of the fortress. Before he reached the massive gates he was leaning his head upon his hand in mute meditation, when he was asked, what were his emotions. Raising his mild, and mournful eye, he replied, "I feel something *nameless* in me."

Into a deep, and dark dungeon within the old castle of Buda, he was let down to pass the lonely years. Amid the noisome, unwholesome vapors exhaled from its cavernous depths, other state prisoners had surrendered existence deemed dangerous to the government; and tyrants hoped that the same silent homicide would now add another victim to its list of murdered freemen. Poison or assassination might have been used as in centuries before, to despatch the Hungarian, but the pestilential air of a dungeon was often as efficacious, and less revolting to the refined cruelty of modern times. Solitary cells, and slow disease have been substituted for the more merciful chalice and poniard. Kossuth understood his danger, and felt his privations, but his great heart was strong. Like Lafayette at Olmutz, suffering under the pressure of the same arm, he uttered no repining and suppressed emotion which might permit his captors to triumph in his sufferings. Thank God! his mind was yet free. With manly earnestness he petitioned to be supplied with books. For twelve cheerless months, his prayer was unheard. In his own words, since:

"The first year, they gave me nothing to read, and nothing to write with: in the second, they came and told me it would be granted to me to read something, but that I must not make my choice of any political books, but only an indifferent one. I pondered a little, and knowing that a knowledge of languages was the key to sciences, I concluded that perhaps it might be useful to get some knowledge of the English language, so I told them I would name some books which would not partake in the remotest way, with politics—I asked for an English Grammar, Shakspeare, and Walker's Dictionary. The books were given, and I sat down without knowing a single word, and began to read the "Tempest," the first play of Shakspeare, and worked for a fortnight to get through the first page. I have a certain rule never to go on in reading anything without perfectly understanding what I read; so I went on, and by-and-bye became somewhat familiar with your language. Now I made that choice because I was forced not to choose a book of any political character. I chose books which had not the remotest connection with politics, but look what an instrument in the hand of Providence became my little knowledge of the English language which I was obliged to learn, because forbidden to meddle with politics."

So, while amid horrors that baffle description, he was preparing for his coming "*nameless*" future —his glorious mission. A directing Providence, in permitting him to tread the dungeon floor, passed him through an ordeal which annealed and polished his immortality for its splendid part—

"On Life's broad field of battle!"

In his long hours of solitary thought, he discovered the steady light of those ultimate principles, which are stars in the moral firmament. They shone down upon him the more clearly, as did Paradise to Milton, because of surrounding gloom.

But the perishable frame was smitten by the mildew of its humid home. His unyielding spirit strug gled to stay the progress of disease, which became so palpable, that daily walks under the eye of an officer, were allowed him upon the bastions of the fortress. This checked the progress of his decline, and with the companionship of Shakspeare, he mastered the mysterious harp of the human heart, whose chords he has touched so well.

We ask, without cant, but with solemn feeling, if the finger of God is not visible in this discipline and its issue? Kossuth became at once consecrated in the popular mind as a martyr. Liberal subscriptions were raised through the country for his mother and sisters, whom he had supported by his exertions, and who were now left without protection. Numerous public meetings were held in his behalf. The people, nobles and peasantry alike, instinctively recognized their friend, and defended his cause. The waves of popular sentiment in his behalf swept along the plains and slopes of Hungary. At Vienna, with sympathy for the man, the democratic feeling was deepened into a bond of union. Associations were formed there, and in all the chief towns and villages of the Maygar land, to sustain the natural rights of humanity against the arrogant pretensions of reigning despotism.

In the second year of his imprisonment, Austria again needed Hungarian assistance. The threatening aspect of affairs in the East, growing out of the relations between Turkey and Egypt, determined the great powers to increase their armaments. A new Hungarian Diet was to meet, and Austria signified her intention of demanding an additional levy of eighteen thousand troops. But the people who beheld the Constitution trampled in the dust of scornful princes, in the captivity of its defenders, were indisposed to meet the royal demand unless atonement were made for flagrant wrongs. A large body of delegates were chosen, pledged to refuse the supplies unless concessions were made, among which was a general amnesty of prisoners, with direct reference to Wesselenyi and Kossuth. The Government was advised by the most sagacious of the conservative party to liberate the captives with the exception of Kossuth, and to do this before the meeting of the Diet, that the release might not be a condition which would kindle a flame of excitement. But fearful of the appearance of yielding to popular clamor, the Cabinet temporized and did nothing. The Diet was opened and the contest waged during six months. The opposition controlled the Chamber of Deputies, while the Government party held the power in the House of Magnates. The struggle developed so fully the settled hostility of the nation, that Metternich and the Cabinet were alarmed, and in haste to obtain the regiments of men and close the refractory Diet. In 1840, a royal rescript suddenly made its appearance, granting the required amnesty, attended with conciliatory remarks, which immediately divided the vote for the Government claim. This management of the court naturally weakened the influence of the Hungarian Magnates, since they were exposed to the charge of being more despotic than even the Cabinet of Metternich itself.

Kossuth issued from prison on the 16th of May, 1840, after a captivity of three years; bearing in his emaciated frame, his pallid face, and sunken, glassy eye, traces of severe mental and physical suffering. But an elastic constitution, and inflexible will, had saved him from the hopeless wreck, Austrian vengeance usually made of noble forms and souls. A vast multitude had gathered under the shadow of Buda's political inquisition, to welcome the captive. That night, he was escorted through the town by a procession of torch bearers; in their lurid blaze, lighting upon the exciting scene, Austria might have beheld beacons "of quite another sort," a few years later to illumine the crimson plain.

He found his companion, the aged Wesselenyi, blind; another was a maniac, and three more were ready to die with disease contracted in their loathsome abodes. But his heart leaped for joy when he found that these sufferings of himself and companions, had awakened the people, revealing the divine beauty of liberty, and nerving them for the conflict, he, prophet-like, knew was near.

Soon after his release, Kossuth repaired for a time to the watering place of Parad, among the Matra mountains, to recruit his shattered health.

"His imprisonment had done more for his influence than he could have effected if at liberty. The visitors at the watering place treated with silent respect the man who moved about among them in dressing gown and slippers, and whose slow steps and languid features disfigured with yellow spots, proclaimed him an invalid. Abundant subscriptions had been made for his benefit and that of his family, and he now stood on an equality with the proudest Magnates. These had so often used the name of the 'martyr of the liberty of the press,' in pointing their speeches, that they now had no choice but to accept the popular verdict as their own.

"Kossuth, in the mean while, mingled little with the society at the watering place; but preferred, as his health improved, to wander among the forest-clad hills and lonely valleys, where, says one who there became acquainted with him, and was his frequent companion—'the song of birds, a group of trees, and even the most insignificant phenomena of nature furnished occasions for conversation.' But now and then flashes would appear which showed that he was revolving other things in his mind. Sometimes a chord would be casually struck which awoke deeper feelings, then his rare eloquence would burst forth with the fearful earnestness of conviction, and he hurled the sentences instinct with life and passion. The wife of the lord-lieutenant, the daughter of a great Magnate, was attracted by his appearance, and desired this companion of Kossuth to introduce him to her house When the desire was made known to Kossuth, the mysterious and nervous expression passed over his face, which characterizes it when excited. 'No,' he exclaimed, 'I will not go to that woman's house; her father subscribed four pence to buy a rope to hang me with!'"

On the 10th of January, 1841, Kossuth was married to Teresa Mezlenyi, who has since proved herself to be " *conjux conjuge nobilissimo digna.*" She was the young daughter of a nobleman, and inspired with admiration for his political career, and with sympathy for his fate, had with her mother, called upon him in prison. A correspondence began—the mutual affection, which was the result, gave to Kossuth an amiable and devoted wife. It was a strangely romantic marriage, associated thus with dungeon horrors. But the accents that came like the carol of the bird of Chillon, to his prison-gate, were ever after the æolian undertone of his stormy life.

Kossuth had pined in the twilight that steals through grated windows, for daring to unmuffle the people's voice; again free, he resolved to redeem the press. It was a bold measure, and unknown in oppressed Europe, where for ages the aspirations of humanity had been stifled. A bookseller of Pesth, had received permission from Government to issue a periodical; and on New-Year's day, 1841, appeared the first number of the Pesti Hirlap, (Pesth Gazette.)— Kossuth was invited to be its principal editor. It was published four times a week, but its rapidly increasing subscription list, soon made it a daily paper. Its circulation rose rapidly to five, six, eight, ten, twelve thousand copies. The name, LUDWIG KOSSUTH, sent the Pesth Gazette, like the beams of morning, to the dwellings of Hungary. The peasantry were electrified by remembered accents, that found an echo in their weary hearts; the unlettered formed clubs, and nightly listened to the reading of editorials breathing their own free thoughts. The great object before the mind of Kossuth was his country's independence but he knew that intelligence must precede, and the season of preparation herald the fruition of his hopes. The serf must become nature's nobleman, before the lifted hand of Austria could confer freedom to the nation. He was, therefore, the unshrinking champion of the rights of the lower and middle classes, against the exclusive privileges and immunities of the Magnates. He demanded that the house tax, should be paid without distinction of classes, not excepting the highest nobility. This levelling and fearless proposition, raised a hostile party among the nobles, who established a rival paper. Sustained by Government influence, it wielded tremendous power. When Kossuth was nominated as member from Pesth for the Diet of 1843, it defeated his election. But this neither mortified the unsuccessful candidate, nor weakened his influence with the masses. He continued his devotion to the press, while he was an active member of the local Assembly of the Capital. Untiringly advocating the concession of privileges unjustly monopolized by the Magnates, he urged the multiplication of schools, and the organization of municipalities, and progress in whatever educated the people.

Austria was not idle. She foresaw the next stride of the bold leader. In 1844, the ministry was changed, and as a consequence, the Liberals of 1838 were displaced by Imperialists. This was followed by the removal of Kossuth from the editorial chair of the Hirlap. He now gave himself earnestly to the emancipation of the serfs, and the enfranchisement of the trade of Hungary, from the prohibition to import none but Austrian manufactures, and export no Hungarian goods to Austria. An association was formed, called the bedetgyle, pledged to consume no Austrian goods until the tariff was reformed. The effect of this was immediately felt. Austrian manufacturers, to preserve their trade, had to transplant their factories to Hungary. To repress this new-born and dreaded spirit, the Court at Vienna spared no resource of tyrannical rule. It was an attempt as vain as that to still volcanic throbbings. The leaders of reform from all parts of the kingdom were assembled at Pesth, during the quarterly fairs of 1846–7. These were thronged by the common people, before whom the measures of reform were publicly and repeatedly discussed, and in every detail determined. Kossuth was the life and soul of the movement. His able speeches increased daily his popularity. His eloquence was a complete, burning utterance of practical views—of grievances, and their remedies.

Nor was he alone in the deepening struggle for rights. The venerable Wesselenyi, whose dungeon had thrown over him the midnight of hopeless blindness, was traversing the kingdom, to fan and concentrate the patriotic flame, spreading through the Magyar's domain. The cottage door flew open at his coming, and warm palms were pressed to his own. It was the Baron's noble revenge for his darkened orbs, to cheer and stir his countrymen, with his unpalsied tongue.

CHAPTER III.

COUNT BATTHYANYI—KOSSUTH IS ELECTED TO THE DIET OF 1847—MEASURES FOR REFORM—AUSTRIAN SLANDERS—KOSSUTH IN DEBATE—THE FRENCH REVOLUTION—KOSSUTH'S SPEECH—ADDRESS TO THE THRONE—OUTBREAK IN VIENNA—ACTION OF THE DIET—DEPUTATION TO THE EMPEROR—NEW MINISTRY FORMED—DARK PICTURES—THE WAR OF RACES—CAUSES—DESCRIPTION OF THE RACES IN HUNGARY—LAWS PASSED BY THE DIET—TESTIMONY OF DISTINGUISHED WRITERS.

COUNT LOUIS BATTHYANYI, one of the most prominent Magyar Magnates, subsequently President of the Hungarian Ministry, and the most illustrious martyr of the Hungarian cause, was at this juncture, the cordial friend of Kossuth and his system of reform. He brought him forward in 1847, as one of the two candidates from Pesth for the Diet about to assemble.

The Government party, aware that they were in a decided minority, limited their opposition to defeat, if possible, the election of Kossuth. Stratagem was the last resort. The liberal party nominated Szentkiraly and Kossuth. The Government party also named the former. The royal administrator, who presided at the election, decided that Szentkiraly was chosen by acclamation; but that a poll must be held for Kossuth. Before his intention of being a candidate was known, the liberals had proposed M. Balla as a second delegate. He at once declined in favor of Kossuth. Notwithstanding, the Government party cast their votes for him, to draw off a portion of the Liberal party from the support of Kossuth. M. Balla loudly, but unavailingly protested against the stratagem; and when, after a scrutiny of twelve hours, Kossuth was declared elected, Balla was the first to applaud. That night, Kossuth, Balla and Szentkiraly were serenaded by the citizens of Pesth, and, descending to the street, they walked arm in arm among the crowd. The Government faction was foiled completely. Instead of sowing discord among the candidates they had united them more cordially together, and witnessed the election of the man whom they most hated and feared. The Royal Administrator was censured for not having prevented the ominous issue; but the bitter reproaches he met were simply the language of enraged men at a triumph they could neither hinder nor change.

Kossuth took his seat in the Diet: and here begins an era in his history. He was no longer the uninfluential representative of an absent Magnate, but elected by the suffrages of his people, he could vote and speak for himself and his country. The eyes of the nation were upon him. On no other man did the people lavish so enthusiastically their wealth of love and confidence, and above none darkened as threateningly the frown of a quailing Government. The most prominent seat in the Diet was conceded him. A more accomplished parliamentary orator and debater never rose in Parliament or Senate Chamber. He made a series of attacks upon the policy of the Austrian Cabinet, with distinguished skill and effect. He was regarded then by all parties and the entire people, the most finished and forceful orator that had appeared on the floor of the Hungarian Diet. "His speeches," says an enemy, "were, even at that time, like burning arrows which he hurled into kindred minds, thereby urging them to a fanatic enthusiasm. His oratory was like a large battery, with heavy pieces of ordnance, whose discharge did the most fearful execution. The poisonous sting of his interpolations, his despotic power in the house, and his intrigues out of doors, formed in themselves a power— so to say, an army—against the stand-still policy of Metternich." He is spoken of as the orator " with the flaming tongue," who hurled his fiery projectiles at the heads of his quailing adversaries, as though he revelled in his power to kill and make alive.

Modern history furnishes nothing comparable with the scenes which transpired in that assembly. Under the glance of his haughty foes, Kossuth stood in conscious power, battling an Empire with his eloquent tongue. He swept objections away as the lion brushes the cobwebs of morning from his path. His pauses were not from exhaustion, but reminded one of the remark applied to an English orator; that his momentary stops, "were like the recoil of ordnance after discharge." He might fail to convince, but he always was *heard* with mute wonder.

There were three parties in the National Assembly; the old Conservatives, unwilling to break the ties that bound them to Austria, or to sever the chains of the people—the Progressives, who were determined to do both—and the extreme socialistic Reformers, who, on the ruins strown by the Democrats, like an architect amid the fragments of a splendid structure, wished to rebuild the civil and social fabric. Kossuth identified himself with the middle party. He scorned the parasitical policy of the first, and distrusted the theories of the last; but, whatever his differences with either, he soon fused them by the furnace-glow of his eloquence, into a grand Hungarian Federation.

"Kossuth's policy, as unfolded in a programme published in 1847, had two aspects; the one relating to foreign and international affairs, and the other to the domestic administration. With regard to Austria, it simply asserted that the independence and integrity of the kingdom should be maintained on the old basis of the laws and Constitution, but that the king should act, not through foreigners, but native Hungarians. Nothing like a revolt, however, from the Austrian connection was proposed. The patriots meant merely to go back to the old system, under which they had some opportunity of managing their own affairs. They even professed the warmest attachment to the throne, so long as they were permitted the exercise of their rights, dating back some eight hundred years. They were not then either rebels or revolutionists, but erred rather on the side of devotion to law and order.

"But their internal policy showed that while they could be tolerant, moderate, and even too loyal to a House which had inflicted so many wrongs upon them, they were determined to be fearless and just in respect to the people. They proclaimed their objects in the following propositions :

"1. That all the peasants of the Kingdom, whatever might be their religion or race, should be at once exempted from all urbarial dues and obligations to their landlords, for which the latter were to receive an indemnity from the State.

"2. That, without exception of religion or race, all the inhabitants of the country, noble and non-noble, should be declared equal before the law.

"3. That every inhabitant whose income amounted to ten pounds, (fifty dollars,) which included all persons not vagabonds or State paupers, should possess the elective franchise.

"4. That every inhabitant should bear his equal proportion of the expense of the Government, by being taxed on his income.

"5. That the Hungarian Diet, not the Chancery at Vienna, should decide on the employment of the public revenue.

"6. That the revenue and other National interests, should be put into the hands of a Cabinet of native Ministers, who would be responsible to the people, whose interests they represented.

"Besides these more general principles, it was proposed that all real estate should be held responsible for its owner's debts; that the whole tithing system, which had been so oppressive to the poor, should be abolished; that the nobles, though they were about to relinquish more than half their possessions, should be taxed on what remained; that the Jewish and foreign inhabitants should no longer be subject to special legislation, but be brought under the laws common to all the citizens; and that eight millions of dollars should be immediately expended in works of internal improvement.

"These laws were all regularly carried through both Chambers, and five millions of serfs raised in one day to the dignity of landholders and free citizens, the most generous and sublime legislative act on record!"*

These points should be distinctly noticed by those who have delighted to charge upon Louis Kossuth

---

* Godwin.

an alliance with the nobles to keep the peasants in their long-continued subjection. Never was a more false, malicious fabrication circulated by Austrian hate. And yet, there are some professedly wise men among us, who have made themselves a target for ridicule in believing it. Of other Austrian slanders in the same vein, we shall have something farther to say when we speak of the "War of Races."

Owing to the mismanagement of the Imperial Ministry, a general stagnation of trade prevailed through the country. The National Bank was distrusted, and its notes refused in Hungary and Bohemia. The disorder caused by this induced a motion of inquiry in reference to the Bank. This was made by the conservative deputies from the county of Raab, upon the 4th of March, two days after the news of the French Revolution of February had reached Presburg, where the Assembly was holding its sessions. Kossuth rose to speak upon it. The tidings from Paris had profoundly impressed him. In his deeply impressive manner, he uttered what every Hungarian felt, but which no Hungarian had dared to speak:

"I am happy and grateful in seconding the motion of the honorable member for Raab, although I am firmly convinced that the extraordinary features of the present time compel us to take our leave of private bills. I second his motion because I think it a fit opportunity to entreat you to be alive to the enormous responsibility of the moment, and to raise the policy of the parliament to a level with the times. The local question in relation to the Bank I will not now discuss. It is true, Magyars, Austria has embarrassed us long enough.

But this is a secondary matter. What we ought to ask for, is the budget of the Hungarian receipts and expenditures, which have hitherto been mixed up with those of our neighbors. We ought to ask for the constitutional administration of our finances. We ought to ask for a separate and independent financial board for Hungary; for, unless we have this the foreign government which rules us without our advice, is likely to embarrass our finances almost to hopelessness. In a recent speech, touching the relations of Austria to this country, I expressed my conviction, that the constitutional future of our nation will not be secure, till the King is surrounded by constitutional forms in all the relations of his government. I expressed my conviction, that our country was not sure of the reforms it desired at home; that we could not be sure of the constitutional tendencies of those reforms, and of their results so long as the system of the monarchy, which has the same prince that we have, remains in direct opposition to constitutionalism, and so long as that privy council, which conducts the general administration of the monarchy, and which has an illegal and powerful influence on the internal affairs of the country, remains anti-constitutional in its elements, its composition and its tendency. I expressed my conviction, that, whenever our interests conflict with the allied interests of the monarchy, the differences thus created, can be removed without danger to our liberty and welfare only on the basis of a common constituency. I cast a sorrowful look on the origin and the development of the bureaucratical system of Vienna. I remind you that it reared the fabric of its marvellous power on the ruins of the liberty of our neighbors; and recounting the consequences of this fatal mechanism, and perusing the Book of Life, I prophesy it in the feeling of my truthful and faithful loyalty to the royal house, that that man will be the second founder of the House of Hapsburg, who will reform the system of government on a constitutional basis, and re-establish the throne of his house on the liberty of his people."

In still bolder language, he continues:

"Mighty thrones, supported by political sagacity and power, have been overthrown, and nations have fought for and won their liberty, who three months ago could not have dreamed of the proximity of such an event. But for three whole months we are compelled to roll the stone of Sisyphus incessantly and without avail; and my mind I confess is clouded with almost the grief of despair, at witnessing the languid progress which the cause of my country has made. I see with sorrow so much power, so true and noble a will toiling at this ungrateful and unrequited task. Yes, honorable deputies, the curse of a stifling vapor weighs upon us,—a pestilential air sweeps over our country from the charnel-house of the Viennese council of state, enervating our power, and exciting a deadening effect upon our national spirit. But while hitherto my anxiety has been caused by seeing the development of the resources of Hungary checked by this blighting influence, to the incalculable injury of my country, by seeing the constitutional progress of the nation unsecured, and that the antagonism which has existed for three centuries between the absolutist government of Vienna, and the constitutional tendency of the Hungarian nation, has not up to this day been reconciled, nor ever can be reconciled, without the abandonment of either the one or the other,—my apprehension at the present time is increased by other causes, and a fear weighs upon my mind, lest this bureaucratic system, this policy of fixedness, which has grown to be part and parcel of the Viennese council of state, should lead to a dissolution of the monarchy, compromise the existence of our dynasty, and entail upon our country, which requires all her powers and resources for her own internal affairs, heavy sacrifices and interminable evils.

"Such is the view I take of present affairs, and regarding them in this light, I deem it my urgent duty to call upon this honorable assembly seriously to direct its attention to the subject, and to devise means of averting the danger which threatens our country. We, to whom the nation has entrusted her present protection and her future security, cannot and dare not stand idly by and shut our eyes upon events and their consequences, until our country is gradually deluged by a flood of evil. To prevent the evil is the task to which we are called; and satisfied I am, that if we neglect our duty, we shall be responsible for the ill that may result from our neglect, in the sight of God, before the world, and to our own consciences. If persisting in a perverse policy, we allow the opportunity for effecting a peaceable settlement to pass, and neglect to make the free and loyal sentiments of the representatives of this nation heard, we may repent it when the die has been irrevocably cast, when the embarrassment has proceeded so far as to leave us only the choice between an unconditional refusal, or sacrifices which no one can calculate; but repentance will then come too late, and the favorable moment which was allowed to pass in listless inaction will be gone forever. As a deputy of this assembly, I for one will have no share in this responsibility, although as a citizen of our country, I may be obliged to participate in the consequences of a tardy repentance."

In this speech was foreshadowed a revolution. It was talked of in whispers at Presburg and Vienna; for keen-sighted men could now catch the distant oncoming of the fearful struggle. Said Count Pulsky when he heard of it: "Next autumn our fields will no more be tilled by soccage; feudal institutions will disappear in Europe."

Kossuth concluded his speech by moving an "Address to the throne," in which a series of reformatory measures were urged. "Among the foremost of these was the emancipation of the country from feudal burdens—the proprietors of the soil to be indemnified by the state; equalizing taxation· a faithful administration of the revenue to be satisfactorily guaranteed; the further development of the representative system; and the establishment of a government representing the voice of, and responsible to the nation." Not a word was uttered in reply, and the motion was unanimously carried.

The great design of Kossuth at this period, was to procure an entire change in the imperial administration. By this he anticipated not only the liberation of Hungary, but that of all the states in the Austrian Empire. To his own land he wished their old constitution restored, and to the others he desired new constitutions to be granted, upon the same basis. That Hungary must be free, was to him a settled point; but he clearly saw that freedom could not be, and retain connection with Austria, unless that Power should yield forever and entirely its despotic functions. It was an absurdity to dream of a constitutional King and a tyrannical Emperor, united in the same man. Yet it was precisely this that was attempted when Ferdinand took upon himself the coronation oaths of the King of Hungary. But if the constitutional King might also become a constitutional Emperor, then all that was required for freedom might be gained.

This was Kossuth's grand scheme of bringing all the Austrian States into one confederaey, with the Emperor's powers limited and prescribed by a free constitution. He no more contemplated at first a
Washington and

relation, provided its ancient constitution could be preserved.

With this secured to Hungary, "It was then," said he, "the proper and holy mission of our nation, as the oldest member of the empire, and possessing a constitutional form of government, to raise its voice in behalf of those sister nations under the same ruler, and who are united to us by so many ties of relationship. Lovers of freedom, we would not ask liberty for ourselves alone—we would not boast of privileges that others did not enjoy, but desired to be free in fellowship with free nations around us. This motion was inspired by the conviction that two crowns—a constitutional and despotic crown—could not be worn by the same head, any more than two opposing dispositions can harmonize in the same breast, or than a man can be good and evil at the same time."

In his speech above quoted, and in the address to the throne, moved with it, those truths were distinctly defined. They had fallen with a profound meaning upon his hearers, but the Diet was not ready for action. The leaven was working, and the quick eye of the orator discovered the issue. The Cabinet of native ministers, which in the first ages had always resided at the Magyar capital, and attended to Hungarian questions, had been removed to the Austrian Court, and reduced to a little bureau of clerks, called a Chancery, a creature of imperial caprice.

The impossibility of independence under this system, was hinted in his speech, yet the crisis in popular feeling had not come. A few days after, followed the Austrian Revolution A Democratic mine was sprung in Vienna itself. The masses inflamed by Kossuth's speeches in the Diet, had risen with fierce determination, and boldly demanded their trampled rights. The troops refused to fire upon the excited populace, and the Emperor, terror-smitten, was the toy of their wrath.

With the news from Paris ringing like a knell in his ear, and the wild shouts of his own subjects drowning every other echo, while the host surged and swayed around his own palace, as waves clasp a summit, his cowardly heart yielded to fear, what conscience would not have wrung from his unwilling hand. An imperial manifesto was issued, conceding all that his people had asked. Metternich was dismissed, liberty of the press was restored, the publicity of the law-courts was ensured—trial by jury was granted, and the promise given of a representative and free constitution, according to Kossuth's idea, which, suggested by him, the Viennese patriots unyieldingly demanded. The tidings of this successful insurrection, went like lightning to Presburg. The rumor of the outbreak was heard with amazement. Kossuth alone was ready for the storm. With great courage, wisdom, and eloquence, he arose before the representatives, who were dumb with painful surprise, and calmly yet most earnestly urged the proposition, to send a deputation from their body to the Emperor, requiring an immediate dissolution of the Chancery, and the restoration of the

Cabinet in its place, as guaranteed by the Constitution. His tones grew strong and trumpet-like, his face was luminous with quenchless fire, and with a graceful sweep of his arm, he pointed to the ministerial seats, made vacant by despotism, and exclaimed:

"For six hundred years, Magyars, we formed a constitutional state, we will, therefore, that from this moment, ministers again sit upon these benches, to hear and answer our questions. From this day forth, Magyars, we wish to have a Hungarian ministry!"

He resumed his seat. There was none to break the stillness. Each member, thrilled with the solemn appeal, and absorbed with the interests at stake, communed with his own thoughts.

There was a sublime impressiveness in the surprise. The balance, with Hungary in one scale, and Austrian claims in the other, wavered before the breath of that single orator. The pause was brief. It was the forethought of noble minds, stirred by vital truths, more burningly spoken than ever before by human lips. The response was unanimous—the decision made. A committee was chosen to repair to the palace. Kossuth was at the head of this band of heroic men; he appeared at Vienna on the 13th of March, 1848. The people hailed him as the *father* of their country, and their rejoicings were heard unceasingly in the streets of the Capital. They gave to his unostentatious embassy, the glory of a triumphal entry, and lifted him in their strong arms into the palace. There he confronted the startled

NEW MINISTRY FORMED.

and trembling counsellors of the monarch, and *him*, the indignant impersonation of absolute principles. The glittering train of attendants circled away in that royal apartment, and the splendor of a throne against which five centuries had vainly beat, was over them all. The prisoner of Buda gazed without a blush or a fear upon him whose captive he had been, and thought only of the millions of Hungarians, whose freedom and future greatness were in his hands. It was an hour of moral grandeur seldom witnessed by King or Courtier.

Kossuth modestly, but with the tone of a determined heart, urged his demands. The Emperor listened; the orator finished, and waited with the tranquillity of a summit reposing in the serene heaven, while girdled with storms, for the reply. The monarch hesitated—the courtly throng curled the lip in scorn—but as the sound of many waters came the voices of the moving masses. This wild clamor gave to the eloquence of the advocate, the energy of conviction. Ferdinand granted the request, and Count Louis Batthyanyi, received the command to form immediately a cabinet. Let Hungary and the world write their names on imperishable tablets.

COUNT LOUIS BATTHYANYI, Prime Minister.
BERTALAN SZEMERE, Home Affairs.
LOUIS KOSSUTH, Finances.
FRANCIS DEAK, Justice.
GENERAL LAZAR MEZSAROS, War.
GABOR KLAUZAL, Trade.
COUNT STEPHEN SZECHENYI, Public Works.

Baron Iosef Eotvos, Public Instruction.

Prince Paul Esterhazy, Minister around the person of the King, and entrusted with the regulation of international concerns between Hungary and the Austrian provinces, and therefore called Minister of Foreign Affairs.

What Ferdinand had yielded, was extorted by cowardly fear—he quailed before the fierce resolves of the people. While yet the solemn vows were at his lips, he was meditating the basest perjury. He had given to Hungary her demand, but had plotted her total extinction as a nation. The means employed to blot a brave nation from separate existence, disclosed a heart unvisited by justice or mercy.

Metternich's policy had been to preserve the Austrian ascendency in Hungary by kindling jealousies among the races. Union was prevented, and Metternich believed that no one race would venture alone on rebellion. This demoniac resort was perfectly adapted to the genius of the Hapsburg dynasty. It prevailed after Metternich had left its councils. And, while yet the shouts of rejoicing rang along the valleys, and the bonfires were burning on the hills of the Maygar land, Ferdinand sent abroad his agents to do the work of assassins, stab the country in the dark, by bringing together in deadly conflict those who were peacefully dwelling within their boundary lines. The Croats, the Servians, the Wallachs, Sclaves, the Wends, the Saxons, by arguments and gold, appeals to traditional and religious

THE WAR OF RACES. 73

prejudice, and by all the reckless instrumentalities which power is quick to handle and jealousy ready to believe, were persuaded that the Magyars designed only their own elevation at the expense of the rest. Absurd and shameful pretence; yet the races, blinded and stimulated by the prestige and power of the empire, rose in bloody insurrection.

Much has been said upon this civil contest, and many have been deceived by Austrian tales; it may therefore be well, to give farther proof of the assertion concerning the origin of the Hungarian War.

First, a distinct conception of the races is indispensable.

The Magyars of Hungary are the principal race, though not a majority of the whole population. They number 5,000,000. The Wallachs number 2,317,340; the Saxons, 1,422,168; the Slovacks, 2,220,000; the Ruthenes, 350,000; the Wends, 50,000; the Croats, 1,352,966; the Servians, 943,000; and the Sclavonians 1,000,000.* The Sclavic is not applied to any specifically, but is a generic term, including the Slovacks, the Croatians, the Servians and the Sclavonians. These different races have not been mingled to any extent, but have preserved their distinct identity through all the periods of Hungarian history. The Magyars have generally been dominant in the Government, although their neighbors have had a representation in the Diet. The question then is,

---

* Hanfler's Map of the Austrian Possessions.

whether the efforts of Kossuth and his confederates in the Diet of 1848, were to preserve this ascendency of the Magyars at the expense of other races. This is the charge distinctly made by Austrian writers, and reiterated by papers devoted to the same interest in England and America. A charge so grave ought to rest on the clearest evidence; but we conceive it to be unsustained by any proof whatever. For during the whole of the period now in question, there was no act passed by the Diet, without regard to the complete equality of the different classes represented. The Magyars struggled to elevate all to a higher position of freedom and independence. The nobles of other nations had always stood by the side of the Magyars, having an equal voice in the Assembly, while in this Diet, the peasants of all the races enjoyed the same equality. Political distinctions were abolished, and it is worthy of particular remark and admiration, that this grand movement was introduced and consummated by the Maygars themselves. The race which has been charged with oppression, was the one by which the principle of equality, of civil rights for all, was made a practical principle. In proof of this we cite the following from Alison, written with the laws of this period before him:

"By unanimous votes of both houses, the Diet not only established perfect equality of civil rights and public burdens amongst all classes, denominations and Races in Hungary and its Provinces, and perfect toleration for every form of religious worship, but, with a generosity perhaps unparalleled in the history of nations, and which must extort the admiration even of those

TESTIMONY OF DISTINGUISHED WRITERS. 75

who may question the wisdom of the measure, the nobles of Hungary abolished their own right to exact either labor or produce in return for the lands held by urbarial tenure, and thus transferred to the peasants the absolute ownership, free and forever, of nearly half the cultivated land in the kingdom, reserving to the original proprietors of the soil such compensation as the Government might award from the public funds of Hungary. More than five hundred thousand peasant families were thus invested with the absolute ownership of from thirty to sixty acres of land each, or about twenty millions of acres amongst them. The elective franchise was extended to every man possessed of capital or property to the value of thirty pounds, or an annual income of ten pounds—to every man who has received a diploma from a university, and to every artisan who employs an apprentice. With the concurrence of both countries, Hungary and Transylvania were united, and their Diets, hitherto separate, were incorporated. The number of representatives which Croatia was to send to the Diet was increased from three to eighteen, while the internal institutions of that province remained unchanged, and Hungary undertook to compensate the proprietors for the lands surrendered to the peasants to an extent greatly exceeding the proportion of that burden which would fall on the public funds of the province. The complaints of the Croats, that the Magyars desired to impose their own language upon the Sclavonic population, were considered, and every reasonable ground of complaint removed. Corresponding advantages were extended to the other Sclavonic tribes, and the fundamental laws of the kingdom, except in so far as they were modified by these acts, remained unchanged.

" The whole of these acts passed in March, 1848, received the royal assent, which, on the 11th of April, the Emperor personally confirmed at Presburg, in the midst of the Diet. These acts then became statutes of the kingdom, in accordance with which the new responsible Hungarian ministry was formed, and commenced the performance of its duties with the full concurrence of the emperor-king and the aid of the Archduke Palatine. The changes that had been effected were received with gratitude by the peasants, and with entire satisfaction, not only by the population of Hungary Proper, but also by that of all the Sclavonic provinces. From Croatia more especially, the expression of satisfaction was loud and apparently sincere."

This testimony is decided, and is strengthened by the following from Klapka:

"Our parliamentary Opposition (headed by Kossuth) was at all times a strenuous advocate of the Servian nationality and religion; and in March, 1848, when the Opposition carried its most liberal Constitution, and when that Constitution was sanctioned by the King, it afforded the safest guarantee against the persecution and opposition of the Servian people. By virtue of the new Constitution, the peasant of Servia, like the peasant of Hungary, was raised to the rank of a Freeman and Citizen of the State. A voluntary surrender of property was made to him. His national existence was guaranteed by a free and independent Municipal Constitution. The Servian soldiers on the frontier were, according to the despotic regulations of the frontier service, incapable of holding landed or any other immovable property; they were ill-treated and whipped by the Austrian officers. The new Constitution raised them from the lowest depths of misery. The Hungarians received them as friends and brethren, for the Hungarian character was at all times a stranger to national animosity and religious intolerance. The Servians were by no means blind to the advantages of their new institutions. They received them with exultation. The colors of Hungary and Servia fluttered from their steeples. The Servian towns sent deputations to the Parliament, to offer their thanks and congratulations."

CHAPTER IV.

SPECIAL PRIVILEGES GRANTED TO CROATIA—PERFIDY OF AUSTRIA—JELLACHICH APPOINTED BAN OF CROATIA—HIS MOVEMENTS—SCLAVIC UNION AND EMPIRE—SERVIAN REVOLT—HORRID CRUELTIES—KOSSUTH SENDS AN ARMY TO QUELL THE INSURRECTION—RESULT—TOKENS OF A HASTENING STORM—KOSSUTH'S DISCERNMENT—JELLACHICH PROPOSES TO INVADE HUNGARY—REMONSTRANCE OF THE MINISTRY—DUPLICITY OF THE KING—ROYAL MANIFESTO.

CROATIA had less reason than any other province to complain of the legislation. She had previously possessed a national or general Assembly for the regulation of her internal affairs, and was federally represented in the Diet by three deputies. Her executive was held by a Governor under the old feudal title of the Ban. She differed materially from Hungary Proper, in respect to religious freedom; for Croatia would tolerate no public Protestant worship. But in the wise policy of the Hungarian Diet, while they extended in the widest sense, freedom and equal laws, and the old feudal offices of the State were abolished in Hungary, the dignity and power of the Ban of Croatia were continued. Besides, the influence of Croatia in the Legislative Assembly, was increased by allowing her to send eighteen instead of three representatives. Croatians were called to fill the State employments of their country. The use of their language was guaranteed in their official business; and Hungary promised to examine all additional demands preferred. In her liberality, a step beyond justice was taken, by yielding to the religious intolerance of the province, by maintaining the ancient supremacy and exclusive domination of the Roman Catholic faith.

Let it now be especially noted, that in the general joy felt by the nation at the passage of these acts, and those above referred to, the masses partook without distinction. As they received the royal sanction, a universal acclamation echoed from the banks of the Drave, to the Carpathian summits, in which none but Austrian hirelings refused to join. These two facts, then, are sufficiently clear; first, that the various races had every reason to be satisfied with the legislation of the Diet; and second, that they really *were so*. What then were the elements of discord and revolt? Why should the sword so soon leap from its scabbard to sunder the ties of this brotherhood, wrought with generous care? It was not because of the Magyar's wish to lord it over the Croat or the Serb. No historical fact can be more triumphantly established. Subsequent events have shown the rising to have been the result of Austrian intrigue. The insurrectionary movement was guided at Vienna. Louis Gay, a Croat journalist, devoted to Austria, was sent by the Government to his countrymen, to create hostility against the Hungarians, and so prepare the way for Hapsburg oppression. Others followed him, and the plot was briskly prosecuted. The Sclavic delegation, which had been sent to express the gratitude of the provinces to their Magyar benefactors, had returned to their homes to be met by the emissaries of an unprincipled court, who, with demoniac skill, were busily reviving the buried dissensions of the races.

The first point urged in opposition to the Magyars, was the decree of the Diet of 1832, respecting the future language in which the business of the Assembly should be transacted. Before that time the Diet had been a confused Babel of provincial tongues; and it was to remedy the evil, that the Assembly determined to select a language to be used officially in national affairs. What dialect should be chosen but the Magyar? This was spoken by twice as many people as used any other, and was the native tongue of the great majority of the representatives. It was, therefore, judiciously and justly selected.

Gay and his associates went back to this act, and, perverting its meaning, pointed to it as the interpreter of the more recent legislation of the Diet. "Behold," said they, "the Magyars have taken away your language, and they would now remove your nationality also. They would merge your existence in theirs, that they may become the more glorious thereby. True, they have given you some advantages, but these are only to lure you on the more readily to your own destruction as individual races. Every other race is to be swallowed up in the Magyar, as every other language has been excluded from the National Diet for that. Rise, and throw off the yoke before it shall have become so closely fastened to your necks that resistance will be in vain." Still farther splendid visions of Sclavic supremacy were held before the mind. A union of all the Sclavic races, was the day-dream of the Croat. To take the power from the Magyars, and give to the Sclaves forever a predominance in the National Councils, was the glorious reward offered for a brief struggle. Ignorant and jealous—in every respect inferior to the Magyars, the Sclaves were exposed to the delusive power of such appeals.

Threatening unrest began to appear about the first of June. Leading members of the Servian aristocracy met at Karlowicz, and formed a "Central Committee of the Servian nation." They drew up a paper, entitled—Demands of the Servian People—and sent it on to Pesth by an angry delegation. The Hungarians were amazed. Some of the more discerning saw the hidden spring of the movement, and pitied, more than they blamed, their deluded countrymen. Hoping that mild treatment might yet win them to union, they carefully abstained from reproaches in return, and hoped that delay would dispel the illusion, and cool the passions of their indignant neighbors. Instead, there were isolated acts of revenge, followed by murder, and soon these became frequent and brutal. At length came open insurrection, and, as when the torch touches a magazine, fast upon the first blaze of popular excitement, the work of vengeance ran through the Servian and Wallachian provinces, a fraternal and horrible slaughter. The sanguinary atrocities are without a parallel. The Servians and Wallachs fell like a troop of tigers upon the Magyars and Germans found in their confines, who, stung with revenge, returned the bloody attack.

The Servians in their warfare emulated the French Papists under Charles IX., on St. Bartholomew's Day when the sluices of Paris ran blood. No age or condition was spared their avenging and savage assaults. At midnight, families were awakened to shriek and die under the assassin's club; sleeping infants were torn from maternal arms, and their unoffending forms trodden beneath the enemy's feet; quickly followed upon the imploring mother the relentless stroke. Sex, tears, and decaying health were no protection in the lawless murder of innocence and beauty. Houses were burned around their inmates, and the fruitful plains were desolate behind the invaders. Villages disappeared—" the fields and flocks of the unprepared and unresisting inhabitants, were destroyed by these infuriated rebels. The voice of lamentation was spread over many districts. A cold shudder convulsed the Magyar nation."

While such was the terror and suffering in the Banat and the Bacska, Croatia and the southern provinces were ripening for a similar gory harvest. Austrian interference had destined Croatia as the central scene of a tragedy, whose heroic victims were the Magyars. To control the movement, the corrupt and ambitious court selected the Baron Joseph Jellachich, a Croatian by birth, who had been Colonel of a Croat regiment in the army of Italy. He was appointed Ban of Croatia, and with instructions and authority to lead the revolt, and to make it a final settlement with the Magyars. To the credit of Jellachich, it may be recorded, that his heart revolted from this deliberate treachery; but overcome by the promises of Government, and moved by the tears of the Archduchess Sophia, who, clasping him in her arms, declared that without him they were lost, he consented to enter upon the diabolical mission. Once committed, he prosecuted the work with energy; he was not a man to falter from his purpose. With conscience driven to consent or silence, he was fitted for the butchery of his countrymen. In many things his abilities and character would commend him to admiration. He was a poet, a scholar, and a wit. He was a bold, chivalrous and generous officer, highly popular among his soldiers, possessing an easy address and a fervid, enthusiastic mode of utterance, which won the affection of the masses in his native province. His office of Ban, gave him the command within the limits of Croatia, and he hastened to use his supremacy for his royal master.

His first official act was to declare the new Hungarian Ministry unauthorized to review Croatian affairs, and forbid the magistrates who were his satellites, to recognize or hold intercourse with that Assembly. By letters and personal appeals, he taught resistance to Magyar legislation. He assured his countrymen that open revolt would meet with encouragement and favor from the king. The Servian rebellion was quoted, and the probable union of the Sclavic races was still the theme. The subtle poison transfused into the veins of society, spread gradually but surely, till the blood was on fire, leaping through all its channels with fever madness. Meanwhile, Kossuth and his brave people, were neither ignorant nor careless of the footsteps of their foe. He felt, with them, a heart throb at every echo of coming conflict.

The tidings of the insurrection of May 14th, had reached the Ministry, succeeded with frequent tales of barbarities committed by the Serbs,* which blanched the cheek of manhood. The inventive genius of cruelty among them, surpasses the satanic devices of the Neronic persecution.

"They bored out the eyes of men, cut off the flesh in strips, roasted them alive on spits, and buried them up to their necks, and so left them to be eaten by crows and swine. Still more horrible, crying yet louder for Heaven's vengeance, they ripped open women big with child, and trampled the fruit of the womb before the eyes of the dying mother."†

These increasing horrors demanded from the Ministry decisive, immediate action. An army was organized and marched to the scene of blood. The instructions given to the troops, in which we distinctly discern the amiable spirit of the great leader, Kossuth, were to proceed with moderation in their treatment of the Serbs. He knew that with their unexampled

---

* It will be understood that Serb and Servian are synonymous.

† "I affirm, on my conscience," says Pragay, "and without exaggeration, that hundreds upon hundreds of examples in each kind of these barbarities occurred."

atrocities, they were yet "more sinned against than sinning;" and hoped that mercy, attending and prevailing over justice, might restore them to amity and faith. The forces sent, met the insurgents, and in numerous engagements were generally successful. The martial character of the Hungarians is unsullied. Of skill beyond their opportunities, and bravery unyielding, recent annals are gloriously mournful proof. The Serbs might have seen the hopelessness of resistance, but blinded by folly, and goaded on by human and invisible demons, they paused only when conquered, to renew more fiercely the havoc upon recovered strength. When the campaign closed, and the Hungarian troops were withdrawn for a wider field, the volcano was calmed a moment, *at the crater* only.

The struggle began with the Serbs; but to Kossuth's prophetic eye, it was then no more than the herald-cloud of the tempest. With deep concern he watched Croatia, and his pulse quickened with a strange and sad foreboding, as the plot thickened and blackened under the wing of royal treachery.

The preparations of the Ban compelled the Ministry to notice his designs. Statutes passed by the votes of Croatian representatives, were contemptuously unregarded; and the delegate despatched to remonstrate against the violations of compact, was denied a reception. Preparations for war were made, and in defiance of all law, Jellachich had convoked a Croatian Assembly, by which he was designated the Ban and military chieftain of the province. In this he was not without the secret co-operation of

Ferdinand, who was devoting his infantile mind, aided by counsellors, to the single necessity of smiting down uprising liberty, before whose radiant form his crown waxed dim.

Kossuth could not believe his fears of such harmony between the king and Ban, and sent a deputation to solicit royal aid. His representations were so earnest that Ferdinand must either drop his mask and take a hostile attitude, or declare for the Hungarians, and denounce Jellachich, who was plainly guilty of treason to the State. Owing to recent reverses of his army in Italy, he dared not challenge the fiery Magyars, and to hush the murmurs of apprehension, and farther to conceal his maturing plans, he resolved to condemn the Ban. There never was a blacker deed of treachery than this monarch perfected. With a smile upon his lips, and words of sympathy on his tongue, his heart was a hell, burning with traitorous thoughts towards the nation whose rights he had sworn to defend. Jellachich was formally summoned to his presence to make his plea, and a royal manifesto was issued declaring him a traitor, and depriving him of his honors. A part of this curious document we quote, partly for the proof it furnishes, in connection with subsequent events, of Ferdinand's duplicity, and partly for the convincing evidence it contains, that the Hungarian war was battling for freedom. Every word of it is a clear and unanswerable defence of the Magyar against the disaffected Sclaves. Having announced the sadness with which "*his paternal heart"* had learned of their rebellion, the document proceeds:

"With you, Croatians and Sclavonians! who, united to the crown of Hungary for eight centuries, shared all the fates of this country; you, Croatians and Sclavonians, *who owe to this very union the constitutional freedom, which alone amongst all Sclavonic nations you have been enabled to preserve for centuries;* we were doomed to be mistaken with you, *who not only have shared in all the rights and liberties of the Hungarian Constitution,* but who besides—in just recompense of your loyalty. until now stainlessly preserved—were lawfully endowed with peculiar rights, privileges, and liberties, by the grace of our illustrious ancestors, and *who, therefore, possess greater privileges than any whosoever of the subjects of our sacred Hungarian crown.* We were mistaken in you, *to whom the last Diet of the kingdom of Hungary and its dependencies, according to our own sovereign will, granted full part in all the benefits of the enlarged constitutional liberties, and equality of rights.*— The legislation of the crown of Hungary has abolished feudal servitude, *as well with you* as in Hungary; and those amongst you, who were subjected to the soccage, have without any sacrifice on their part become free proprietors. The landed proprietors receive for their loss, occasioned by the abolition of soccage, an indemnification, which you with your own means would be unable to provide. The indemnification granted on this account to your landed proprietors, will be entailed upon our Hungarian crown estates with our sovereign ratification, and without any charge to yourselves.

"*The right, also, of constitutional representation was extended to the people with you no less than in Hungary;* in consequence of which, no longer the nobility, alone, *but likewise other inhabitants* and the Military Frontier, *take part by their representatives in the legislation common to all,* as much as in the municipal congregations. *Thus you can improve your welfare* by your immediate co-operation. Until now, the nobility contributed but little to the public expenses, henceforward the proportional repartition of the taxes amongst all inhabitants is lawfully established, whereby you have been delivered from an oppressive charge. Your nationality and municipal rights, relative to which ill-intentioned and malicious reports have been spread with the aim of exciting your distrust, are by no means threatened. On the very contrary, both your nationality and your municipal rights are enlarged, and secured against any encroachment; as not only the use of your native language, is lawfully guaranteed to you forever, in your schools and churches, but it is likewise introduced in the public assemblies, where the Latin has been habitual until now.

" Calumniators sought to make you believe that the Hungarian nation desired to suppress your language, or at least to prevent its further development. We ourselves assure you, that these reports are totally false, and that it is recognized with approbation, that you exert yourselves to develop and establish your own mother tongue, renouncing the dead Latin language. The legislature is willing to support you in this effort, by providing adequately for your priests, to whom is entrusted the spiritual care of the soul, and the education of your children. *For eight centuries you have been united to Hungary. During this whole time the legislature has ever dealt with due regard to your nationality.* How could you, therefore, believe that the legislature, which has guarded your mother-tongue for eight centuries, should now bear a hostile aversion to it ?" * * *

After more in the same vein, the decree proceeds in the following strain of concentrated perjury :

" We, the King of Hungary, Croatia, Sclavonia and Dalmatia —we, whose person is sacred to you—we tell you, Croatians and Sclavonians, the law, too, is sacred, and must be considered so ! WE HAVE SWORN TO THE ETERNAL KING OF ALL KINGS, THAT WE OURSELVES WILL PRESERVE THE INTEGRITY OF OUR HUNGA-

RIAN CROWN, AND OF OUR CONSTITUTION, AND THAT WE WILL NO LESS OBEY THE LAW, THAN WE WILL HAVE IT OBEYED BY OTHERS. WE WILL KEEP OUR ROYAL OATH!"

The swiftly passing events that followed, tell how well the kingly oath was kept.

CHAPTER V.

EFFORTS OF JELLACHICH—OPENING OF THE NEW HUNGARIAN DIET—SPEECH OF THE PALATINE—KOSSUTH'S SPEECH—THE KING WITHDRAWS HIS DENUNCIATION OF JELLACHICH—SURPRISE OF THE HUNGARIANS—DEPUTATION TO THE KING—EVASIVE ANSWER—THE SIGNAL OF CONFLICT.

JELLACHICH left his sovereign but not his army. He artfully treated the whole affair at the palace, as a courtly farce. The mandate to submit to the Hungarian Ministry, and disband his regiment, was afterward received; but the day this order was despatched, Count Latour, the Minister of War, *transmitted to him* 50,000 *guilders for the payment of his troops*, besides arms and ammunition. These supplies, it is now proved, were continued.*

Jellachich received the two despatches the same hour; and in the light of the fact, *read the manifesto.* A smile of disdain played around his proud lip at the harmless thunder of the monarch, darkened by a shade of remorse while conscience pointed to the basely inglorious part he was stooping to play. The Ban, to be sure of his men, sent to the Scla-

---

* Schutte.

vacks in the North inviting them to join the invasion.

The Sclavacks were neither fools nor knaves, and refused. "The Magyars," said they, "have done everything that could be done, by voluntarily resigning their hereditary rights and power into the hands of all the people, without distinction of sect or race, for the general good. None of your purposes nor plans can induce us to abuse such unprecedented generosity; and though Sclaves, we are yet opposed to any Sclavic establishment, under the shadow of the Russian Empire, at whose despotic rod such an establishment would have to cower and be a slave. No. The Magyars have laid the foundation of all the freedom that any tribe, or any religion, can maintain. Upon this foundation, as brothers and friends, let us together build, thankful to that noble race by whose magnanimity we have the opportunity to be free." Notwithstanding this failure and rebuke, the influence of the Ban extended East and West, until the Wallachians of Transylvania, and the inhabitants of Croatia and Sclavonia, waited his signal to rise in arms against the Magyars.

The Hungarians sent a new deputation to the Emperor-King, beseeching his Majesty to come in person to Pesth, on the occasion of the approaching Diet, and convince the enemies of Hungary that he was sincere in his proclamations; but the prayer was unheard. They farther requested the Archduke John to address himself directly to the Croats.

declaring that Ferdinand frowned upon the insurrection; but he deigned no reply.

Hungary began to comprehend her condition. Kossuth boldly affirmed his belief, that the Hapsburg was playing a Judas-game. "It has never been otherwise," said he, "their solemn oaths have been broken, their sacred pledges violated, ever since they have worn the Hungarian crown. There is perfidy now as there has always been."

To gain farther time, another trick of deception was palmed upon the Hungarians. On the 2d of July, the National Diet, which was really the first representation by the suffrages of the people, was opened at Pesth. The Archduke Palatine read the address dictated by Ferdinand, in which the sceptred traitor continued his dastardly dealing. The document is interesting, but we quote only the portion bearing on the present issue:

"In the name, and as representative of our glorious reigning King Ferdinand V., I hereby open the present Diet. The extraordinary circumstances in which the country has been placed, make it necessary to summon at once a meeting of the Diet, without waiting for the completion in detail of all the propositions and administrative measures which the responsible Ministers of the Crown were charged and directed by the past Diet, to prepare and complete. Croatia rose in undisguised sedition; in the Districts of the lower Danube, bands of armed rebels have broken the peace of the country, and while *it is the sincere wish of his Majesty to avoid a civil war*, his Majesty is, on the other hand, convinced that the assembled representatives of the nation will regard it *as their first and chief duty to provide all the means required to restore the troubled tranquillity of the country*, to preserve the integrity of the Hungarian realm, and maintain the sacred inviolability of the law. The defence of the country and the state of the finances will therefore form the chief subject towards which, under these extraordinary circumstances, I call the attention of the assembled representatives. His Majesty's responsible Ministers will submit to you propositions relating to these points. His Majesty entertains the confident hope that the representatives of the nation will adopt speedy and appropriate decisions upon all matters connected with the safety and welfare of the country.

"His Majesty has learned with deep feelings of regret and displeasure,—although he in his hearty paternal desire for the happiness of this country, *following solely the impulse of his own desire, sanctioned during the last Diet*, by giving them the royal assent, *those laws which were necessary to the progress of the country to prosperity*, under the demands of the time,—yet that, especially in Croatia and on the Lower Danube, evil-disposed rebellious agitators have excited the inhabitants of those countries, speaking different languages, and holding different creeds, with false reports and terrorism to mutual hostility, and have driven them, under the *calumnious representation* that these laws were not then sanctioned out of the free will of his Majesty, to oppose the ordinances of these laws and the legal authorities—that some even have gone so far in rebellion as to announce that their violent resistance to those decrees is for the good of the royal house, and takes place with the knowledge of his Majesty.

"For the tranquilization of the inhabitants of those districts, of all tongues and creeds, I therefore hereby declare, *under the special commission of his most gracious Majesty, our lord and King, and as his representative*, that his Majesty is firmly resolved to maintain intact, by his royal power, the integrity and inviolability of his crown against all attacks from without, and against all discord within the realm, and to assert and enforce at all times the laws he shall have sanctioned. And as his Majesty will allow no one to curtail the freedom assured by the laws to the inhabitants of the country, his Majesty *expresses his displeasure* with the daring conduct of all those who venture to assert that any illegal act or disobedience shown to the law can have taken place with his Majesty's knowledge or in the interest of his royal house."

This had weight with the weaker members, but did not for a moment deceive Kossuth, the watchman of the night. His transcendent mind saw within the veil, and the future became palpable before him. He could not then with success, in open parliament accuse the King of what he felt to be the fearful truth. But he might prepare his beloved people for coming danger. The stirring hope attuned his eloquent voice. Rising with his theme, while the gloom of a grandly solemn future hung upon his pathway, he uttered predictions and warnings with the modest yet confident tone of inspiration.

His speeches combine the Arabian fervor of Mohammed, and the religious earnestness of Cromwell. The blending of resistless persuasion, sweetest poetry and penetrating views of political economy, is the wonder of the orator. The dry details of finance caught a glow from his enthusiasm, and he could make them fire-brands to the train of slumbering thought in his auditory. He made a most elaborate and awakening speech before the Diet on the 11th of July, 1848. He alluded to it in the opening of his recent Birmingham speech.* The passages selected embody the sentiments uttered with so marvellous effect.†

---

* See Appendix.   † The omissions are not starred.

"GENTLEMEN:—In ascending the tribune to demand of you to save our country, the greatness of the moment weighs oppressively on my soul. I feel as if God had placed into my hands the trumpet, to arouse the dead, that—if still sinners and weak —they may relapse into death! but that they may wake for eternity, if any vigor of life be yet in them. Thus, at this moment, stands the fate of the nation! Gentlemen, with the decision on my motion, God has confided to your hands the decision affecting the life or the death of our people. But it is because this moment is most important, that I am determined not to have recourse to the weapons of rhetoric; for, however opinione in this house may differ, I find it impossible not to believe—impossible not to feel the conviction—that the sacred love of our country, and such a feeling for her honor, independence, and liberty, as to render this assembly ready to sacrifice its last drop of blood, are common to us all in an equal degree. But where such a feeling is common, there no stimulus is required: cool reason alone has to choose amongst the remedies. Gentlemen, the country is in danger! Perhaps it would suffice to say thus much; for, with the dawn of liberty, the dark veil has dropped from the nation. You know what the condition of our country is; you know that besides the troops of the line, a militia of about 12,000 men has been organized; you know that the authorities have been empowered to place corps of the National Guard on a war footing, in order to establish an effective force to defend the country, and to punish sedition, which is rife on our frontiers. This command found an echo in the nation. How could this have been unless the nation felt that there is danger? This in itself is an evident proof that the presentiment of danger is general. Nevertheless, gentlemen, I think I ought to give you a general, if not a detailed sketch of the state of our country.

"At the dissolution of the last Parliament, and when the first responsible Cabinet entered on its functions with an empty exchequer—without arms, without means of defence; it was impossible not to see and to grieve in seeing the terrible neglect which the interests of the country had suffered. I myself was one of the many who for years have called upon the executive power and the nation, to be just at length to the people, for the day would come when it would be too late for justice. The feeling for justice, of patriotism perhaps, and general enthusiasm, may yet avert from our heads the full force of the fatal word, 'Too late!' Thus much is certain, that the nation and the executive power have retarded justice; and that by this very delay, the moment when first they became just to the people caused the overthrow of all existing institutions.

"Entertaining, as I do, such sentiments, I am obliged to throw a transient glance on the relations between Hungary and Croatia. Gentlemen, you are aware that the nation has granted all its rights and privileges to Croatia, and that already at a time when it only conferred its own rights on the most favored nationalities. Since Arpad, Hungary possessed no right whatever in which Croatia, from the date of her alliance with us, did not participate. But besides having shared with us every right, Croatia obtained in addition, and at our expense too, particular privileges. I find in history, that the large parts of great empires have reserved for themselves certain rights—that Ireland, for instance, possesses less than England; but that the greater part of a whole nation should deny itself rights in favor of a small minority, is a fact which stands isolated, but not the less glorious, in the relations of Hungary with Croatia. Where is a reason to be found that, even if we take up arms to quell the disturbance, we should feel in our own hearts the conviction of having ourselves provoked the disturbance? In the past no such reason exists; nor has, perhaps, the last Parliament, which opened a new epoch in the life of the nation, caused any change whatever in the late and so particularly favorable circumstances of Croatia. I say, no! The rights we have acquired for ourselves, we have likewise acquired for Croatia; the liberty that was granted to the people, was likewise granted to the Croats; we extended the indemnity allowed by us to our nobility, at our own expense, to Croatia—for that country is too small and powerless to raise herself the indemnity.

"With regard to nationality, Croatia entertained apprehensions—though produced by various conceptions and by erroneous ideas—for the Parliament has expressly decreed that in public life the Croats should have the fullest right to make use of their own language in accordance with their own statutes; and thus their nationality has been sanctioned, by this public recognition. Their municipal rights the Parliament has not only not impaired, but extended and augmented.

"Is there a greater privilege than that of regulating the election of representatives, which representatives are convoked to frame laws, to grant and to protect liberty? And the Parliament has said:—'You, our Croatic brethren, shall decide among yourselves how to elect your representatives!' By this measure, the last Parliament has consolidated the municipal independence of Croatia. If, therefore, in the past, no reason can be found to excuse this rebellion, surely the acts of the last Parliament offer none.

"I will not deny that Croatia has to complain of special grievances which, up to this day, remained without redress; but neither the Cabinet nor the Nation have occasioned them—they are simply an heir-loom which the old Government left behind. The nation, however, has always made these grievances its own, and left nothing untried to amend them, as it would have done if they had indeed been its own. And this was certainly one of the causes why we invited the Ban, on his nomination by His Majesty, to co-operate with the Cabinet in accomplishing the speedy removal of the grievances, for we were conscious not only of our authority, but of our duty to re-establish the law where it is injured. But by his revolt the Ban has prevented the Cabinet from communicating its decree to the Croats respecting their petition laid before His Majesty in the Provincial Diet in 1845. Under all these circumstances, the Cabinet, nevertheless, has not omitted to do what it considered necessary to pacify Croatia and its fellow-citizens. The past Parliament conferred the franchise on the military frontier—and thus gave them a right which they never had possessed. To effect its realization, the Cabinet has not only made such arrangements as were in its power, but has left no means whatever untried by which the population of the frontiers might be gained. But they—these unfortunate, deluded men—replied with sedition, with rebellion, so that no further opportunity offered itself to realize the benefits which, weeks ago, we felt inclined to bestow.

"Of their nationality I have already spoken. Concerning its official duties, the Cabinet, from the very outset, selected a number of individuals from the provinces, without making any party distinction—nay, for the Croatian affairs it has, in various branches of the administration, formed distinct sections, which are not yet filled up, because the tie between us has been forcibly torn.

"If a people thinks the liberty it possesses too limited, and takes up arms to conquer more, it certainly plays a doubtful game—for a sword has two edges. Still I can understand it. But if a people says, Your liberty is too much for me, I will not have it if you give it me, but I will go and bow under the old yoke of Absolutism—that is a thing which I endeavor in vain to understand.

"Another affair is the Servian rebellion in the lower countries. Words cannot trace its motives! Croatia, although a land bound to the Hungarian crown, which cannot loose the binding tie without committing high treason, is nevertheless a distinct land.— But he that wishes to establish on the territory of Hungary a distinct power, is so great a traitor, so arrant a rebel, that he can only be answered with the rope of the 'Statarium.' But, gentlemen, the shedding of blood is, even in case of guilt, a matter of great importance. While the Government, therefore, took into consideration, that to force the misguided masses into the horrors of a civil war, merely on account of the faults of some ambitious criminals, would, in these excited and revolutionary times, be an act for the omission of which we should deserve the approbation of God and man, we have, even in this respect, left nothing untried. We have, therefore, made preparations for the realization of all those wishes which in this case could possibly present themselves.

"The third of the circumstances, gentlemen, which exhort us to place the country in a state of defence, is the position of the countries on the Lower Danube. As I exact from every nation, with regard to Hungary, not to interfere with her internal affairs, so the Hungarian will not meddle with the internal affairs of those nations. I only mention that on the banks of the Pruth a mighty Russian army has appeared which can turn to the right and to the left, which can act as a friend and as an enemy; but even because either one and the other is possible, the nation must be prepared.

"Finally, gentlemen, I must allude to our relations with Austria. I will be just, and therefore I find it but natural that the Government of Vienna feels grieved at its inability further to dispose over Hungary. But even if natural, grief is nevertheless not always just; still less does it follow, that from sympathy with grief the nation should incline to permit any of its rights to be alienated.

"Yes, gentlemen, most undoubtedly such movements take place which have for their object to restore to the Viennese Government, if not all, at least the departments of war and finance; the rest will soon follow. If, then, they once have the power of the purse and sword, they will soon have power over the whole nation. The Croatian movement is evidently connected with this scheme, for Jellachich has declared that he cares not for liberty, and that it is all the same to him whether or not the Government at Vienna again obtains possession of the departments of War and Finance. And in the last days the veil of these public secrets has been lifted without reserve. The Viennese Ministers have thought proper, in the name of the Austrian Emperor, to declare to the Cabinet of the King of Hungary, that, unless we make peace with the Croats at any price, they will act in opposition to us. This is as much as to say, that the Austrian Emperor declares war to the King of Hungary; or to his own self. Whatever opinion you, gentlemen, may have formed of the Cabinet, I believe you may so far rely on our patriotic feelings and on our honor, as to render it superfluous on my part to tell you that we have replied to this menace in a manner becoming the dignity of the nation. But, just when our reply was on its way, a second note arrived which clearly stated what a horrible man the Minister of Finance must be to refuse a grant of money to the rebel Jellachich. For since Croatia has broken out in open rebellion, I have of course suspended the remittance of money to the Commander-General, at Agram. I should not be worthy to breathe the free air of Heaven—nay, the nation ought to spit me in the face—had I given money to our enemy. But the gentlemen of Vienna hold a different opinion; they considered my refusal as a disgusting desire to undermine the monarchy. They have put their shoulders to the wheel, and transmitted to the dear rebel 100,000, so they say, but in reality 150,000 florins in silver. This act, gentlemen, might excite the whole House to an angry spirit, to national indignation—but be not indignant, gentlemen, for the ministry which by adopting such a miserable policy believed for a time to prolong its precarious existence, exists no longer. The Aula has crushed it. And I hope, whoever the men may be that compose the next Ministry, they will understand that, without breaking their oath of allegiance to the Austrian Emperor, who is likewise King of Hungary, and without siding with the rebels against their Lord and master, they cannot in future adopt that policy without also bidding defiance to Hungary, which, in that case, would throw the broken alliance at the feet of Austria, which feeds rebellion in our own country, and that we would look for friends in other quarters!

"Gentlemen, I have no cause to complain of the Austrian nation; I wish they had power and a leader, both of which have hitherto been wanting. What I have said refers to the Austrian Ministry. I hope that my words have also been heard at Vienna, and that they will exert some influence on the policy of the new Ministers.

"The Austrian relations, the affairs of the countries on the Lower Danube, the Servian disturbances, the Croatian rebellion Pansclavonian agitators, and the reactionary movements—all these circumstances taken together cause me to say the nation is in danger, or rather, that it will be in danger, unless our resolution be firm! And in this danger, where and with whom are we to look for protection? Are we to look to foreign alliances? I will not form too low an estimate of the importance of relations with foreign countries, and I think that the Cabinet would be guilty of a dereliction of duty, if, in this respect, we were not to exert ourselves to the utmost of our power.

"In the first moments of our assuming office, we entered into correspondence with the British Government, and explained that Hungary has not, as many have attempted to promulgate, extorted rights and liberties from her king, but that we stand on common ground; with our Lord and King we have further entered into an explanation of the interests we have in common on the Lower Danube. On the part of the British Government we have received a reply, such as we might have expected from the liberal views, and from the policy of that nation. In the meanwhile we may rest convinced that England will only assist us if, and as far as she finds it consistent with her own interests.

"As for France, I entertain for the French, as the champions of liberty, the most lively sympathy, but I am, nevertheless, not inclined to see the life of my nation dependent upon their protection and their alliance. France has just seen a second 18th Brumaire. France stands on the threshold of a Dictatorship; perhaps the world may see a second Washington; it is most likely that we shall see a second Napoleon rising out of the ashes of the Past. This much is certain: France can give us a lesson that not every revolution is for the interest of Liberty, and that a nation *striving for liberty can be placed under the yoke of tyranny most easily when that liberty exceeds proper limits.* It is, indeed, a most lamentable event for such a nation as the glorious French nation undoubtedly is, that in the streets of Paris the blood of 12,000 citizens has been shed by the hand of their fellow-citizens, May God preserve us from such a fury in our own country. But whatever form the affairs of France may assume—whether that man whom Providence has placed at the head of that nation becomes a second Washington, who knows to reject the crown, or a second Napoleon, who, on the ruins of the people's liberty, erects the temple of his sanguinary glory; one thing is certain—that France is far from us. Poland relied on French sympathy; that sympathy existed, but Poland is no more!

"The third is the German empire. Gentlemen, I say it openly, I feel that Hungary is destined to live with the free German nation, and that the free German nation is destined to live with the free Hungarian nation, in sincere and friendly intercourse, and that the two must superintend the civilization of the German East. From this point of view, then, we have thought of a German alliance, and as soon as Germany made the first step towards her Unity by convoking the Frankfurt Parliament, we considered it to be one of our first duties to send two of our countrymen (one of whom has now been elected President by this House) to Frankfurt, where they have been received with the respect which is due to the Hungarian nation. But just because the Frankfurt Assembly was still struggling for existence, and because that body had not developed itself with which negotiations could have been brought to a result, (this can only be done with the Ministry to be constituted after the election of the Regent,) there is even now one of our ambassadors in Frankfurt to negotiate, as soon as official relations can with propriety be opened, respecting the league which we desire to enter into with Germany—though with the proviso that we will not abate a hair's breadth from our rights, from our consistency, from our national freedom, for the sake either of liberty or of menaces, from whomsoever they may proceed.

"The danger, therefore, is great; or rather, a danger threatening to become great, gathers on the horizon of our country, and we ought, above all, to find in ourselves the strength for its removal. *That nation alone will live which in itself has suffi-*

cient vital power; that which knows not to save itself by its own strength, but only by the aid of others, has no future.* I therefore demand of you, Gentlemen, a great resolution: Proclaim that, in just appreciation of the extraordinary circumstances on account of which the Parliament had assembled, the nation is determined to bring the greatest sacrifices for the defence of its crown, of its liberty, and of its independence, and that in this respect it will at no price enter with any one into a transaction which even in the least might injure the national independence and liberty, but that it will be always ready to grant all reasonable wishes of every one. But in order to realize this important resolution, either by mediating, if possible, an honorable peace, or by fighting a victorious battle; the Government is to be authorized by the nation to raise the effective strength of the army to 200,000 men, and for this purpose to equip immediately 40,000 men, and the rest as the protection of the country and the honor of the nation may demand. The expense of raising an army of 200,000 men, its armament, and its support for one year, will amount to forty-two millions of florins—but that of raising 40,000 men, from eight to ten millions of florins. Gentlemen, if you assent to my motion, I propose within a few days to lay before the House a detailed financial plan; but I here mention beforehand, that nothing is further from my thoughts than to ask of the nation a taxation of forty-two millions of florins; on the contrary, my plan is that every one shall contribute according to his means, and if that will not cover the expense, we shall be obliged to let our credit make up the deficiency. I rejoice at being able to declare that the plan which I mean to propose is based upon an estimate which agrees with the rates of taxation as fixed a century ago by Maria Theresa for Transylvania, and which in reality is much more moderate. Should my plan be adopted, and should the House make an especial proviso that the readiness for the sacrifice on the

---

* These words of 1848 are a prophecy and a condemnation of what Austria did in 1849.

part of the Representatives of the nation shall not dwindle away without result, the nation will be able to bear the burden, and to save the country. In case the imposed taxation should not suffice for the establishment of a military power— such as circumstances urgently demand, I claim the power for the Executive to open a credit to any amount which the Representatives may deem necessary. This credit shall supply the deficiency either as a loan, or by the issue of paper-money or by some other financial operation.

" These are my proposals! Gentlemen, I am of opinion that the future of the nation depends on the resolution of the House on my motion; and not alone on that resolution, but in a great measure on the manner in which we form it. And this is the reason, Gentlemen, why I refrained from mixing this question with the debate on the address. I believe, if a nation is threatened on every side, and if it feels in itself the will and the power to repel the danger, that the question of the preservation of the country ought not to be tacked to any other question.

"This day we are the Ministers of the nation; to-morrow, others may take our place: no matter! The Cabinet may change, but thou, O my country! thou must forever remain, and the nation, with this or any other Cabinet, must save the country.— But in order that this or any other set of men may be able to save it, the nation must develop its strength. To avoid all misunderstanding, I declare solemnly and expressly, that I demand of the House 200,000 soldiers, and the necessary pecuniary grants.

" Gentlemen, what I meant to say is, that this request on the part of the Government ought not to be considered as a vote of confidence. No, we ask for your vote for the preservation of the country! And I would ask you, gentlemen, if anywhere in our country a breast sighs for liberation, or a wish waits for its fulfilment, let that breast suffer yet a while, let that wish have a little patience, until we have saved the country. This is my request! You all have risen to a man, and I bow before the nation's greatness! If your energy equals your patriotism,

I will make bold to say, that even the gates of Hell shall not prevail against Hungary!"

The *four hundred* representatives had listened with the fixedness of statues to the profoundly eloquent speech; and before his last words had ceased to echo in the spacious hall, Paul Nyary rose, and shouted in a voice which resounded through the apartment, "We give it." Catching the inspiration, the whole assembly rose, and raising their right arms toward Heaven, exclaimed in a voice of thunder, *Megadjuk!* "We give it! We give it! LIBERTY OR DEATH!" When the tempest of excitement had subsided, the President announced that the motion was unanimously adopted.

But the address did more than secure supplies for War. It was a shaft of meridian light upon minds accustomed to twilight, revealing the lion's lair, towards whose Golgotha, the victim with undecided step was moving. Jellachich had been to Innspruck, and was received by the Emperor with quiet approval. No punishment was attempted, no threats offered; he was yet the Ban of Croatia, in the face of the solemn manifesto by which he was ostensibly shorn of his baronial dignity and military glory. Kossuth and the ministry remonstrated in vain; the Hungarian nation was dumb with amazement and alarm.

To make a last endeavor at reconciliation, Batthyanyi, Prime Minister, repaired to Vienna, where Jellachich was openly attending the Imperial court the conference between them was protracted. This occurred in July.

"In this conference, Batthyanyi requested Jellachich to name the demands of the Croats. The Ban refused to enter into any negotiations with the Hungarians until they relinquished the concessions made them by the king in the month of March, of a separate ministry for the departments of war and finance; he demanded that these departments should once more be placed under the control of the Austrian ministry. Batthyanyi replied, that this was a question between Hungary and Austria, and once more desired Jellachich to name the desires of the Croatian people. The Ban, in his character of champion of the 'unity of the Austrian Empire,' remained obstinate, and demanded the surrender of the independence of Hungary as the condition upon which he would agree to suspend his hostile preparations. The conference remained, of course, without result."

Batthyanyi returned to Kossuth, and his mission was the subject of repeated interviews between the patriots. Further proof of Austrian designs would be superfluous as evidence after confession of guilt. The Hungarian ministry could look upon the naked, homicidal plot. The Servian insurrection was permitted, to try the temper and leanings of the Hungarian army, while it was intended by treason and generalship, to occupy the attention and paralyze the power of hostile forces.

Jellachich was to concentrate an army behind the Drave, to invade Hungary whenever the Italian struggle would make it safe to advance with

"Death's music and the roar of combat," upon unoffending Hungary. Money was furnished and all the munitions of war supplied from the Imperial arsenals. Says Schutte:

"As early as the 13th of August, the Austrian Minister of War believed the preparations of Jellachich so far advanced, that he sent him the necessary means for crossing the Drave, two complete pontoon bridges, which were carried through Vienna on more than a hundred wagons to the Gloggnitz railroad."

The laws passed upon Kossuth's motion to increase the army and supplies, were carried to the capital, for the royal sanction, by Batthyanyi and the Minister of Justice. The time passed without reply, while along the frontier the tokens of conflict were thickening. Kossuth was alarmed; the Diet again by a deputation claimed the signature of Ferdinand to statutes securing the life of Hungary; asked the recall of Austrian troops, and that foreign forces appointed to defend their native soil, should be allowed to guard its boundaries. Lastly, they again requested the monarch to visit his kingdom, and restore peaceful order.

The deputation received an evasive reply. But while the ministers were in Vienna, the reckless monarch, without apprising them, forwarded on the 31st of August, a letter to the Palatine, directing him to send members of the Hungarian Diet to the capital to negotiate with the Austrian Ministry, for the consolidation and unity of the empire, and to open correspondence with the Croats to conciliate them.

THE SIGNAL OF CONFLICT. 107

The King declared it an indispensable preliminary that Jellachich should sit in the conference, and warlike preparations cease.

Finally, in the same message, a communication was made to the Hungarian Ministry, of a note from the Austrian government, concerning the relations to obtain between Austria and Hungary. It was urged that the liberal provisions of the law of 1848 were opposed to the legal position of the nations, and detrimental alike to the interests of both. With shameful baseness, the concessions were declared illegal and of none effect, under the pretext that they were not consented to by the responsible Austrian ministry; and though sanctioned by the royal word on the 11th of April, and again formally recognized in the speech from the throne on the 2d of July, it was announced they would be modified, so that a central power could be established at Vienna.

Of this the deputation were profoundly ignorant; but while waiting at Vienna, news came on the 4th of September, that the Emperor-King had withdrawn his decree against Jellachich, and reinstated him in office. The deputies looked upon each other silently, while the tidings spread. The kindling eye, the compressed lips, the deepening frown, revealed the repressed indignation within. They left Vienna with the red feather mounted in their black hats, and proceeded directly towards Hungary. The tri-color standard which had accompanied them had disappeared, and the crimson alone waved before their homeward steps.*

---

* The Hungarian colors are the same as the Italian colors, viz.: "Red, White and Green." The red color alone means War.

CHAPTER VI.

JELLACHICH CROSSES THE DRAVE—WAR INEVITABLE—THE HUNGARIAN MINISTRY RESIGN EXCEPT SZEMERE—KOSSUTH JOINS HIM—A NEW CABINET DEMANDED—ARCHDUKE STEPHEN CALLED TO THE COMMAND OF THE ARMY—LAST ATTEMPTS AT CONCILIATION—THE ARCHDUKE RESIGNS—KOSSUTH'S SPEECH—VOLUNTEERS HASTEN TO THE CAPITAL—MURDER OF COUNT LAMBERG—BATTHYANYI RESIGNS—BATTLE OF SEPTEMBER 29TH—THE BAN'S RETREAT AND PROMOTION—INSURRECTION AT VIENNA.

THE spires of Schonbrunn disappeared from the sight of the insulted deputation, and the tremulous tones of the treacherous Ferdinand, were forgotten in the music of the noble guard's farewell; "*Soon as necessary, we shall all come to Hungary.*" At nightfall of that day, there was a warlike scene on the banks of the Drave. Jellachich's army of more than 40,000 men, was in motion. The camp-fires were reflected by burnished arms, and gave to the red uniform of the savage peasantry, its sanguinary significance. The Ban fully committed to the Hapsburg usurpation, sends along the lines the command to cross the Rubicon. A shout broke upon the evening air, and the invading host marched to Hungarian soil. Whether Jellachich designed more than the purpose he announced, to subdue the revolution and establish the Empire, cannot be known. Blinded by the influence of the Camarilla,* and expecting an easy conquest, he formed, with the Emperor's approval, his legions upon the Magyar plains. To suppose he anticipated the desolation which followed, the intervention of Russia, and the Croatian disasters, would make him an outlaw of darker type than the brutal Haynau, whose taste and profession were undisguised. But Austria evidently expected the Ban's advance would be followed by an outbreak in Pesth, and the emergency concentrating power in Kossuth's hand, would give occasion for the proclamation of martial law; from which the transition to centralization would be speedy and certain.

The Hungarian Ministry saw that war was inevitable and their influence with the Emperor gone. September 13th all but Szemere had resigned, who, as Minister of the Interior, only awaited the formation of a new Cabinet.

Jellachich continued his march, sweeping before him the Magyar detachments sent to reconnoitre his movements, and spreading alarm among the people. Kossuth was entreated to resume his office and share

---

* "*Spanish*—a little chamber. A kind of secret cabinet not recognized in the constitution, and generally composed of the relations of the prince, priests, intriguing women, &c. In the present instance, the most prominent members of the Camarilla were Cibini, one of the ladies of the court, and the Archduchess Sophia."
—PRAGAY.

the augmenting burden of State with the solitary Szemere. True to his country's voice he obeyed, amid the joyful salutations of the excited multitudes. Courier succeeded courier, in bringing intelligence of hourly increasing danger. Kossuth calmly proposed financial measures to meet the expenses of protracted conflict, while the sound of Jellachich's approaching army, threw the shadow of doubt and fear upon every spirit but his. The conservatives yet unwilling to take the field of battle, craved of the Archduke a new Cabinet, to escape if possible the impending storm. Count Batthyanyi was commissioned to choose the Ministry, which he consented to do upon condition that his choice should be confirmed by the King. The Count to unite the forces and guard the nationality of Hungary, besought the Archduke, who was officially Captain-General of the realm, to take the command. His compliance awakened the liveliest enthusiasm among the troops. But their number was few, in contrast with the foe, who hung like an avalanche above an Alpine hamlet, along the highway to their beautiful capital. Another delegation was sent to Vienna, to solicit an arbitration chosen from both Diets. The Hungarian petitioners were spurned from the very door of the Austrian Assembly.

Batthyanyi was untiringly active to obtain conciliation. He pressed upon the Emperor through Count Francis Pulszky, the imperative necessity of an immediate withdrawal of Jellachich's regiments, if he would have the formation of a new Cabinet possible.

Instead of regarding the respectful and earnest appeal, Ferdinand forwarded a message to the Archduke, requesting him to avoid collision with the Ban. The final resort of Stephen was an attempted interview with Jellachich. This was prevented by the soldiery of the Ban, who exclaimed to their willing chief, pausing on the river's margin in sight of the Hungarian General, "We do not permit it!"— The avenue of possible peace was rudely closed forever. The Palatine returned to his army terrified and hopeless. In the struggle before his little band, he saw nothing but defeat and slaughter. Resigning his commission to General Moga, he hastened to Vienna, thence to his maternal estates, in Germany, to find inglorious retirement beyond the flow of blood and the clash of fratricidal arms. Batthyanyi was also in despair. It was an awful crisis with ravaged Hungary. Like the Hebrews on the Red Sea's shore, with a vastly out-numbering enemy behind and the waves before, there seemed to every mind but one, no path for the hunted Magyars.

Louis Kossuth was unvisited by fear. His argus eye comprehended the encircling perils, and beheld the way forward, over which floated God's bright and guiding cloud. He addressed his countrymen to inspire their hearts of Oriental mold, with patriotic fire. His design was not to unfold the details of commercial interest, and define the aggressions of Austria; but to inflame his desponding brethren with the ardor that paved the pass of Thermopylæ with the forms of heroic men. He alluded to former predic-

LAST ATTEMPTS AT CONCILIATION. 113

tions of the treachery of the Hapsburg, and the swift fulfilments; then proceeded with his trumpet-call to battle.

"Hear! patriots hear!

"The eternal God doth not manifest himself in passing wonders, but in everlasting laws.

"It is an eternal law of God's that whosoever abandoneth himself will be of God forsaken.

"It is an eternal law that whosoever assisteth himself him will the Lord assist.

"It is a Divine law that swearing falsely is by its results self-chastised.

"It is a law of God's that he who resorteth to perjury and injustice, prepareth his own shame and the triumph of the righteous cause.

"In the name of that fatherland, betrayed so basely, I charge you to believe my prophecy, and it will be fulfilled.

"In what consists Jellachich's power?

"In a material force, seemingly mighty, of seventy thousand followers, but of which thirty thousand are furnished by the regulations of the military frontier.

"But what is in the rear of this host? By what is it supported? There is nothing to support it!

"Where is the population which cheers it with unfeigned enthusiasm? There is none.

"Such a host may ravage our territories, but never can subdue us.

"Batu-Chan deluged our country with his hundreds of thousands. He devastated, but he could not conquer.

"Jellachich's host at worst will prove a locust-swarm, incessantly lessening in its progress till destroyed.

"So far as he advances, so far will be diminished the number of his followers, never destined to behold the Drave again.

"Let us—Hungarians—be resolved, and stones will suffice to destroy our enemy. This done, it will be time to speak of what further shall befal.

"But every Hungarian would be unworthy the sun's light if his first morning thought, and his last thought at eve, did not recall the perjury and treason with which his very banishment from the realms of the living has been plotted.

"Thus the Hungarian people has two duties to fulfil.

"The first, to rise in masses, and crush the foe invading her paternal soil.

"The second, to remember!

"If the Hungarian should neglect these duties, he will prove himself dastardly and base. His name will be synonymous with shame and wickedness.

"So base and dastardly as to have himself disgraced the holy memory of his forefathers—so base, that even his Maker shall repent having created him to dwell upon this earth—so accursed that air shall refuse him its vivifying strength—that the corn-field, rich in blessings, shall grow into a desert beneath his hand—that the refreshing well-head shall dry up at his approach!—Then shall he wander homeless about the world, imploring in vain from compassion the dry bread of charity. The race of strangers for all alms will smite him on the face. Thus will do that stranger-race, which seeks in his own land to degrade him into the outcast, whom every ruffian with impunity may slay like the stray dog—which seeks to sink him into the likeness of that Indian Pariah, whom men pitilessly hound their dogs upon in sport to worry.

"For the consolations of religion he shall sigh in vain.

"The craven spirit by which Creation has been polluted will find no forgiveness in this world, no pardon in the next.

"The maid to whom his eyes are raised shall spurn him from her door like a thing unclean; his wife shall spit contemptuously in his face; his own child shall lisp its first word out in curses on its father.

"Terrible! terrible! but such the malediction, if the Hungarian race proves so cowardly as not to disperse the Croatian and Serbian invaders, ' as the wild wind disperses the unbinded sheaves by the way-side.

"But no, this will never be; and, therefore, I say the freedom of Hungary will be achieved by this invasion of Jellachich. Our duty is to triumph first, then to remember.

"To arms! Every man to arms; and let the women dig a deep grave between Veszprem and Fehervar, in which to bury either the name, fame, and nationality of Hungary, or our enemy.

"And either on this grave will rise a banner, on which shall be inscribed, in record of our shame, 'Thus God chastiseth cowardice;' or we will plant thereon the tree of freedom everlastingly green, and from out whose foliage shall be heard the voice of the Most High, saying, as from the fiery bush to Moses, 'The spot on which thou standest is holy ground.'

"All hail! to Hungary, to her freedom, happiness, and fame.

"He who has influence in a county, he who has credit in a village, let him raise his banner. Let there be heard upon our boundless plains no music but the solemn strains of the Rakoczy march. Let him collect ten, fifty, a hundred, a thousand followers—as many as he can gather, and marshal them to Veszprem.

"Veszprem, where, on its march to meet the enemy, the whole Hungarian people shall assemble, as mankind will be assembled on the Judgment Day."

The nation was now fully aroused. Volunteers arrived in Pesth from hill and valley. While German officers and soldiers deserted the Hungarian army to join the Austrian host, by the expurgation it increased the strength of the uncorrupted friends of Hungary. Gray and bearded men with youths in their minority gathered around the threatened Constitution of St. Stephen, armed with whatever they could wield in the coming fight. Scythes, hatchets and pikes, were among the equipments of an army too poor and in too hot haste, for better weapons.

Count Latour, Austrian Minister of War, wrote to the Commander of Comorn, a strong Hungarian fortress, to submit to the Ban. True to his race and land, he replied, "that the King legally conveyed his orders by his Hungarian Ministry, and that therefore no order could be accepted from his majesty's Austrian Ministry."

The Magyars were emerging from the mist of deception and reviving in courage. Fast upon the mockery of the Hungarian Diet, which marked all the manœuvres of Jellachich under the royal smile, came the appointment of Count Lamberg, "Commander-in-chief of all troops in Hungary." This decree was in the face of the Constitution, having the countersign of no Hungarian Minister; it was a bold attempt to gather the reins of government from the necks of the people, and bind them to the Sceptre. Remonstrance was in vain. The Austrian General, as if to aggravate the outrage, instead of repairing to the Hungarian army, went directly to Pesth, to receive the homage of the soldiers and direction of the Diet.

The Cabinet, in consequence of failing to obtain Ferdinand's sanction, had been merged into a "Committee of Defence," under the control of Count Batthyanyi. He was therefore the proper officer to countersign the commission of Lamberg. Whether the Count would have done so or not is of little importance. For if he had, it would have only been an expression of his extreme conservative policy; and without this legal form, Count Lamberg boldly claimed his authority. Upon his appearance in Pesth, the most intense and angry excitement prevailed. With popular opinion and rights under his feet, he set out for Buda, the stronghold of the Capital. The populace knew not how daring might be his designs on the garrison. It was ru mored that he would displace the National Guards, and give up the Castle to Austrian soldiers.

Kossuth was addressing the Diet upon the means of opposing the progress of the Ban, when an outcry in the streets announced the uprising of the populace. Armed with scythes, and mad with indignation, they rushed toward the fortress. But soon as they saw its gates guarded by faithful men, they began to disperse. Count Lamberg was crossing the bridge of boats over the Danube. To some of the mob he was known, hurled from his carriage, then smitten down, and his body dragged along the pavements of the Capital.

The next day, Kossuth moved in the Diet, an address to the Emperor, expressing their sorrow at the tragedy, and reminding him that these scenes of horror followed illegal acts forced upon an exasperated people. This murder made a wide and deep sensation. Count Lamberg was esteemed both in the army and among the magnates. Count Batthyanyi, overcome with sad forebodings, left his seat as Prime Minister, and hastened to tender again his resignation to the King. But he did not abandon his suffering country.

He consulted Count Pulszky whether he should enter the army, or visit European cities and correct public opinion, perverted by the slanders of enemies to Hungarian independence. He finally decided to equip his servants and take the field.

Thwarted in his purpose by a fall which disabled his arm, he was compelled to seek retirement. Hearing that he was accused at Pesth by the progressive party, of regarding too favorably Count Lamberg's appointment and Jellachich's march, and also of unwisely resigning his responsible office, he wrote in self-vindication the following touching letter to Kossuth:

"Dear Friend,—For six months full of difficulties, I have been worn out by the cares of public concerns. The first feeling, after I withdrew from the government, yielding to the power of circumstances, is bitterness. What can be more bitter to a true patriot, than to be accused of duplicity against the fatherland, when it is encircled by intrigues and endangered by manifold treason?

"If anybody disapproves my politics, it does not afflict me in the least. But nobody shall accuse me of having misused my influence to endanger the independence of my country.

"My whole past life—an open book since the first beginning of my public career—should prove sufficient against every suspicion. But as my last stay at Vienna occasioned suspicions, I will simply state its causes.

"You, dear friend, know well, that I went to the camp with the consent of the Committee of Defence, and of several deputies then assembled at my house. I wanted to speak with Lamberg, and persuade him, if possible, not to forsake the legal path. As, however, he was not in our camp, and as I presumed him to be in the camp of Jellachich, I sent Major Bubna to the enemy, with the knowledge of General Moga, ordering him to invite General Lamberg, in my name, to an immediate interview; but if Lamberg should not be in the enemy's camp, then my presence among our army was not to be mentioned at all. Bubna did not find Lamberg in the camp of Jellachich, but trusting that the Count would soon arrive, the Major, without my order or knowledge, made an armistice. I only mention this circumstance, because the negotiation of this armistice was attributed to me, in order to raise suspicions against me.

"Meanwhile, the deputies sent by the Diet to the camp, arrived with the resolution; which was not only founded on distrust of me, but likewise might possibly have the most prejudicial influence on the army.*

"I explained this to the deputies, and advised them, before they took any further steps, to consult on the matter with the 'corps of officers.' They did so. The officers corroborated my opinion, that it would not be safe to communicate to the soldiers the resolution of the Diet. With this the deputies complied, after the officers had declared, that in case of any attack from Jellachich, notwithstanding the Royal manifesto, by which the continuation of the contest was interdicted, they would not lay down their arms until all hostile troops should have left the Hungarian soil. I was then anxious to return to Pesth. But on the road I learnt by a courier the murder of Count Lamberg. Simultaneously the messenger delivered to me three autograph letters from his Majesty, directed to myself.† In these letters I was directed to countersign the appointment of Lamberg as unlimited Royal Commissary; further, the appointment of George Mailath as Stadtholder of Hungary, and likewise the order authorizing the dissolution of the Diet. I speedily hastened back to speak personally with Jellachich, and convince him of Lamberg's appointment; (since he had always declared the Royal manifesto [to that effect] false and counterfeit,) and to persuade him to leave the country with his troops. As in this I did not succeed, I proceeded directly to Vienna, actuated by two motives.

"First, I wished to express my judgment concerning the unlawfulness of the autograph letters I had received; and, secondly, I was anxious to make matters up in respect to the sad end of Lamberg, lest arbitrary will and bad intention should snatch at this deed as a

---

* This was the resolution of the Diet on the 27th of September, declaring the uncountersigned nomination of Count Lamberg illegal, and himself a traitor if he should make use of it, and traitors all those who should obey it.

† The above-mentioned documents had, after the murder of Lamberg, all been found upon him.

pretext for a *coup-d'état*. I likewise went to Vienna, because I thought that there the crisis of our affairs would take place; and I wanted to arrest at its very source the danger which might threaten my fatherland.

"I therefore spoke to Wessenberg, (to whom I had always been directed,) and told him that our laws did not recognize any Lieutenant, and that according to the law, the Diet could only be prorogued or dissolved after the discussion on the budget was ended. In regard to Lamberg, I told him, that since a criminal inquisition regarding this sad event had been ordered, it could not be turned into a pretext for a *coup-d'état;* so much the less, as the Diet had expressed its condemnation of the deed. At the same time I pointed out to Wessenberg, how they themselves in Vienna had *indirectly* occasioned the murder of Lamberg, by their disregard and avoidance of the lawful forms. To prevent the renewed occurrence of such unlawfulness, I requested that the appointment of Baron Vay to be Prime Minister should be sent to me, and that I would consider it my duty to countersign it.

"On the following day I got an autograph letter from his Majesty, in which my resignation was accepted, and the appointment of Baron Vay to be Prime Minister was sent to me. But also another document was included, in which I was desired to countersign the appointment of Baron Recsey to replace Prince Eszterhazy. This last I naturally did not; as the resigning Prime Minister can only countersign the appointment of his successor, who can then of himself compose his cabinet, and propose the names of his colleagues to the King. This I declared to Wessenberg in a letter, and at the same time exhorted Baron Recsey not to give himself up to be used as a tool for a *coup-d'état*. Recsey promised to follow my advice. Not long afterward I was informed of the notorious manifesto, which, countersigned by Recsey, overthrew the independence of Hungary.

"I went to Recsey, and reproached him, in the presence of witnesses, with his fickleness and the unlawfulness to which he had lent his hand. In respect to the manifesto, I declared that this was a breach of every legal proceeding, and a declaration of war against Hungary, so that no other path was left to Hungary but to provide for its self-defence.

"After this I left Vienna, and proceeded by Soprony to my estate, where I equipped myself, and armed my servants and my former peasants. I then set out to the battle-field, that as a true son of my beloved fatherland, I might not only by my advice, but likewise by the devotion of my blood and life, prove my faithfulness to my country.

"Providence, however, disposed otherwise of me, as in consequence of an unlucky fall I am doomed to inactivity. But I trust that my bruised arm will soon recover strength enough to be used against the enemy who is ravaging the country, that I may take part in the glory of victory, or, if so it must be, in the glorious death of our fatherland.

"I yet may add that I never did anything without the consent of the other ministers, and that I never listened to the proposal of measures by which the laws of 1848 might have been injured. This I have proved in my private, public, and official actions."

Count Lamberg's murder, and Batthyanyi's resignation, encouraged Jellachich to advance more rapidly. September 29th the two armies met near the vineyards of Sukoro, which lay green and quiet under a smiling sky. The proud Ban anticipated a victory with resistance so faint, that the iron hail should scarcely mar the foliage of the plain. But the sons of Hungary were there from the legal brief and the patient's couch, to fall under her banner. The inhabitants of the surrounding country had gathered to witness the conflict. The Croats were 40,000 strong, and General Moga's force about 5,000. The order to fire was given by Jellachich, and returned promptly by his foe. A long cannonading succeeded, and the volumes of smoke fringed with fire, rolled over the unyielding combatants. Then the Ban's fierce cuirassiers made their charge, and were beaten back as a rock flings back the surge. Again they charged with desperate energy and the rage of disappointed valor. The artillery opened gapes which were quickly filled; the swords drank blood, and the scythes mowed down their ranks of living men. And so till night came down, the locust swarm of Croatia were in close struggle with the undisciplined Hungarian soldiery. Suddenly, there was a rush of the Magyars upon the foe—the final onset of the heroic band. A moment the shock was sustained by the stung and astonished cuirassiers of the Ban, and the billow of bravery went over the prostrate enemy, forced to the waters of Lake Velentze, in their rear. The sounds of discord died on the evening air—the clouds of vapor sank away from the vineyards of Sukoro, whose confines were red with the wine of carnage. And there stood the little army who had guarded the ark of freedom amid the fury of their first mighty battle, wondering at the triumph their own hands had won.

With the greater Hannibal, Moga committed a fatal mistake in refusing to permit his impatient soldiers to follow up the victory. Jellachich requested an armistice of three days, which was granted. The invader, under cover of darkness, decamped and fled toward the Austrian frontier. He escaped with the permission of his captors, to slay more defenders of rights dearer than a fleeting existence—protectors of national honor and a religious faith.

In this "*flank movement,*" as Jellachich termed his flight, he was met, October 3d, by a detachment of National Guards of the Southern District, commanded by Vidos, a representative in the Diet, and completely routed. On the 5th, the other division of the Croatian force, numbering 12,000 men and twelve pieces of ordnance, was overtaken by the rising people under Gorgey and others, and surrendered. The trophies taken at Pesth were sixty officers, twelve cannon, and eleven thousand muskets. The citizens in their rejoicing, could not mourn for the "unreturning brave;" but they made the capital ring with enthusiastic demonstrations of brightening hope for Hungary.

Jellachich with the remnant of his army reached the Austrian dominions, and was fairly in the grasp of the monarch who three months before had declared him a traitor. But instead of an execution, there appeared, October 4th, this Royal Manifesto:

"We, Ferdinand I., Constitutional Emperor of Austria, &c., King of Hungary, Croatia, Sclavonia, Dalmatia the Vth of this name, to the Barons, to the High-Dignitaries of the Church and State, to the Magnates and Representatives of Hungary, its dependencies, and the Grand Duchy of Transylvania, who are assembled at the Diet, convoked by ourselves in our free and royal town of Pesth, our greeting:

"To our deep concern and indignation the House of Representatives has been seduced by Kossuth and his adherents to great illegalities; it has even carried out several illegal resolutions against our royal will, and has lately, on the 27th of September, issued a resolution against the commission of the Royal Commis sary, our Lieutenant Field-Marshal, Count Francis Lamberg, appointed by ourselves to re-establish peace. In consequence of which, this our Royal Commissary, before he could even produce his commission, was in the public street violently attacked by the furious mob which murdered him in the most atrocious manner. Under these circumstances, we see ourselves compelled, according to our royal duty, for the maintenance of the security and the law, to take the following measures, and to command their enforcement:

"First. We dissolve the Diet by this our decree; so that after the publication of our present Sovereign Rescript, the Diet has immediately to close its sessions.

"Secondly. We declare as illegal, void, and invalid, all the resolutions, and the measures of the Diet, which we have not sanctioned.

"Thirdly. All troops, and armed bodies of every kind, whether national guards, or volunteers, which are stationed in Hungary, and its dependencies, as well as in Transylvania, are placed by this our decree, under the chief command of our Ban of Croatia, Sclavonia and Dalmatia, Lieutenant Field-Marshal Baron Joseph Jellachich.

"Fourthly. Until the disturbed peace and order in the country shall be restored, the Kingdom of Hungary shall be subjected to martial law; in consequence of which, the respective authorities are meanwhile to abstain from the celebration of congregations, whether of the counties, of the municipalities, or of the districts.

"Fifthly. Our Ban of Croatia, Sclavonia and Dalmatia, Baron Joseph Jellachich, is hereby invested and empowered as Commissary of our Royal Majesty; and we give him full power and force, that he may, in the sphere of Executive Ministry, exercise the authority, with which as Lieutenant of our Royal Majesty, we have invested him in the present extraordinary circumstances.

"In consequence of this our Sovereign plenipotence, we declare that whatsoever the Ban of Croatia shall order, regulate, determine and command, is to be considered as ordered, regulated, determined and commanded by our royal authority. In consequence of which, we likewise by this graciously give command to all our ecclesiastical, civil and military authorities, officers, and High Dignitaries of our Kingdom of Hungary, its dependencies, and Transylvania, as also all their inhabitants, that all the orders signed by Baron Jellachich as our empowered Royal Commissary, shall be by them obeyed, and enforced, in the same way as they are.bound to obey our Royal Majesty."

The republican principle had been growing in strength and vigor among the students of the University of Vienna, professional men, and the poorer classes generally. The rejection of two dignified deputations from the Hungarian Diet by the Court, deepened the popular feeling. And when the appointment of Jellachich, the ravager of guiltless Hungary, was known, placing under his military rule the freemen of the Magyar domain, the excitement waxed hot. He was a defeated traitor; and what had those who loved liberty to anticipate from him?

The reactionary mission of the Ban was apparent. The people assembled in masses of 10,000 in the Odeon, to hear the harangues of Dr. Tauseman on the depredations of the Croats. The 5th he made a tremendous speech on "Jellachich before the gates of Vienna." The immense concourse cheered the orator and retired, with no visible tokens of coming earthquake. There was *thought* out of sight, and the upheaving elements were at work. A battalion of troops were ordered to leave the capital and join the

Ban. Reluctantly they complied, exclaiming, "The Hungarians are our brothers, not our foes!"

Reaching the railway station, they were surrounded by excited crowds, among whom were many of the National Guards. General Bredi persisted, against the remonstrances from the masses, in obeying the imperial mandate. The throngs blocked the path of the troops, and were commanded to retire. They still pressed around the soldiers, and the word "fire!" was given. Several of the Guards fell; the rest who were armed and the citizens, returned the shot. Bredi fell from his horse a corpse, and the soldiers retired. The alarm spread, and general insurrection followed, until the streets ran blood. Amid the ringing of alarm-bells, the ceaseless thunder of cannon, and the wild tumult of desperate battle, Count Latour, who from his official position was deemed responsible for the sanguinary scene, was seized and hung by the infuriate populace.

The troops were defeated, the arsenal stormed, and the King was a fugitive from the palace of Vienna; terror-stricken and cowardly in his departure from resolute subjects, upspringing from his oppressive hand, like the recoil of a massive spring from a giant's relaxing grasp.

CHAPTER VII.

THE PROGRESS OF THE STRUGGLE—GAIN AND LOSS OF THE INSURRECTION—BEM'S ARRIVAL—KOSSUTH MARCHES TO PRESSBURG—SIEGE OF VIENNA—THE HUNGARIANS ADVANCE TOWARDS THE AUSTRIAN FRONTIER—BATTLE OF SCHWECHAT—LAST APPEAL BY THE CATHOLIC BISHOPS—EXECUTIONS—CONDITION OF THE TWO ARMIES—ABDICATION OF FERDINAND.

ON the morning succeeding the convulsion which drove Ferdinand to Olmutz, there was a strange tranquillity, a calm above the feverish throb of hearts, whose fiery impulses were tamed only by success, unknown in the annals of revolutions. Business was unchecked in its flow. The locomotive thundered on—the telegraph transmitted its messages—and busy wheels were numberless in the streets of Vienna. But liberty had raised her drooping form amid the carnage of the few past hours; and the sight rejoiced the masses. The struggle was now plainly between Hungary and Austria—freedom and despotism. The Sclavic portion of the Viennese democracy, whose influence decided the rejection of the last deputation from the Hungarian to the Austrian Diet, were no longer deluded. The " Constituent Assembly," beholding the vacant throne, declared itself sitting "*en permanence.*" It forbade the entrance of imperial troops into the Capital along the railways; issued a proclamation to the people, congratulating them upon the triumphs of the insurrection; and sent an address to Ferdinand, imploring him to return to his loyal subjects, and prevent the threatened result of his absence, civil war. These official acts, identified the Assembly with the revolutionary party, and prompt measures would have secured the glorious conquest of popular rights. But delay paralyzed the energies which needed only a guiding spirit. General Auersperg, commander of the city, had retired with the remnant of the army to the Glacis, or declivity, between the Capital and Champaign, and frowned harmlessly upon the conquered metropolis. A brave leader of the impatient people, could have dislodged him without the shedding of blood.

Jellachich's force was reduced to a powerless company of exhausted Croats, and might have been scattered like autumnal leaves before the blast. But both Hungarian and Austrian patriots were unused to the strategy of war.

The Assembly, bewildered and timid, threw the responsibility of decisive work upon the Common Council; and they, in turn, leaned helplessly upon the National Guards. This interval of hesitation, gave Auersperg, Jellachich and Prince Windischgratz, time to join their divisions of the royal army, and by recruits strengthen their blockade of the Capital.

Meanwhile, the Hungarians in hot pursuit of the Ban, had halted on the Austrian boundary, and the Committee of Defence waited for a formal invitation from the Assembly, before venturing across the line. This body was not sufficiently committed to the revolution to make the request, and the masses, though armed and panting for the strife, dare not dissolve the Assembly. While standing upon the question of legality, gazing anxiously towards each other, the friends of freedom saw the golden moment passing. The tide of affairs so hopeful, turned sadly against Hungary. It was an emergency which knows no law of expediency or forms of diplomatic propriety; and had the patriots seen it then, as since, the tricolor might have waved from Pesth to Vienna.— Count Francis Pulszky, a noble Hungarian, was despatched to the Austrian Capital. He found the National Guard, which, overshadowed by common consent the Diet and Assembly, virtually without a Commander. In five days, they had changed Generals three times, and at length chose Messenhauser, whose greatest quality was the tact of hostile display, and a fruitless waste of powder. Pulszky entered the room of the Permanent Committee of the Diet in the Palace, and was saluted with the earnest question:—" Will the Hungarians come?" The Count's reply disclosed the extreme caution of the ministry at home:—" As soon as desired by the Austrian Diet.'. After unavailing interviews with the Common Council and Guards, he returned. At this juncture, Bem, a brave Pole, arrived at Vienna, *en route* to Hungary.

He had served under Davoust and Macdonald, in the campaign of 1812, and possessed of a splendid mind, he was a valuable accession to the cause of freedom. He loved the heroic and fiery Magyar, and was in haste to lead on his battalions under the tri-colored banner.

The Viennese saw in this northern Lafayette, their leader, and, thronging into his apartment, urged his acceptance of the command and defence of the Capital. Waving his enthusiastic preference of an Hungarian appointment, he yielded to the popular clamor. At Pressburg there was the activity of preparation for the combat with Austria. Men of snowy beard and stooping form were by the side of ardent boyhood throwing up entrenchments with haste too intense for tumult; hospitals for the wounded were erected, and supplies were despatched to the army encamped along the right bank of the Danube, between Kopcseny and Parendorf. The brave Klapka fortified the heights of the town, and animated, with his unfaltering courage, the troops. While the ministry at Pesth were deliberating and undecided whether to join the Viennese, around whom dangers gathered rapidly, Kossuth was mustering twelve thousand volunteers and thirty cannon; and with this force marched on to Pressburg. He immediately reviewed the regiments, and learning from Count Pulszky the chaotic condition of affairs in the Capital, who suggested an interview with Bem and union of design, he sent a letter to the generous Pole, requesting his presence in the Hungarian camp. The Courier escaped the vigilance of the Austrian and Croat, passing through the enemy's country safely, and reached the friends of the revolution. The message fell into the hands of Messenhauser, the commander of the Guards; his undetermined spirit anticipated yet an agreement with the Court, and he suppressed the communication. Of course, Bem did not hasten to the waiting Magyar, and the failure was a sad one for freedom. What might not have been hoped from the consultation and simultaneous onset of Kossuth and Bem?

October 24th, Kossuth arrived at Parendorf, the rendezvous of Hungarian troops. Assembling the entire army, he glanced along the silent lines, while the interests at stake, and his country's doubtful future, swept over the horizon of his lofty mind. Upon the deeds of those men, hung the independence and glory of an ancient race. The Danube rolled by, a solemn emblem of the rushing tide of decisive events. He felt deeply, and spoke with no thought of himself; "my bleeding country!" was his tearful exclamation. His voice rang over the tented plain like a trumpet of certain and *shrill* sound; stirring the blood of veterans, to whom the thunder of war was familiar music.

Extending his hand toward the public way, he closed his sublime oration in these words: "Magyars, there is the road to your peaceful homes and firesides. Yonder is the path to death; but it is the path of duty. Which will you take? Every man shall choose for himself. We want none but willing soldiers!" The great body of that host, comprising thirty thousand Hungarians, shouted, "Liberty or Death!" Then the officers of each regiment, were required to signify in writing whether they would remain in the service of Hungary, and fight the common foe, or leave the ranks. A hundred officers, principally foreigners, retired with the pledge not to engage in a war against their comrades for six months.

On the 27th, a council of war was held, and while General Moga, and inferior commanders, opposed strenuously aggressive movements, the roar of cannon came on the breeze from Vienna. It startled Kossuth; it was a demand for immediate action. The proposition to send a force against a Gallacian invasion designed to kindle another Sclavonic insurrection, was urged by the conservative party. Gorgey voted for advancing, and ambitiously desiring the Generalship, pressed the necessity of appointing an officer whose reputation should be security *against treachery*. Then louder came the noise of artillery, borne heavily by the passing wind to that council-tent. Kossuth replied to the question of marching unsolicited to the Capital, already under the iron hail of assault: "Though Hungary stood in no connection with Vienna, yet it is a duty of honor to hasten to the aid of the Viennese, as they have risen in opposition to the war against Hungary. If we win a battle, it will decide the fate of the Austrian monarchy, and of all Germany; if we lose one, it will not discourage the nation, but will spur it to the greater sacrifice. But to be passive at the very threshold of the scene of action, would lower the Hungarians with foreign countries, and in the country itself would cool enthusiasm." The simple argument closed the debate; the decision was to advance without delay.

The next day, the Hungarian army crossed the frontier of Austria, and planted her flag upon hostile soil Of their 25,000 men, 10,000 were raw volunteers, undisciplined and almost unarmed. Prince Windischgratz, the commander-in-chief of the enemy, had 70,000 trained soldiers. For twenty days the Viennese had held the city against the augmenting enemy, whose fortifications darkened the encircling plains. The echo of artillery was the hourly tocsin of the siege, and at night a circle of fire revealed the embrace of the beleaguering host. On the evening of the 28th the Hungarian army had reached the river Fischa, and pitched their tents. On a solitary hill, they kindled a mighty signal fire, whose ascending flames could be seen with telescopes from the tower of St. Stephen, in the bombarded Capital. The sky reddened in the glow of the conflagration which *telegraphed* to the Viennese the coming of brave warriors to their rescue. Around a feebler glow, under the interlocking forest-trees, sat Kossuth and his Generals, eating roasted potatoes and lard, and discussing the prospects of Hungary. They lay down on the dry foliage and snatched a brief repose. Resuming with the flush of dawn their march, at close of day they were encamped on the slopes near Schwechat. And when the fires burned dimly in the spreading light of the next slow morning, a thick, gray mist covered the valleys. Nothing was visible in the direction of Vienna, nor did the booming of guns announce the preparation of the revolutionists for combat. The Magyars were altogether ignorant that measures of capitulation had been commenced, and waited impatiently to meet the enemy. As the clouds broke away, and the sunlight fell again upon their camps, the roar of cannon from the Austrian legions, announced that conflict was at hand.

"Hurrah!" rang along the Hungarian lines, and the brave fellows seemed to hear it returned from the distant turrets of St. Stephen. For two hours a ceaseless cannonading followed without decided effect. Major Guyon then charged impetuously upon Mannsworth and took it, while the right wing rushed on against the opposing Croats, and with a shout of victory swept aside the battalions of the Ban. An advance of the left wing would have made the storming of Schwechat another conquest. The Hungarian centre was opposite that of the enemy, and Kossuth perceiving at a glance the advantage of securing the position held by the Austrians, ordered Gen. Moga to bring forward his force and take the entrenchment. He refused, and Kossuth immediately offered the mutinous General his own carriage to convey him home, as he could no longer retain command. Gorgey, who had bravely led the vanguard, and was the most conspicuous hero then on the field, was named Commander by Kossuth on the spot. Delay permitted a concentration of the enemy's cavalry, and the day was lost.

And no sound of strife reached the ear from Vienna, and not a banner floated from the ramparts or frowning walls. The ominous stillness was painful to Kossuth, who with Pulszky, rode by Moga's side continually. Unwilling to abandon the field, though this General urged a retreat, the fearless patriot dared the storm of battle, that the Viennese might not lose the possibility

BATTLE OF SCHWECHAT.

of escape and victory. The advancing troops of Windischgratz, left no longer a doubt concerning the fate of the Capital. There was no battle strife there, or the Austrians would have other work to do, than a universal gathering around the Hungarian bands. At four o'clock two bomb-shells fell among a few regiments of peasants, armed only with scythes, who had stood for hours defenceless before the artillery of the foe.

A panic spread like an electric shock, and, making a rapid flight, they broke and disordered the right wing, which had nobly sustained the overwhelming force of the royal troops. The command for retreat was sounded, and within the unbroken curve of the left wing, aided by a reserve, they were covered from the shots of the enemy. Kossuth hastened after the terrified Guards. Checked for a brief time, they were again seized with sudden alarm, and rushed headlong from the camp, bearing with them the battalions in their path. By that strange fatality which sometimes saves and again destroys an army, the Austrians did not improve their victory, and annihilate the Hungarians as they might have done; but allowed their distracted foe to leave unpursued the fields of Schwechat. Count Pulszky, a hero, a statesman, and a most amiable citizen, led off the rear guard of the right wing. About two hundred Magyars lay dead where they fiercely fought, and four hundred of the imperial soldiers had fallen. Six hundred lifeless forms are a small offering on the altar of Mars, but enough to sadden the contemplative mind, with pictures drawn from two worlds, of the consequences which followed the slaughter.

During this deadly strife, the Bishops of the king dom, had been in solemn consultation and prayer at Pesth. They added the impressiveness of religious obligation to the last appeal made in their nation's behalf to the soulless despot, whose chain was on the neck of the resisting Magyar. Their eloquent address deserves a place among the memorials of that crisis in human well-being:

"Sire! Penetrated with feelings of the most profound sorrow, at the sight of the innumerable calamities, and the internal evils which desolate our unhappy country, we respectfully address your Majesty, in the hope that you may listen with favor to the voice of those, who, after having proved their inviolable fidelity to your Majesty, believe it to be their duty as heads of the Hungarian Church, at last to break silence, and to bear to the foot of the throne their just complaints, for the interests of the Church, of the Country and of the Monarchy.

"Sire! We refuse to believe that your Majesty is correctly informed of the present state of Hungary. We are convinced that your Majesty, in consequence of your being so far away from our unhappy country, knows neither the misfortunes which overwhelm her, nor the evils which immediately threaten her, and which place the throne itself in danger, unless your Majesty applies a prompt and efficacious remedy, by attending to nothing but the dictates of your own good heart.

"Hungary is actually in the saddest and most deplorable situation. In the south, an entire race, although enjoying all the civil and political rights recognized in Hungary, has been in open insurrection for several months, excited and led astray by a party which seems to have adopted the frightful mission of exterminating the Magyar and German races, which have constant ly been the strongest and surest support of your Majesty's throne. Several thriving towns and villages have become a prey to flames, and have been totally destroyed; thousands of Magyar and German subjects are wandering about without food or shelter, or have fallen victims to indescribable cruelty, for it is revolting to repeat the frightful atrocities by which the popular rage, let loose by diabolical excitement, ventures to display itself.

"These horrors were, however, but the prelude of still greater evils, which were about to fall upon our country. God forbid that we should afflict your Majesty with the hideous picture of all our misfortunes. Suffice it to say, that the different races who inhabit your kingdom of Hungary, stirred up, excited one against the other by infernal intrigues, only distinguish themselves by pillage, incendiarism, and murder, perpetrated with the greatest refinement of atrocity.

"Sire! The Hungarian nation, heretofore the firmest bulwark of Christianity and civilization against the incessant attacks of barbarism, often experienced rude shocks in that protracted struggle for life and death; but at no period did there gather over her head so many and so terrible tempests, never was she entangled in the meshes of so perfidious an intrigue, never had she to submit to treatment so cruel, and at the same time so cowardly—and yet, oh! profound sorrow! all these horrors are committed in the name, and, as they assure us, by the order of your Majesty.

"Yes, Sire, it is under your Government, and in the name of your Majesty, that our flourishing towns are bombarded, sacked and destroyed. In the name of your Majesty, they butcher the Magyars and Germans. Yes, Sire! all this is done; and they incessantly repeat it, in the name and by the order of your Majesty, who nevertheless have proved, in a manner so authentic and so recent, your benevolent and paternal intentions toward Hungary—in the name of your Majesty, who in the last Diet of Pressburg, yielding to the wishes of the Hungarian nation, and to the exigencies of the time, consented to sanction, and confirm by your royal word and oath, the foundation of a new Constitution, estaolished on the still broader foundation of a perfectly independent Government!

"It is for this reason the Hungarian nation, deeply grateful to your Majesty, accustomed also to receive from her King nothing but proofs of goodness really paternal, when he listens only to the dictates of his own heart, refuses to believe, and we her chief pastors, also refuse to believe, that your Majesty either knows or sees with indifference, still less approves, the infamous manner in which the enemies of our country and of our liberties compromise the kingly majesty, arming the populations against each other, shaking the very foundations of the Constitution, frustrating legally established powers, seeking even to destroy in the hearts of all, the love of subjects for their sovereign, by saying that your Majesty wishes to withdraw from your faithful Hungarians the concessions solemnly sworn to and sanctioned in the last Diet, and finally, to wrest from the country her character of a free and independent kingdom.

"Already, Sire! have these new laws and liberties, giving the surest guarantees for the freedom of the people, struck root so deeply in the hearts of the nation, that public opinion makes it our duty to represent to your Majesty, that the Hungarian people could not but lose that devotion and veneration, consecrated and proved on so many occasions up to the present time if it were attempted to make them believe that the violation of the laws, and of the Government, sanctioned and established by your Majesty, is committed with the consent of the King.

"But if, on the one hand, we are strongly convinced that your Majesty had taken no part in the intrigues so basely woven against the Hungarian people, we are not the less persuaded, that that people, taking arms to defend their liberty, have stood on legal ground, and that in obeying instinctively the supreme law of nations, *which demands the safety of all*, they have at the same time saved the dignity of the throne and the monarchy, greatly compromised by advisers as dangerous as they are rash.

"Sire! We, the chief pastors of the greatest part of the Hungarian people, know better than any others their noble sentiments; and we venture to assert, in accordance with history, that there does not exist a people more faithful to their monarchs than the Hungarians, when they are governed according to their laws.

"We guarantee to your Majesty, that this people, such faithful observers of order and of the civil laws in the midst of the present turmoils, desire nothing but the peaceable enjoyment of the liberties granted and sanctioned by the throne.

"In this deep conviction, moved also by the sacred interests of the country and the good of the Church, which sees in your Majesty her first and principal defender, we, the Bishops of Hungary, humbly entreat your Majesty patiently to look upon our country now in danger. Let your Majesty deign to think a moment upon the lamentable situation in which this wretched country is at present, where thousands of your innocent subjects, who formerly all lived together in peace and brotherhood on all sides, notwithstanding differences of races, now find themselves plunged into the most frightful misery by their civil wars.

"The blood of the people is flowing in torrents—thousands of your Majesty's faithful subjects are, some massacred, others wandering about without shelter, and reduced to beggary—our towns, our villages are nothing but heaps of ashes—the clash of arms has driven the faithful people from our temples, that have become deserted—the mourning Church weeps over the fall of religion, and the education of the people is interrupted and abandoned.

"The frightful spectre of wretchedness increases and develops itself every day under a thousand hideous forms. The morality, and with it the happiness of the people, disappear in the gulf of civil war.

"But let your Majesty also deign to reflect upon the terrible consequences of these civil wars; not only as regards their influence on the moral and substantial interests of the people, but also as regards their influence upon the security and stability of the monarchy. Let your Majesty hasten to speak one of those powerful words which calm the tempests!—the flood rises, the waves are gathering, and threaten to engulf the throne!

"Let a barrier be speedily raised against those passions excited and let loose with infernal art among populations hitherto so peaceable. How is it possible to make people who have been inspired with the most frightful thirst—that of blood—return within the limits of order, justice, and moderation?

"Who will restore to the regal Majesty the original purity of its brilliancy, of its splendor, after having dragged that Majesty in the mire of the most evil passions? Who will restore faith and confidence in the Royal word and oath? Who will render an account to the tribunal of the living God, of the thousands of individuals who have fallen, and fall every day, innocent victims to the fury of civil war?

"Sire! our duty as faithful subjects, the good of the country, and the honor of our religion, have inspired us to make these humble but sincere remonstrances, and have bid us raise our voices! So, let us hope, that your Majesty will not merely receive our sentiments, but that, mindful of the solemn oath that you took on the day of your coronation, in the face of Heaven, not only to defend the liberties of the people, but to extend them still further—that mindful of this oath, to which you appeal so often and so solemnly, you will remove from your royal person the terrible responsibility that these impious and bloody wars heap upon the throne, and that you will tear off the tissue of vile falsehoods with which pernicious advisers beset you, by hastening with prompt and strong resolution, to recall peace and order to our country, which was always the firmest prop to your throne! in order that, with Divine assistance, that country, so severely tried, may again see prosperous days; in order that, in the midst of profound peace, she may raise a monument of eternal gratitude to the justice and paternal benevolence of her King.

"Signed at Pesth, the 28th Oct. 1848.

"THE BISHOPS OF THE CATHOLIC CHURCH OF HUNGARY."

Fogarassy, who bore this pathetic message to Ol

mutz, was dismissed with the coolness of tyranny unsoftened by the amenities of common life. The tidings of his scornful rejection reached Pesth before he arrived. The Bishops then lifted their despairing voice to their flocks. How completely do their paternal words answer the Austrian calumny that civil conflict in Hungary was the disorder the *benevolent* Ferdinand would suppress.

"When six months ago, our constitution, eight centuries old, was modified at the Diet, of Pressburg, according to the exigencies of the times and the wishes of the nation, and its benefits extended to all the sons of our native land, without distinction of class, language or creed; when the independent government sanctioned by the King, received its powers, no one could have believed it possible ever to attack that free constitution, *or to excite* the other races against the Hungarians.

"We exhort you, dear brethren in Christ, to be of unflinching fidelity to your country, of courageous devotion to her defence, of sincere obedience to the authorities, who in this hour of danger, are obliged to ask you for greater service than heretofore. Be convinced that they are endeavoring to win your liberty, and with it your happiness on earth. Consider it your most sacred duty to submit yourselves to the legal authorities of the country; to live amongst them in peace and love, mutually to assist each other, to sustain the weak, to encourage the timid, to punish the enemies of order. Have patience and courage, and hope in the grace of God, which, far from allowing you to sink under the weight of battle, will recompense your perseverance by the blessings of peace. To Him, the Eternal King, the Immortal Lord, invisible and wise, be glory and praise forever and ever. Amen!"

Such was the unusual and noble attitude of the Catholic Church of Hungary during the struggle;

a hierarchy whose tendencies are everywhere toward centralization—and which has been always the wall of fire around thrones. In Vienna victims were falling before the executioner's hand. Prince Windischgratz, not naturally cruel, systematically selected his men for sacrifice, according to the dictates of policy; the *moral* power of their example on the rebels.

The eloquent Blum, among German democrats, a leader whose fame was universal, was the first citizen devoted to the gallows. A brave Pole must die to avenge the havoc of Bem, and his aid-de-camp Jelovizki was taken. Of the National Guards, Baron Sternau was seized and made a target for the riflemen. Doctor Becher represented the Press in this tragedy, and was hurried to his doom. A young Jew and disciple of Hegel, followed to the place of slaughter; then went a poor Hungarian. Soon after, the half-hearted patriot Messenhauser, an Austrian officer who dared to join the revolutionists, passed to execution, contrary to law and express order for three days' delay of sentence, to gratify the relentless purpose of Windischgratz. While these objects of despotic vengeance were following each other to violent death, the condition of Hungary was perilous and disheartening. Seventy-five thousand soldiers under the Prince, were around Vienna: twelve thousand, commanded by Simonich, darkened the Moravian boundary; and fifteen thousand, led by Schlick, guarded the Gallacian frontier. Puchner and his associate generals, were entrenched

CONDITION OF THE TWO ARMIES. 143

in Transylvania; while the Serbs hung menacingly along the Banat. The strong-holds of Arad, Esseg and Temesvar, were in the power of the enemy. So that from nine points at the same moment, the artillery of Austria was aimed at the palpitating heart of poor Hungary, isolated and unaided in her gloomy hour.

Those environed Magyars remind us of scenes which have transpired in a northern wilderness. A conflagration spreading in summer time has swept along the mountain ridges until every tree has become a spire of flame, and the roar of the advancing element filled the gorges. Chased from their quiet lair, the deer have descended to the valleys, and tremblingly awaited the issue of the invading fire, which narrowed continually their green domain, and lit up the sky with the hue of wrath.

But for Hungary there was help in her chief. LOUIS KOSSUTH was at the head of the Committee of Defence, with genius equal to the dangers that thickened about his trembling people. He left Gorgey to discipline his troops at Pressburg, by daily drills and skirmishes, and went over the land to secure the munitions of war. To supply the want of sulphur for powder he gathered pyrites from the copper mines, and the powder-mills began to hum with activity. Foundries illumined the nightly sky with beacons of ceaseless glow; and the mechanics, as if by a sudden and supernatural impulse, made boots and uniforms for the unclad volunteers. "Wherever Kossuth stamped his foot, there sprang up a soldier." The battalions multiplied at his call, and were drilled for action with astonishing haste and precision. He planned financial securities, wrote countless despatches, and in person visited the masses, setting their pulses on fire for combat around their altars and constitution. The 1st of December, Bem set out for Transylvania, where the hostile preparations were most alarming, promising the Diet at Pesth, that with his 8000 men " he would in a fortnight invade Transylvania; would first beat Wardner, and take Dees, the key of the country, and after that Kolosvar. When he had achieved this, he would pursue and chase away Urban, from the Wallach districts next to Bukovina; and as soon as he had thus effected a junction with the faithful Szekelys, he would drive the Austrians out of the Saxon land at the point of the bayonet." The brilliant prophecy awakened a smile in the Diet. The next day, after the departure of the Polish hero, December 2d, Emperor Ferdinand abdicated his throne at Olmutz; his brother Francis Charles in turn renounced his royal claim, and the sceptre passed to the delicate hand of his son, *nineteen years old*. The oppressive spirit of the Hapsburg dynasty was represented by that unbearded boy, before whom Hungary must stand bleeding; and unless victorious, at length clasp her chains and bow at his feet; a lion in the strong meshes of a juvenile yet ruthless hunter.

CHAPTER VIII.

SKIRMISHES WITH THE AUSTRIAN ARMY—KOSSUTH AND COUNT PULSZKY—THE CONFLICT OPENS—A DEPUTATION DESPATCHED TO PRINCE WINDISCHGRATZ WITH PROPOSALS OF PEACE, AND ARE DETAINED PRISONERS—TRANSFER OF THE GOVERNMENT TO DEBRECZEN—COUNCIL OF WAR—PLAN OF DEFENCE—GORGEY'S MARCH—STORMING OF THE DEFILES OF BRANIEZKO—PROGRESS OF THE ARMIES—BATTLE OF KAPOLNA—KOSSUTH'S PRAYER—BEM—PERCZEL—HUNGARIANS ADVANCE TOWARDS GODOLLO—MARCH OF THE HUNGARIANS TOWARDS PESTH—BATTLE OF TAPIOBIESKE—BATTLE OF ISASZEG—RENDEZVOUS AT GODOLLO—BATTLE OF WAITZEN—DECLARATION OF INDEPENDENCE—JOY OF THE PEOPLE.

DURING the first half of December but little was accomplished besides brief battles with the enemy. Damianics defeated the Serbs on the frontier of the Banat; in the defiles of Dukla, General Schlick routed the Hungarians under Colonel Alexander Pulszky, but their retreat was covered by a company of Poles, who took prisoner the chief of Schlick's staff. It was like the affair of Bunker Hill in the Colonial Revolution; according to Austrian confession, "a victory dearly bought." General Meszaros, Minister of War, now commanded the forces against Schlick, and was also defeated. Kossuth was anxious still to spare the country a long and bloody struggle, and wrote to Mr.

Stiles, U. S. Envoy at Vienna, imploring him to secure from the Prince an armistice with the Hungarian army. Windischgratz declined to treat, demanding unconditional surrender. On the 16th of December, the same day that the entire Austrian army entered Hungary from the Upper Danube, and the horrors of a winter campaign brooded over the frozen soil and streams, Count Pulszky, after a private conference with Kossuth, was sent to Gorgey at Pressburg, to ascertain if rumors of the advancing foe were true.

In an open carriage, wrapped in the peasant's mantle of sheep-skin, he glided like Napoleon's courier, over the undulating country. Gorgey had crossed the Danube, and defeated in severe engagements, halted at Altenburg. Pulszky returned to Pesth. Kossuth meanwhile, closely secluded in his dwelling, was intensely active; conferring with members of the Diet which was in session, and writing often all night without an intermission of repose. His intellect seemed to compel the body to endure this ceaseless mental friction without derangement. Gorgey marched from Altenburg to Kaab, an important port, where he concentrated his forces. Upon the approach of the enemy, he retreated towards Buda, to join Perczel, advancing with 6000 men from the Drave.

But Perczel was not allowed to pass the Ban, who hovered upon his march. At Moor they met, and after a desperate fight, in which the Hungarians displayed Spartan courage, Jellachich was victorious. It was sad tidings for Hungary. The disasters affected the nation as did the darkest crisis in the

American war. Noble hearts sank with despair, and prayers for help went up from Catholic and Protestant homes. In this dismal hour, which gave to the bearing of Prince Windischgratz the scornful arrogance of an avenging conqueror, whose work was done, it was thought expedient to send a deputation to the camp of the Prince, and propose to negotiate a peace.

Count Louis Batthyanyi and four others were the appointed representation, who proceeded to the Austrian head-quarters. In defiance of laws sacred to savages, Windischgratz ordered them arrested prisoners of the realm; and with treacherous indignity demanded still unconditional submission. All but Batthyanyi were soon released. He was too conspicuous, influential and wealthy to be spared. Austrian treachery thirsted for his blood, and her avarice for his fortune. To the interrogatives of his relentless foes, he replied, "Let me be confronted with the Archduke Stephen, the Palatine of the Kingdom, who shamefully deserted his post. I have done nothing but to carry into practice those measures which he, the Palatine, and fully authorized agent of the King, has constantly approved."

Nothing was now left for Hungary but to bare her breast to the shock of battle, on whose devastating and gory prosecution depended the triumphs of freedom, or the slavery of the Magyar race. Gorgey, who, since the defeat at Schwechat, had commanded the main army, was encamped near Buda, on the road to Kaab. On the 1st of January, 1849, a council of war was held at Pesth, composed of the Committee of Defence, Gorgey, Perczel, Lazar, and Vetter, acting Secretary of War, who presided. It was decided to transfer the seat of government to Debreczen; to remain and stake a decisive battle under the walls of Buda would be rash, if not fatal, without the aid of the division in the lower country, which had just conquered the Serbs.

In the plan of defence unanimously adopted by the Generals, was the assembling of the troops upon the banks of the Theiss, to guard that river against the royal battalions. Gorgey, with 20,000 soldiers, was directed to march towards Upper Hungary, and by attracting the attention of Windischgratz, deceive him respecting the designs and movements of the Hungarians. The feint was perfectly successful. The Prince, after taking possession of Pesth, watched narrowly Gorgey's progress, barely saluting with a detachment or two, the Magyars mustering beside the sweeping Theiss. Arsenals and foundries were opened, while the new recruits continued streaming in, and were enrolled by regiments.

Meszaros being routed at Kashau, Klapka was sent to take command, and after three brilliant actions, checked the enemy's approach to Debreczen, and protected the new capital. Gorgey fought his way through from Waitzen to Ipolysag, thence from one mountain city to another, till he reached Zips county. At Iglo, he was surprised by the Austrians, but after a scene of carnage in the streets, advanced triumphantly towards Epiries. It was necessary to pass the defiles of Braniezko, whose steeps, deemed impregnable, were occupied by Schlick. Gorgey entered the gorge, and pointed his brave troops to the threatening heights, bristling with bayonets, and covered with artillery. The order to assault was given, and with a shout the heroes rushed up the cliffs of fire. The storming waxed furious, and the defiles echoed with more fearful uproar than ever the surrounding squadrons of the tempest made in that fastness, and it was wreathed with more consuming lightning than fringes the meeting clouds. Upward moved the dark lines of living men over the descending bodies, until *one fourth* of the assailants were slain; and the Austrians were flying from this Thermopylæ in disorderly haste.

February 6th, Gorgey was at Epiries, and the communication with Debreczen and the Theiss, complete. General Dembinski, a patriotic Pole, thoroughly educated, and who had received a captaincy from Napoleon in the invasion of Russia, came from Paris, his residence for several years, and joined the Hungarian army. At this time he was appointed Commander-in-Chief of the troops—a circumstance that first distinctly developed Gorgey's towering ambition.

A deeply concerted plan of operations was laid by Kossuth and his Generals, for prosecuting vigorously the unavoidable struggle. Before its consummation, Prince Windischgratz, by slow marches, pressed forward to Erlau, and the 25th of February, the hostile armies met on the plain of Kapolna. Gorgey, stung by Dembinski's superior position, hazarded the prospect of victory by a blunt refusal to obey orders. The effect of this quarrel on the eve of battle was disastrous. Yet there were terrible deeds of slaughter and bravery on that day. For six hours without intermission the impetuous battalions closed, and mowed down a harvest of death. The cannon sent forth an unceasing roar, and the rattling of musquetry with the clang of bayonets and scythes was mingled with shouts and groans. The Hungarians retained possession of the ground; and on the following day, the strife was renewed. As the sun went down, the tide of victory turned toward the Austrian flag.

Night at length hushed the music of carnage, and silence, excepting the moan of the dying, settled upon the red field of Kapolna. Many brave fellows were laid in their narrow abode with the pomp of military interment; beneath the booming of artillery, and the drooping banner of Hungary. Kossuth afterward visited the mounds of his buried comrades. "He stood by the last resting-place of many of his dearest friends, and of thousands whose fearless hearts but a few short hours before beat in unison with his own in its high aspirations after national liberty and glory. Kossuth raised his face to heaven, and uncovered his head, an action in which he was imitated by all present; a smile of unearthly beauty played round his lips—it was not kindled by joy, but by faith—as he clasped his hands together, and, with a bearing that can never be forgotten, uttered the prayer, of which the following is a translation from the German:"

"Exalted Ruler of the Universe, God of the warriors of Arpad, look down from Thy starry throne upon Thine unworthy servant, from whose lips the prayer of millions ascends to heaven, extolling the infinite power of Thine Omnipotence. My God, Thy bright sun shines above me, whilst beneath my knees rest the bones of my fallen brothers. Thy stainless azure over-canopies us; but beneath, the earth is red with the sacred blood of the children of our fathers. Let the fructifying beams of Thy glorious luminary shine upon their graves, that the crimson hue may be replaced with flowers, and the last resting-place of the brave be still crowned with the emblems of Liberty. God of my fathers and of my race, hear my supplications: let Thy blessing rest upon our warriors, by whose arms the spirit of a gallant nation seeks to defend Thine own precious gift of freedom.

"Help them to break the iron fetters, with which blind despotism would bind a great people. As a freeman, I prostrate myself before Thee on these fresh graves of my slaughtered brethren. Accept the bloody offering which has been presented to Thee, and let it propitiate Thy favor to our land. My God, suffer not a race of slaves to dwell by these graves, nor pollute this consecrated soil with their unhallowed footsteps. My Father! my Father! mightier than all the myriads of earth— the Infinite Ruler of heaven, earth, and ocean—let a reflex of Thy glory shine from these lowly sepulchres upon the face of my people. Consecrate this spot by Thy grace, that the ashes of my brothers who have fallen in this sacred cause may rest undisturbed in hallowed repose. Forsake us not in the hour of need, great God of battles! Bless our efforts to promote that liberty of which Thine own spirit is the essence; for to Thee, in the name of the whole people, I ascribe all Honor and Praise."

This beautiful petition is what we should expect

from the genius and heart of Kossuth. Though Windischgratz refused to follow up a victory so doubtful, Dembinski was strangely disheartened, and began his retreat under a deadly rear-guard fight; he fell back to Porosslo, thence hastened to the Theiss. Here he was desired to resign his command, and General Vetter was chosen to fill the vacancy.

March 4th, the New Constitution of the Austrian Empire, wiping out the last traces of the Constitution of St. Stephen, was issued from Olmutz, exasperating and stimulating the people to throw themselves across the track of the gigantic enemy, asking no favor but the chances of a fair combat, and final victory, or death at the cannon's mouth.

Clergymen refused to read the proclamations of Windischgratz, according to royal mandate, in the churches. In one instance, a pastor finally compelled to obey, persuaded the soldiers to stand beside him with fixed bayonets; he thus withdrew the attention of his hearers entirely from the despised message. Deeds of valor were performed by daring sorties upon the foe, resembling the feats of Putnam and Marion of glorious memory.

March 8th, Klapka marched to Szolnok as reserve to Damianics and Vecsey, who in a brilliant action dispersed the Austrians under Karger and Ottinger The charges of Damianics were like the resistless sweep of the elements, and the day was a proud one for Hungary. About 500 prisoners, and a great variety of military stores, were carried from the stained and trodden field. The result sent a thrill of hope and joy over the land. It was seen that an inferior force battling for *the right* might anticipate victory.

Kossuth repaired to head-quarters, and reviewed the brave troops, thanking them in the name of the nation, and with his electric tones summoned them to more splendid conquests. With revived courage offensive measures were renewed to retrieve Dembinski's errors. Gorgey, who had crossed the Theiss, and accomplished the *trajet* with the main force at Fured, upon the sudden illness of Vetter was advanced to the chief command. He was the oldest General next to Vetter, and his bravery unquestioned. During these operations in the North, Bem had been fulfilling his prediction, on the plains of rich and beautiful Transylvania. Kossuth's wisdom was never more apparent than in sending Bem to this hostile province. The dauntless Pole overswept the country like an Alpine avalanche in its descent; the opposing battalions melted away before him, and each day was the record of a victory.

At the village of Piski, February 9th, he had fought a battle, which was unrivalled in fierceness and heroism through the campaign. The stake, was possession of the town, and the bridge over the Strehl. After a temporary defeat at Hermannstadt, March 3d, he returned by a flank movement on the 14th, and with 9000 men, stormed and took the garrison defended by a force of 10,000. Bem's trophies were several hundred prisoners and eight cannon. The following despatches forwarded to Debreczen, disclose his successes and subsequent plans:

"March 15th.—In my despatch I had the happiness to mention, that I had sent a corps against the Rothenthurm Pass, in order as effectually as possible to cut off the communication of the enemy with Wallachia. The division could not, however, advance far, as the whole Austrian army was in Freck, and consequently separated only by a mountain-ridge from the defile, and thus my troops were threatened on the flank as they advanced. Nevertheless I got possession of this defile by a circuitous movement; and I shall not only defend this, but at the same time press the enemy in the direction of Cronstadt, from whence they will have great difficulty to pass the Carpathians in case they endeavor to fly to Wallachia.

"I shall commence these military operations this very day, etc., etc. BEM."

"Head-quarters, Rothenthurm, 16th of March.—My operations yesterday, for driving the Russians from the Rothenthurm Pass, were crowned with such success, that the same night at eleven o'clock, we dislodged the Russians from this strong position. The 15th of March, the birthday of national freedom, could not be celebrated more worthily. At five o'clock this afternoon, the Russians took to the wildest flight, heels over head. Four Austrian generals, Puchner, Pfarsman, Graser, and Jovich, have fled with three companies to Wallachia. I have myself very carefully inspected the Rothenthurm Pass, and made such dispositions, that the Russians will find a difficulty in re-attempting to force their way through it. I have despatched another division of my army in pursuit of the Austrians, who according to the reports given by the prisoners we have taken, have fled dispirited and in disorder toward Cronstadt. Their main force is at Fogarasch, but the rearguard has only just quitted Freck. The enemy broke down the bridge over the Olt behind them which checked our pursuit for a time. Now, after the bridge has been restored, I shall continue the pursuit with all possible vigor. I hope to take Cronstadt in the course of three or four days, whereby the imperial Austrian army will be in part annihilated, in part dispersed, and at all events rendered incapable of disturbing the internal rest of this country. It will then be an easier task to reduce to obedience the single Wallachian bands, which still make their appearance.

"Postscript.—After the taking of Cronstadt I shall immediately set out with a division for Hungary.

"BEM."

It must be remembered in estimating the splendor of Bem's campaign, that his 10,000 men, were both poorly armed and disciplined, principally raw recruits, and hundreds swinging scythes and hatchets; with whom, in an incredibly short period, he reconquered a whole province. Besides cutting his way through a hostile population on every hand, along with Puchner's superior army, he drove across the frontier, 15,000 *Russian* auxiliaries. The last particular disclosed what was soon after officially declared, that the Autocrat was to have a part in the horrid game of Austrian invasion, and secure the immolation of Hungary in the destroying arms of the Hapsburg Moloch.

Bem's greatness and gallantry, are no more conspicuous than his humanity. He treated prisoners of war with kindness, and his soldiers with affection. Kossuth was honored by the impetuous Pole; whose admirers may point triumphantly to the pages of impartial history, for testimony against the reiterated calumnies of the German and English Press. Perczel, who, after leaving Dembinsky's army, took command of the division at Szegedin, was equally victorious. He made a heroic assault upon Sz. Tamas, and carried that position, swept the Roman entrenchments, and relieved the threatened garrison of Peterwarasdin. Somewhat deficient in military science, he was daring, courageous and unyielding, with fearlessness stamped upon his warlike mien, and boundless self-reliance apparent in his bearing, both on the contested field and in the guarded camp.

April 1st, the army of Hungary was concentrated between Gyongyos and Kapolna, directed toward Pesth, but designing to turn upon the enemy and outflank the strong entrenchments of Bag and Aszod. The corps of Klapka, Damianics, and Aulich, accordingly advanced, and were joined by General Gaspar, the successor of Gorgey upon his promotion to chief command, who the same day encountered Schlick, and drove his division behind Hatvan. Godollo was the last important position on the highway to Pesth, and it was determined to take this outpost of the Capital. Klapka hastened forward to the river Tapio, crossed by a single bridge leading to the town of Tapiobieske. A small force only was discernible guarding the place. The village was at the base of a mountain between which and the river, were dangerous quicksands. Klapka ordered the army across the bridge, to storm the town. But suddenly, when within cannon-shot, every dwelling became a redoubt, and opened a wasting fire upon the Hungarians. Jellachich was in ambush there, and a hasty flight alone saved the battalions so unexpectedly surrounded. Klapka with a part of his staff rode into a quagmire, and he escaped by the disguise of his coarse apparel, taken from a captured Serbian, and which he wore through the campaign of that eventful winter. In less than an hour, the village was carried, and the tri-color at nightfall waved over a thousand killed and wounded warriors of the fiercely contested field. On the 5th, it was ascertained that Windischgratz with the royal army was entrenched at Isaszeg. Preparations for a general engagement were commenced. On the heights, one hundred and twenty cannon looked gloomily down upon the valley, where lay the fortified village shaded by an extensive forest. Klapka advanced upon one side, Damianics from the other, while Aulich lay between, fronting the woods. About noon of the 6th, the battle began.

The Hungarians made a murderous onset upon the forest, and three times were driven back by a vastly superior foe. At length Aulich and Gaspar's cavalry came up, when again the charge upon the forest was made, and the enemy vanished before them, like the blasted leaves beneath their feet, when swept by flame. The victors entered the village burning at ten different points, the torch of a desperately bloody contest. Along a line of five miles, artillery thundered, musketry blazed, and men fell in ridges between the hostile ranks. Then followed the assault upon the fortress, which an officer engaged in the conflict, calls the "Gibraltar of the Country."

Right in the hot breath of ordnance, and the tempest of balls from the heights, the Magyars took the garrison, and planted the tri-color in the glow of the setting sun.

Thousands were silent that eve, with ghastly aspect, imploring burial. Again a delay in the advance of Gen. Gaspar's regiments upon the Godollo road, saved the Austrians from a more ruinous, if not fatal rout. Prince Windischgratz was compelled to retreat to Pesth, and gathered his forces on the Rakos field, to wait farther attacks of the victorious Gorgey.

In the morning, the Hungarian army marched rapidly forward towards Godollo, the last position of the enemy which could offer resistance on the highway to Pesth. The disasters at Isaszeg, left the flank of the Austrians exposed to attacks, and Godollo was abandoned except by the lingering corps, who were soon driven from the field. The Hungarians, exhausted by frequent battles and long marches, halted at Godollo. A council of war was held, attended by Kossuth. It was determined to direct the campaign against the Austrian force blockading Comorn, the "Key of Hungary."

To deceive the Austrians, 10,000 men under Aulich, were left behind to watch Pesth, while Gorgey and Klapka, Damianics and Gaspar, advanced by forced marches towards Comorn, which had been severely pressed since December. These battalions commenced their movement on the 8th of April, and after four engagements rescued the Capital, but were obliged to leave Buda in the hands of the enemy's

BATTLE OF WAITZEN.

garrison, numbering about 6,000 men. The next day, Gorgey marched upon Waitzen, lying between his army and Comorn, and held by 12,000 troops. Aware of Gorgey's approach, the foe waited behind a range of sandy hills, for the moment of attack. Damianics rushed forward in the driving rain which set in, and when Klapka advanced, the lines were reeling before the heroic onslaught. The town was soon stormed and taken.

The Magyars took 800 prisoners, several cannon, and other military equipments, leaving General Gotz among the slain, and themselves losing no more than thirty in the short but sanguinary battle.

Kossuth was elated with the success of Hungarian arms, whose conquests he had witnessed surpassing the wildest dream of his illumined spirit. He had met and cordially embraced Gorgey, whose bravery thrilled the soldiery with enthusiasm, and filled the land with shouts of joy and adulation. To crush conspiracies and cabal among conservatives tired of war, and also to hasten the issue that now flamed like the sun before his patriotic mind, he proposed the DECLARATION OF INDEPENDENCE.

The 14th of April dawned a day decisive and immortal in the annals of Hungary.

She was henceforth to take her rank among the independent states of the earth, or the light of her nationality was to go out in the gloom of oppression's night. The crisis of her destiny had arrived. On the morning of this day, the Hungarian representatives gathered in the Protestant church of Debreczen.

It was no magnificent temple, with splendid decorations, whose gorgeous shows conceals the purity of worship, but a plain edifice, whose unadorned simplicity better harmonized than pictured image or sacerdotal pomp, with the grandeur of the scene about to transpire. Within that sanctuary, the worldwide interests of humanity were now centering. The decision pending was to be like the pebble dropped into the ocean, whose circling waves were to reach the remotest shores of that invisible deep of popular feeling which is sweeping away ancient thrones and hoary wrongs. With becoming solemnity the representatives of a struggling nation, met in this house of prayer to deliberate upon the formal question of Hungarian Independence. The United States had boldly declared themselves a free and sovereign people, in the very face of the serried hosts of the mightiest nation the world then knew, and why should not Hungary follow the example! This was the theme before them. Never was a sublimer spectacle beheld in that temple, than this assembly, bowed in supplication for the help of the God of battles, both while they deliberated, and when they went to deadly strife. The voice of prayer was uttered by men who felt that in Jehovah alone was their strength.

The worship over, silence reigned till Kossuth rose, and, in his always impressive manner, rendered more so by the momentous hour, addressed the Assembly. He reported the victories that had attended the Hungarian arms; and then, in tones of impassioned eloquence and ardent patriotism, he recounted their wrongs. In startling colors he pictured the centuries of their own sufferings and sacrifices for that proud dynasty whose iron sway had pressed their noble lineage to the dust. As he unrolled this mouldering record of deception and unrequited toil, and pointed to each act as a warning spirit which they should heed, the Magyar blood quickened its flow, and every heart was ready to seal with its warm wellspring the eternal divorce. In the name of their country and their God, he summoned them to break away from the fetters rusting on their limbs; and, rising in offended majesty, take their place among the free nations of the earth.

As a formal declaration of their rights and resolves, he submitted to the Assembly the following

"DECLARATION RELATIVE TO THE SEPARATION OF HUNGARY FROM AUSTRIA.

"We, the legally constituted representatives of the Hungarian nation assembled in Diet, do by these presents solemnly proclaim, in maintenance of the inalienable natural rights of Hungary, with all its dependencies, to occupy the position of an independent European State—that the House of Hapsburg-Lorraine, as perjured in the sight of God and man, has forfeited its right to the Hungarian throne. At the same time, we feel ourselves bound in duty to make known the motives and reasons which have impelled us to this decision, that the civilized world may learn we have taken this step not out of overweening confidence in our own wisdom, or out of revolutionary excitement, but that it is an act of the last necessity, adopted to preserve from utter destruction a nation persecuted to the limit of the most enduring patience.

"Three hundred years have passed since the Hungarian nation, by free election, placed the House of Austria upon its throne, in accordance with stipulations made on both sides, and ratified by treaty. These three hundred years have been, for the country, a period of uninterrupted suffering.

"The Creator has blessed this country with all the elements of wealth and happiness. Its area of 100,000 square miles presents in varied profusion innumerable sources of prosperity. Its population, numbering nearly fifteen millions, feels the glow of youthful strength within its veins, and has shown temper and docility which warrant its proving at once the main organ of civilization in Eastern Europe, and the guardian of that civilization when attacked. Never was a more grateful task appointed to a reigning dynasty by the dispensation of Providence than that which devolved upon the House of Hapsburg-Lorraine. It would have sufficed to do nothing that could impede the development of the country. Had this been the rule observed, Hungary would now rank amongst the most prosperous nations. It was only necessary that it should not envy the Hungarians the moderate share of constitutional liberty which they timidly maintained during the difficulties of a thousand years with rare fidelity to their sovereigns, and the House of Hapsburg might long have counted this nation amongst the most faithful adherents of the throne.

"This dynasty, however, which can at no epoch point to a ruler who based his power on the freedom of the people, adopted a course towards this nation, from father to son, which deserves the appellation of perjury.

* * * * * * *

"Confiding in the justice of an eternal God, we, in the face of he civilized world, in reliance upon the natural rights of the Iungarian nation, and upon the power it has developed to maintain them, further impelled by that sense of duty which urges every nation to defend its existence, do hereby declare and proclaim in the name of the nation legally represented by us the following :—

"1st. Hungary, with Transylvania, as legally united with it

and its dependencies, are hereby declared to constitute a free, independent, sovereign state. The territorial unity of this state is declared to be inviolable, and its territory to be indivisible.

"2d. The House of Hapsburg-Lorraine—having by treachery, perjury, and levying of war against the Hungarian nation, as well as by its outrageous violation of all compacts, in breaking up the integral territory of the kingdom, in the separation of Transylvania, Croatia, Sclavonia, Fiume, and its districts from Hungary—further, by compassing the destruction of the independence of the country by arms, and by calling in the disciplined army of a foreign power, for the purpose of annihilating its nationality, by violation both of the Pragmatic Sanction and of treaties concluded between Austria and Hungary, on which the alliance between the two countries depended—is, as treacherous and perjured, forever excluded from the throne of the united states of Hungary and Transylvania, and all their possessions and dependencies, and is hereby deprived of the style and title, as well as of the armorial bearings belonging to the crown of Hungary, and declared to be banished forever from the united countries and their dependencies and possessions. They are therefore declared to be deposed, degraded, and banished forever from the Hungarian territory.

"3d. The Hungarian nation, in the exercise of its rights and sovereign will, being determined to assume the position of a free and independent state amongst the nations of Europe, declares it to be its intention to establish and maintain friendly and neighborly relations with those states with which it was formerly united under the same sovereign, as well as to contract alliances with all ther nations.

"4th. The form of government to be adopted for the future will be fixed by the Diet of the nation.

* * * * * * *

"And this resolution of ours we shall proclaim and make known to all the nations of the civilized world, with the conviction that the Hungarian nation will be received by them amongst the free and independent nations of the world, with the same friendship and free acknowledgment of its rights which the Hungarians proffer to other countries.

"We also hereby proclaim and make known to all the inhabitants of the united states of Hungary and Transylvania, and their dependencies, that all authorities, communes, towns, and the civil officers both in the counties and cities, are completely set free and released from all the obligations under which they stood, by oath or otherwise, to the said House of Hapsburg-Lorraine, and that any individual daring to contravene this decree, and by word or deed in any way to aid or abet any one violating it, shall be treated and punished as guilty of high treason. And by the publication of this decree, we hereby bind and oblige all the inhabitants of these counties to obedience to the Government now instituted formally, and endowed with all necessary legal powers.

"DEBRECZEN, APRIL 14, 1849."

The propositions were received with applause, and adopted by acclamation. The representatives were irrevocably pledged to National Independence. The multitude without, excited by the expected event, had gathered around the temple, and caught the sublime decision with a shout of exultation, which rolled like thunder through the crowded streets. From city to city leaped the glad tidings; village and hamlet repeated the stirring notes, till every hearth-stone from the Drave to the Carpathian peaks had become warmer and brighter, in the air and beams of liberty.

This great step needed another before it could attain the desired consummation. A man was required to take the reins of Revolution and guide the car of freedom along its bloody path.

There was but one intellect in the nation equal to the work, and he stood forth so pre-eminent that no other name was whispered. The thoughts of every deputy turned spontaneously towards him who had proposed the Declaration, as "THE MAN FOR THE HOUR." It was no time for party jealousy, and with the unanimity which had distinguished their proceedings, they appointed Kossuth upon the same day, "PRESIDENT GOVERNOR OF HUNGARY."

CHAPTER IX.

BATTLE OF NAGY SARLO—POSITION OF AFFAIRS IN HUNGARY—RE-
JOICINGS AT PESTH—KOSSUTH AT DEBRECZEN—MESSAGE TO THE
ARMY—RUSSIAN INTERVENTION—STORMING OF BUDA—GORGEY—
HUNGARIAN ARMY—WALLACHIAN INSURRECTION—GOVERNMENT
REMOVED TO PESTH—MILITARY MOVEMENTS—THE PALATINAL
HUSSARS.

MAY 18th, the Hungarian army crossed the swollen and rapid current of the Gran, upon a bridge hastily constructed of floating timbers and the ruins of buildings, and the following day, unexpectedly, met a large division of the enemy at Nagy Sarlo. Klapka was in the advance, and Gorgey in the rear, making the transit of the bridge. Without waiting for his battalions, the 22,000 recruits dashed forward to the combat against 34,000 Austrian troops. The fight was desperate, and for a while doubtful.

The swaying, reeling columns were seen under the folds of the black and yellow,* and then beneath those of the tri-color. At length the Hungarian left wing closed with the enemy's right, and decided the fortunes of the day. Damianics then swept round the

---

* Austrian colors.

BATTLE OF NAGY SARLO.

garrison, and soon silenced the batteries. The Austrians threw themselves upon the centre of the hostile forces, and after a destructive encounter, made their retreat, under hot pursuit. In this contest, General Klapka found himself in arms against his own brother, Captain Klapka, who adhered to the imperial cause. This was a mournful feature of the revolution. Father and son, brothers and friends, met in the slaughter, who had always before clasped hands in affection.

The revolutionary army lost 800 in killed and wounded, and took 3000 prisoners in addition to the uncounted dead on the field. Tidings of the victory reached Pesth, and General Welden, who had succeeded Windischgratz in the chief command, withdrew from Pesth on the 23d, and left General Henzi with a strong garrison at Buda. General Guyon, the hero of Schwechat, was appointed by Kossuth to the command of Comorn, and before the arrival of the army, had revived the courage of the garrison, around whose works the bomb-shells and red-hot balls of the enemy had been flying for months. This strong-hold lies at the confluence of two branches of the Danube, near the national frontier, and on the eastern extremity of the island of Schutt. Along the land side, or Palatinal line, is a semicircle of ramparts, and on the river banks, bastions increase the protection of the waters. Upon the approach of the army, the besiegers on the left bank of the Danube withdrew, and the fearful entrenchments of the Sandberg, were to be the scene of the decisive struggle. Soon after midnight, the storming of these works began. General Guyon marched out of the garrison with his troops into the field. The sky was lit up with flying shells, and the fortress shook with the thunder of artillery. The Austrians sustained with their accustomed discipline and bravery, the enthusiastic onset of the patriots, till about 8 o'clock in the morning, when they gave way, and the fortifications were under the Hungarian banner.

With Comorn relieved and rejoicing, we pause to glance at the position of Hungarian affairs; the crisis in the war of independence. The army had made a brilliant manœuvre, which will be recorded among the marvels of martial strategy. After a retreat for months before the superior force of the enemy, crushing hope, and sapping the strength of the army, the patriots suddenly halted, and wheeling upon the exulting foe, rolled back the tide of victory. The Austrians were defeated in every battle, and hurried their march across the plains over which they had swept with nodding plumes, shouting in their visionary conquest and hopeless annihilation of the democratic forces.

In Vienna, the courtly circles had discussed the overthrow of the lawless hordes of Hungary, and smiled at their attempt to measure swords with Austria. The press repeated the gossip, and mingled with the sentiments of pity for the unfortunate and mad adventurers, the eloquent reproof. But when the gates of Comorn were wide open to the footsteps of the undisturbed and triumphant Magyars, there was the deepest mortification, and a resort to falsehood to cover the shame of defeat. The flight of the

Imperial battalions was represented as an artful stratagem, designed to hasten the ultimate ruin of the rebels. The climate of the country was affirmed to be destructive, and the tidings of retreat across the Danube, with the desertion of Comorn, an exaggeration. The truth at length prevailed over the delusion of unprincipled courtiers. It was evident that Hungary had conquered with undisciplined regiments and gleaming scythes, the royal troops, deepening the halo of her ancient glory. But we may drop a tear over this hour of success. It was grand, yet fatal. There lay Vienna, corrupt and trembling with the expectation of hearing soon the artillery of an avenging enemy, whose approach would again spring the mine of popular fury beneath the throne. On the other side, were the walls of Buda, whose iron-bound munition of rock, had long been the central fastness of Hungary, and within which were the brave troops of the Austrian Henzi. To storm Buda, the romantic and royal castle of the land, would be a difficult and splendid exploit. But a greater, and the only successful expedition, would be an advance upon Vienna. Entrenchment there would cripple the enemy, and furnish supplies. The decision between the adventures, was entirely in the hand of Gorgey. He determined at all hazards to gratify his boundless and base ambition. He anticipated a post at the head of the War Department, and the fascination of Buda's historical glory would make the conquest a crowning honor in his heroic campaign. He had talent, but no *heart*, and like the greater Napoleon, when France was at his disposal, he was haunted with the proud dream of a Dictator's reign. Three days of useless delay passed, when, April 29th, Gorgey issued his orders for the march to Buda. Colonel Poltenberg was despatched to watch the flying Austrians, and a part of the garrison at Comorn directed to dislodge those royalists who had taken up a position on the Island of Schutt. Gorgey disclosed his secret plot against Kossuth by directing the plan of attack independent of the President's legitimate power. At this time, Pesth was occupied by the brave, chivalrous and amiable Aulich. From balconies, belfries and doors, waved the Hungarian flag; the people, delirious with delight, crowded the streets, throwing flowers in the path of the soldiery, and making the welkin ring with cheers. Their Buda only was solitary and gloomy, under the Austrian colors. At Debreczen, the new seat of government, Parliament and people had recovered from despondency, and participated in the general gratulation. The seats of the Upper House were again filled by representatives from all the counties. Unfortunately, the members wasted renewed energies in fruitless debates and enactments, when united and decided appeals to the nation, attended with appropriate legislation, would have sustained their Chief, and saved the country's cause.

In Parliament, the want of efficiency, and in the army the absence of harmony, gave to external enemies a might otherwise impossible, and which rendered powerless the unexampled courage of the common warriors. It is proper here to add a passing no tice of Kossuth's life at Debreczen. In one spacious room his secretaries were constantly employed, and in another he received strangers. He was brief, and carefully listened to those who addressed him. His industry and despatch were amazing. He was always at work. Calls often continued, and despatches arrived till past midnight. He has indited a letter in German, another in French, and a third in Magyar at the same time, besides answering interrogations, and busily writing himself. If the physician entered to inquire after his feeble health, he extended his left arm, and while the medical adviser felt his pulse, with his right hand he moved the pen without a momentary pause. Toward morning, his secretaries sometimes fell asleep from mere exhaustion, and he would bid them retire, till he called for their services; which occurred before the dawn of day. He frequently took no nourishment during the hours of business but a medicinal liquid he kept by his side. His recreation was a brief pastime with his children on the greensward of spring, or a drive into an adjacent grove with his faithful wife. The peasantry shouted "Eljen Kossuth!" whenever he appeared on the way to Parliament, or returned to his dwelling, and were ready to form a breastwork before cannon and bayonets at his command. It is related of a peasant, that meeting another in a public-house, he drew from his pocket a two-florin note on Kossuth's Hungarian Bank, and said, "He is too good, he is too good, and would not injure any creature, and this will be his death. Why does he treat the prisoners so well, and prevent any harm being done them, while they would exterminate us all, and destroy Hungary if they could? But he cares for his enemies as if they were his own children. Look ye, here he has had printed, you see, on this note, German, Serbian, Croatian, and God knows what besides, in order that not a human soul should be deceived. But what are the others to us? If I had been he, I would have written on it 'Eljen Kossuth! Ket forint!' (Long live Kossuth! Two florins.) We should all have understood it, shouldn't we? But no, he is too good. Jesus Christ be with him!"

General Klapka visited Governor Kossuth at Debreczen, who expressed his fears that Buda might resist the Hungarians, and the precious moment of decisive advance upon the troubled enemy be lost forever. The resignation of Meszaros, of whose orders Dembinski in Upper Hungary complained, and which other generals disregarded, elevated Klapka to the War Department of the Cabinet; at his suggestion, more energetic measures were adopted. They are set forth in the Resolution which follows, forwarded to the commanders of the various divisions:

"The probability of a Russian invasion, and the considerable reinforcements which have lately poured in to the Austrian armies, make it incumbent upon the Government, with all its powers, to provide for the defence of the country. On the representations of General Klapka, the Secretary at War, I have therefore resolved as follows:

"The military forces of the nation are to act in concert and co-operate with the combined plan of defence adopted by the Government.

MESSAGE TO THE ARMY. 173

"The arbitrary and fanciful character of operations which some commanders, regardless of the direction of the campaign, have adopted must be done away with.

"For this purpose, the commanders of forces shall have the general plan of the campaign communicated to them. Each commander will likewise receive his separate instructions, informing him of the part his corps is to take in the operations.

"Immediately after the capture of Buda, or in case of a failure, immediately after the establishment of a blockading corps round that fortress, and the arrangement of the other corps on the Upper Danube, General Gorgey will proceed to this place to take the lead in the War Office, for the purpose of establishing the preparations for the defence of the country on a broad and solid foundation.

"The commanders of the various corps have hitherto taken it upon themselves to remove, translocate, appoint, and grant medals and orders to military officers. For the future, they are bound to appeal to the War Office, and in the higher grades to the Governor of the country for confirmation. On the field of battle alone shall the commanders be entitled to reward the merits of individuals, according to the best of their opinion.

"This Resolution of the Council of Ministers, and its confirmation by the Governor of the country, shall at once be communicated to the army and the military authorities throughout Hungary.   KOSSUTH."

Austria had published the proclamation of Russian intervention, while Gorgey was fortifying himself with 30,000 troops before Buda. The murderous measure drove Count Stadion at the Capital mad, who foresaw the horrors it involved. The declaration exhibits the reciprocal fear and determinations of European Sovereigns.

"The insurrection in Hungary has within the last months grown to such an extent, and its present as pect exhibits so unmistakably the character of a union of all the forces of the revolutionary party in Europe, that all states are equally interested in assisting the Imperial (*i. e.* Austrian) Government in its contest against this spreading dissolution of all social order. Acting on these important reasons, His Majesty the Emperor's Government has been induced to appeal to the assistance of His Majesty the Czar of all the Russias, who generously and readily granted it to a most satisfactory extent. The measures which have been agreed on by the two sovereigns are now executing."

This addition of 130,000 Russians, increased the enemies of Hungary to 300,000 men, most of them disciplined troops, opposed by 135,000 patriots, half armed, and with only 400 pieces of artillery. But the *masses* were the strength and hope of the righteous cause under God; they were ready for any summons but to surrender.

Kossuth addressed himself with resistless eloquence to the people; urged their mustering in numbers equal to the allied foes, armed with knives, pitchforks, scythes and hatchets. He proclaimed a public fast as did our forefathers, who thus sought the indispensable aid of Jehovah in the hour of danger and approaching battle. After a bold and unavailing correspondence of Gorgey with Henzi, the commandant of Buda, the storming of the fortress was fixed at midnight of the 16th of May.

General Aulich was ordered to break through the Castle Gate into the Park, thence enter the fortress;

General Knezich and the third corps were directed against the Vienna Gate and its bastions, and other divisions commanded to take the remaining assailable points. At 2 o'clock in the morning the order for general assault was given. The solid columns advanced into the tempest of bombs, grenades and red-hot balls, poured from the garrison. To increase the terrible sublimity of the scene, immense piles of wood were set on fire by the Austrians, and the conflagration illumed the entire field of conflict. Beneath the lurid sky, the Danube rolled like a tide of lava against Buda's reddened walls, and on its bosom floated like fearful phantoms the fire-ships towards the pontoon bridge. Around these, gleamed the numberless batteries, whose volleys shook the hills, and sent the tidings of deadly combat over the distant plains, in the continual thunder that drowned the wild hurrahs of the meeting foes. Against previous stipulation, and with strange delight in Vandal deeds, a fierce cannonading was opened upon lovely Pesth, to demolish its finished blocks of buildings, and blacken its quiet beauty. The brave Honveds,* were cut down by ranks, but their comrades returned with shouts to the charge.

The gray dawn began to appear over the clouds of smoke tinged with the lightning of battle, and the strong-hold of Buda stood impregnable, though scarred and trembling before the shock. The lad-

---

* " Home defenders, the Hungarian militia."—KLAPKA.

ders were removed from the walls, and the commanders retired with their troops to their former entrenchments. General Nagy Shandor, complained of Gorgey's management, and conferred with Kossuth on the subject. The bitterness of hatred to Kossuth, was apparent in every act of Arthur Gorgey, who was then accused of treachery. At Debreczen, the indignation toward him and his declining fame, stung his proud spirit. He mustered his forces and made another and resistless assault upon Buda. His Honveds mounted the scaling-ladders in a blaze of artillery, and descended like a tornado upon the garrison.

General Henzi fell in the breach, pierced with balls and bayonets; Colonel Allnosh, attempting to spring a mine under the suspension bridge, by the explosion was cast a mutilated corpse at a distance from his ghastly commander. Aulich, Knezich, and young, gallant Leiningen, covered themselves and the arms of Hungary with glory. It was a dazzling victory for the despised rebels. Kossuth issued the following proclamation :

" Praise to the holy name of God! Praise to the heroes of the National army, who sacrifice their lives to the liberation of our country!

" *The fortress of Buda is in our hands !*

" The Government has received the following official report of this important event :—

"'BUDA, 21st May, 5 o'clock, A.M.

'The Hungarian colors are flying from the towers of Buda Castle! The honveds are scaling the walls of the fortress on ladders! The enemy's 24 pounders have hoisted the white flag;

STORMING OF BUDA.

"'The first attack, which was commenced at midnight, was directed against the Vienna Gate. The Castle Gate and the breach were attacked at one o'clock in the morning, and continued to the break of day. A murderous fire was directed upon our honveds, from the bastions, towers, and houses. Heavy stones were thrown down upon them; but their devoted courage overcame the resistance of the enemy.

"'The fire of the Austrian troops, though fierce and continuous, has done less execution than might have been expected. But at this moment a street fight is commencing which is likely to lead to a great sacrifice of life. The enemy retreats from the bastions on the side of the Schwabenberg. One of their detachments holds out in a position near the Wesseinburg Gate. Through the breach the honveds pour into the fortress. The fire of artillery and musketry is already silenced in this part of the town, but strong discharges of small fire-arms are heard from the Pesth side of the fortress.

"' 6 o'clock 30m. A.M.
"' A powder magazine has exploded. The street fight still continues in the fortress.

"' 7 o'clock, A.M.
"' The firing has ceased on all sides. *Buda is conquered!*'

"May the nation gather fresh courage and enthusiasm from the example of this success! May the combat which is still impending be short, and the liberation of the country complete! Peals of bells throughout the country, proclaim the victory of Hungarian arms. Pray to God, and thank him for the glory he has vouchsafed to grant the Hungarian army, whose heroic deeds have made it the bulwark of European liberty!

"Debreczen, 22d May, 1849.
"The Governor of the Commonwealth,
"LOUIS KOSSUTH."

The storming of Buda under Gorgey, turned the current of popular feeling at Debreczen. Upon motion of Szemere, Prime Minister, the Parliament voted to present the thanks of the country to him and his invincible army, accompanied with "the grand cross of the Hungarian order of military merit" to Gorgey.

The proud General, concealing his enmity towards Kossuth, which made favors a burden from him, replied to the committee of award, with plausible dissimulation, that "his principles would not allow him to accept a mark of distinction; that the mania for titles and orders was already rife among the officers of his army, and that for the purpose of calling them back to the early purity of their purposes and tendencies, he felt it incumbent on himself to set them an example."

To maintain the conquests gained, and prepare for further campaigns, it was decided that, "Dembinsky should protect Upper Hungary against the Russian invasion—the main army resting on Comorn; the right should extend to the mountain cities, the left to the Bakony range; the southern army under Vetter, was to remain in Baksa on both sides of the Danube, until Bem, with a part of his forces from Transylvania, should be advanced on a line with the other armies, when he was to take the chief command and resume the offensive. It was additionally resolved to form an army of reserve, at Szolnok, and also arranged that 22,000 troops, under Klapka's command, should be disposed in a fortified camp at Comorn: if the main army were repulsed and pursued these were to operate in the rear.

"In pursuance of this design, Klapka left the ministry of war, and assumed command of the fortress and troops in and about Comorn."

At this period, the insurgent Wallachians again rose upon the Magyars, under the incendiary influ ence of Austrian agents, who persuaded the infatuated people that the Hungarian war was prosecuted to absorb their language and distinct nationality, from which nothing but exterminating insurrections could save them.

Shoguna, a bishop, was the leader of the revolt. Unsuccessful mediation was attempted, and an unparalleled scene of slaughter followed. Churches on every hand were bonfires, houses were pillaged, women ravished, harvest-fields wantonly desolated, and a hundred Magyar villages laid in ashes. The sky was red above a crimson earth, and shrieks were the music of the general murder of helpless families.

Meanwhile Gen. Bem attacked and routed the second time, Malkowski's corps of 10,000 men, chasing him across the Wallachian frontier, and joined Perczel who had defeated the Servians, and was besieging Temesvar. Dembinski with 10,000 troops was encamped at Eperies and Kashau; the defiles along the line of Transylvania were strong'v fortified, and the divisions which stormed Buda advan.ed to the banks of the Waag and Upper Danube.

Parliament returned to the re-conquered capital; Baron Haynau, the modern Nero, was invested with the supreme command of the hostile forces; General Gorgey was promoted to the Hungarian War Department, which he established at Buda, retaining in his vaulting ambition also his command in the army. To combine the honor of the two offices, he formed a Chancellery at head-quarters, which ever after, especially under the influence of Bayer, hindered the operations of the army, and increased the gulf of inexcusable alienation from Governor Kossuth. Gen. Klapka, after his resignation in favor of Gorgey, was appointed Commander of the camp and fortress of Comorn, the battalions on the Island of Schutt and right bank of the Danube.

Additional changes were made in official appointments, and on the whole, the prospects of the Hungarian army were passing under eclipse in the beginning of June. A message from Kossuth to Klapka gives a condensed view of the condition and designs of the country.

"THE GOVERNOR OF THE COMMONWEALTH TO GENERAL KLAPKA.

"MY DEAR GENERAL:

"The Government has at length arrived at Pesth. The people received us with exulting enthusiasm—for in our persons they cheered the idea of national liberty and independence.

"1 have received your two letters of the 2d and 3d June, and I reply to them as follows:

"I believe that the plan of operations which you submitted to the Cabinet Council at Debreczen, and which we accepted, was the result of an understanding between yourself and your friend Gorgey, and I had no reason to doubt but that after your departure for Comorn this plan would be brought to execution. I calculated the forces under your command to be—

The Garrison of Comorn	8000 men.
Kmetty's Corps	4000 "
Damjanitsh's Corps	7500 "
Poltenberg	8000 "
Making a total of	27,500 men.

"But even if the corps under the command of Damianics had, for strategical purposes, been ordered to the left bank, (a movement which might always have served to cover Comorn from that side,) I relied on your having still 20,000 men, and that you would have no difficulty in recruiting their strength to the number of 5000 more.

"But if this is not the case, I confess that I cannot but entertain serious apprehensions, and I must entreat you to come to an understanding with the Secretary of War, and to induce him to a speedy execution of the said plan of operations; for though firmly convinced of the importance of Comorn, I cannot, if that place is to be regarded merely as a fortress, and not as a great entrenched camp, but consider it a serious loss that your talents, which require a larger sphere of action, and which, in this time of general exertion, are indispensably necessary to the country, should be condemned to the keeping of Comorn, which would be quite as safe in other hands.

"I am in hourly expectation of the return from the Banat of Minister Vukowitsh. He will form one of the results of the recruiting of a corps of from 12 to 16,000 men. Unless this force is to be placed under the command of Bem, there is no objection to its joining your army. But even if they are to join you, it is necessary that your forces be recruited by new enlistments. For this purpose it is indispensable that the War Office, and by means of that office I, myself, am continually to be informed of the numbers actually in the battalions, and of the number of recruits which have been sent to you. I recommend this affair to your particular notice.

"Under to-morrow's date I mean to issue instructions for sending (for the use of your recruits) 1000 suits of summer regimentals for the corps of Comorn, as well as for that at Raab A second supply of regimentals will follow in the course of next week.

"I did not by any means find such an extent of preparations here as I had been led to expect from the promises of Lukats, &c But even in the most favorable case, I think it necessary to establish at Comorn a manufactory of weapons and percussion caps.

to construct powder mills, and to set down a commission of **Equip-ment.**

"For this purpose I recommend to you Mr. Szekely, who, you know, is a clever and honest man. If you think you can make use of him as commissioner of goods or purveyor of stores, I beg you will inform me of it, and I will send him to you.

"The bearer of this is instructed to pay you 1000 florins. Another remittance to the same amount will follow the day after tomorrow.

"You will use all your energies in the construction of the works and fortifications. I will take it upon myself to let you have the money, and the commissioner Ujhazi is instructed to provide you with the laborers and implements.

"As to the question between an offensive and defensive warfare, I am firmly convinced that the longer we delay acting on the offensive, the more prepared will the enemy be to meet us, and the more difficult will it be to succeed. In the development of resources, the enemy has less obstacles to conquer than we have, especially since the want of weapons is becoming painful. In my opinion, it would have been very advantageous if we had made use of the time in which the Russian intervention was preparing, for the purpose of attacking the Austrians, who were then isolated : or, at least, for the purpose of advancing on the Laytha. But whether or not the latter movement is still advisable, depends upon the powers at the enemy's disposal. If the statement of 15,000 men on the left, and 25,000 on the right bank, be true, we might, indeed, by a prompt and energetic movement, attack them on either shore. I propose to confer on this matter with Gorgey.

"But the most important point of the operations is, that Comorn may be placed in a most efficient state of defence.

"General Lahner has sent several thousand muskets to Comorn to be repaired, but I do not believe that your factory will suffice to do the work with sufficient despatch. If such be the case, you wil. please to send a part of these muskets back. I mean to put them into the hands of the Pesth gun-makers.

"General Lahner has likewise sent 500 cwts. of saltpetre to Comorn, to be used in the fabrication of gunpowder. Your powder-mill is still to be built: when can it work? I think General Lahner would have acted more judiciously if he had sent this transport of saltpetre to some place where the powder-mills are actually at work. Whenever yours is so, I will take care that you are plentifully supplied with materials.

"Yours sincerely,

"PESTH, June 7th, 1849.   KOSSUTH."

It was with Hungary in 1849 as with America in 1776. The comprehensive mind and disinterested affection for his country of a single man, was the defence and hope of the nation.

The Austrians were recovering from the mortifying paralysis of overwhelming defeat, and sustained by the locust swarms of Russia, meditating anew the annihilation of Hungary. The fears Kossuth expressed in his letter to Klapka, darkened during every moment of Gorgey's delay to act according to the wishes of the Government and Generals at Pesth, and hasten to avert the calamity which must attend the concealed plans and wasted time of the haughty chieftain. At this crisis, an exciting and romantic display of heroism broke like a gush of sunlight through clouds, upon the army and people. A company of 120 Palatinal hussars in Upper Austria, sympathizing with their brethren in the Hungarian army, seized a favorable hour, and dashing away toward the interior of their surrounded country, cut through opposing troops, marched along mountain slopes and deep defiles, and made their rapid flight to Papa, to enlist under the tri-colors of the Commonwealth. The perils, fatigues and escapes of these warriors, the bravest in the ranks of either host, remind us of the tales of the Crusaders, and the knight-errantry of past centuries. There was an electric thrill in the advent of the hussars, and Klapka promoted the sergeant who led them to a lieutenancy, and decorated him with the "third class of the Order for Military Bravery."

On the 12th of June the Austrians reached Csorna, under General Wiss. To discipline Colonel Kmetty's division, they were ordered to meet the enemy crossing the Raab; they made a forced march of thirteen hours, and at five o'clock the next morning appeared before the village where the hostile troops were drawn up in order of battle. The command to charge was given, and an impetuous struggle followed. The Hungarian hussars and Austrian lancers closed with the fearless desperation of mountain tigers. They fought like men who forgot that on any others depended the victory. When Csorna was carried by the columns on the south, every *fifth* hussar lay in his blood, pierced with wounds. General Wiss fell, and about 200 of his troops.

By this time Haynau, with his main Austrian force, held Pressburg; Grabbe was marching toward the cities dotting the mountainous region, and Prince Paskienitsbe with his Russian host was at Dukla. Forty thousand more of the troops of the Autocrat were advancing toward Transylvania, while Jellachich, re-conquering the ground won by Perczel in the Batska country, moved forward with his Cro-

ENGAGEMENT AT ZSIGARD.

tians. These mighty armies were uniting around central Hungary, and sweeping on to force the encircled Magyars to decisive conflict—a general battle on Hungarian plains. Gorgey could no longer beat time; he must either make defensive preparations, and protract the war, or concentrate his battalions, and stake the issue upon a bold assault upon the gigantic foe. Gorgey plainly should have maintained the defensive, strengthened his position at Comorn, and compelled the Austrians to disclose their designs. In this attitude, while strengthening his force, he could have watched the enemy, and taken them by suprise when divided by reconnoitering detachments. But Gorgey seemed infatuated; blind with Haman's jealousy of a nobler mind, which cast his own in shade, he resolved to act aggressively, and sacrifice the manifold advantages in his grasp, for the doubtful experiment of offensive battle. In the selection of his field, he exhibited an insane carelessness of results. He marched his second and third corps, upon the marshy plains that lie between the Waag and Danube, to fight a superior force strongly encamped on the right shore of the Waag. Advancing along the river towards Zsigard, and after successful skirmishes by the way, they had a general engagement there. A deadly conflict terminated in the defeat of the Hungarians. Notwithstanding, Gorgey prepared for another battle under similar difficulties, and on nearly the same ground.

The gallant Klapka wrote an earnest protest to the

plan of operations, from which we give an extract to show the feeling of able Generals toward Gorgey:

"My dear Friend:—

"Some weeks ago, when I drew up the plan for the defence of the country, I had cause to believe that it would obtain your approbation. I am sorry to find that I was mistaken, and that your views differ from mine. I have for some time been convinced of this fact, by your directing the first corps to the Neutra; and my conviction has been strengthened by the late offensive movements of the second corps in the Shutt, and across the 'Neuhausel arm.' Give me leave, therefore, to submit my views to you, not as an officer who serves under you, but as a friend.

"In the first instance, situated as we are, I must pronounce against any hasty movement in the offensive. An offensive war, with frequent defensive reactions—such is our task at this moment. It is the highest task, while it is the simplest in a national warfare. If we can but succeed in gaining time to recruit and concentrate our forces, we need not fear for an opportunity to annihilate the enemy's power; such an opportunity will, in that case, occur in the regular course of things. For God's sake, do not let us resign ourselves to illusions! Only a practical review of our condition—a calm and deliberate survey of the dangers which on every side surround us, can enable us to work the salvation of the country.

* * * * * * *

"I protest that we ought not to be too greedy of victory, but that we ought, in the South, as well as here, to re-form our available forces, so as to make them a guarantee to our cause, in order to avoid the necessity of staking the present and future welfare of the country on a single and desperate cast.

"Let me therefore entreat you, at your earliest convenience, to give existence and shape to the lower army, and to consign its command to energetic and trustworthy hands. As for this part of the country, let Comorn be the hinge on which our operations turn; our position round that fortress is much more likely to awe the enemy than our feigned assumption of offensive warfare. It is the latter which the Austrians most desire, since it eventually will turn to their own advantage. Do not let us be deluded. The Imperialists are likely to hold back for some time, for the purpose of inducing us to leave our positions. What guarantee have we for the result of the contest, if we fall into this trap? And if the fate of war turns against us, who is to restore to the army its courage and confidence? Let the Austrians attack *us*, since they would conquer Hungary, and attack they will and must, though they do not at all seem to like the idea of such a thing, here on the Upper Danube.

"The perseverance in so imposing an attitude of defence as our present, is, in my opinion, what circumstances command us to do. Nor ought we to swerve from this line of action—or *in*-action if you please—until circumstances are changed, and until we have completed our preparations.

"In conclusion, let me entreat you again to send forces—no matter where they come from—to the Drave.

"KLAPKA.
"RAAB, 18th June, 1849."

But Gorgey was never swerved by counsel, from a favorite plan. On the 20th, he took command in person of the Hungarian troops bivouacking at Aszod. It was his purpose to make a grand onslaught upon the enemy, and regain the glory lost, while he added laurels to his own brow. The dense fog early rolled away, revealing to the long lines of Austria, the Magyars in battle array. At 10 o'clock, Colonel Ashboth made a powerful charge without waiting for Gorgey, and the cannonading of the hostile battalions opened like the explosion of a magazine. Colonel Mandi drove their cavalry to Pered, where a halt was made, and preparations for the heat of contest.

Pered was guarded by several Imperial battalions, and two batteries. Colonel Ashboth planned an assault with five battalions and two batteries. It was apparent that here would be decided the fortunes of the day, and the attack was commenced with great deliberation and courage. The Hungarian troops went steadily forward through a storm of grape and grenades, till an advanced battalion reached the church. Then a masked battery was opened by the enemy, and the volleys of discharge cut the brave ranks like hail upon the vernal herbage. Ashboth saw with agony the retreat that followed, for upon their success hung the cause of the Magyars on that battle-field. He rallied his flying troops, and again led them to the charge. Right before the blaze of the decimating tempest, he swept the principal street, and every rood of land, and every threshold reddened with the tide of carnage. The legions closed in mortal combat, as if the terrific scene were one of personal encounter. Foes fell in each other's arms, outstretched in slaughter, and the blood of many nations mingled in the sluices. The Austrians toward noon began to reel before the furious charges of the Magyars, and at 2 o'clock, P. M., were hastening in disorderly retreat toward Galantha. The patriotic troops held the torn tri-color above the dead and wounded that paved the streets of scathed and blackened Pered. Gorgey appeared at this juncture, and wounded in spirit because Ashboth had charged without his order, removed the hero from command. Meanwhile a Russian force of 15,000 troops arrived from Pressburg, putting two battalions against each one of the Magyars. Besides, the Hungarians had gone thirty-six hours without their rations. But Gorgey determined to attempt to break the enemy's line. At ten o'clock on the morning of the 21st, the Austrian artillery opened a fire upon Pered, while at Kiralyrev Gorgey ordered an attack. The royalists yielded to the attack at first; but uncovering their batteries, they poured in a destructive fire.

The Hussars retreated, and the Austrians made a furious pursuit. The scene between Kiralyrev and Pered was a confused intermingling of cuirassiers and lances. Bohemians, Poles, Austrians and Magyars, killing and charging in a general and horrible running fight. Suddenly, from the fields of Pered, an unexpected blaze of musketry welcomed the foe, and in a panic of fear, they fled from the bleeding yet victorious hussars. Yet there lay two grand columns of the enemy between the villages; and Gorgey leaving Pered to meet them, that place was attacked and carried, which was followed by the taking of Kiralyrev; the Magyars made an orderly retreat toward Aszod. Attempting to force their way through Kiralyrev, there was another mortal strife, and after three desperate charges, Gorgey succeeded, piling ghastly bodies upon the esplanades of flowers and the hearthstones of home. In these battles, Hungary lost 2,500 men, and Austria at least as many. This holocaust was fearful, and without great results to the cause of freedom. Gorgey had let the glorious moment of confident hope pass for bloody experiments, and

henceforward Hungary hastens with transient conquests to her fall.

Klápka had been skirmishing with the enemy on
the right bank of the Danube, sometimes pursuing
and again retreating, with the unceasing sound of
the fierce cannonading at Pered, resounding over
his desponding and weary battalions. At Aszod
bridge, the Imperialists again came upon the Hungarians and were defeated, though an earlier and united attack would have routed—perhaps destroyed the
patriotic army. Gorgey hastened to the Waag in a
peasant's cart, like a subdued lion, chafing under defeat and dispirited in view of the awful future. The
Austro-Russian forces were elated by recent success,
and concentrating their strength, left Pressburg, and
moved forward upon Raab. It was another momentous crisis, to which the Central Chancelry of Gorgey
and himself were strangely blind. Colonel Bayer
was at the head of that Board, a temporizing, suspi-
cious man, whose suggestions always outweighed
with Gorgey, the oracular voice of Kossuth. Instead
of marching troops to Raab, with the advantages of
position and equal numbers, the divisions were idle or
ordered to less important posts, while "the Butcher"
Haynau, was advancing. Raab is a finely built city
of 20,000 inhabitants, at the confluence of the rivers
Raab and Rabnitz with the Danube, and a common
centre of highway to the Hungarian capitals, and the
Austrian cities.

Its fortifications were old as the Turkish wars of
the 16th century, of which the French in 1809 spared

only a single bastion guarding the Raab. Upon the garrison of 6,000 soldiers, the Austrians marched on the 27th of June, with 40,000 troops. The assault began at noon, and at six P. M., when Klapka arrived at Dove Inn, near the city, Gorgey was rallying his flying battalions. The brave Colonel Kossuth held his ground against eight times his number of men. The fight was bloody, powder-carts exploded, ordnance were crushed to the soil slippery with gore, and the artillery cut down by ranks. Thus that band, shouting " Eljen Kossuth !" "Hurrah for Hungary !" as often before, bore for hours the surges of battle, beating furiously upon them as the ocean smites a cliff that falls only because it *must*.

The Magyars fell back to Dove Inn on the Gonyo road, where Gorgey assumed in person the command. General Klapka departed via Comorn, for Pesth, to confer with Kossuth. The rapid succession of disasters, and progress of the Russians in Transylvania and northern Hungary, threw the nation into a maze of anxiety and terrific apprehensions. Klapka passed through crowds gathered on the banks of the Danube, to hear the last tidings from the scene of conflict. With his brave heart oppressed and bleeding for Hungary, he entered, July 1st, the silent streets of the Capital; a few weeks before, along those streets, surged the tide of humanity to sounds of music, and rending the air with shouts of gladness.

Kossuth bitterly lamented the operations upon the Upper Danube, and the influence of Colonel Bayer. General Perczel went into a blaze of passion respecting

Gorgey's movements. Governor Kossuth urged a retreat of the northern forces, to join Visockis' division, and concentrate on the Theiss or Moros. He regarded this plan as the only possible means of averting the impending ruin from his pillaged country. Gorgey promised to obey the order, and then arranged his own plan of again meeting the enemy. The Government resolved to remove him, and appoint Meszaros, who was a patriot, but had lost the confidence of the army in his ability to guide the campaigns. The following despatches were sent by a courier to Klapka after his departure from Pesth for Comorn:

"My dear General :

"Gorgey has broken his word, which he pledged to a minister of state and two generals.

"He shall remain Secretary-at-war, but the chief command cannot be allowed to rest another moment in his hands. The Field-Marshal-Lieutenant Meszaros has been appointed to that post.

"Perhaps Gorgey will refuse to obey. That would be infamous! It were treason—as, indeed, the breach of his word, and his blind submission to Bayer's influence, is akin to treason.

"General! the liberty of our country and the liberty of Europe depend upon there being at this moment no dissensions, no party quarrels in the army.

"In you I respect a Roman character. Our country and our liberty above all! Support General Meszaros. My reasons I mean to communicate to you. God and history will judge us.

"I am sure, General, I shall not be deceived in you.

"Kossuth,
"Governor of the Commonwealth.

"Pesth, 1st July, 1849."

"The Governor of the Commonwealth to General Klapka.

"By these presents, I inform you, that, by the authority which the country has given me, and with the counsel and assent of the council of ministers, I have this day, in the name of the people, appointed the Field-Marshal-Lieutenant Lazarus Meszaros to be Commander-in-chief of all the troops of our country. And with these presents, I decree and ordain in the name of the people, that the armies, corps, divisions, garrisons of fortresses, and all other forces, whatever their names or denominations may be, shall yield an unconditional obedience to the orders and instructions of the said Lazarus Meszaros, and shall consider it their bounden duty to recognize him, the said Lazarus Meszaros, as their lawful Commander-in-chief; and whoever shall act against his orders, that man is, and shall be considered, a traitor to the country.

"In the name of liberty and the people, I summon you by your patriotism, of which your heroism and devotion have given such signal proofs, that you shall see this decree punctually executed by your corps, and do all you can to preserve the union, which, in the present dangerous moment, can alone save our country, and indeed the liberty of Europe, and to co-operate now, as you did formerly, for the salvation of our country and of liberty, with your tried fidelity, loyalty, heroism, and disregard of all personal feelings; and for the same I give you the thanks of the country, the high rewards of self-esteem, and the verdict of history : with my sincerest respects.

"The Governor of the Commonwealth,
"Louis Kossuth"
"For the Secretary-at-War,
"Szemere,
"President of the Cabinet.

"Pesth, 1st July, 1849."

General Klapka reached Comorn the 2d, and at eight o'clock A.M., the Austrians and Russians advanced upon the entrenchments, held by 22,000 men. This camp without the fortress, lay along a range of hills on the banks of the river, the most elevated of which is the Monostor—the Mount Defiance of their strong fortifications. Here Gorgey should have rallied his strength, and beaten back the foe. But he either failed to see, or did not care what might be the issue of losing that strongest ground in possession of the troops. Through the vineyards of Szony the bayonets gleamed, swiftly followed by the sweeping battalions of the young Emperor, who, encouraged by late victories, had placed himself at the head of the allied army. They carried the outposts, and displayed triumphantly the black and yellow banner on the walls. At this moment of peril Gorgey appeared in the entrenchments, and revived the enthusiasm of the Hungarians. Wherever the danger deepened, and balls flew the most thickly, Gorgey's erect and haughty form was seen, a sneer of disdain upon his lips for the foe, blended with a smile of contempt for death. The Austrians advanced upon Monostor, but after half-girdling it with bodies, retreated. The left wing marched upon Szony, and over piles of slain men, reconquered the village. The beautiful vineyards around it were a wine-press of hearts, and countless groans were there instead of the vintage song. At half-past six o'clock, Haynau advanced upon the Hungarian centre, and was met by the hussars, who dashed like a cataract upon the cavalry. Swords and bayonets crossed and flashed through blood, and the wild hurrah drowned the tones of Ragotzky's march, to which the soldiers charged. Gorgey was wounded in the head, and left the field. Over heaps of the slain, the combatants fired their last shot at nine

RETREAT OF THE AUSTRIANS.

o'clock P.M. The Austrians retreated to their former position, and Szony was in the hands of the Hungarians.

Nearly 2,000 Magyars had fallen, and a still larger number of the Austrians. It was unfortunate for the cause of Hungary, that the despatches ordering Gorgey's recall had reached Comorn, and were known among the troops, while the fearless General lay wounded; the halo of this brilliant engagement around his couch of suffering, to the ardent Magyars, cast his manifold sins into the shade of forgiving forgetfulness.

CHAPTER X.

GORGEY RETAINS COMMAND—CSANYI'S INTERVIEW WITH KLAPKA —GORGEY'S AMBITION—KOSSUTH—BATTLE OF COMORN—KLAPKA AT THE FORTRESS—BATTLE OF HERKALY—KOSSUTH'S RESIGNATION IN FAVOR OF GORGEY—SURRENDER AT VILLAGOS— SCENES AT PESTH AND COMORN—CAPITULATION OF THE FORTRESS—EXECUTIONS—KOSSUTH'S FLIGHT—HIS FAREWELL TO HUNGARY—RESIDENCE AND SCENES AT WIDDIN—HE REFUSES TO RENOUNCE HIS PROTESTANT FAITH—LETTER TO LORD PALMERSTON—BEM'S CHARACTER AND DEATH—KOSSUTH REMOVED TO KUTAHIA—MADAME KOSSUTH JOINS HIM—EMBARKATION ON BOARD THE MISSISSIPPI—DIFFICULTIES AT MARSEILLES—SAILS FOR ENGLAND.

A COUNCIL of war was called, in which General Klapka acted as mediator between the government and the army. The officers declared their confidence in Gorgey, and unanimously assented to Klapka's proposition of petitioning Kossuth to permit Gorgey to retain his command and resign the Department of War. This calmed the excitement; Nagy Shandor and Klapka set out for Pesth. The Governor and his advisers decided to compromise the matter, by Gorgey's resignation of the War Office and obedience to Meszaros as commander-in-chief, while he remained at the head of the army of the Upper Danube. The venerable Csanyi saw his country's hastening doom in Gorgey's deeds and continued influence. Taking Klapka by the arm during a conference at Kossuth's residence, he invited him to a separate apartment; and when they were alone, tears of agony filled the furrows of his haggard face, and he assured Klapka that the nation was on the verge of an abyss. But salvation was possible, he added, "if Gorgey would consult his *heart* as well as his head," and break away from the charm of Bayer's guilty policy. In conclusion, he remarked with great emotion: "As for me, I am old. I have nothing to lose! If Pesth is again given up, I shall again be the last who leaves it. Perhaps I'll go to Szegedin, and even to Arad; but beyond Arad I will not go. I am too old to be an exile. I do not care what will happen to me,— it is the thought of my country which harrows my soul!"

Klapka returned to Comorn, which he reached in the night after his departure from Pesth. He found Gorgey recovering from his wound, and handed him the orders of Government, over Kossuth's hated name. He ran his eagle-eye over the decrees, and a shadow like that of a rising storm-cloud passed across his ample brow. But his wonted self-command returned after brief reflection, and the marble impassiveness of expression uniformly his, excepting in the rage of battle or passion, concealed the bitterness of his spirit. He then proposed an expedition upon the right bank of the Danube, through the serried ranks of the enemy's overwhelming host. This would divide the force which should be concentrated on the line of Pesth, and keep the army with the Government. He was opposed in the Council of War, but by withering sarcasm aimed at the pride of military character, he succeeded in carrying the main plan of campaign.

Since the moment Gorgey received his orders from the Hungarian Committee of Defence, without royal or martial influence over his ambitious nature, he felt with Napoleon, that upon his greatness and military skill, hung the fate of Hungary. The want of promptness and decision in the revolutionary Ministry at times, increased this haughty independence, which at length directed his aspiring genius against the pure and disinterested Kossuth. Besides, he viewed everything from the height of military glory, and had no confidence in the invincible strength of the common people, the rock of Kossuth's reliance and confident hope. Consequently he was reserved and mysterious even to his friends, while he treated contemptuously the Government. But, as not unfrequently in the world's history, by the fascination of his brilliant mind, and his bravery in conflict, he held to the last the affections and enthusiastic faith of his battalions, and returned it with ripening designs, involving the destiny of the Hungarians and the liberties of Europe.

At this crisis, Gorgey was prostrated with a burning fever. Kossuth urged a junction of Perczel's 10,000 troops ready to cross the Theiss, and Visocki's division which had reached Czegled, with Klapka's forces, and a suppression of dissensions and intrigues in the army of the Upper Danube. These indispensable movements, with the general uprising of the masses, would give promise even then, of the nation's rescue from the embrace of a merciless enemy. Nagy Shandor immediately left the fortress with the first corps, and Klapka was preparing to follow, and meet the advancing battalions upon the left bank of the Danube, which was free from hostile troops, when intelligence came that Gorgey was offended with Shandor's march without his order, though too ill to advise upon the necessity for immediate action, and that the commander-in-chief had tendered his resignation. General Klapka was entreated to recall the troops, and, yielding to Gorgey's plan of retreat, retain him in the army. Fatal concession! the mistaken patriots who urged it, learned their error on the scaffold. On the 11th of July, after delays which augmented the power of the allied army, the decisive battle began under the walls of Comorn. The Government had removed from Pesth to Szegedin, and the Austrians had reached Buda. The Magyars fought well, opening avenues through the lines of the foe, which were instantly filled with the exhaustless troops of the Empires combined in this crusade against freedom. Gorgey looked down from the heights of his entrenchments upon the fierce charges cutting down almost to a man the staffs of his bravest generals, until he was reluctantly convinced that to break through the coil of the victorious foe, whose grasp he had invited, was impossible. The alternative was now between the defensive at Comorn and retreat. At noon of the 13th, the rear of Gorgey's division crossed the Waag bridge, and Klapka, with deathless heroism, like a lion returning to his lair, prepared to defend his fortress, and make Comorn the last bold castle of Hungarian rights, on which should play the sunset glory of liberty.

Gorgey encountered the Austrians at Waitzen, and after temporary victory was obliged to retreat, and continue his flight towards the Theiss. A rear-guard fight with the pursuing enemy, and the fatigues of the march, diminished the battalions one fifth before reaching Tokaj. Kossuth was watching the aspect of affairs with sleepless anxiety, and started to meet the retreating army, and by his wondrous accents reanimate them, and save if possible from defeat, but the approach of the hostile detachments prevented, and he returned to Arad. The burden of military operations fell upon Klapka, who determined to attack the Austrians at Csem and Herkaly, and at least by diverting the invading forces, support the southern army. The assault was brilliant; Klapka moved forward from Csem, which was abandoned at his approach, and joined Sehulz and Jonik at Puszta-Herkaly. General Klapka ordered his storming columns forward upon the enemy's entrenchments blazing with ceaseless discharges, while Sehulz with unparalleled bravery, shouting "Eljen a Magyar!" led his small cohort through the driving hail of grape and musketry, to the parapet of the Austrian works. Victory perched tearfully upon the torn tri-color, floating over heaps of manly forms. A thousand Austrians were lying in their blood, and a thousand more were prisoners of war, among whom were forty-eight officers. In addition, twelve field-pieces were taken, 3,000 muskets, and 2,000 head of cattle. Klapka advanced to Raab, where wreaths of flowers were showered upon his hussars, and peasants white-haired with age crowded round the hero, asking earnestly if the time for *the people to rise* had come.

Alas! Kossuth had yielded to the pressure of calamity before the news of these glorious deeds reached him, and resigned his high office to Gorgey.

It was Kossuth's transparent honor and patriotism that decided him in his estimate of Gorgey's character. He hoped to satisfy the traitor's ambition, and save the country by resigning in his favor, conferring a Military Dictatorship upon him in whose hands was virtually the trailing standard of Hungarian freedom. Kossuth set forth his convictions in a last address.

"KOSSUTH TO THE NATION.

" After the unfortunate battles. wherewith God, in these latter days, has visited our people, we nave no hope of our successful continuance of the defence against the allied forces of Russia and Austria. Under such circumstances, the salvation of the national existence, and the protection of its fortune, lies in the hands of the leaders of the army. It is my firm conviction that the continuance of the present Government would not only prove useless, but also injurious to the nation. Acting upon this conviction, I proclaim, that—moved by those patriotic feelings which, throughout the course of my life, have impelled me to devote al. my thoughts to the country—I, and with me the whole of the Cabinet, resign the guidance of the public affairs; and that the supreme civil and military power is herewith conferred on the General Arthur Gorgey, until the nation, making use of its right, shall have disposed that power according to its will. I expect of the said General Gorgey—and I make him responsible to God, the nation, and to history—that, according to the best of his ability, he will use this supreme power for the salvation of the national and political independence of our poor country and of its future. May he love his country with that disinterested love which I bear it! May his endeavors to re-conquer the independence and happiness of the nation be crowned with greater success than mine were!

"I have it no longer in my power to assist the country by actions. If my death can benefit it, I will gladly sacrifice my life. May the God of justice and of mercy watch over my poor people!

Louis Kossuth,
S. Vuckorits,
L. Csanyi,
M. Horvath."

Gorgey, upon receiving the honors of supreme control of imploring, devastated Hungary, gave his message to the people, in which with a religious hypocrisy, he indicates succeeding events.

GORGEY TO THE NATION.

"Citizens!

"The Provisional Government exists no longer. The Governor and the Ministers have voluntarily resigned their offices. Under these circumstances, a Military Dictatorship is necessary, and it is I who take it, together with the civil power of the state.

"Citizens! whatever in our precarious position can be done for the country, I intend to do, be it by means of arms or by ne-

SURRENDER AT VILLAGOS. 203

gotiations. I intend to do all in my power to lessen the painful sacrifice of life and treasure, and to put a stop to persecution, cruelty, and murder.

"Citizens! the events of our time are astounding, and the blows of fate overwhelming! Such a state of things defies all calculation. My only advice and desire is, that you shall quietly return to your homes, and that you eschew assisting in the resistance and the combats, even in case your towns are occupied by the enemy. The safety of your persons and properties you can only obtain by quietly staying at the domestic hearth, and by peacefully following the course of your usual occupations.

"Citizens! it is ours to bear whatever it may please God in His inscrutable wisdom to send us. Let our strength be the strength of men, and let us find comfort in the conviction that Right and Justice *must* weather the storms of all times.

"Citizens! May God be with us!

"ARTHUR GORGEY."

"ARAD, 11th August, 1849."

The same day upon which this proclamation was dated, he obtained a pledge from the commanders under him to submit to his arrangements of any prospective movement, under the impression that he would secure by Russian aid deliverance from Austrian power. The deceiver repaid them for their confidence on the 13th, at Villagos, where the Russian General Rudiger, according to the message of Gorgey, "that the main Hungarian army was willing to surrender unconditionally," appeared to receive the submission of 24,000 picked troops, and an immense park of artillery. The Hussars and Honveds were entirely unaware of the terms of surrender, but were assured by the deluded officers that their arms would be restored, and Russia unite with them in placing the Grand Duke Constantine on the throne of Hungary.

The battalions of the Autocrat were amazed at this sudden turn of events. Gorgey, Kiss, and other officers were treated with marked cordiality, and entertained splendidly. Csanyi, ex-minister, and many brave comrades, strangely deceived by these displays, went to the Russian Camp, and voluntarily surrendered. The Russians first delivered Arad to Haynau, and this lifted the curtain of the nation's tragedy. When the heroic ranks were ranged in two solid columns, on each side of the Szollos road, the scene was heart-rending. Staff officers swept along in splendid uniforms, but silent and sad, excepting occasionally a mournful word of cheer. Magyar curses were muttered fiercely by pallid lips, and wild lamentation arose from ten thousand living monuments of despair. The "Red-cap" Honveds, who "understood only one command—'Elore,' forward, and their wild battle-cry, 'Eljen a Magyar,'" gazed mutely and despairingly upon each other. The brave hussars, stood with their hands grasping convulsively the slackened rein, and dropping a hot tear upon the mane which had been scathed in the fire of battle. While the cloudless sun of August poured its beams on these wailing battalions, the Hungarian Dictator was having *repartee* with a *beautiful girl*, and around him circled his magnificent staff. When the grand and solemn cavalcade began to move, Gorgey mounted his charger, and rode into the ranks, and proclaimed, "that he no longer felt it in his power to defend the army, but if any was found willing to assume the command he would gladly yield to him."

A veteran captain, springing forward in a flood of grief, begged Gorgey to let the army cut their way through the hostile army. The *traitor* replied it was no time to joke, and passed on. A new gush of agony followed. Soldiers who had never faltered while comrades were shot down by their side in ranks, wept, kissed their tried steel, and fell in each other's arms, sobbing a farewell. Some tore the saddles from their steeds, and shot the war-horses which had borne them over bloody and victorious fields. Gorgey rode proudly amid the outcry of his too faithful host, calmly gazing on the spectacle his treachery had furnished, and urging their march. Night came down, and beneath the long twilight shadows of their bayonets encircling in pyramids the tri-color, the soldiers, weary of life, lay down on the dewy grass to troubled dreams.

The march was soon sounded again, and under their Russian escort, the Hungarian troops moved forward on their eight days' gloomy travel to Sarkad. The Imperialists now moved down upon Comorn, which was under the command of Gen. Klapka. On the 20th of August, they encamped before the forest of Atsh, and sent to the fortress the demand of surrender, urged by a letter from Gorgey. Afterward Haynau despatched a letter

" To Mr. Klapka, for the time being, Commander in Comorn.

" Messrs. Thali and Katona, the messengers whom you sent

to this place, have been convinced by ocular demonstration, and by the assurances of the captive chiefs of Gorgey's corps, that, after the victories which the imperial army, under my command, obtained at Szegedin and Temeshvar, as well as at Lugos and Deva, the corps which were opposed to me have been dissolved; that the chiefs of these corps, and most of the officers and men, with the whole of the artillery, are in our hands. Gorgey's corps, too, is disarmed: his officers, men, and stores, are in my power.

"There is not, therefore, anything like a so-called Hungarian army. The fortress of Comorn is thrown upon its own resources. You can have no hope to receive mercy at our hands, unless you make a voluntary and immediate surrrender.

"The fate of your troops depends upon your decision. You will but expose them to useless tribulation, if, misled by an erring craving for military glory, and at your own responsibility, you continue your rebellious resistance against your legitimate king and lord.

"I therefore summon you immediately to surrender the fortress to Field-Marshal Lieutenant Csorich, the Commander of the blockading army, and to avoid the heavy responsibilities which any delay of the surrender must necessarily bring on your head.

"Head-quarters at Old Arad, 27th August.
"The Commander-in-Chief of the
Imperial Royal Army,
"HAYNAU, Feldzeug-Meister."

Instead of yielding, Klapka prepared for resolute defence. Assaults upon outposts were made, and thousands of printed bills offering safe-conduct home to deserters, were smuggled into the garrison. Klapka was obliged to execute many brave fellows who accepted the offer, as examples. His own life was perilled by a disguised assassin, who was discovered and hung. He attempted to confer with Peterswarasden, but his messengers never reached the fortress The first tidings he received, was that Peterswaras-den, the last bulwark of Hungary besides Comorn, had surrendered unconditionally to the allied forces early in September. This event blotted out the last ray of hope within the walls of the unyielding Klapka's stronghold. His hospitals were filled, yet there he held aloft the nation's flag, environed by more than a hundred thousand hostile troops. But resources of every kind failed, nothing was left but conditions of capitulation. Klapka's correspondence with Haynau, and his stirring, affectionate messages to his heroic garrison, displayed the nobility of his heart, and the sublime courage which could endure despair, rather than surrender to a treacherous enemy. Before he submitted the terms of surrender, he drew up the entire garrison on parade, then marched to funeral service for the countless dead; in his own touching words: "For the last time my troops met under arms; for the last time were they assembled beneath the victorious banners which so often led the way through the fiercest contention of battle. The *Requiem* which was chanted for our comrades was chanted for us, for we all buried our happiness and our hopes. When the service was over, and when the first division defiled before me in sorrow and silence, it seemed as if the soldiers felt that my grief was even greater than their own, and rallying for the last time, their trembling lips uttered a loud and thundering *Eljen!* to the beloved and forlorn—to our Country!"

The conditions of capitulation are given below.

1. The garrison are to be allowed freely to withdraw, without arms; the swords of the officers to remain in their possession.

Foreign passports shall be granted to those officers who have formerly served in the imperial army; to those who do not ask for passports to other countries, a free dismission to their homes—excepting such as voluntarily enter the imperial service.

A free residence at their homes shall be granted to the Honved officers not previously in the imperial service, without restriction as to their future conduct and occupation.

An amnesty is granted to the rank and file of the imperial regiments, and to those individuals who have been meantime promoted. They are to remain unmolested, and no legal prosecution shall hereafter be conducted against them.

2. Passports abroad shall be furnished to all who apply for them within thirty days.

3. One month's pay to the officers, and ten days' wages to the rank and file, according to the rates of the Austrian service, shall be paid in Austrian national bank-notes.

4. For the settlement of the various obligations entered into by the garrison, as shown by their orders on the military chest, the sum of 500,000 guilders, *convention's munze*, (about $250,000,) shall be paid in Austrian bank-notes.

5. The sick and wounded in Comorn, and in the hospitals, shall be properly cared for.

6. Private property, both real and personal, shall be generally retained by the owners.

7. The place, time, and manner of giving up the arms, shall be hereafter determined.

8. All hostilities shall immediately cease on both sides.

CAPITULATION OF THE FORTRESS.

9. The fortress shall be given up according to the usages of war after a mutual ratification of the conditions.

Puszta-Herkaly, Sept. 27th, 1849.
Haynau, M. P.

Takats, captain.
Gasparetz, captain.
Mednyansky, colonel.
John Pragay, colonel.
Stefan Rutkay, colonel.
Count Otto Zichy, colonel.
Count Paul Esterhazy, colonel.
John Janik, colonel.
Sigmund Szabo, colonel, commandant in the town.
Joseph von Kaszonyi, colonel.
Francis Asserman, colonel, commandant in the fortress.
George Klapka, commander-in-chief of fortress and troops.

A true copy of the original,
Comorn, Sept. 29, 1849.

Szillanyi, lieut.-colonel, chief of the general-staff.

Oct. 3d, Klapka assembled the Wurtemberg hussars on the right bank of the Danube, and after thanking them for their patient bravery, inquired if any wished to enlist under the Imperial flag. Tears were falling like rain, and a deep silence followed. It was broken by an old Serjeant, who calmly exclaimed, "General! we have faithfully served our country. We will support it again, if need be; but *never*, NEVER will we go to the Austrians!" In the sunset glow of the 4th, the black and yellow banner of Austria flaunted from the dark walls of Comorn, where the Tri-color last waved defiantly in the air of fallen Hungary. The next morning Klapka, with his "Warrant of Safety," hastened to Pressburg, to wait for a passport to England, where he now lives in hope of the approaching hour of fresh revolution along the banks of the Danube.

The next day, is memorable in the annals of time. It was Haynau's *auto-da-fe*, when he cancelled with blood his oath to spare the Hungarians. Thirteen Generals and staff officers were either executed or shot. The daring Kiss and three comrades, at daybreak fell before the balls of the riflemen. The gallant, impetuous, noble old Aulich, was the first on the scaffold, dying without a shade of fear passing across his brow. Young Leiningen soon followed, having refused means of escape because a dear relative was among the condemned. A soldier offering him a flask, he answered, "I want no wine to give me courage,—bring me a glass of water." The aged Csanyi, who so sadly predicted the issue of Gorgey's treachery, stood beneath the rope not a thousand rods from the spot where he declared to Klapka his choice of death rather than exile. Handing his coat to a poor man, he arranged the fatal noose with his own hand. When asked for his defence, he said, "I have to complain that the accusation is incomplete. I request to add, that I was the first to press the resolution that the House of Hapsburg-Lorraine should be declared *to have forfeited the throne of Hungary !*" Jeszenak's last words were— "I die tranquilly for my fatherland, and *know that our deaths will be avenged !*"

Damianics impatiently and scornfully inquired, as he mounted the scaffold, "How is it, that I the *first in the fire*, am here the last?" Toward sunset, the dignified Count Louis Batthyanyi, who had lain for nearly a year in prison, tried, acquitted, and again brought to trial, and at length condemned to be hung for treason, was marched to the place of execution. The day before, he tenderly bade adieu to his wife, and during the night, recoiling from the inglorious exit of the scaffold, wounded his neck with a dull poinard he had concealed. It was decided, therefore, to shoot the noble martyr. He was a distinguished victim, and the multitude pressed up to see him die. He stood a moment, with his white locks gleaming in the light of departing day, then stretching forth his hands, he exclaimed, "God bless my country!" His last accents were lost in the report of rifles, and Batthyanyi fell pierced with three bullets. So these sons of Liberty died like ancient Romans and Greeks, and Justice shall yet make inquisition for their blood.

We add the names of the heroes slaughtered on that and succeeding days.

In Memory

OF THE DEFENDERS OF CONSTITUTIONAL LIBERTY IN HUNGARY,

Who, after the surrender of the Hungarian Army to the Russians, were put to death by Austrian executioners. Their honored names are dear to the lovers of Liberty founded on Law.

Count Louis BATTHYANYI, Prime Minister.
LADISLAUS CSANYI, Minister of Commerce.
Baron SIGISMOND PERENYI, President of the House of Peers.
Baron JESZENAK, Lord-Lieutenant of the County of Nyitra.
SZATSVAY, Member and Secretary of the Diet.
Prince WORONYIECZKY.
CZERNUS, Councillor of State.
Major MURMAN.
Major ABANCOURT.

PRISONERS OF WAR, given up by Russia to the Austrian Executioners, and who were hanged or shot at Arad on the 6th October, 1849

General AULICH, Minister of War.
Lieut. Gen. ERNEST KISS.
General DAMIANICH.
General NAGY SANDOR.
General DESSEWFFY.
General Count LEININGEN, Cousin of Her Majesty Queen Victoria.
General Count VECSEY.
General TÖRÖK.
General LAHNER.
General Baron PÖLTENBERG.
General KNESICH.
General SCHVEIDL.
General Count LAZAR.
Colonel KAZINCZY.

As fit interludes to these tragical and barbarous scenes, pure and noble women were publicly *whipped* to satiate the Austrian appetite for blood.

Gorgey, the betrayer, lives in an obscure Austrian village, upon the munificent pension of 60,000 florins a year from the monarchs at whose feet he laid the constitution and banner of Hungary. The peasants shun him in his daily walks, like the presence of an evil genius, and his name, with Benedict Arnold's, is the scorn of the world!

Kossuth left his country, when his presence could no longer retrieve her fortunes. Before his unwilling departure from the betrayed and desolate land of his birth, he knelt upon the soil hallowed by the memories and bloodshed of ages, and with arms extended as if to embrace the spreading plains, he kissed the green sod ; then lifting his aspirations to God, he pronounced the following thrilling Farewell to Hungary :

"God with thee, my beloved Fatherland! God with thee, Fatherland of the Magyars ! God with thee, land of tortures ! I shall not be able to behold the summits of thy mountains ; no more shall I be able to call my Fatherland the soil where, on the mother's heart I imbibed the milk of Freedom and Justice !

"Pardon me, my Fatherland, me who am condemned to wander about far from thee, because I strove for thy welfare. Pardon me, who no more call anything *free*, than the small space, where I am now kneeling down with a few of thy sons. My looks fall upon thee, O, poor Fatherland! I see thee bent down with sufferings! I now turn them to futurity; thy Future is nothing but a great grief!—thy plains are moistened with crimson gore, which will soon be blackened by unmerciful devastation and destruction, as if to mourn over the numberless conquests, which thy sons have achieved over the accursed enemies of thy hallowed soil. How many grateful hearts lifted up their prayers to the throne of the Almighty! How many tears have flowed which would even have moved hell to compassion! How many streams of blood have run, as proofs, how the Hungarian loves his Fatherland, and how he can *die* for it! and yet hast thou, beloved Fatherland, become a slave!

" Thy beloved sons are chained and dragged away like slaves by those who are destined to fetter again everything that is holy; to become serviceable to all that is unholy! O, Lord, if thou lovest thy people, whose heroic ancestors thou didst enable to conquer under Arpad, amid so manifold dangers, I beseech thee, and implore thee, O, humble them not!

" Behold, my dear Fatherland, thus speaks to thee thy son in the whirlwind of troubles and despair, on thy utmost boundary!

" Pardon me, if the great number of thy sons have shed their blood for my sake, or rather for thine, because I was their representative: because I protected thee when on thy brow was written in letters of blood the word ' DANGER,' because I, when it was called unto thee, ' Be a slave,' took up the sword for thee; because I girded on my sword when the enemy had the audacity to say, ' Thou art no more a nation,' in the land of the Magyars!

" With gigantic paces time rolled on—with black, yellow letters Fate wrote on the pages of thy history, ' Death!' and to stamp the seal upon it, it called the Northern Colossus to assist. But the reddening morning dawn of the South will melt this seal.

" Behold, my dear Fatherland, for thee, who hast shed so much of thy blood, there is not even compassion; because, on the hills which are towered by the bones of thy fallen sons tyranny earns her bread.

"O, see, my dear Fatherland! the ungrateful, whom thou didst nourish from the fat of thy plenitude, has turned against thee, against thee has turned the traitor, to destroy thee from head to the sole of thy foot! But thou, noble nation, hast endured all this—thou hast not cursed thy fate, because in thy bosom over all suffering, HOPE is enshrined.

"Magyars! turn your looks not away from me; for even at this moment my tears flow only for you, and the soil on which I am kneeling yet bears your fame.

"Thou art fallen, truest of nations! Thou art thrust down under thine own blow! not the weapon of a foreign enemy, which has dug thy grave; not the cannon of the many nations, brought up against thee—they have tottered back at thy Love to thy Fatherland! not the Muscovites, who crawled over the Karpathites, have compelled thee to lay down thine arms. O no! sold, thou wast, dear Fatherland. Thy sentence of death, beloved Fatherland, was written by him, whose love to his country I never questioned for a single moment. In the bold flight of my thoughts, I would rather have doubted the existence of a good man, than I should have thought he could have become the traitor to his Fatherland.

"And thou hast been betrayed by him, in whose hands a few days ago I laid the Government of our country, sworn to defend thee with the last drop of his blood. He became a traitor to his country because the color of gold was dearer to him than that of blood, which was shed for the independence of the Fatherland. The profane metal had in his eyes more value than the Holy God of his land, who forsook him, when he entered into a covenant with the associates of the Devil!

"Magyars! my dear fellow-sons of the same country! Do not accuse me, because I was compelled to cast my eye on this man, and to vacate my place for him. I was compelled to do so, because the people confided in him, because the army loved him, and he had already attained to a position, in which he could have proved his fidelity! and yet the man abused the confidence of the nation, and in return for the love of his nation treated them with contempt.

"Curse him, people of the Magyars! curse the heart which did not dry up when it attempted to nourish him with the moisture of life!

"I love thee, Europe's truest nation! as I love the freedom for which thou fought so bravely! The God of liberty will never blot you out from His memory. Be blessed for evermore! My principles were those of Washington, though my deeds were not those of William Tell! I wished for a free nation—free as God only can create man—and thou art dead, because thy winter has arrived; but this will not last so long as thy fellow-sufferer, languishing under the icy sky of Siberia. No, fifteen nations have dug thy grave, the thousands of the sixteenth will arrive to save thee!

"Be faithful as hitherto, keep to the holy sentences of the Bible, pray for thy liberation, and then chant thy national hymns when thy mountains re-echo the thunder of the cannons of thy liberators! God be with you, dear comrades and fellow-sufferers! The angels of God and of liberty be with you. You may still be proud, for the lion of Europe had to be aroused to conquer the rebels! The whole civilized world has admired you as heroes, and the cause of the heroic nations will be supported by the freest of the free nations on earth!

"God be with thee, sacred soil! drenched with the blood of so many of thy noble sons! Preserve these sacred spots, that they may give evidence before the world for you, before the people, that will come to your succor! God be with thee, young King of the Magyars, forget not that thy nation has *not elected thee!* There lives in me still the hope that a day will come, on which you will see the confirmation of the word—if it even be on the Ruins of Buda!

"The blessing of the Almighty, my dear nation, rest upon thee. BELIEVE—LOVE—and HOPE!"

It is farther related that when he stood upon the verge of his fatherland, a fugitive from the wrath of the oppressor, he was met by Dushek, the Treasurer of Hungary, having in his possession two and a half millions of dollars, in gold and silver, of his country's funds, which he offered to lay at the feet of his unfortunate Governor. He urged Kossuth to accept the treasure, with an eloquence which was responded to by many of the companions of his flight. Behind him he had left his home; his broad lands he knew would be confiscated by those who had sought his blood. His fortunes and his country fell together. If he refused to accept the means offered him of personal comfort and ease, Austrian coffers would be enriched by the additional booty. Why not snatch from the grasp of a tyrant, an equivalent for the property he had been compelled to leave? The temptation was great, and few would have resisted. But the persecuted patriot, friendless and poor, spurned the offer without a momentary wavering. "That treasure is none of mine," said he, "it belongs to the Treasury of Hungary. Whatever may be its fate, I have no right to touch its smallest piece, and this I cannot, will not do." Kossuth proceeded to his exile and poverty, while Dushek returned to the army of Austria, and with the gold his Governor had spurned, purchased existence.

Toil-worn and weary, his heart bowed by the weight of sorrows, Kossuth and his brave companions, numbering about five thousand men, crossed the frontier at Orsova, on the 18th of August, and sought upon Turkish soil, an asylum which their own country no longer afforded. It was a touching sight when the band of patriots landed on the right bank of the Danube, and then sadly turned to take a farewell look toward their bleeding and betrayed, but not yet con quered land. Tears fell "from eyes unused to weep," while sighs revealed the anguish of noble souls. The Pacha of Widdin had previously given Kossuth assurance that he should be the guest of the Sultan, and thither the footsteps of the exiles were directed. On their way the acclamations of the Turkish peasantry fell with mournful cheer upon their ears. They were regarded as a bulwark against the tide of Russian invasion; and a common interest gave the Magyars a cordial greeting from the Mussulmen.

The reputation of Kossuth had preceded him, and was more familiar to the Orientals than the fame of any other chieftain excepting Bonaparte. Their warm imagination had clothed him with resplendent powers, and he was said to act like a second Roustan, "wise in council and just in judgment, but scattering hosts with his red cimeter." Though the wildest tales respecting the Hungarian struggle had spread along the frontier, he, and occasionally Bem, were the only heroes known in connection with it. Kossuth Effendi* was almost deified in their ardent thoughts.

As the company entered Widdin they were received with becoming honor. The orders of the Sultan had been explicitly transmitted to the Pacha, and the exiles were treated with great courtesy. A change, however, occurred in the mode of their entertainment. Austrian and Russian spies had followed them; despotism even there hunted the conquered Hungarians.

---

* Master. Among the Turks this term is applied to an officer of high rank.

The Sultan's generosity was genuine, but his subordinate at Widdin, the almoner of his favors, was more easily influenced by the enemies of Hungary. Russian gold was mighty with the Pacha, while to promises and threats, the Sultan was alike unyielding. The immediate object, however, was gained. The Pacha was induced for personal profit to withhold the Sultan's munificence. The exiles were still furnished with the necessaries of life, but the luxuries they had received were quietly withdrawn. In the camp, provisions were distributed to the soldiers, but without beds, clothing, fire-wood, or even hay upon which to repose. They suffered intensely. The cholera broke out and swept away nearly four hundred of the exiles. Every day the dead-cart, drawn by heavy oxen, went creaking through the infected streets with its ghastly load.

The author of " Revelations of Russia," who visited Kossuth at Widdin, pleasantly describes the retreat of the exiles.

"I returned with Kossuth into his dwelling, and will at once proceed to narrate to you how he was lodged and treated. A mud wall with heavy oaken gates separated from the street (or rather from the triangle I have mentioned) this habitation, which consisted of a single apartment—the reception-room of its owner—whose real abode was in the chambers of his harem, a separate building in an inner court. On account of this custom, the best houses in provincial Turkish towns afford but little accommodation to male visitors, the reception-room, which is accessible to the public, being little more cared for, even by officials of rank, than with us the chambers, or the office in the Inns-of-Court, or bye-lanes of the city, by the luxurious lawyer, or the opulent merchant. Kossuth's *char-à-banc* was a narrow yard. Two Hussars were grooming his horse under an open shed, and the owner of the house, a portly Turk, was sitting on a small platform smoking his chibouque complacently. Colonel Asboth, the young Count Dembinski, and his interpreter, constituted all the attendance for which his single chamber afforded possible accommodation. This one room was of tolerable size, surrounded on three sides by a divan, and covered for about three fourths of its extent by a carpet, on the edge of which inferiors in rank and the Albanian servitors of the host deposited their yellow boots or red slippers before trespassing on its precincts. Cloaks, papers, bridles, and the contents of Kossuth's slender baggage, were exposed in great disorder about the divan, which constituted at night the bed of the ex-president, governor, his secretary, and interpreter. Three wooden chairs and a small deal table were the only articles of furniture introduced in honor of the guest.

Kossuth's host was chief of the police;—a Turkish officer was in attendance to accompany him whenever he walked out on foot, a horse soldier in case he chose to ride, and two or three Albanian attendants brought in, as he called for it, ice-water, or the chibouque. Under the pretence of solicitude for his safety and marks of honor, it was clear that M. Kossuth was closely watched, and all his applications for a more convenient odging were, at this time, neglected or evaded.

"Kossuth's dinner was brought in. It consisted of a Hungarian dish cooked by the wife of a Hungarian soldier. It was served in a brown earthenware dish, and partaken of with an iron spoon. After dinner, Count Dembinski came back with his Countess, and the conversation took a lighter turn.

"Within the precincts of the fort, or citadel, I found Meszaros, the Perczels, Bem, old Dembinski, Guyon, Count Zamoyski, Mr. Longworth, and a number of officers lodged. Outside the fortress, but within the city walls, Count Casimir Batthyanyi, his lady, his cousin, and many more Hungarians, were quartered. The soldiers, the Polish and Italian legions, were encamped on the shore of the Danube. The camp was surrounded on three sides by a cordon of Turkish infantry, and the refugees were permitted to circulate wherever they pleased within the enclosure formed by the camp and the city. To pass beyond the gates, even with escort, into the open country, was, however, a favor only occasionally claimed by the Batthyanyis."

Kossuth occasionally visited the soldiers, but could not relieve their sufferings, nor could he promise to the survivors personal safety, and gave no delusive hopes of the future. His own position was one of sad privation. The Pacha, under Russian control, took pains to isolate him from the world, by cutting off and intercepting intelligence from abroad.

The demands of Russia against the Magyars increased in number and severity. The Czar, throned mid the resources of his vast dominion, yet feared the tones of Kossuth's voice and the might of his uplifted arm. A formal requisition was made upon the Sultan for the extradition of the exiles. In this Russia took the lead, while the feeble voice of her Austrian satellite echoed the claim.

Constantinople now became the scene of deep interest to the cause of human progress. It was not simply the life of Kossuth and his companions, but a great principle which was at stake. Despotism would plant its iron heel more firmly upon the neck of crushed Hungary, and hated liberty.

The Czar's requisition upon the Sublime Porte was accompanied with the threat of a Russian invasion. But the Sultan was strongly enlisted in behalf of the heroes who had thrown themselves upon his protection. High-minded and generous, he shrunk from the deed of cowardly cruelty.

In the Divan an exciting discussion arose on the disposal of the Hungarian refugees. Reschid, the minister, who favored their protection, and reprehended compliance with the request of Russia, suddenly inquired, "What if they turn Mahometans?" It was unlawful to deliver a Mussulman to his enemies. The English Government would give no assurance of help, if the refusal to deliver up the exiles resulted in aggression. Lord Palmerston was governed rather by regard to public opinion, than the suggestions of his own enlightened mind, in the policy pursued. The Sultan with sublime independence, said he would rather lose 500,000 soldiers than make the cowardly concession.

But Reschid and others of the ministry, sustained by radical Mahometans, despatched a messenger to Widdin with the degrading proposition which he had suggested, who visited separately the chiefs in their quarters. An intense excitement ran through the encampment. Bem, whose religion was hatred to Russia, and to whom promotion in the Sultan's disciplined army was attractive, immediately accepted the offer. Whole ranks of subalterns and soldiers followed the Pole. At this solemn crisis, Kossuth assembled a council in his room, and rising with impressive dignity, said, "That he did not pretend to control the conduct of any of his compatriots. That every man's religious convictions were a matter that rested only between himself and God—that consistently with that sincerity and truth, to which he had always rigidly adhered, he could hold out no hope that if they refused the offer made them, their extradition could be averted, and that if given up to Austria, he knew its Cabinet too well to allow them to cherish for a moment the illusion that any mercy would be shown. But, nevertheless, for his own part, he would, when asked to abjure the faith of his forefathers, through terror of the executioner, welcome rather the gibbet and the block, and curses on the tongue which should dare propose to him anything so infamous."

It was well spoken; and was enough alone to bind his brow with the crown of martyrdom. He unburdened his full heart in a letter to Lord Palmerston, from which extracts on this subject are given:

"WIDDIN (Turkey), Sept. 20.

"Your Excellency is no doubt already informed of the fall of my country—unhappy Hungary, assuredly worthy of a better fate.

"It was not prompted by the spirit of disorder, or the ambitious views of faction; it was not a revolutionary leaning which induced my native country to accept the mortal struggle maintained so gloriously, and brought, by nefarious means, to so unfortunate an end.

"Hungary has deserved from her kings the historical epithet of 'generous nation,' for she never allowed herself to be surpassed in loyalty and faithful adherence to her sovereign by any nation in the world.

"Nothing but the most revolting treachery, the most tyrannical oppression, and cruelties unheard of in the words of history—nothing but the infernal doom of annihilation to her national existence, preserved through a thousand years, through adversities so numerous, were able to arouse her to oppose the fatal stroke aimed at her very life, to enable her to repulse the tyrannical assault of the ungrateful Hapsburgs, or to accept the struggle for life, honor, and liberty, forced upon her. And she has nobly fought that holy battle, in which with the aid of Almighty God she prevailed against Austria, whom we crushed to the earth, standing firm, even when attacked by the Russian giant, in the consciousness of justice, in our hope in God, and in our hope, my lord, in the generous feeling of your great and glorious nation, the natural supporter of justice and humanity throughout the world. But this is over: what tyranny began has been by treachery concluded; on all sides abandoned, my poor country has fallen, not through the overwhelming power of two great empires, but by the faults, and I may say the treason, of her own sons.

"To these untoward events, I pray God that my unhappy country may be the only sacrifice, and that the true interests of peace, freedom, and civilization through the world, may not be involved in our unhappy fate.

* * * * * * *

"His Majesty the Sultan, was so gracious as to give a decided negative to the inhuman pretensions of our extradition demanded by Russia and Austria.

"But a fresh letter from his Majesty the Czar arrived in Constantinople, and its consequence was the suggestion sent to us by an express messenger of the Turkish Government, that the Poles and Hungarians, and in particular myself, Count Casimir Batthyanyi, Minister of Foreign Affairs of Hungary, under my government, and the Generals Meszaros and Perzcel (all here,) would be surrendered unless we chose to abjure the faith of our forefathers in the religion of Christ, and become Mussulmans. And thus five thousand Christians are placed in the terrible alternative either of facing the scaffold, or of purchasing their lives by abandoning their faith. So low is already fallen the once mighty Turkey, that she can devise no other means to answer or evade the demands of Russia.

"Words fail me to qualify these astonishing suggestions, such as never have been made yet to the fallen chief of a generous nation, and could hardly have been expected in the nineteenth century.

"My answer does not admit of hesitation. Between death and shame the choice can neither be dubious nor difficult. Governor of Hungary, and elected to that high place by the confidence of fifteen millions of my countrymen, I know well what I owe to the honor of my country even in exile. Even as a private individual I have an honorable path to pursue. Once governor of a generous country—I leave no heritage to my children—they shall, at least, bear an unsullied name. God's will be done. I am prepared to die.

* * * * * * *

"Time presses—our doom may in a few days be sealed. Allow me to make an humble personal request. I am a man, my lord, prepared to face the worst; and I can die with a free look at Heaven, as I have lived. But I am also, my lord, a husband, son, and father; my poor true-hearted wife, my children, and my noble old mother, are wandering about Hungary. They will probably soon fall into the hands of those Austrians who delight in torturing feeble women, and with whom the innocence of childhood is no protection against persecutions. I conjure your Excellency, in the name of the Most High, to put a stop to these cruelties by your powerful mediation, and especially to accord to my wife and children an asylum on the soil of the generous English people.

"As to my poor—my loved and noble country—must she, too, perish forever? Shall she unaided, abandoned to her fate, and unavenged, be doomed to annihilation by her tyrants? Will England, once her hope, not become her consolation?

"The political interests of civilized Europe, so many weighty considerations respecting England herself, and chiefly the maintenance of the Ottoman Empire, are too intimately bound up with the existence of Hungary for me to lose all hope. My lord, may God the Almighty for many years shield you, that you may long protect the unfortunate, and live to be the guardian of the rights of freedom and humanity. I subscribe myself, with the most perfect respect and esteem,

(Signed) "L. KOSSUTH."

The spirited Sultan relieved the foreign powers from farther solicitation from Kossuth and his companions. He determined to guard his guests, and soon after removed them to Schumula, thence to Kutahia in Asiatic Turkey, to lend the appearance of captivity to their residence in this foreign fortress. It hushed the clamor of Austria, and prepared the way for the exile's freedom.

Madame Kossuth had not been inactive. She followed the flight of the chief in her wandering love and thoughts; and with woman's heroism under great calamities, she resolved to gather her children about her, and make the perilous journey to his solitude.

She is a retiring and true woman, whose ambition does not transcend the sanctuary of home. Her trio of offspring had been entrusted to the care of a female cousin, during Madame Kossuth's absence to attend her husband in the campaign. When the Governor signed his abdication at Arad, he sent a faithful friend for the children. The mother remained to receive them. On their way they were all captured, and hurried to an Austrian prison in Pressburg. Madame Kossuth was taken sick, and death was apparently near. Her unoffending children were closely guarded by soldiers, and restrained in the very pastime of life's morning, to them overcast by a premature storm. After two months' imprisonment, the cold and horrid Haynau called upon the captives to enjoy the spectacle of their grief; the juvenile victims of his demoniac vigilance recoiled from his savage mien, and with a smile of triumph he left them the memory of his hated presence.

Madame Kossuth recovering, and having no possible power to interpose for her children, turned her steps toward Turkey. For *four months* she wandered from hamlet to hamlet, disguised in a peasant's apparel, and secreted often without food; a solitary fugitive from despotic vengeance. The common people disregarded the proclamation forbidding shelter and aid to the flying wife of Kossuth. On the 16th of January she arrived at Schumula, worn and weary, to embrace the splendid object of her pilgrimage. After six months' incarceration, the sons and daughter of the Magyar Chief, on application of Madame Meszelenyi, his sister, were given up to her and their grandmother, who has since died in prison, to be kept under the surveillance of the police at Pesth. The people thronged to see them, and lavish on the wondering children the love they cherished for the illustrious father. Food and tokens of boundless enthusiasm, were laid before them, who innocently replied, "Kossuth never left his children; he will come back again." These dangerous demonstrations of popular interest decided the Government to send the "young rebels" to Kutahia. In May, 1850, they left Pesth, amid the farewell shouts and tears of thousands, and hastened to their home upon the confines of Asia.

During the summer of 1850, Bem was seized with a slow fever. His piercing eye grew dim, and his strength failed, with intervals of convalescence, till November. Extremely unwilling to use medical prescriptions, and careless of himself, he sank rapidly, and on the morning of Dec. 10th, passed from the excitements of time, with his Mahometan faith, to the unseen realm.

His physician describes his last hours:—"Toward noon he had an attack of faintness, which lasted twenty-five minutes. When I had succeeded, after some effort, in arousing him from this, he was aware that he had had a serious swoon. 'You give yourself a great deal of trouble,' said he, 'but what God has ordered man cannot change.' About 8 o'clock in the evening he pressed General Kmety by the hand, thanking him for his friendship, and said, 'Gentlemen, I beg for rest.' He turned in the bed, and slept for three hours very quietly. He then awoke, spoke a few words, and again fell asleep. His friends all surrounded his bed, and he appeared to be enjoying such a refreshing slumber, that we all hoped to see him awake with renewed strength. But it was otherwise written in the book of fate. His pulse grew weaker and weaker during the sleep—I attempted in vain to awake him—and he died without a struggle about two o'clock in the morning. According to the custom of the country, an examination of the body was not permitted."

He was buried with military honors, though not the usage of the country. He was about sixty years old, and appeared much worn by the exposure and toil of a stormy life. Bem was an intellectual man, but thoroughly and with absorbing passion a soldier. More bold than cautious, he was yet successful in nearly all important battles. After he embraced Islamism, he devoted his restless energies to his adopted land, the Sultan whom he admired, and the religion of the Prophet, toward whose Mecca his head was solemnly laid, to wait the resurrection dawn.

On the afternoon of September 7th, 1851, the U. S. steamship Mississippi, according to the accepted offer of this Government to convey the Hungarian refugees to our shores, sailed from Constantinople up the Dardanelles. A Turkish frigate also left her moorings in the Bosphorus for the port of Gemlik, where Kossuth and his comrades from Kutahia were to embark for the American vessel. Mr. Holmes of the U. S. Legation, as a mark of respect, and to hasten the embarkation, called on Gov. Kossuth, and officially announced the arrival of a national steamer in the Dardanelles to receive him. Madame Wagner only had died at Kutahia; her constitution was broken in attempts to rescue Lady Kossuth and children from Austrian power.

When the Turkish vessel reached the Dardanelles, Capt. Long paid his respects to Kossuth. No sooner did his feet press the deck of the Sultan's steamer, than the loud "Eljens!" of the Hungarians greeted him. The transfer to the Mississippi was made without delay. When Kossuth went aboard the U. S. ship, and stood beneath the stars and stripes, the officers and crew formed a circle around him. The scene was subduing. His form of medium height was erect, his large blue eye filled with tears, and his pale face suffused with a glow of intense emotion. To the native dignity and grace of his person, and the expression of unused power, there was added the gushing sympathy of the man of feeling. His fascinating smile, which comes when demanded, like a burst of sunlight through an open casement, was a soft illumination of joy too deep for any language but tears.

Capt. Long attempted to address Kossuth, but his utterance failed in the rush of feeling. A tear shone in the eye of every sailor, and the Captain could only say, "Sir, you are welcome! Sir, you —— three cheers for Kossuth!" When the sea had trembled to the shouts, Capt. Long began again to speak, but the accents died away in "three cheers more for Kossuth!" Tranquillity soon returned to the deck of the noble bark, and Kossuth retiring with his family to his comfortable and pleasant rooms, the Mississippi struck with her strong arms the romantic waters of the Dardanelles; the foaming wake lengthened swiftly, and the minarets of the Sultan's domain disappeared in the haze of the distance, while a greater than Cæsar was borne away amid the perils of the sea!

At Marseilles, a popular exhibition of enthusiasm alarmed the U. S. Consul, Hodge, followed as it was by the disgraceful opposition of France, and a difference arose between Capt. Long and Kossuth, which has been slanderously perverted by Austrian emissaries. Kossuth's letter to Mr. Hodge, confirmed by the subordinate officers of the Mississippi, is a manly vindication of his unsullied name.

Referring to the excitement, he writes the Consul:—
"In the afternoon, a hundred boats were floating around the Mississippi, singing national songs, offering garlands of laurel to me, garlands of immortals to America, and shouting 'Hurrahs!' to the Republic, to the United States of America, and to myself. Called forth by the shouts of the people, I mounted on the deck, and uncovering my head, bowed to thank the people, without speaking one single word. I was surprised to see the captain of the frigate walk along the deck, without even waving his cap to acknowledge the cheers given to America; but my surprise was still heightened, to see Capt. Long accost me in a reproaching manner,—that I am compromising him by staying on deck. I answered, 'I hope I will meet a generous welcome from your people also, and I am sure you would not have me repulse it. I am in the very position here. I will, in honor and conscience, feel bound thankfully to acknowledge everywhere the sympathy I meet; and am confident that your people and your Government

can but approve this, and feel in no way compromised to learn that the people of Marseilles did, in a graceful manner, cheer the United States and cheer myself. You knew whom you received on board your ship; and I beg to be assured that I have the sentiment of what is due to you and convenient to me. It appears we have different views about what may be thought compromising to your position. So I free you from the embarrassment, and entreat you to land me wherever you please. But, as long as I have the honor to be on board your ship, you have to command, and your commands shall be obeyed.' And I left the deck, and caused all my companions to do the same. The people upon the boats continued to cheer yet for a while, then went away peaceably as it came, without the consolation of a single acknowledging sign from the Mississippi.

"These are the incidents of our staying in the Bay of Marseilles."

At Gibraltar, Kossuth determined to make a hasty visit to the shores of England, who had united with a Republic in obtaining the freedom of the exiles. Forbidden by France to cross her plains he was compelled to take a steamer for Southampton. France in her fawning to despots, and fear of the contagion of a patriot's passing steps, foreshadowed in that act, the usurpation which afterwards cast a constitution and the rights of the people beneath the chariot wheels of the younger Napoleon.

CHAPTER XI.

RECEPTION IN ENGLAND—ENTHUSIASM—BANQUETS AT WINCHES
TER AND SOUTHAMPTON—MAGNIFICENT WELCOME IN LONDON—
VISITS BIRMINGHAM—EMBARKATION FOR AMERICA—ARRIVAL AT
STATEN ISLAND—THE PAGEANT IN NEW YORK—BANQUETS—
VISIT TO PHILADELPHIA—BANQUETS AND SPEECHES—VISIT TO
WASHINGTON.

On the 23d of October, about noon, the steamer Madrid neared the entrance of Southampton Water. A throng had gathered upon the pier heads and along the shore, impatiently waiting the vessel's landing. The Hungarians among the multitude, recognized Kossuth with the first glimpse of his noble form, and as the ship passed into harbor, their acclamations was the signal of his presence. Then from the electrified spectators rose immediately the loud and repeated cheers—England's welcome to the Exile of freedom. When the Madrid was fairly in her moorings, and the safe arrival of Kossuth was a palpable reality, his excited countrymen wept at the sight of their leader, making every expression of joy too deep for the power of speech. With grateful courtesy, the Magyar Chief bade adieu to the Captain and ship's company, escorted ashore by the Mayor of Southampton, and followed by his attendants. The moment his feet pressed the wharf, the Hungarians surrounded him. Venerable men, hung on his neck in tears, while others seizing his hand kissed it with affection. Soon as they gave way to the increasing crowd, the cooler Englishmen extended their hands to touch the palm unsullied by a dishonorable deed. Through files of enthusiastic strangers, he reached the carriage drawn by four beautiful horses, furnished by the Mayor of the city. Behind it were the barouches of his family and attendants. They rolled away amid one continued storm of cheering, while the grand procession increased at every revolution of the wheels. From the Hungarians sprinkling the moving mass, and wildly shouting in their gladness, was heard distinctly in foreign accent, "Eljen Kossuth! Eljen Kossuth!" The windows along the streets were filled with faces bright with welcome, and white handkerchiefs waved like numberless wings in the air, which rang with the jubilant chime of bells from the belfreys of the churches. A single mighty impulse of gratulation and rejoicing animated the lengthening cavalcade. Kossuth stood with uncovered head at the back of his carriage, calm yet evidently intensely alive to the cordial greeting; while his countrymen again grasping his hand laid it with a warm baptism on their bosom. Reaching the Mayor's city residence, Kossuth and suite entered, and soon he re-appeared in the balcony of a window. The immense concourse beneath sent up a prolonged and deafening shout. Again and again the heavens echoed with cheers. At length they died away into silence, and the Exile stepped forward to give the people of England his first utterance to them, of Magyar fire and feeling.

With a clear mellow voice, and graceful energy, he began with an apology for his "bad English," although his accent and command of the language were remarkably good. Interrupted with frequent cheers, he proceeded:

"Seven weeks ago I was a prisoner in Kutayah, in Asia Minor; now I am a free man; because glorious England chose it—that England which the genius of mankind selected for a monument of its greatness, and the spirit of freedom took to be its happy home. Cheered by your sympathy, which is the anchor of hope to oppressed humanity, with the view before me of your freedom, your greatness, and your happiness, and with the consciousness of the misfortunes of my native land in my heart, you must excuse me for the emotion I feel—the natural consequence of so striking a change, and of such different circumstances. Excuse me that I am not able to thank you so warmly as I feel for the generous reception with which you have honored me, and of which I feel that I an undeserving. I only say, may God Almighty ever bless you and your glorious land. Let me hope you will be willing to bestow on me a ray of hope on my native land by this your generous reception. May England ever be great, glorious, and free! But let me hope, by the blessing of Almighty God, and by your steady, persevering and generous aid, that England, though it ever remain the most glorious spot on earth, may it not long remain the only one where freedom dwells. Inhabitants of the generous town of Southampton, in shaking hands with your Mayor, our best and truest friend, I

SPEECH AT SOUTHAMPTON. 235

have the honor to thank you with the deepest respect—you the inhabitants of this industrious, enlightened, noble-minded, and prosperous borough of Southampton."

Madame Kossuth was then led by the Mayor to the edge of the balcony, and the cheering of the assembly was renewed. She retired exhibiting the deepest emotion.

Her children were then led to the edge of the balcony, and saluted with a new burst of enthusiasm. The Mayor thanked the concourse for their unsolicited, orderly and kind reception of Kossuth; who added a brief address, and closing with "an impressive God bless you all!" retired. The people slowly and reluctantly dispersed to their homes, to repeat the illustrious name which had aroused the free spirit of Britain.

Toward evening, the citizens assembled in the Town Hall, to present Kossuth their address, and hear his eloquent voice. When he entered the large hall, evidently worn and weary, he was greeted with tumultuous acclamations. After listening to the panegyrics with which he was received, he thanked the Mayor, Corporation and town of Southampton, for their generous welcome, and continued:

"Mr. Mayor and gentlemen of the municipality of the town and borough of Southampton, excuse me, an unpretending stranger, for not being able in your own language duly to express the warmest sentiments of thanks and gratitude for the honor of your generous welcome, and for those generous sentiments which you, Mr. Mayor, were pleased to address me. I was already before my arrival bound by lasting gratitude to the town of Southampton for numerous tokens of the most high-minded sympathy with the cause of my dear native land, and of protection to its exiles; and, being prepared for the honor of this occasion, you will excuse a few words, I may say inspired by your presence, and said to you without any preparation.

"It is indeed an honor to be welcomed by the people of England in this noble town. It is the highest gratification to me that it was the municipality of the first town I had the honor to meet, which receives me in such a generous manner. It is not on this day only, but from my early youth, that this glorious country had a mighty share in my destiny. I was used to look on England as on the Book of Life, which had to teach me and the nations of Europe how to live. Through three centuries the house of Austria has exhausted against Hungary the arts of open violence and secret intrigue, and it was our municipal institutions which still, among the most arduous circumstances, conserved to Hungary some spirit of public life and some part of constitutional liberty. It was at the time when this fatal sickness of political feeling to centralize every power and to tutor the people into this notion of political wisdom—when this fatal sickness, I say, spread over the continent, and made its way even to my own country, so that it became almost the fashion, and almost a mark of intelligence to bend towards the doctrine of centralization, that I, my humble self, with a few friends who stood by me, struggled against this storm—against those rushing waves coming over the spirit of Europe, because I regarded, and I ever shall regard, municipal public life as a public benefit, without which there is no practical freedom whatever, and for the loss of which I think all Ministerial responsibilities and Parliamentary privilege but a pitiful equivalent.

"In this land is seen the finest fruits of this conquest of liberty; the glory outside, the freedom within, unwithered by the blighting finger of centralization. When I first read the French constitution

SPEECH AT SOUTHAMPTON.

I foretold that great and glorious French nation should have to go through many storms, because it did not abandon its fatal principle of centralization; and because it is only in municipal institutions freedom can be developed. That is my conviction. Sir, I hope England will be forever ' great, glorious, and free ;' but when I look to history, and see what is this land and the English race, the only single one which is free in both hemispheres of the world, and when I look for the key of this freedom, I readily confess I believe that it is not only those municipal institutions, which are not absorbed by the propensity to centralization, which so conserved that freedom though under different forms of government,—here in England, under a monarchical form, in America under a republican form,—that it was not those institutions only, but the spirit of the people embodied in those institutions, which made these two great offsprings of a mighty race great, glorious, and free. Therefore it is with the highest satisfaction I receive this address from your hands, and from the corporation of Southampton. As to my own humble self, conscious of no merit, and never aspiring to whatever reputation, but to that of a plain honest man, faithful to the duty of a true friend of freedom and of a patriot, I could not forbear to feel perplexed to see myself the object of such undeserved honors, were I not aware that this manifestation is intended rather openly to countenance that principle of freedom, of justice, of popular rights, for which my nation has valiantly struggled, and which you so happily enjoy.

" It is a glorious position the English race holds—almost the only one that is free—it is the only one, the freedom of which has neither to fear the changes of time nor the ambition of man, provided it keeps to its institutions, provided that the public spirit of the people continues to safeguard that which is best for the exigencies of the time, and that their manly resolution never fails to meet those exigencies in time. This watchfulness and resolution being the chief guaranty of your country's greatness and happiness, I take for the most consoling hope to oppressed humanity ; for I have the most firm conviction that the freedom and greatness of England are in intimate connection with the distinies and liberty of Europe.

"It is not without reason that my native land, and all oppressed nations look up to you, as to the elder brother to whom the Almighty has not in vain imparted the spirit to guide the tide of human destiny. There is one thing that is a prominent feature in your race,—a result of no small importance in our struggles,—that the sentiments of this race are spreading over the world, and that it is not the least of the glories you call your own, that the people of England appear to be resolved to take the lead in the new direction of the public opinion of the world, out of which the highest blessings will flow. The generous sympathy of the people of England for my bleeding, struggling, down-trodden, but not broken, native land, is one, but not the only one manifestation, by which England shows she is ready to accept this glorious *rôle* of the elder brother of humanity.

"This country, though it has not to fear any direct attack on its own liberty, still knows that its welfare and prosperity, founded as they are on the continued development of your genius and industry, cannot be entirely independent of the condition of other nations. The people of England know that in neither social nor political respects can it be indifferent whether Europe be free or groaning under Russia and her satellites; the people of England are conscious of their glorious position—it knows that, while it conserves its freedom, it cannot grant the privilege to Russo-Austrian despots to dispose of the fate of Europe, but must have its weight in the balance of the destinies of Europe, or England would no more be an European Power. And it is this knowledge which is the source of hope and consolation to my oppressed country, as well as to all the fellow-nations of Europe, for by the principle on which your freedom continues, and on which your happiness is founded, and by your generous sentiments, we are assured that let the people of England once throw their weight into the balance of the fate of Europe, then they will never assist despotism, but freedom; not injustice, but right; not the ambition of a few families, but the moral welfare and dignity of humanity.

SPEECH AT SOUTHAMPTON. 239

"Such were my expectations of the public spirit of Britannia, which you, by your generous address, have raised to the level of conviction by assuring me you have the belief and hope that those principles for which we have struggled have a future in my own native land. Seeing you to entertain this hope and belief is almost like a victory itself, because this manifestation cannot fail to influence in the most effectual manner the public spirit of my nation, and to double her perseverance and my own in her cause. And, besides the prophecy of freedom is almost realized, for when the people foretell it, you have the self-confident power to make good your own words.

"I hope the Almighty will grant, before I leave this country and cross the ocean, and go to the young giant, the younger brother of your mighty race, and thank him for the generous protection bestowed on me, and entreat his brotherly hand for the future of Europe and of my own country, that I shall see established in full activity and spread over these glorious isles, some of those mighty associations by which you carry the triumph of every great reform and of every great principle in your constitution. I hope to see some of those associations lending its attention to the solidarity of the independence of Hungary, with the hope that the peace of Europe and the future of these glorious isles will take for its aim to give a practical direction to the sympathy of the people for my poor down-trodden country—that the people of England will look upon my unhappy land, and that they will reduce to a ruling principle that sentiment of the public spirit of Britannia which evidently shows itself to be ready to accept the solidarity of the destiny of mankind, and especially of the liberty of Europe itself.

"I thank you for the generous wishes you have bestowed on me. To me, life in itself is not of value—but only so much as I can make some use of it to the liberty and independence of my own country, and to the benefit of humanity; and, though I have to decline all praises bestowed on my own personal character, as I am conscious I have nothing done but only that which

I considered my own simple duty to do, while I am sorry my modest faculties could not equal my devotion to my native land; still I take this expression as an encouragement to go on in that way which I took for the aim of my life, and which I hope the blessing of the Almighty and the sympathy of the people of England, and of all generous hearts over the world, may help to carry to a happy issue. Let me, in pronouncing a most sincere wish for the happiness, greatness and freedom of these glorious isles—let me repeat what I take to be a most glorious sight to see—your gracious Queen representing on the throne the principle of liberty, and let me hope the acknowledgment of this principle will not only have a future in Europe, but that the time draws near when we shall have to applaud the success of those endeavors which now live in your generous sympathy, even in adversity and misfortune. But it is a much greater merit to acknowledge a principle in adversity than to pay a tribute to its success.

"Excuse me that my words cannot flow more freely: my tongue has been devoted to my own native land. I have not had time to secure to myself a greater knowledge of the western civilization of Europe, but my life has been devoted to admiration of England; never was there a man who appreciated better your institutions than myself, and you never will meet a man more faithfully attached to you, and who has a warmer sentiment of thanks and gratitude towards you, and towards your glorious land of liberty."

He was then presented with a splendid silk banner, wrought by Hungarians in New York, and transmitted to England, to be sent forward to the field of battle. It was detained in a Custom House for non-payment of duty, until the plains of Hungary were overswept by the hordes of modern Northmen. Kossuth received the national flag with great feeling, and said: "I receive it, gentlemen, as a most valuable trust entrusted to the people of Hungary; and I swear to you—whatever may be my fate—cowardice or ambition shall never tarnish this flag."

Oct. 25, the Mayor gave him a magnificent banquet at his cottage near Winchester. On that occasion he made his great exposition of the Hungarian Revolution, in a logical, clear, and fervidly eloquent speech, which was frequently interrupted by the cheers of a select audience, thrilled too intensely for the calmness of an ordinary debate.

This festive occasion was followed with a banquet given by the people of Southampton, Oct. 27. Kossuth's reception there was no less enthusiastic and brilliant than the more limited display at Winchester. His address enchained the auditory; its only interludes were the waves of emotion that found utterance in the universal language of applause. In London, the welcome was equally warm and flattering. Before his appearance in public, Nelson's Monument up to the fluted shaft, the iron balustrade of Northumberland-house, and Trafalgar Square were black with people; and above all, hats were waving and arms swaying, while the air resounded with the countless voices of the expectant throng.

The Hungarian tri-color floated from the dwellings, and every avenue was the pathway of a triumphal procession. It was like the coronation day of Kings. The great metropolis of Europe was thoroughly alive with excitement, and its millions seemed on the march. When the officials, with Lord Dudley Stuart, followed by Kossuth, emerged from the residence of the exile, a general burst of enthusiasm hailed him; "Long live Kossuth!" "Down with Austria!" saluted his ear with stirring emphasis. The Magyar perhaps never presented a more commanding appearance. He wore a blue braided uniform, and a green hat and feather, which he lifted with perfect composure and dignity of manner, in response to the shouts of welcome. The cortege progressed slowly on account of the pressure of the people, who at different points completely blocked the highway.

At Piccadilly, Charing-cross, the Strand and Temple-bar, the procession, which was hours in passing, was increased by thousands. The open windows displayed groups of beautiful women, and the demonstration of feeling on every hand, was unbounded. At length the carriage of Kossuth drew up before Guildhall, and a shout arose from the multitude, which was caught up by the concourse within the ample and crowded edifice. The object of all this pageantry only was tranquil; and his pale face, luminous with intellect, added to the interest his presence awakened. When he entered amid the tempest of applause, every person in the spacious court, arose and stood till he reached the platform; and when silence was obtained, he addressed with undiminished fire the captivated throng.*

Kossuth's grandest oratorical display in England, was doubtless his speech at Birmingham, Nov. 12th.

---

* Appendix.

An immense concourse had assembled in the Musical Hall to welcome the Hungarian Leader, and sit down with him to a sumptuous and splendid banquet. A member of Parliament gave the health of Kossuth, as a toast. Soon as stillness could be obtained, the nation's guest replied in a strain of eloquence, rarely if ever equalled. Scorching sarcasm, and plaintive pathos were expressed in finished style, and with burning power. The people were at times affected to tears, and when he resumed his seat, were ready to shout as did the admirers of the Roman Prince—"It is the voice of a God!"*

Kossuth visited Manchester and delivered there another speech of great power.† Notwithstanding he had been malignantly assaulted by a popular Daily paper, he was everywhere treated with respect and homage accorded to no foreigner before, at least in the modern history of England. Upon the announcement of his intended departure for America on the 20th of November, the Mayor and Council of Southampton passed the following resolution:—

"The members of this committee cannot refrain from hereby recording their admiration of those patriotic and strictly constitutional sentiments which he has everywhere and on all occasions enunciated to the people of this country, and of those prompt and unqualified denials which he has given to the unfounded calumnies of the abettors of despotism and tyranny, whether resident of this or other countries, as well as the surpassing eloquence and irresistible truthfulness with which he

---

* See Appendix. † Ibid.

has placed before the British public the countless wrongs and the crushing oppressions of his beloved country, and the claims which it has on the sympathy, moral and energetic influence of all lovers of freedom throughout the world. Most gratifying has it been to this Council to have observed from day to day since the arrival of that great and distinguished man in our port, since the 23d of October last, that the admiration of his public good and private worth, and of his vast sacrifices for those great and undying principles of liberty which he so ably and so worthily represented, first publicly expressed to the Mayor and Corporation of Southampton, have been everywhere most enthusiastically re-echoed by the millions of the British people.

"For the purpose of further expressing our most profound and increased admiration of so illustrious, high-minded and gifted an asserter of the rights of human freedom, and our deepest sympathy with the people of whom he is so distinguished an ornament: and after having carefully read and considered the statements of his traducers, and the manly replications with which they have been instantly met, this Council resolves to invite his Excellency to a *dejeuner*, on Thursday next, previously to his departure on his great mission to the United States of America, hoping and believing that his visit to England of the Old world, and to the United States of the New, will greatly tend, sooner or later, more closely to unite the two great sections of the Anglo-Saxon race, in the vindication and maintenance of human rights and freedom; and trusting that, by the blessing of Providence, he will, ere long, be restored to his country and home, and there realize, in the emancipation of his beloved nation, the most ardent wishes of his noble and generous soul, and the complete and enduring consummation of his transcendent exertions and labors."

After a rough voyage across the Atlantic, during which Kossuth suffered from prostrating illness, the Humboldt reached Staten Island at 1 o'clock in the morning of December 5th. Signal guns had an nounced her approach, and a deputation were waiting to board the vessel, and receive the distinguished stranger. After the firing of salutes, and the usual greetings, Dr. Doane, at whose mansion on the Island, Kossuth and his suite were to remain until preparations were made to give him an appropriate welcome in New York, made a brief and beautiful address.

Kossuth replied:—

"I cordially thank you for the generous sentiments, and for the kind words in which they have been conveyed. I trust you and the people of the United States of America will yet see Hungary free. I am glad to hear that such an interest was taken here in the struggles of my people, and she will yet be as free as she deserves to be. You offer me a free and generous welcome, and I am proud to meet you and to thank you that I am at liberty by the generosity of the United States. I know that every man who longs for freedom in Europe, as well as in this nation, has a kind feeling for Hungary. I am thankful for the generous action taken for my liberation by America, which you say is an infant country, but I say no! She is a giant, and though she has only been a short time in her growth, some seventy-five years, she has done more than other nations who have been one thousand years in existence, and as the power of steam has blotted the word distance from the dictionary, with regard to crossing the Atlantic, I hope and trust that American generosity and American sympathy will not see the day far distant, when the word shall be given to all Europe, which shall make it free, and give it perfect liberty. I give you my hand, and I hope you will not be disappointed in me. If I am a straight-forward man, and have been true to those principles which you in the United States revere, and though my country is not so great as yours, nor are my people so happy and free as you are, still I hope we shall meet with your favor and your sympathy in the cause of our nation."

In a few moments more, he touched American soil. A carriage was waiting to convey him to his spacious apartments, from which was presented a glorious view of the Bay, Rivers, and City of New York.

The next day, Staten Island was a scene of rejoicing. Deputations called on the Magyar, ladies were presented, and a magnificent procession formed. He was escorted to a large pavilion erected expressly for his appearance before the enthusiastic Islanders, who poured into the broad circle, as if the spirit of Washington, by some metempsychosis, had re-appeared in foreign guise.

Saturday, December 6th, was selected by the authorities of New York to celebrate Kossuth's arrival, and make a grand demonstration of American sympathy and homage. The morning was cloudless and serene, the air bracing, and gladness visible in the faces of the moving thousands. At 9 o'clock the steamer Vanderbilt, decorated with the flags of the United States and Hungary, touched the wharf at Castle Garden to receive the city officials and gentlemen in company, who were to invite the Exile across the Bay. The waters sparkled in the golden light, and like a mighty mirror, reflected the signals of jubilee that began to multiply on its tranquil bosom. The vessel was soon floating before the residence of the Governor, and after the preliminaries of salutation and embarkation were over, a general shout rose from the spectators, who recognized the object of their applause by his Hungarian dress. The Band then played spiritedly "Hail to the Chief;"—

ARRIVAL AT NEW YORK.

and under the roar of cannon, the Vanderbilt moved off toward the New York shore. While passing Governor's Island, a salute of 31 guns was fired, and the thunder of the artillery answered by the ship. At New Jersey, 120 guns echoed along the bay, whose rim was excited people. Passing the Navy Yard, the North Carolina and Ohio played Yankee Doodle, then fired salutes; while aloft on the masts and yards of vessels, the marines and seamen were waving their tarpaulins and shouting to the top of their voices.

Thus amid incessant displays of congratulation, the Vanderbilt sweeping round by Jersey City returned to Castle Garden. The Battery never before offered a sight so glorious. A *hundred thousand* persons were there, over and amid whom banners waved from every angle, while the cheers of that host made the smiling heavens ring. Upon the Magyar's entrance into the ample structure, another tumultuous shouting rose, and reverberated, until the roof seemed to tremble above the tide of sound that ebbed, only to swell with redoubled power. After partial silence was gained, Kossuth pronounced his eloquent address to the Republican masses of the New World.

"I am yet half sick, gentlemen; tossed and twisted about by a fortnight's gale on the Atlantic's restless waves; my giddy brains are still turning round as in a whirlpool, and this gigantic continent seems yet to tremble beneath my wavering steps Let me, before I go to work, have some hours of rest upon this soil of freedom, your happy home. Freedom and Home, what heavenly music in those two words! Alas, I have no home, and the freedom of my people is down-trodden. Young Giant of Free America, do not tell me that thy shores are an asylum to the oppressed, and a home to the homeless exile. An asylum it is, but all the blessings of your glorious country, can they drown into oblivion the longing of the heart, and the fond desires for our native land? My beloved native land! thy very sufferings make thee but dearer to my heart; thy bleeding image dwells with me when I wake, as it rests with me in the short moments of my restless sleep. It has accompanied me over the waves. It will accompany me when I go back to fight over again the battle of thy freedom once more. I have no idea but thee; I have no feeling but thee. Even here, with this prodigious view of greatness, freedom and happiness, which spreads before my astonished eyes, my thoughts are wandering toward home; and when I look over these thousands of thousands before me, the happy inheritance of yonder freedom for which your fathers fought and bled,—and when I turn to you, citizens, to bow before the majesty of the United States, and to thank the people of New York for their generous share in my liberation, and for the unparalleled honor of this reception, I see, out of the very midst of this great assemblage, rise the bleeding image of Hungary, looking to you with anxiety whether there be in the lustre of your eyes a ray of hope for her; whether there be in the thunder of your hurrahs a trumpet-call of resurrection. If there were no such ray of hope in your eyes, and no such trumpet-call in your cheers, then woe to Europe's oppressed nations. They will stand alone in the hour of need. Less fortunate than you were, they will meet no brother's hand to help them in the approaching giant struggle against the leagued despots of the world; and woe also to me. I will feel no joy even here, and the days of my stay here will turn out to be lost to my fatherland—lost at the very time when every moment is teeming in the decision of Europe's destiny. Citizens, much as I am wanting some hours of rest, much as I have need to become familiar with the ground I will have to stand upon before I enter on business matters publicly, I took it for a duty of honor, not to let escape even this

FIRST SPEECH IN NEW YORK. 249

first moment of your generous welcome, without stating plainly and openly to you what sort of a man I am, and what are the expectations and the hopes—what are the motives which brought me now to your glorious shores. Gentlemen, I have to thank the people, Congress and Government of the United States, for my liberation from captivity. Human tongue has no words to express the bliss which I felt when I—the down-trodden Hungary's wandering chief—saw the glorious flag of the stripes and stars fluttering over my head—when I first bowed before it with deep respect—when I saw around me the gallant officers and the crew of the Mississippi frigate—the most of them the worthiest representatives of true American principles, American greatness, American generosity—and to think that it was not a mere chance which cast the star-spangled banner around me, but that it was your protecting will—to know that the United States of America, conscious of their glorious calling as well as of their power, declared by this unparalleled act to be resolved to become the protectors of human rights—to see a powerful vessel of America, coming to far Asia, to break the chains by which the mightiest despots of Europe fettered the activity of an exiled Magyar, whose very name disturbed the proud security of their sleep—to feel restored by such a protection, and in such a way, to freedom, and by freedom to activity, you may be well aware of what I have felt, and still feel, at the remembrance of this proud moment of my life. Others spoke—you acted; and I was free! You acted; and at this act of yours, tyrants trembled; humanity shouted out with joy; the down-trodden people of Magyars—the down-trodden, but not broken, raised his head with resolution and with hope, and the brilliancy of your stars was greeted by Europe's oppressed nations as the morning-star of rising liberty.

"Now, gentlemen, you must be aware how boundless the gratitude must be which I feel for you. You have restored me to life—because, restored to activity; and should my life, by the blessings of the Almighty, still prove useful to my fatherland and to humanity—it will be your merit—it will be your work. May

Kk

you and your glorious country be blessed for it. Europe is on the very eve of such immense events, that however fervent my gratitude be to you, I would not have felt authorized to cross the Atlantic at this very time, only for the purpose to exhibit to you my warm thanks. I would have thanked you by facts contributing to the freedom of the European continent, and would have postponed my visit to your glorious shores till the decisive battle for liberty was fought, if it were my destiny to outlive that day. Then what is the motive of my being here at this very time? The motive, citizens, is that your generous act of my liberation has raised the conviction throughout the world, that this generous act of yours is but the manifestation of your resolution to throw your weight into the balance where the fate of the European continent is to be weighed. You have raised the conviction throughout the world, that by my liberation you were willing to say, 'Ye oppressed nations of old Europe's continent, oe of good cheer; the young giant of America stretches his powerful arm over the waves, ready to give a brother's hand to your future.' So is your act interpreted throughout the world. You, in your proud security, can scarcely imagine how beneficial this conviction has already proved to the suffering nations of the European continent. You can scarcely imagine what self-confidence you have added to the resolution of the oppressed. You have knit the tie of solidarity in the destinies of nations. I cannot doubt that you know how I was received by the public opinion in every country which I touched since I am free, and what feelings my liberation has elicited in those countries which it was not my lot to touch. You know how I, a plain, poor, penniless exile, have almost become a centre of hope and confidence to the most different nations, not united but by the tie of common sufferings. What is the source of this apparition unparalleled in mankind's history? The source of it is, that your generous act of my liberation is taken by the world for the revelation of the fact that the United States are resolved not to allow the despots of the world to trample on oppressed humanity. It is hence that **my liberation was cheered, from Sweden down to Portugal, as a ray** of nope. It is hence that even those nations which most desire my presence in Europe now, have unanimously told me, 'Hasten on, hasten on, to the great, free, rich, and powerful people of the United States, and bring over its brotherly aid to the cause of your country, so intimately connected with European liberty;' and here I stand to plead the cause of the solidarity of human rights before the great Republic of the United States. Humble as I am, God, the Almighty, has selected me to represent the cause of Humanity before you. My warrant to this capacity is written in the sympathy and confidence of all who are oppressed, and of all who, as your elder brother, the people of Britain, sympathize with the oppressed—my warrant to this capacity is written in the hopes and expectations you have entitled the world to entertain, by liberating me out of my prison, and by restoring me to activity. But it has pleased the Almighty to make out of my humble self yet another opportunity for a thing which may prove a happy turning-point in the destinies of the world. I bring you a brotherly greeting from the people of Great Britain. I speak not in an official character, imparted by diplomacy, whose secrecy is the curse of the world, but am the harbinger of the public spirit of the people, which has the right to impart a direction to its government, and which I witnessed, pronouncing itself in the most decided manner, openly—that the people of England, united to you with enlightened brotherly love, as it is united in blood—conscious of your strength as it is conscious of its own, has forever abandoned every sentiment of irritation and rivalry, and desires the brotherly alliance of the United States to secure to every nation the sovereign right to dispose of itself, and to protect the sovereign right of nations, against the encroaching arrogance of despots, and leagued to you against the league of despots, to stand together with you, godfather to the approaching baptism of European liberty.

"Now, gentlemen, I have stated my position. I am a straightforward man. I am a republican. I have avowed it openly in the monarchical but free England; and am happy to state that I have nothing lost by this avowal there. I hope I will not lose here, in republican

America, by that frankness, which must be one of the chief qualities of every republican. So I beg leave, frankly and openly, to state the following points:

"First, that I take it to be the duty of honor and principles not to meddle with whatever party question of your own domestic affairs. I claim for my country the right to dispose of itself; so I am resolved, and must be resolved, to respect the same principle here and everywhere. May others delight in the part of knights-errant for theories. It is not my case. I am the man of the great principle of the sovereignty of every people to dispose of its own domestic concerns; and I most solemnly deny to every foreigner, as to every foreign power, the right to oppose the sovereign faculty.

"Secondly, I profess, highly and openly, my admiration for the glorious principle of union, on which stands the mighty pyramid of your greatness, and upon the basis of which you have grown, in the short period of seventy-five years, to a prodigious giant, the living wonder of the world. I have the most warm wish that the star-spangled banner of the United States may forever be floating, united and one, the proud ensign of the mind's divine origin; and taking my ground upon this principle of union, which I find lawfully existing, an established constitutional fact, it is not to a party, but to the united people of the United States that I confidently will address my humble requests for aid and protection to oppressed humanity. I will conscientiously respect your laws, but within the limits of your laws I will use every honest exertion to gain your operative sympathy and your financial, material and political aid for my country's freedom and independence, and entreat the realization of those hopes which your generosity has raised in me and my people's breasts, and also in the breast of Europe's oppressed nations.

"And, therefore, thirdly, I beg leave frankly to state that my aim is to restore my fatherland to the full enjoyment of that act of declaration of independence, which being the only rightful existing public law of my nation, can nothing have been lost of its rightfulness by the violent invasion of foreign Russian arms, and which therefore, is fully entitled to be recognized by the people of the United States, whose very resistance is founded upon a similar declaration of independence?

"Thus having expounded my aim, I beg leave to state that I came not to your glorious shores to enjoy a happy rest. I came not with the intention to gather triumphs of personal distinction, or to be the object of popular shows; but I came a humble petitioner in my country's name, as its freely chosen constitutional chief. What can be opposed to this recognition, which is a logical necessary consequence of the principle of your country's political existence? What can be opposed to it? The frown of Mr. Hulsemann—the anger of that satellite of the Czar, called Francis Joseph of Austria; and the immense danger with which some European and American papers threaten you, and by which of course, you must feel extremely terrified, that your minister at Vienna will have offered his passports, and that Mr. Hulsemann leaves Washington, should I be received and treated in my official capacity? Now, as to your Minister at Vienna, how you can combine the letting him stay there with your opinion of the cause of Hungary, I really don't know; but so much I know, that the present absolutistical atmosphere of Europe is not very propitious to American principles. I know a man who could tell some curious facts about this matter. But as to Mr. Hulsemann, really I don't believe that he would be so ready to leave Washington. He has extremely well digested the caustic pills which Mr. Webster has administered to him so gloriously; but after all I know enough of the public spirit of the sovereign people of the United States, that it would never admit to whatever responsible depository of the executive power, should he even be willing to do so, which, to be sure, your high-minded Government is not willing to do, to be regulated in its policy by all the Hulsemanns or all the Francis Josephs in the world. So I confidently hope that the sovereign of this country, the people, will make the declaration of independence of Hungary soon formally recognized, and that it will care not a bit for it if Mr. Hulsemann takes to-morrow his passports, bon voyage to him. But it is also my agreeable duty to profess that I am entirely convinced that the Government of the United States shares warmly the sentiments of the people in that respect. It has proved it by executing in a ready and dignified manner the resolution of Congress in behalf of my liberation. It has proved it by calling on the Congress to consider how I shall be treated and received, and even this morning I was honored by the express order of the Government, by an official salute from the batteries of the United States, in such a manner in which, according to the military rules, only a republic, high official capacity can be greeted.

"Having thus expounded my aim, I beg leave to state that I came not to your glorious shores to enjoy a happy rest—I came not with the intention to gather triumphs of personal distinction, but because a humble petitioner, in my country's name, as its freely chosen constitutional chief, humbly to entreat your generous aid; and then it is to the aim that I will devote every moment of my time with the more assiduity, the more restlessness, as every moment may bring a report of events which may call me to hasten to my place on the battle-field, where the great, and I hope the last battle will be fought between Liberty and Despotism. A moment marked by the finger of God to be so near that every hour of delay of your generous aid may prove fatally disastrous to oppressed humanity, and thus having stated my position to be that of a humble petitioner in the name of my oppressed country, let me respectfully ask, do you not regret to have bestowed upon me the high honor of this glorious reception, unparalleled in history? I say unparalleled in history, though I know that your fathers have welcomed La Fayette in a similar way; but La Fayette had mighty claims to your country's gratitude;—he had fought in your ranks for your freedom and independence, and what still was more, in the hour of your need. He was the link of your friendly connection with France—a connection, the results of which were, two French fleets of more than thirty-eight men of war, three thousand gallant men, who fought side by side with you against Cornwallis, before Yorktown; the precious gift of twenty-four thousand muskets, a loan of nineteen millions of dollars, and even the preliminary treaties of your glorious peace, negotiated at Paris by your immortal Franklin. I hope the people of the United States, now itself in the happy condition to aid those who are in need of aid, as itself was once in need, will kindly remember these facts; and you, citizens of New York, and you will yourselves become the La Fayettes of Hungary. La Fayette had great claims to your love and sympathy but I have none. I came a humble petitioner with no other claims than those which the oppressed have to the sympathy of free men, who have the power to help—with the claim which the unfortunate has upon the happy, and the down-trodden has to the protection of eternal justice and of human rights. In a word, I have no other claims than those which the oppressed principle of freedom has to the aid of victorious liberty. Then I would humbly ask, are these claims sufficient to ensure your generous protection, not to myself, but to the cause of my native land—not to my native land only, but the principle of freedom in Europe's Continent, of which the independence of Hungary is the indispensable keystone.

"If you consider these claims not sufficient to your active and operative sympathy, then let me know at once that the hopes have failed with which Europe's oppressed nations have looked to your great, mighty and glorious Republic—let me know at once the failure of our hopes, that I may hasten back and tell Europe's oppressed nations, 'Let us fight, forsaken and singlehanded, the battle of Leonidas; let us trust to God, to our right, and to our good swords; there is no other help for the oppressed nations on earth.' But if your generous Republican hearts are animated by the high principle of freedom and of solidarity in the destinies of humanity—if you have the will, as, to be sure, you have the power, to support the cause of freedom against the sacrilegious league of despotism, then give me some days of calm reflection, to become acquainted with the ground upon which I stand—let me take the kind advice of some active friends on the most practical course I have to adopt—let me see if there be any preparatory steps taken in favor of that cause which I have the honor to represent; and then let me have a new opportunity to expound before you my humble requests in a practical way.

"I confidently hope, Mr. Mayor, the Corporation and citizens of the Empire City will grant me the second opportunity. If this be your generous will, then let me take this for a boon of happier days; and let me add, with a sigh of thanksgiving to the Almighty God, that it is your glorious country which Providence has selected to be the pillar of freedom, as it is already the asylum to oppressed humanity.

"I am told that I will have the high honor to review your patriotic militia. Oh, God! how my heart throbs at the idea to see this gallant army enlisted on the side of freedom against despotism; the world would be free, and you the saviours of humanity. And why not? These gallant men take part in the mighty demonstration of the day, proving that I was right when I said that now-a-days even the bayonets think. Citizens of New York, it is under your protection that I place the sacred cause of freedom and independence of Hungary."

The subsequent pageant, it is impossible to describe with fidelity.

"Everywhere along the line of march the most lively enthusiasm was manifested. The waving of banners, of handkerchiefs, hats, &c.; the cheers and recognitions from windows, balconies, and all standing places, were ample evidence of the deep sympathy of the people for the great Exile and his cause.

"When the procession reached the American Museum, the scene was in the highest degree magnificent. Never before was its equal witnessed in this City. It was such a scene as New York alone in the New World, and but few cities in the Old, could produce. On reaching that point, the open space of the

SCENES IN NEW YORK.

Park burst upon the view. In front was our beautiful Broadway, straight as an arrow, with thousands of variously colored flags suspended from, and wreaths of evergreens decorating the hotels and store-buildings. In the distance stood the spire of Grace Church. On the right, Park Row and Chatham-st. presented a long avenue of fine buildings, likewise decorated in a magnificent style, with the stars and stripes, the Cross of St. George, and the Hungarian flag, entwined in harmony. On the left, was the massive Astor House, every window of which was filled with admirers of the great hero. While the eye was taking in these, it was arrested by the Park itself, with its thousands of human beings, its fine fountain, and the City Hall, ornamented with flags, and its portico festooned with drapery, and seen through the trees. The *coup d'œil* thus presented, was grand and imposing. Kossuth calmly viewed the scene, but was in a moment startled by a shout of welcome from the Astor House. He looked up and saw every gentleman in the windows and on the porch of that hotel huzzaing and waving his hat in a phrenzy of enthusiasm, the ladies saluting him with equal fervor. Kossuth was taken by surprise. He gracefully bowed, not once, but twice, thrice, a dozen times. But the scene did not end here. The procession was temporarily arrested by the immense crowd. Again loud huzzas were expressed for Kossuth by thirty thousand persons of all classes, ages, and sexes. The Hungarian exiles who followed immediately after Kossuth's carriage, came in for their share of applause; they, too, were cheered frantically. They returned the compliment. They waved their Hungarian banner in recognition. Again the voices were raised in honor of the great Magyar, and again the Magyar flag was lowered. Again were shouts of applause, and the Hungarian exiles, not satisfied with lowering their flags this time, cheered as loud as the rest.

"So dense was the multitude in Broadway, and so great was the pressure, that thousands upon thousands were forced out of the procession into the side-streets, and parallel streams of human beings rushed up Nassau-st., on one side, and Greenwich on the other; and, after reaching the Park, vast numbers pressed into Church-st., Elm, and Centre-sts., in order to get a little ahead, so as to obtain a sight of the procession. For the entire route of the procession through Broadway and back through the Bowery, the people filled every available spot long before the procession started. All along the line of march, and indeed throughout the city generally, business was suspended, and the whole demonstration was one of the greatest, most important, and most enthusiastic ever given."

The Sabbath was carefully regarded by Kossuth, the friend of religion no less than of liberty. He refused to receive deputations or visitors, and with his family attended St. Bartholomew's Church, accompanied by the Mayor of the city. The succeeding days were devoted to the delegations and individuals from surrounding towns, and those remote from the metropolis. From the Exile's replies to these numerous addresses, a few extracts are taken illustrative of the great qualities of his character. A hundred clergymen of the Methodist Episcopal Church, waited upon him with a dignified welcome, in which reference was made to the test of his Christian faith in Turkey. Kossuth said:

"I take no merit for what I did. Every honest man would do the same—that is not worthy being mentioned. If man be not truly faithful to his God and to his religion, would he be faithful to his country? I have always acknowledged, and will ever acknowledge, my unspeakable confidence in a God, as the richest source of consolation, and the most solemn of all my hopes for the future. I am so entirely convinced of the justice of my cause, that it seems not possible but that the blessings of the Almighty God must fall upon it.

"Every act of Divine Providence takes a course, which apparently cannot be understood by weak men's minds. But by-and-by circumstances break forth, which, even in our misfortunes, make us realize the Christian's trust, and shows us that God blesses the world. All our misfortunes are only the means to come to that end which God in his divine providence has marked for us. And now I have full confidence for my country's future. I have very strong reasons to convince me of that. These reasons form the motives of my hope and trust, and nothing gives me such consolation as that there is a God in heaven who is a just and good God, and who will not allow a just cause to die, to become annihilated. It is out of the soul that I draw my force and strength, which enables me to go on in all duty and honor for my country's cause; a duty sanctified by religion; a duty prescribed by our religion to every member of Mankind—prescribed by the great injunction which is the foundation of brotherhood on earth—' Thou shalt love one another.' "

A committee from Newburgh invited the Magyar to visit their romantic village, Washington's headquarters during the Revolution.

He made the following beautiful response:—

"GENTLEMEN: I return my most hearty thanks to you and those who have commissioned you to do me this honor (which I highly value) for your generous sentiments and kindness. My memory is roused to the remembrance of what effects to mankind's liberty have been produced by your revolutionary struggle, when you recall to my mind that you have come from the head-quarters of your great Washington. If I am not mistaken in my recollection, we are within four days of the anniversary of his death. The 14th day of December is the day on which Washington died. That day ought not to be a day of mourning and sorrow, because to die is the fate of every man, and Washington was subject to the common fate of humanity as well as others. But to see a man die in his full age—going down the horizon as clear and pure as he did, and had reason to do—that is a circumstance that must fill with joy the hearts of such people as you are. Such was the halo of glory that surrounded the death of Washington, and the anniversary of his departure from this life is not a day of mourning and sorrow. The greatest merit of Washington is not that he rejected the offer of a coterie to accept the crown of the United States. I would rather be surprised if he had accepted it, for what value is a crown to a free man—to a man like Washington, who was the great instrument in the hands of God of making his country free? Therefore I do not regard that as the greatest deed of his life—there are others far greater. However, as the time and the place you offer me to speak to the inheritors of that freedom for which Washington fought, are very appropriate, and I feel the great influence these circumstances have upon me, it is the wish of my heart to go to your town; but, from the immense demand upon my time, you can hardly expect to have your wish gratified; and these circumstances suggest to me that I shall hardly have the honor of doing it. The events of Europe are pointed out by the finger of God—the words *mene! mene! tekel upharsin,*' are written so plainly on the wall that we know not the hour when the trumpet of the resurrection of the enslaved millions shall sound. And so I must be guided by that advice, and I cannot select my own ground or time. But you will take into consideration the shortness of the period that may be allowed me to give practical effect to my mission, and to secure the advancement of those principles for which you have expressed almost a religious respect. I will be compelled, therefore, to go, not where my presence is most gratifying to myself, or to others, but wherever it is best for the cause."

He was waited upon by the Industrial Congress, and in the course of his speech, remarked:

"Sorrowful as that past may be to which you allude in your address, and unhappy as the present condition of my country may appear to be, I am a Christian, who in no case despairs of the justice and mercy of God, who knows that however unfavorable circumstances and the ways of Divine Providence for the welfare of humanity may seem, that still there is good even in every misfortune. A mighty benefit results from the struggle of Hungary, greater perhaps in its momentary failure than it would have been in case of a better fate. By victory we might have established the independence of our country, but the misfortunes of Hungary serve as the means of a wider union among nations, and of giving a broader sphere to that spirit of brotherly love which promises the greatest benefit to the future of humanity. In our own land, for instance, there has been in some parts a low and prejudiced condition of the popular intellect, which to conserve in its low and dependent state is always the care of despotism; there have been mutual antipathies which despotism has cherished among the citizens of the same country, which antipathies broke out at the very hour when I and my friends, battling against the Austrian Government, had succeeded in replacing the common expression by common liberty. By our failure this antipathy has been swept away, and unity of feeling, and of hostility to the common enemy, has succeeded it. I took opportunity from certain expressions in your address to mention these few words, and as I take your address as a declaration of sympathy with the cause which I have the honor to represent, I give you the assurance of the gratitude of myself, my companions and of those at home, who have not only experienced the same sufferings as we, but now see and feel every moment at home the tortures of these oppressions which now overwhelm our unhappy country, while we who are in exile have the happiness to see humanity in other countries in such a condition which raises the hope that an era has now arrived in the history of mankind, when the mutual interests and relations of peoples are recognized, and that no nation will now stand alone.

* * * * * * *

"I declare—and man of no condition or station can be offended at the declaration—that while we welcome, and gratefully acknowledge sympathy and support for the cause of Hungary and liberty from whatever quarter it comes, at no moment, and in no place is it so dear, as when it comes from the working classes. Because I consider that the most noble charter of man's dignity is labor; and because, knowing this, I must be well aware that when working men, whose greatest treasure is their time and their work, stop their work and devote their time to express sympathy for the poor exile, it is because they connect him with the cause of universal liberty. Therefore, I must, through my whole time, appreciate this meeting as a very dear treasure of my wandering life. Finally, let me hope that you will use your influence, and your constitutional privilege in such a manner as might lead to some effectual benefit for the cause in behalf of which you have here expressed your interest and sympathy."

On the evening of Dec. 11, the Corporation of New York gave Governor Kossuth the Municipal

Dinner, in the spacious hall of the Irving House. The literati and various professions were represented, the decorations were appropriate, and the whole scene honorable to the renowned Magyar, the cause he represents, and to the American people. Upon this occasion he made a most thrilling and elaborate speech, vindicating his appeals to the free hearts of this Republic, answering thoroughly the ungenerous assaults of papers and politicians upon his character and motives, and giving another illustration of his versatile and extraordinary talents.* His profound knowledge of our institutions and glorious constitution, amazed his delighted auditory, and added new radiance to a star of solitary splendor.

On the evening of the 15th, he met his brethren of the editorial profession, at a magnificent banquet. He who had been a hunted captive for his love to an unshackled press, stood in modest majesty, and with a full heart, before the assembled journalists of New York; the humble editor of the Pesth Gazette, was the master spirit of minds whose influence is felt around the globe, and shapes a nation's destiny. His speech was greatly applauded, increasing the admiration of his exhaustless powers and fascinating eloquence.† The next evening he addressed the military companies in Castle Garden. The spacious amphitheatre was filled with soldiers in varied uniform, presenting with their contrasted equipage and trappings, a splendid scene. Kossuth appeared in rich,

---

* See Appendix.   † Ibid.

yet simple uniform, with a burnished sword, whose scabbard flashed by his side. Never before had the metropolis made a national display so dazzlingly beautiful. We quote the passages in Kossuth's speech that were peculiar to the occasion, and effective in delivery:

"I am now rather a soldier than an orator; but you are citizen soldiers, a glorious title, to which I have the ambition of aspiring. So I hope you will kindly excuse me if I do not give you an elaborate speech, but rather endeavor to speak to you as soldiers—forward and plain, without any pretensions to skill. Do you know, gentlemen, the finest speech I ever heard or read? It is the address of Garabaldi, to his Roman soldiers of the last war, when he told them:—'Soldiers, what I have to offer you is fatigue, danger, struggling and death—the chill of the cold night, the open air, and the burning sun—no lodgings, no munitions, no provisions—but forced marches, dangerous watch-posts, and continual struggling with bayonets against batteries. Those who love freedom and their country follow me.' That is the most glorious speech I ever heard in my life. But, of course, that is no speech for to-day. I will speak so, when I again meet the soldiers of Hungary to fight once more the battle of freedom and independence. And before God, I know there is no Hungarian who would not follow his Governor. So it must be, and so it will be. There is another fine speech which I remember. It is that of the old Covenanter, who spoke to his soldiers these words: 'Now, boys, trust in God, and keep your powder dry.' Gentlemen, that must be my motto for to-day. I will put my trust in God; but I don't know if my sickness will not cast some damp on my powder. If it does, you must excuse me. General (turning to General Sandford), I have had the high honor to review the First Division of the New York State Militia, and to receive their marching salute. Allow me, before all, to compliment you on their discipline, skill, military attitude, and the general appearance of the gentlemen who are commanded by you

To be sure, General, it is no flattering compliment—it is an acknowledgment of a fact; and I say that in no European army your division would have been regarded as not of the regular soldiers. There are two other things which have struck me on this occasion. The first is the firm character and resolute attitude of the gentlemen you command, and who are organized to maintain social order. Secondly, the readiness of the people to comply with it. This I take, gentlemen, as a proof of the validity of free institutions. While in other countries, not so happy as yours, not provided with such institutions as yours, obedience to every public authority is only enforced by fear— here obedience is a principle. The people feel honored in complying with their public duty, the source of which is the people themselves. Republicanism—your Republic—proves to the world that social order is most firmly founded on liberty, and it is a free people that are the surest guarantee of social order in a State. There are among the gentlemen whom I have the honor to address, a regiment which had, I am told, not long ago, to fulfil the difficult duty of restoring public order on a certain occasion; and it was that very regiment, during the marching salute which I received, that was most cheered by the people. Now this fact is as glorious to the regiment as it is honorable to the people. To-day, if I am not wrong, is the anniversary of the great fire in New York, which happened in 1835, on the 16th of December. Since that time, New York has risen more splendid than it was before, and has spread on a large scale. Now, this gigantic development of this great city is only possible on the basis of social order. In the maintenance of order, public authorities must have their merit. The support of the people has its own, but it is also no little glory to the military that social order exists. General (addressing General Sandford), I thank you for the explanation of the organization and discipline of this gallant division. Europe has many things to learn from America. It has to learn the value of free institutions. It has to learn the expansive power of freedom—it has to learn the practical value of self-government, as opposed to centralization

But cne of the most important lessons you give to Europe, is in the organization of the militia of the United States. You have the best organized army in the world, and yet you have scarcely a standing army at all. That is a necessary thing for Europe to learn from America—that great standing armies must cease. But they can only cease when the nations are free, because great standing armies are not national institutions—they are the instruments of despotism, and the ambition of tyrants. The very existence of tyranny imposes on Europe great standing armies. When the nations once become free, they will not want them, because they will not war with each other. Freedom will become a friendly link among nations. But as far as they will want them, your example shows that the popular institution of the militia, like yours, is the most powerful and the most mighty means of national defence. Thirty-seven years ago, a great battle was fought at New Orleans; that showed what a defence your country has in its militia. Nay, more, your history proves that this institution affords the most powerful means of offensive war, should war become indispensable. I am aware, gentlemen, that your war with Mexico was chiefly carried on by volunteers. In Hungary, my brave companions here have some claim to renown for bravery, but it is my duty to confess that those who fought in that war have a high claim to brilliant bravery. Often they had to fight one against four. A handful of men at such a distance, in a foreign land, having a gallant foe to contend with (because it was among a warlike population), and so victorious! That war, gentlemen, and those victories are a remarkable page in the military history of mankind. I know, gentlemen, what a distinguished part the volunteers of New York took in that war. I know that seven regiments were offered, but only two accepted. I know what a glorious part they took at Vera Cruz, Cerro Gordo, Contreras, and Molino del Rey. I know how they were distinguished at Cherebusco, at Chapultepec, and how they partook of the immense glory of entering—a gallant handful of men—the metropolis of Mexico. And who were these volunteers? Who were those from New York city and of other regiments? They were of your militia, the source of that military spirit which is the glory of your country, and its safety when needed in time of war or social disorder. I learned all this from the United States, and it was my firm intention to carry out this militia organization in Hungary. My idea was, and still is, to do so, and I will endeavor, with the help of God, to carry it out. My idea is, there are duties towards one' native land, common to every citizen, and public instruction and education must have such a direction as to enable every citizen to perform his duties to his native land. One of these duties is to defend it in time of danger, to take up arms for its freedom and independence and security. My idea is to lay such a foundation for public instruction in the schools, that every boy in Hungary shall be educated in military skill, so as to prepare him for the duty of defending his native land. It is not my intention to have separate schools for teaching military science; not at all. My opinion is that every boy must be taught to know as much as is necessary for the defence of his native land, and those who feel inclined to adopt the profession of arms, might be established in higher public schools and universities, so as to complete their education, as is the case in the professions of the bar, and physic, and the pulpit. But I would have no distinction among the citizens. To defend our country is a common duty, and every one must know how to perform it. Taking the basis of your organization as an example for Hungary, Hungary would have at least one million of men ready to defend it against the oppression of any power whatever. That the militia of Hungary, thus developed, would be the most solid guardian of my country's freedom and independence, we havê shown in our past struggles. The glorious deeds which the unnamed demi-gods of the people achieved, proves what with provious preparations, they could do in defence of their native land. Often they have gone into battle without knowing how to fire or cock a musket; but they took batteries by their bayonets, and they achieved glorious deeds like those that are classed among the deeds of immortality. We have not either wish or inclination for conquest. We are content with our native land, if it be independent and free. To the maintenance of that independence and freedom, we have established by law, the institution of the National Guard. It is like your militia, and I like to say often to my people, that I consider the organization to be like a porcupine, which goes on quietly, but when attacked or when danger approaches, stretches forth its thorns. May God Almighty grant that I may soon see developed in my native land, the great institution of a National Guard to that extent that the power of Hungary may become the indispensable basis of the freedom of Europe.

* * * * * * *

"I thank you for your generous sympathy, and for the reception and welcome of my companions, the devoted sons of Hungary, who were ready to sacrifice life and fortune to the independence of their native land. There are several among them who were already soldiers before our struggle, and they employed their military skill in the service of their country. But there were others who were not soldiers, and whose patriotism only led them to embrace the cause of their native land, and they proved to be brave and efficient supporters of the freedom for which they fought. Thanking you for the sympathy you have expressed for them, I promise you, gentlemen, that they will prove themselves worthy of it. I will point out to them the most dangerous places, and I know they will acquit themselves honorably and bravely. As to myself, I have here a sword on my side given to me by an American citizen. This (drawing the sword), being a gift from a citizen of the United States, I take it as a token of encouragement to go on in that way by which, with the blessing of Almighty God, I shall be enabled yet to see again my fatherland independent and free. I swear here before you (raising the sword to heaven), that this American sword in my hand, shall be always faithful in the cause of freedom—that it shall be ever foremost in the battle, and that it shall never be polluted by ambition or cowardice."

The excitement which followed this oath, uttered with startling solemnity, was surpassingly sublime. The 5,000 military rose simultaneously, waving their plumed hats, while the ornaments of gold and silver reflected the blaze of myriad lamps, and the volumes of repeated cheers, like surges breaking upon trembling cliffs, shook the old castle to its base.

His next public address was given in the Plymouth Church, at Brooklyn. Tickets of admission in aid of Hungary were issued, and the ample edifice was full. He commenced his vindication of religious liberty, with a serious dignity befitting the sanctuary of the Most High, associated with the memory of those immortal founders of our Republic, the first to secure perfect liberty of Divine worship to the people. The portion of his address bearing upon freedom of conscience, he introduced with an unaffected acknowledgment of his dependence on the "Father of Lights," apparent in all his public acts:—

"A few minutes after I took my seat I was entirely unprepared to address you in such a manner as would content you I was told that I might rely on inspiration; but inspiration comes only from above. It is not in the power of man to be inspired—man has no power but to be honest—everything else is the gift of Heaven. I, therefore, do not know whether inspiration will do at this moment or not; you will excuse me, therefore, for what I shall say. When I look around me, two considerations force themselves on my mind. The first is, that I am in the house of God; and secondly, that in this holy place, I meet an assemblage of the friends of freedom, who have come to assist the cause of liberty in my fatherland. Therefore, two considerations force themselves on my mind—one religious and the other financial—commercial. As to the religious, I am fully aware that when I was a captive in far-off Asia, when I could not have had the proud dream that the heart of humanity beat with commiseration in my behalf, you, inspired by the noble sentiments of that man whom you have chosen to take care of your religious interests, you raised your prayer to God for me; and now, you show that you remember the sacred words of our Saviour, who said : 'Pray, and be also watchful.' You are watchful respecting the interests of humanity. In my opinion, it is religious in men to do so, because I consider the Christian religion the true source of the liberty of mankind in this world. The great principle which our Saviour taught, was that of equality before God. He said his kingdom was not of this world. He said it was not only the kingdom of salvation, but, by pronouncing his principles, he invited men to provide for themselves an earthly interest—to be free, and to enjoy the bounties of nature, as they are called, and to share the great destiny of mankind—bliss in heaven. I am fully convinced of the truth that the first destiny of our species is to bring about new reforms in Christianity, not in respect to doctrines, but in respect to the great principles of Christianity, which teach us to love our neighbors as we love ourselves, and out of private life, to prevent the interference by one nation with another. That would be a new development of Christianity, giving not only the hope of bliss to man in heaven, but giving him liberty here on earth. The cause of Hungary is strongly connected with the principles of religious liberty in the world.

* * * * * * *

"It was reserved for our revolution of 1848, to show a great development of the glorious circumstances of freedom; that the principle of liberty was common to all, without respect to religion or education, throughout the whole country; so much so that when my nation reposed on my humble shoulders, the heavy duty to govern the land, to show what immense faith I had in that principle of freedom, I nominated the first independent minister of Hungary—a Catholic Bishop—to be Minister of Public Instruction—I, myself, who am a Protestant by profession and by conviction ; and I must say I felt justified in the choice, because the man I selected fully justified the confidence which I reposed in him. He showed, and I, by my choice, showed, that when the institutions of a country are founded on liberty—equality of rights for all—that principles know only citizens in their capacity as such, without regard to their religious professions—the principles of liberty by which even Catholic Bishops are bound to their country, and become patriots. It is only possible, under free institutions, that a man who is a minister of the Word of God according to certain forms, when called upon to perform civil duties, is a religious man no longer, but only a citizen. That is possible under republican institutions alone. You will find no instance in history where a Catholic monarch would have employed a Protestant priest to take care of the public instruction of a whole country, and you would never find a Protestant king to employ a Catholic bishop to take care of public instruction. But in a country where government is founded on liberty, there it is possible ; and in this case the choice I made was not a bad one. I never saw the vitality of liberty better illustrated than in reposing in a Catholic bishop the high interests of public instruction, where an entire equality of rights and full religious liberty were established as the common right of all. And I must say, could the Court of Rome be able to estimate the value of the principle which induced me to act as I did in Hungary, it might become the regenerator of Italy, and my friend Mazzini would not be necessary. But the Court of Rome cannot perceive the principle, and Mazzini becomes necessary, and the temporal power of the Pope is about to fall down forever. That is my conviction. The temporal power of the Pope will probably fall down in the next revolution, which is already felt in the air, and which is pointed out by the finger of God. I say this prophetically. I have read it in the book of Providence, and in the public spirit of humanity. But I must tell you why it was necessary in Hungary to have a minister of public instruction. Here you have no such necessity. It was necessary, because my country's principle was that every church had full right and full liberty to provide for public instruction; and to take care of this great interest of mankind, that every man has a right to be employed in the glorious field of public instruction, but that the country at large has the duty not to relinquish the great interests of mankind to chance—that it is the duty of the country to provide establishments where every citizen can partake of the benefit of public instruction, when, perhaps, no church and no single man can provide it. Our principle, therefore, was, that the country should provide for it; but at the same time that every church and every society had a right also to do it. We wanted liberty of education, but not to make it dependent on the church or on individuals. Therefore, we found it our duty to provide for it as a government matter. Another thing was, that practical men must take things practically.— There were several men belonging to the Greek church who considered it as an oppression of the Hungarian government, that it gave no material aid for their necessities; they would have considered it an oppression, and therefore we declared by law that Hungary offered equal support to all citizens in respect to their religious interests and public duties. My principle it was not; but I was forced to accept circumstances as they were. At the time I was Governor of Hungary I did not cease to be a member of the church, and I always advocated the voluntary principle— that is, not to accept any aid from the public authorities, and therefore to preserve to every man the right to dispose of his own affairs. My principle, and the principle which I consider to be that of the majority of my nation—which, by the blessing of God, and the generous aid of free nations, we will yet carry out—was, and is, that the church shall not meddle with politics, and politics shall not meddle with religion."

The orator's opinion of the extreme views of the "Peace Society," the purity of whose aims none will question, cannot fail to impress the most sensitive foe to the shedding of human blood:

"But I am told there are men of peace who say, after all it is very true—very fine, if you please, but they will have peace at any price. Now, I say, there are many things in the world which depend upon true definitions—and it is not true that they are men of peace who speak so—they are men who would conserve, at any price, the present condition of things. Is that present condition peace? Is the scaffold peace?—the scaffold, on which, in Lombardy, the blood of 3,742 patriots was spilled during three short years. Is that peace? Are the prisons of Austria filled with patriots, peace? Or is the blind murmur of discontent from all the nations, peace? I believe the Lord has not created the world to be in such a peaceful condition. I believe he has not created it to be the prison to humanity, or to be the dominion of the Austrian jailer. No; the present condition of the world is not peace. It is a condition of oppression on the European continent, and because there is this condition of oppression there cannot be peace; for so long as men and nations are oppressed, and so long as men and nations are discontented, there cannot be peace—there can be tranquillity; but it will be the dangerous tranquillity of the volcano, boiling up constantly, and at the slightest opportunity breaking out again, and again, and sweeping away all the artificial props of tranquillity. Freedom is the condition of peace, and, therefore, I will not say that those who profess to be men of peace, and will not help the oppressed to obtain their liberty, are really so. Let them tell truly that they are not men of peace, but only desire to conserve the oppression of nations. With me and with my principles is peace, because I was always a faithful servant of the principles of liberty, and only on the principles of liberty, can nations be contented, and only with the contentment of nations, can there be peace on the earth. With me and with my principles there is peace—lasting peace—consistent peace; with the tyrants of the world there is oppression, struggles, and war."

The next evening he attended a grand banquet prepared by the Bar of New York. With the unfailing freshness which distinguishes his speeches, he discussed the mighty meaning of our Constitution, and exhibited a profound knowledge of our history and institutions, which surprised statesmen and delighted his auditory —and will so affect every American reader.*

The Magyar's farewell to the city of New York, was spoken before the ladies, assembled in Tripler Hall, to behold and hear the exile, they would welcome with woman's generous sympathy and cheerful offerings. The oration was exceedingly chaste in style and rich in thought; the most poetic and touching appeal he has made to American hearts.†

In Philadelphia he was received with pageantry in some respects not inferior to his first reception. Soon after his arrival he was waited upon by Col. PAGE and his company of State Fencibles, who presented the Magyar with a magnificent Maltese cross of gold, in which was set a miniature of Washington bordered with pearls, and appended was a beautiful locket enshrining some of the hair that had streamed in the smoke of freedom's battle. Upon accepting the priceless gift, KOSSUTH said:

"It is with deep emotion that I thank you for the manifestation of your active, operative sympathy in the substantial aid you are pleased to bestow for the benefit of the cause of my down-trodden land, and the cause of so many nations connected with it—but, sir, it is more than thanks, it is more than grati-

---

* Appendix. † Ibid.

tude, it is a sort of religious piety, which I feel when I press to my heart this your precious gift—the likeness and the lock of hair of your great Washington—that glorious star on mankind's moral sky. Overpowered as I am with sentiments, and somewhat worn down with a fever as I am, I scarcely can be able better to show the value I attach to this precious gift than when I promise you, Sir, and you, gentlemen, that in the approaching new struggle in Europe for freedom and independence, I will attach it to the very standard which will necessarily be carried at my immediate side when I in person lead on the bravest of the brave of Hungary to decide the victory of freedom against despotism. So may God ess me, as I give you the assurance that as long as one man is left to stand by that standard,—as long as one drop of bloo is in this heart, that standard which you have hallowed by the likeness and by the lock of hair of the venerable head of your Washington, will be proudly and loftily floating, a terror to despots, a hope to oppressed humanity, and an everlasting source of resolution and heroism to all who love liberty and are ready to fight for it. And short as the life may be which I have to live, I confidently hope I shall see the day I will plant this standard, so adorned and hallowed by you, on the very shrine of Hungary's achieved freedom and independence. I thank you once more; let me hope,—and let me say that this hope is not a vain one, because it is supported by your gallant hands and by the sympathy of the people of the United States,—that the American people will wisely consider that the time draws near when it must decide what course it is resolved to take in respect to this great event—the first blow of which has already once been struck, although by an impious hand, yet nevertheless struck to become, by the providential aid of God, even by its very crime, subservient to virtue and liberty. Let me therefore hope that the time is not far distant when I shall have to write you, that this likeness and this venerable lock of hair from the head of your great leader, has not only led on the heroes of Hungary in the renewed struggle for freedom and independence, but it has also inspired them with the spirit of its genius, of its character, of its success as an army. One thing I swear to you, gentlemen—it will ever inspire this heart."

He afterward addressed the masses in his usually eloquent strain, dwelling with intense interest upon the recent treachery of Louis Napoleon:

"It was strange, indeed, to see this delusion of a past glory like vain and injurious to liberty, lead a great nation astray. But very soon a strange fascination passed, and the French nation saw that the President who swore to maintain the republic was only a pretender. While he was cheered by some, with a shout of hurrah for the Emperor, he was told by the nation that the worst of things would be an empire without glory; and because there once existed a man whom his admirers called Napoleon the Great, there was no occasion for having Napoleon the Little. A bad augury for his imperial dream; so that there remained scarcely any chance for him but to keep yet a while the power of a President, and to raise himself by it to the sacrilegious seat of an usurper. You know how he exhausted every possible plan to secure his re-election. But every device broke to pieces on the rock of the constitution, which explicitly forbade the re-election of the actual President. So, indeed, every man might have foreseen that, having failed in these attempts, he would resort to violence to shatter down that constitution which excluded him from power, and by this exclusion, from the treacherous realization of his ambitious dreams, with a violent stroke, easily to be foreseen and to be foretold. But it was equally easy to foresee and foretell that he would, without any delay, hasten to strike this injurious blow. The moment of his going out of office and of power was fixed by the constitution. He saw that the friends of the republican constitution as well as his dynastic rivals, were day by day preparing, and step by step marshalling their forces; but he knew that the republican party not having yet come to a decision about its common nominee for the Presidency, was not entirely ready to oppose his blow sufficiently. Every moment of delay might compromise his success so there was no alternative but either to hasten this impious blow or to become an honest man, faithful to his word and oath.

"Who would have doubted what course an ambitious Crown Pretender would take, placed in the alternative? And there is yet an essential circumstance not to be overlooked. The Emperor of Russia, and all his openly avowed or secret, but equally obedient satellites, hates the word 'Republic,' everywhere, but chiefly a Republic in that France which, as such, once already, made tremble all the Kings and Emperors of the earth. The Emperor of Russia and his satellites were well aware that a new and peaceful Presidential election would consolidate Republicanism in France, and make it dangerous to their absolutism. They wished to overthrow it, and there was but one alternative for that purpose; either war or a *coup d'état* by their tool, Napoleon. A war would have been dangerous, because, against foreign invasion the French nation knows well how to unite; and the French Republic, attacked by continental despotism, would inevitably arouse all nations of that continent to side with France. They well remember those portentous words of Merlin de Thionville · 'If they send us war, we will send them back liberty!' There was therefore no mistake about the fact that the Czar and his satellites would resort to some more easy, and to them more agreeable alternative, to make the hated French bleed by its own hands —a fratricidal combat—and so murder the Republic by the very man who was appointed its chief guardian. This was an easier part to play for the despots than a war; and a little diplomacy was all the part they had to play. You see, therefore, gentlemen, there was no divinatory power wanted to foretell the Napoleon stroke, as orally I have very often done, since my arrival on your happy shores.

"But why have I chosen this topic for this occasion, which your kindness has offered me? Why have I dwelt so largely upon it? The motive, gentlemen, is, firstly, to show that there is nothing in the news from France of such a nature as to arrest that attention which public opinion of the people of the United States has been pleased to bestow to the question: what course your country has to adopt in its foreign policy in respect to European concerns. But that the news from France transforming my prophecy of being on the very eve of a crisis in Europe into an accomplished fact, brings that question of foreign policy home to your immediate decision, which you cannot more postpone—cannot more delay; because even the very delay of it would be more than a delay; it would be a positive answer given to the expectations of the world—an answer, which not only I, but all the oppressed nations of the European continent would exactly understand to be so much as to say—'The people of the United States, in its private capacity, has good wishes for the freedom of the European continent; but in its public capacity as a power on earth, it declares not to care about it if the public laws of nations are respected or violated by the interference of the strong arm of a foreign power, oppressing the spirit of freedom in whatever country.'

"Well, gentlemen, may be that if it is the will of the sovereign people of the United States to give such an answer to the expressions and hopes of the world, you will see a mournful tear in the eye of humanity, and its heart heaving with a mournful sigh; but the answer must be accepted of course; you are mighty and powerful enough not to care about the laws of nations, the expression of my down-trodden land, and about the farewell of freedom on the European continent. I will not speak of France, nor of the unavoidable consequences of a lost opportunity to save liberty on earth, by offering fair play to our struggle against despotism. No—I will not even object to anything to those who believe that should even liberty and nature's law, and the law of nature's God be beaten down on the earth, that can bring no harm home to you, because you feel you are equal to defend yourself when it will become your own domestic interest to maintain the laws of nature and of nature's God, in your own particular case.

"Well, let it be so, if so you please. I have in the name of oppressed nations, and of down-trodden liberty, urged the people of the United States, not to fight our battles, but to maintain the laws of nations against foreign interference, that down-trodden liberty may have a fair play to fight its own battles with its own force. You answer, 'No.' I reminded the public opinion of your people that your own statesmen say you as a nation have precisely the same interest in international law as a private individual has in the laws of his country.

"Well, you may answer no; you may answer, 'Let every one care for himself and God for all;" we are not the keepers of our brethren in humanity. I took the liberty to remind you that in the hour of your need you asked, accepted and received more from Europe to help you than what I humbly ask for Europe from you. You have asked and received military troops and fleets to fight *your* battles in company with you, and received a negotiated peace by the intervention of France. Well may you advance upon the basis of your independence that you have asked and accepted help, because what you wanted was but in reason. You should help others who are in want.

"You may answer thus, if you please : I have said that by declining to be willing now to allow (speaking in the very terms of your President,) 'that the strong arm of a foreign power should repress the spirit of freedom, in any country,' by declining to be willing now to allow that the laws of nations in which you have the same interest as a private individual in the laws of his own country, should be violated by the armed interference of foreign powers with the sovereign right of every man to dispose of his own domestic concerns. I have said that by declining this, and inviting England to unite with you in this policy, as it has united with you, when in the South American question you thought it your interest to adopt such a policy, and to unite with England for it; I have said that all this will bring you in no complication, in no war; because you are powerful, and the word of the powerful will be respected. Well, you may answer me, that you don't believe me, that you are not conscious of your power, that you fear Russia, that you know that Russia does not fear you and will not respect your word; that you would rather be on friendly terms with the Czar, than rejoice in the liberality and independence of Hungary Italy, Germany, and France.

All this you may answer if you please. Dreadful as it is, I will wipe off the tear of sorrow from my eye, and say to my brethren, let us pray, and go to the Lord's last supper, and then to battle and to death, there is no help for us but in the trust to God and our own good swords. I will leave you with the old Roman *moribundi salutant*—the dying bid you farewell! and in bidding you this farewell, I will bless you with the warmest wishes of my heart, and pray to God that the Sun of Freedom may never decline from the horizon of your happy land.

[Here Kossuth was affected to tears, and the audience were deeply moved. The whole assemblage rose to their feet, and joined in hearty cheers. The scene was a most exciting one.]

"I will not argue more about the policy of not meddling with European concerns; but, one thing, gentlemen, you must permit me to remark, and that is, that if the people of the United States intend to give such an unfortunate answer to my humble request, as I was about, by supposition to say, then you may well adjourn the decision, because you have already answered by not making any decision at all; but if, happily, the people of the United States are willing to decide otherwise, then let me entreat you to do it, because soon it may be too late. The struggle has commenced in Europe, the revolution has broken out; every day of delay is a decision too late.

"One thing permit me to say: When a man is swimming and about to reach the shore of salvation, and a robber ready to throw him into the watery grave, and you say, 'Look! look! the poor man will indeed be drowned! we sympathize with him, and we will to-morrow—after to-morrow—in a month—consider, should we allow or not allow him to be thrown into the waves: we will adjourn the question.' Your very adjournment is a decision, and to be sure a very negative one. Hungary—nay, the European continent, is in that very condition.

"I am on my way to Washington. If the Congress adjourns its decision in respect to your policy pointed out to its considera tion by the President of e United States—if your National Government delays to answer my humble request, I will understand it; it is a negative. So much is done. History has seconded my humble requests, and history is recording the answer of the people, Congress and Government of the United States. No answer at all will be also recorded. It is an answer too clear to be misunderstood.

"My task here is nearly done. It was a duty imposed upon me by Providence, by the confidence of nations; by the voice of the people from Sweden down to Italy, and from Hungary across to Portugal, by the expectations caused on my liberation by your gracious aid. The confidence may fail—the voice of Europe die like the sound of the wanderer's step in the desert, and the expectation turn out to have been in vain. I am in the hands of God, and no man is too humble to become an instrument in the hands of Providence, if it be God's will. So I have done what it was my duty to do. So much at least nobody can lay to my charge, that I have not dealt fairly and openly, or left any doubt as to what I wish, request, and humbly ask.

"I am in Philadelphia, the City of Brotherly Love, the city founded by William Penn, whose likeness I saw this day in a history of your city, with this motto under it, " *Si vis pacem para bellum*," prepare for war if thou wilt have peace. A weighty memento indeed, joined to the name of William Penn; and I am in that city which is the cradle of your independence; where, in the hour of your need, the appeal was proclaimed to the laws of nature and of nature's God, and the appeal for help from Europe, which was granted to you. I stood in the Independence Hall, whence the spirit of freedom is whispering eternal words of history to the secret recesses of your hearts. Man may well be silent when from such a place history so speaks. So my task is done: with me the pain, with you the decision, and, let me add with the poet, " the moral of the strain."

In accordance with a resolution of Congress inviting him there, he proceeded with the same unsought triumphal progress which had attended him since he reached our shores, to Baltimore; and again spoke in behalf of his native land. The 30th he arrived at the Capital, and was welcomed to the Legislative Halls of the Nation, under whose flag he left the domain of the Sultan, to send again his clarion voice of freedom around the globe!

After a shamefully protracted debate upon the propriety of admitting beneath the dome of liberty the Washington of Europe, whose foot was already on the threshold, he was formally greeted as the nation's guest. The collision of opinions and the tumultuous discussion of such a question, are humiliating exhibitions to the exile and his comrades, of the degeneracy of our legislative representation. It shows the people how selfishness and wrong-doing for fame and wealth, influence deliberations within the walls hallowed by the departed patriots of '76.

On the last day of the past year, Webster introduced Kossuth and suite to President Fillmore, at the Executive Mansion. The interview was short, and the following addresses, the only matters of interest that transpired on the occasion. Kossuth said,

"Enlightened by the spirit of your country's institutions, when we succeeded to consolidate our natural and historical State's right of self-government by placing it on the broad foundation of democratic liberty:

"Inspired by your history when we had to fight for independence against annihilation by centralized absolutism:

"Consoled by your people's sympathy when a victim of Russian interference with the laws of Nature and of Nature's God:

"Protected in exile by the Government of the United States supporting the Sultan of Turkey in his noble resolution to undergo the very danger of war rather than leave unprotected the rights of humanity against Russo-Austrian despotism:

"Restored by the United States to life because restored to freedom, and by freedom to activity in behalf of those duties which, by my nation's unanimous confidence and sovereign will, devolved upon me:

"Raised in the eyes of many oppressed nations to the standing of a harbinger of hope, because the star-spangled banner was seen cast in protection around me, announcing to the world that there is a nation alike powerful as free, ready to protect the laws of nations, even in distant parts of the earth and in the person of a poor exile:

"Cheered by your people's sympathy so as freemen cheer not a man whatever, but a principle,

"I now bow before you, Sir, in the proud position of your great nation's guest, generously welcomed by resolution of the Congress of the United States, with equal generosity approved and executed by your Excellency:

"I beg leave to express my fervent thanks, in my name and in the name of my associates, who, after having shared my misfortunes, have now the reward to share the honor and the benefit which the great Republic of the United States was pleased to bestow upon Hungary by bestowing it upon its freely chosen chief, when he became a persecuted victim of despotic violence.

"I beg leave to express my fervent thanks in my country's name, and also, which, amidst the sorrows of its desolation, feels cheered by your country's generosity, and looks with resolution to the impending future because it is confident that the time draws near when the eternal code of the laws of nations will become a reality:

"President: I stand before your Excellency a living protestation against the violence of foreign interference oppressing the sovereign right of nations to regulate their own domestic concerns.

"I stand before your Excellency a living protestation against centralization oppressing the State right of self-government.

"May I be allowed to take it for an augury of better times, that, in landing on the happy shores of this glorious Republic, I landed in a free and a powerful country, whose honored Chief Magistrate proclaims to the world that this country cannot remain indifferent when the strong arm of a foreign Power is invoked to stifle public sentiment and repress the spirit of freedom in any country.

"I thank God that he deemed me not unworthy to act and to suffer for my fatherland.

"I thank God that the fate of my country became so intimately connected with the fate of liberty and independence of nations of Europe, as formerly it was intimately connected with the security of Christendom.

"I thank God that my country's unmerited woe and my personal sufferings became an opportunity to seek a manifestation of the spirit and principles of your Republic.

"May God the Almighty bless you with a long life, that you may long enjoy the happiness to see your country great, glorious and free, the corner-stone of international justice, and the column of freedom on the earth, as it is already an asylum to the oppressed.

"Sir, I pledge to your country the everlasting gratitude of Hungary."

The President replied briefly to Kossuth's address, in substance as follows:

"I am happy, Governor Kossuth, to welcome you to this land of freedom; and it gives me pleasure to congratulate you upon your release from a long confinement in Turkey, and your late arrival here. As an individual, I sympathize deeply with you in your brave struggle for the independence and freedom of your native land The American people can never be indifferent to such a contest, but our policy as a nation in this respect has been uniform, from the commencement of our Government; and my own views, as the

CONGRESSIONAL BANQUET. 285

Chief Executive Magistrate of this nation, are fully and freely expressed in my recent message to Congress, to which you have been pleased to allude. They are the same, whether speaking to Congress here or to the nations of Europe.

"Should your country be restored to independence and freedom, I should then wish you, as the greatest blessing you could enjoy, a restoration to your native land; but should that never happen, I can only repeat my welcome to you and your companions here, and pray that God's blessing may rest upon you wherever your lot may be."

The Congressional Banquet was given January 7th, in the hall of the National Hotel. Hon. W. KING, President of the Senate, presided, with KOSSUTH and Speaker BOYD at his right, and Hon. DANIEL WEBSTER on the left. The room was decorated with banners and other appropriate devices. Among the three hundred guests, were the picked politicians of the land, from the Representative Hall to the Cabinet of the President. Talent, wit and beauty were there; for several distinguished ladies graced the scene which followed the removal of the viands. Kossuth's erudite and splendid speech we give in another place.* "The Defender of the Constitution" listened with absorbing interest, and the accents of truth fell with visible effect on the ear of the silent assemblage.

But life at the Capital was not attractive to KOSSUTH. While disheartened and sad amid the chicanery of the political world, he received intelligence that his aged mother, overborne by the calamities which crowded upon her declining years, had sunk to the

---

* See Appendix.

silence and repose of the grave, leaving his sisters in an Austrian prison. KOSSUTH read the announcement with tears, and like all generous, good and gifted men, mourned in unapproachable grief for her who cradled him in infancy, and had to the latest hour borne him on her heart of prayer. But the angel of his spirit here was no more, while Hungary remains a weeper for her slaughtered and exiled children. And rising as often before, in the majesty of Christian faith and heroism, he turns to his dear fatherland, and values existence only as it is precious to the Magyar's ravaged domain.

With a few friends, KOSSUTH called on HENRY CLAY, who is evidently approaching the dark transit to the eternal main; like a noble bark, dismantled by a thousand storms, and freighted with treasures from all lands, drifting away from the tearful gaze of millions who would recover and retain the glorious wreck. The Magyar listened solemnly to the dying accents of the great statesman and orator, and made a brief yet feeling reply. And when KOSSUTH rose to depart, the emaciated form whose pallid face was lit up by the radiance that cannot fade, slowly assumed its commanding attitude before the Exile. Then taking the hand of the chief within one of his own feverish palms, he placed the other upon the shoulder of the Hungarian, and invoked the blessing of Heaven upon him. The tears flowed freely down his cheeks, and KOSSUTH's bosom swelled with struggling emotion, while the venerable Kentuckian added, that every day his life should be spared, his fervent prayers would ascend to Almighty God for the exile's protection and restoration to his native land. And thus they parted, to meet no more till both appear before the King of kings.

Before we leave Governor KOSSUTH in his career of moral conquest, which, though unattended with the roll of the drum and gleam of weapons, is the sublimest triumph of his life, we turn again to the inspiration of pure and brilliant thoughts, falling like a shower of diamonds from his lips. Addressing the Senate of Maryland, he alludes with impassioned language to the deathless names that shine in American history.

"MR. PRESIDENT: The stormy current of my life has offered several moments when the importance of the occasion, connected with associations of historical interest, impressed a deep emotion upon my mind. But, perhaps, never yet in my life has the memory of the past made such a gloomy impression upon me as here.

"I bow with reverential awe before history, in bowing before you, Senators of Maryland, in this glorious hall—the sanctuary of immortal deeds, hallowed by the memories of immortal names.

"Before I thank the living, let me look to those dead whose immortal spirits dwell within these walls, (looking at the portraits that adorn the walls,) living in an unimperishable life in the glory, freedom and happiness of your great united Republic destined, as I confidently hope, to become the corner stone of the future of Humanity.

"Yes, there they are—the glorious architects of the Independence of this republic, grown up to such a giant in such a short time.

"There is Thomas Stone; there, your Demosthenes, Samuel Chase; there, Charles Carroll, of Carrollton, who designedly added that epithet to the significance of his name, that nobody should be mistaken about who was the Carroll who dared the noble deed, and was rewarded by his being the last of his illustrious companions whom God called to the heavenly paradise, after he had long enjoyed the paradise of freedom on earth; and here, William Paca—all of them signers of the Declaration of American Independence, that noblest, that happiest page in manhood's history.

"How happy that man must have been, (pointing to the portrait of Governor Paca,) having to govern this sovereign State on that happy day, when within these very walls was ratified the act which, by the recognition of your very enemy, raised your country to the seat of an independent nation on earth.

"Ye spirits of the departed! cast a ray of consolation by the thundering voice of the nation, over that down-trodden land whose elect chief, a wandering exile, for having dared to imitate the inspiration of your manly hearts, lays the trembling hopes of an oppressed continent before the generous heart of your people— now not only an independent nation, but also a mighty, glorious power on earth.

"Alas! what a difference in the success of two like deeds! Have I not done what ye did! Yes, I have. Was the cause for which I did it not alike sacred and just as yours? It was. Or have we not fought to sustain it with equal resolution as your brethren did? Bold though it be to claim a glory such as America has, I am bold to claim it, and say, yes, we did. And yet what a difference in the result! And where this difference? Only out of that single circumstance, that while you in your struggle met with assistance, we in ours met not even "fair play," because when we fought there was nobody on earth to maintain th laws of nature's God.

"America was silent, and England did not stir; and while you were assisted by a French *King*, we were forsaken by the French *Republic*—itself now trodden down because it has forsaken us!

"Well, we are not broken yet. There is hope for us, because here is a God in Heaven and an America on earth! May be hat our nameless woes were necessary, that the glorious destiny of America be fulfilled—that after it was an asylum for the oppressed, it became, by regenerating Europe, the pillar of mankind's liberty.

"Oh, it is not a mere capricious change of fate that the exiled Governor of that land whose name, four years ago, was scarcely known on your glorious shores, and which now, (oh, let me have the blessings of this faith!) is near the generous heart of America—it is not a mere chance that Hungary's exiled chief thanks the Senators of Maryland for the high honor of a public welcome in that very Hall where the first Continental Congress met, where your great Republic's glorious Constitution was framed, where the treaty of acknowledged independence was ratified, and where you, Senators, guard, with steady hand, the sovereign State rights of your own State united to thirty others, not to make you less free, but to make you more mighty,—to make you a power on earth.

"I believe there is the hand of God in history. You assigned a place in this hall of freedom to the memory of Chatham, for having been just to America by opposing the Stamp Act, which awoke your nation to resistance.

"Now the people of England think as once Pitt the elder thought, and honor with deep reverence the memory of your Washington.

"But suppose the England of Lord Chatham's time had thought as Chatham did; and his burning words had moved the English aristocracy to be just toward the Colonies: those four men there (pointing to the portraits,) had not signed your country's independence; Washington were perhaps a name "unknown, unhonored and unsung," and this proud constellation of your glorious stars had perhaps not yet risen on mankind's sky—instead of being now about to become the sun of freedom. It is thus Providence acts.

"Let me hope, Sir, that Hungary's unmerited fate was necessary in order that your stars should become such a sun. Sir, I stand perhaps upon the very spot where your Washington stood, a second Cincinnatus, consummating the greatest act of his life.

The walls which now listen to my humble words, listened once to the words of his republican virtue, immortal by their very modesty. Let me upon this sacred spot express my confident belief that if he stood here now, he would tell you that his prophecy is fulfilled; that you are mighty enough to defy any power on earth in a just cause, and he would tell you that there never was and never will be a cause more just than the cause of Hungary, being, as it is, the cause of oppressed humanity.

"Sir, I thank the Senate of Maryland in my country's name for the honor of your generous welcome. Sir, I entreat the Senate kindly to remember my down-trodden fatherland.

"I bid you farewell, feeling heart and soul purified, and the re-adoption of my desires strengthened by the very air of this ancient City of Providence."

And thus through the grand constellation of States, Kossuth moves in an orbit all his own, leaving a track more luminous than their glory.

We shall suffer eclipse when he departs to resume a chair more honorable and resplendent than the throne of the Cæsar's; that of

PRESIDENT OF THE REPUBLIC OF HUNGARY.

CHAPTER XII.

KOSSUTH'S MISSION—ELOQUENCE AND CHARACTER.

KOSSUTH came hither to plead for Hungary. By the people of the United States, it was expected that America would be the Exile's home. Had his personal safety and ease been the motives of life, he doubtless would have selected a quiet residence under our stars and stripes, and gathered around him his family, to enjoy the tranquillity for which he intensely longs. But could Washington have left Valley Forge, or the banks of the Delaware for repose in the fairest and most friendly clime of Europe? Neither could Kossuth rest in the time of *his* country's need. With an unselfish patriotism apparent in all his actions, he sank himself in the cause of Hungary; and both in England and the New World, frankly and feelingly announced his mission. When he stood before the masses in Castle Garden, to introduce himself to the people of a hemisphere; he boldly defined his republican principles, then nobly set forth his errand here:

"I beg leave, frankly and openly, to state the following points: FIRST, That I take it to be the duty of honor and principle not to meddle with whatever party question of your own domestic affairs. I claim for my country the right to dispose of itself; so I am resolved, and must be resolved, to respect the same principle here and everywhere. SECONDLY, I profess, highly and openly, my admiration for the glorious principle of union, on which stands the mighty pyramid of your greatness, and upon the basis of which you have grown, in the short period of seventy-five years, to a prodigious giant, the living wonder of the world. I have the most warm wish that the star-spangled banner of the United States may forever be floating, united and one, the proud ensign of mankind's divine origin. And, THIRDLY, I beg leave, frankly to state, that my aim is to restore my fatherland to the full enjoyment of that act of Declaration of Independence, which is fully entitled to be recognized by the people of the United States, whose very existence is founded upon a similar declaration of independence. Thus having expounded my aim, I beg leave to state that I came not to your glorious shores to enjoy a happy rest. I came not with the intention to gather triumphs of personal distinction, or to be the object of popular shows; but I came a humble petitioner in my country's name, as its freely chosen constitutional chief. I came not with the intention to gather triumphs of personal distinction, but to entreat your generous aid; and then it is to this aim that I will devote every moment of my time with the more assiduity, the more restlessness, as every moment may bring a report of events which may call me to hasten to my place on the battle-field, where the great, and I hope the last battle will be fought between Liberty and Despotism. A moment marked by the finger of God to be so near, that every hour of delay of your generous aid may prove fatally disastrous to oppressed humanity."

He believes that England and America, have the moral power, to prevent by their united voice, the ruthless march of Russia upon the Magyar plains. That the United States alone, should take the attitude of protection to Hungary, against the intervention of the Autocrat. How far the application of "the golden rule," to national policy, will harmonize with the first law of nature and nations, self-preservation, is the problem our statesmen will attempt to solve. That it *might* lead to war Kossuth does not deny. Upon this point he remarks, in his address to the BAR:

"But I may be answered, 'Well, if we (the United States) make such a declaration of non-admission of the interference of Russia in Hungary, (because that is the practical meaning of the word, I will not deny,) and Russia will not respect our declaration, then we might have to go to war.' And there is the rub. Well, I am not the man to decline the consequences of my principles. I will not steal into your sympathy by slippery evasion. Yes, gentlemen, I confess, should Russia not respect such a declaration of your country, then you are obliged—literally obliged, to go to war, or else be prepared to be degraded before mankind from your dignity. Yes, I confess that would be the case. But you are powerful enough to defy any power on earth in a just cause, as your Washington's—and so may God help me, as it is true, that never was there yet a more just cause. There was enough of war on the earth for ambition, or egotistical interests, even for womanly whims—to give to humanity the glorious example of a great people going even to war, not for egotistical interest, but for justice, for the law of nations, for the law of nature and of nature's God—and it will be no great mischief after all.

"It will be the noblest, the greatest glory which a nation yet has earned; nobler and greater than any nation yet has earned; and its greatest benefit will be, that it will be the last war, because it will make the laws of nations to become a reality, which nobody will dare violate, seeing them put under the safeguard of all humanity. It will be the last war, because it will make nations contented—contented because free. And what still must be foremostly considered, you have nothing to fear by that war for your own country—for your own security If it were otherwise, I never would have pronounced that wish. But I am certain that there is not a single citizen of the United States, who would not agree with me that there is no plausible issue of that supposed war which could affect the security of your own country. I think, gentlemen, it is time to get rid of the horror to '*review former opinions*,' as Mr. Rush says. I believe it is time to establish that will, and I believe the people of the United States are called to establish it, that policy must be made subservient to justice, international law, and the everlasting principle of right. There is an axiom in jurisprudence, which I hope you will not contradict: 'Laws were a vain word if nobody were to execute them.' Unhappy mankind! that was the condition of thy common laws until now—every despot ready to violate them, but no power on earth to defend them. People of the United States! here I bow before thee; and claim out of the bottom of my National Declaration. Raise thy young gigantic arm, and be the executive power of Nature and of Nature's God; which laws thou hast invoked when thou hast proclaimed thy independence. Protect them; defend them forever—if thou hast to go to war for it! That will be a holier war than ever yet was, and the blessing of God will be with thee."

That the Christian Chieftain is in advance of public opinion in the sublime purity and comprehensive sweep of his views, is evident. But he has taken his position, encircled by immutable principles of right and justice; and calmly waits the issue, leaning upon the arm of the invisible God.

He asks for money, not to cancel the expense of past conflicts, which amounts to $35,000,000; but to prepare for the hastening and decisive hour of liberty's battle. We cannot doubt the fact he affirms, that the next struggle with Austria will be fiery and brief. It is for this "exigence," he purposes to be ready, and is persuaded that myriads in every land will watch the tide of victory, when that death-grapple of despotism in Europe shall come. He dwells with an intensity of sadness upon the possibility that the United States will shrink from crossing the desolating path of Russia among the nations, that finds a responsive echo in every patriotic heart. Whether the mournful adieu he imagined possible in his appeal at Philadelphia, be his or not, the moral influence of his mission will be priceless and abiding.

He has awakened, universally, deeper reflection on the import of our Constitution, and upon human rights, than has before been known amid the feverish excitements of a young and rapidly growing nation.

Whatever are his private views of the strange and melancholy anomaly of American slavery, he has carefully and justly avoided allusion to the institutions of the South. Though Kossuth deeply hates oppression which has pressed out the life-blood of noble ancestors, yet would he not touch a chord of this mighty union. He knows that the brotherhood can not be *dissolved*. It may be severed by the fratricidal sword, and the bleeding fragments lie palpitating beneath the tears of patriots, and the loud scorn of Kings. But the Union cannot be DISSOLVED! And they are dangerous and lawless men, who talk lightly of a deed, which would make the sighing masses of a continent, mourners around the grave of the American Republic, while "Devils gathered to chaunt our funeral song." Kossuth abhors oppression, and at a sacrifice of millions of dollars, on the part of the nobility of Hungary, abolished serfdom at the beginning of his splendid career. But he knows that with our gigantic sins, this broad Empire of States, is the hope of besieged and panting Europe. That *principle*, and not *violence* must correct and purify the inheritance of the Pilgrims, who were willing to concede, what could not be denied without the failure of the grand experiment of an all-embracing Union. At Philadelphia, he thus alluded to the dastardly attempts of citizens here, whose aims have never intersected the wide horizon of his luminous thought, to tarnish his name at home, and paralyze his efforts abroad :

"The Committee of Arrangements received anonymous letters containing printed slips calumniating my personal character, and going even so far as to calumniate the very honor of my nation by stating that it is not me, but Austria, which had freed a population of nine millions in Hungary, and that I was an instrument of the aristocracy to keep these nine millions in bondage. Now, as to myself, I have the consolation of the German Poet :

'Those are not the worst fruits, which the wasps assail !'

but as for the character of our struggle and the immortal honor of my nation, sanctified by the death of thousands of our people—unnamed demigods—and by the blood of our numerous martyrs, that there can be found one single man amongst the millions of humanity, capable to lie so in the very face of the living nation as to call the noon-sun, midnight—moonlight, darkness—fire, ice ; so as to belie history—not of by-gone ages, but of yesterday—stating, not that Nero was a Marcus Aurelian, but that we fought for Aristocracy—and the Despotic, Aristocratic, Jesuitic Austria, has fought for Democracy and liberty; to state that things which were experienced by millions of my countrymen and witnessed by the whole world, did not happen; though the whole living generation of mankind, except the two years' old infant, has seen, heard, and witnessed it—to say that just the contrary happened—indeed, gentlemen, this is a sacrilege for which the human tongue has yet no word, but it is also a great trial to my country to see that it is so highly just, so poor, so virtuous, that our mortal foe, our oppressor, our hangman, cannot even try any plea of not guilty, but by stealing our merit and hanging the mantle of our virtue upon his own impious shoulders. This is indeed a trial unparalleled in history; but let me proudly say, this trial we have merited. Having for me, God, Justice, History—my nation—you—the world—let me have some self-esteem, some humble sentiment of my own moral dignity, and pass over such base calumny with disgust. But the third incident is yet more curious if possible; and the more abominable, because to arrest my movements, a nameless enemy in the dark, intended even to wound the honor of your own fellow-citizens. I received a letter—again a forged one. The gentleman whose name the forger so abused, has declared to me that it is a vile and stupid forgery.

"Now such a letter, and yet a forgery, indeed, is a despicable trick; but though it is a forgery, still there is one thing which forces me to some humble remarks, precisely because I know not whence comes the blow. I am referring to these words. 'Your intervention or non-intervention sentiments are unsuited to the region of Pennsylvania, situated as she is on the borders of several slaveholding States.' I avail myself of this opportunity to declare once more that I never did nor will do anything which, in the remotest way, could interfere with the matter alluded to, nor with whatever other domestic question of your united Republic, or of a single State of it. I have declared frankly and openly several times, and on all and every opportunity I have proved to be as good as my word. I dare say that even the pledge of the word of honor of an honest man should not be considered a sufficient security in that respect. The publicly avowed basis of my humble claims, and the unavoidable logic of it, would prove to be a decisive authority. What is the ground upon which I stand before the mighty tribunal of the public opinion of the United States? It is the sovereign right of every nation to dispose of its own domestic concerns. What is it, I humbly ask of the United States? It is that they may generously be pleased to protect this sovereign right of every nation against the encroaching violence of Russia. It is, therefore, eminently clear, that this being my ground, I cannot and will not meddle with any domestic question whatever of this Republic. Indeed, I more and more perceive that to speak with Hamlet, 'There are more things in heaven and earth than was dreamed of in my philosophy.' But still I will stand upright on however slippery ground, by taking strong hold of that legitimate fence of not meddling in your domestic questions."

It cannot, however, be doubted that Kossuth's sublime aspirations for suffering humanity everywhere, have kindled a more earnest prayer for the peaceful removal of oppression from beneath the stars and stripes; a banner bearing the hue of blood, but not of *race*. He has with subduing fervor rebuked the demoniac spirit South and North, that would cease to think soberly and act wisely, for all classes, climes and coming years; forgetful of the fearful and glorious past, through which sounds continually in the nation's ear, the Farewell of Washington, who though less brilliant than the exile whom we delight to honor has never had a superior on every occasion; and who can have no successor of purer fame. A fame that shines on with the radiance of a Cynosure in the heavens across which comets blaze, and where one star differs from another in glory. Kossuth cannot *stoop* to party corruption and fraud, and has not yet fully comprehended the selfish policy of designing men, who breathe the air of freedom, and were educated under the hallowed influences that stream from the Sanctuary of Religion.

He has revived the remembrance of Puritan Christianity, whose influence has been departing from our land. A defender of the Bible, and necessarily of the Sabbath, he illustrates the historical truth, that a Protestant Faith is indispensable to the success of a popular leader, and a popular government. He has sent abroad anew the eternal verities which have been thrown under the heated wheels of progress, and too nearly forgotten, that in national no less than individual life, "Morality and religion are indispensable supports. In vain would that man claim the tribute of patriotism, who should labor to subvert these great pillars of human happiness, these firmest props of the duties of men and citizens." His distinct utterance of these evangelical sentiments, have gathered about him the clergy of this Republic.

They will embalm the memory of Kossuth in their prayers, whatever be his future on the battle-plain of Kingdoms. No hero and statesman ever shed around his path of glory a more benign and enduring influence. Men devoted to the affairs of commerce—merchants, traders of all kinds, bankers and brokers, find the lower currents in which they have been sailing, crossed by a breeze of heroic feeling. The nobler elements of human nature in them perhaps long slumbering or moving sluggishly, are quickened into fresh life. They gain higher aspirations; they gain a perception of higher duties; they find themselves drawn by diviner sympathies; they feel unwonted satisfaction and joy in experiencing unwonted emotions, but emotions which they know are worthy of human nature; and they find a higher value in their being, in nobler ends to be pursued. They admire the man, nay, more, they unconsciously bless him as the occasion of much good to themselves. It is a sublime and glorious thing for a whole people to come under the potent influence of the thoughts and words of a great and good spirit.

And so does the exile have continually the affection of unnumbered hearts, strangers to him, and he will leave us with a tearful benediction, when the bark that bears him away, disappears upon the infinity of waters; typical of his fame in time, and his immortality beyond, we hope for humanity's sake, its *distant* horizon!

THE ELOQUENCE AND CHARACTER OF KOSSUTH.

Kossuth's personal appearance before a popular assembly is highly prepossessing. His hair lies tastefully above a forehead broad and prominent, his oriental features are distinctly marked by suffering, and his expressive blue eye, has a fascinating light twinkling in its depths, that flashes forth simultaneously with the utterance of a sublime truth or deep emotion. Some one has remarked that "Webster looks as if he knew all the past, Kossuth as if he knew the *present and future.*" The Magyar evidently discerns vividly passing events, even the minutiæ of what is around him, while seer-like, he sadly gazes into the shadows of coming years, whose swift events shall decide the destiny of his fatherland. Much has been said of his smile. There is always, even in his moments of ordinary tranquillity, a pleasant expression, reminding one of the moonlight lingering round a scarred and unyielding castle; but when a sentiment of cordiality or hope rises to his lips, it becomes a smile of great sweetness and power. There is however a dignity of manner that repels undue familiarity. As Washington unconsciously wore the majesty of a transcendant mind dwelling in the atmosphere of moral purity and beauty, so Kossuth has the singular greatness of consecrated genius, "throned upon his brow." His gestures are graceful, and his whole bearing that of a man who has a pressing and solemn work to do.

There can be but one opinion of his oratory. The statesmen and the masses of two continents have listened to his eloquence with parted lips and moistened eye. It is not that he is cheered, and saluted wherever he appears with tumultuous applause, which decides his power in addressing popular assemblies. He uses no rhetorical flourishes to arrest attention—he never appeals to the prejudices of classes in society. He offers no golden Utopia to the suffering poor, and makes no assaults on the rich. He is simple, grave, and deliberate. He often hesitates in translating from

Magyar into English. He stands calmly, and with the sublime dignity of true greatness, and utters *truth*. And yet his auditory are thrilled; he confounds opponents, and warms the stoical.

Reporters have been too excited to proceed accurately with their notes, and a glow of mysterious delight, like an atmosphere, has pervaded the hall through which floated his melodious tones. In England, men who have heard the eloquence of parliament for half a century, and could listen motionless to advocates whose fame is wide as the empire, while making juries weep, have felt their pulses leap to the sound of his voice. They describe his eloquence as "Shaksperean," "Miltonian," and "most thrilling."

"Next week," says the Editor of the *Leeds Mercury*, after describing on Saturday, November 15th, some of the most effective passages of his speeches at Manchester and Birmingham, "may enable us to recover a cool and wise judgment after the too inspiring appeals of the suffering patriot, whose voice yet rings in our ears like a trumpet with a silver sound."

In his native tongue, his fiery words must fall like rockets, each conveying a great thought or elevated sentiment, with the force of unhesitating delivery, and undisturbed flow of ideas. We have watched him with careful and near observation. And while something may be attributed to the oriental romance and historical interest which attend the Magyar, there is beneath this a power unequalled by any departed or living orator. And it is altogether moral and intellectual. The fascination of a great and pure soul, united with that of a starry mind, whose rays stream on all, is the source of his mastery. He holds up in a flood of illumination truths that lie in the chaos of commonest minds—and sweeps with gentle yet familiar hand the chords of human feeling.

In illustration of the grandeur and simplicity with which he scatters "the living coals of truth," we take a few extracts from his speeches. Alluding to the demonstration of sympathy he met, he explains the reason of this unusual excitement in his address at Manchester:—

"There are some who endeavor to contract the demonstrations of sympathy which I have had the honor to meet, to the narrow circle of personality. They would fain make you believe, that there is nothing more in these demonstrations than a matter of fashion, a transitory ebullition of public feeling, passing away without leaving a trace like the momentary bubble; or, at the utmost, a tribute of popular approbation to the bravery of a gallant people in a just cause, and of consolation to their immerited misfortunes. But I say, it is not so. I say, may no nation on earth have reason once to repent of having contemptuously disregarded these my words, only because it was but I who said them. I say, that the very source of these demonstrations is, the instinctive feeling of the people that the destiny of mankind has come to the turning point of centuries: it is the cry of alarm upon the ostensible approach of universal danger; it is the manifestation of the instinct of self-preservation, roused by the instinctive knowledge of the fact, that the decisive struggle of the destiny of Europe was near, and that no people, no country, can remain unaffected by the issue of this great struggle of principles. A great orator has told you that the despotic governments of Europe have become weak. So it is. The despotic governments of Europe feel their approaching death, and therefore they will come to the death-struggle. I am nothing, but the opportunity which elicited the hidden spark—the opportunity at which the pre-existing instinctive appreciation of approaching danger caused in every nation the cry to burst forth—the loud cry of horror. Or else, how could even the most daring sophist explain the fact of the universality of these demonstrations, not restricted to where I am present—not restricted to any climate—not restricted to the peculiar character of a people—not restricted to a singular state organization—but spreading through the world like the pulsation of one heart—like the spark of an electric battery. The addresses, full of the most generous sentiments, which I am honored with in England, are the effects of my presence; but I am but the spark which kindles a feeling which has long existed, from the people of the metropolis down to the solitary hamlets, hidden by neighboring mountains from the vicissitudes of public life.

* * * * * * *

"Is this personal? What have I in my person, in my present, in my future, not to justify, but even to explain this universality of demonstration? Nothing, entirely nothing; only the knowledge that I am a friend of freedom, the friend of the people—so I am nothing but the opportunity for the manifestation of the instinctive feeling of so many nations, that the dragon of oppression draws near, and that the St. George of liberty is ready to wrestle with him. A philosopher was once questioned, how could he prove the existence of God? 'Why,' answered he, 'by opening my eyes. God is seen everywhere; in the growth of the grass, and in the movements of the stars; in the warbling of the lark, and in the thunder of heaven.' Even so I prove that the decisive struggle in mankind's destiny draws near; I appeal to the sight of your eyes; I appeal to the pulsations of your hearts, and to the judgments of your minds. You know, you see, you feel that the judgment is drawing near. How blind are those men who have the affectation to believe, or at least to assert, that it is only certain men who push to revolution the continent of Europe, which also, but for their revolutionary acts, would be quiet and contented! Contented! With what? With oppression and servitude? France contented, with its constitution turned into a pasquinade? Germany contented, with being turned into a fold of sheep, pent up to be shorn by some thirty petty tyrants? Switzerland contented, with the threatening ambition of encroaching despots? Italy contented, with the King of Naples, or with the priestly government of Rome, the worst of human inventions? Austria, Bohemia, Croatia, Dalmatia, contented with having been driven to butchery, and after having been deceived, with having been plundered, oppressed, and laughed at as fools? Poland contented with being murdered? Hungary, my poor Hungary, contented with being more than murdered—buried alive? for it *is* alive! What I feel is but a weak pulsation of that feeling which pervades the breasts of the people of my country. Prussia contented with slavery? Vienna contented? Lombardy, Pesth, Milan, Venice, Brescia, Ragusa, Prague contented? Contented with having been bombarded, burned, plundered, sacked, and their populations butchered! Half of the European continent contented—with the scaffold, with the hangman, with the prison, with having no political rights at all; but having to pay innumerable millions for the highly beneficial purpose of being kept in a state of serfdom! That is the condition of the continent of Europe; and is it not ridiculous and absurd in men to prate about individuals disturbing the peace and tranquillity of Europe?"

Perhaps there is nothing in the range of oratory, and no passage besides in Kossuth's numberless speeches, so grandly touching and beautiful, as that which refers to the effect of his appeal to the Diet of Hungary, July 4, 1848 :—

" Reluctant to present the neck of the realm to the deadly stroke which aimed at its very life, and anxious to bear up against tne horrors of fate, and manfully to fight the battle of legitimate defence, scarcely had I spoken the word—scarcely had I added that the defence would require 200,000 men, and 80,000,000 of florins, when the spirit of freedom moved through the hall, and nearly 400 representatives rose as one man, and, lifting their right arms towards God, solemnly said, 'We grant it, freedom or death!' [The solemnity of gesture and voice with which Kossuth uttered these words, says the reporter, produced a powerful effect on the Assembly.] Thus they spoke, and there they stood in calm and silent majesty, awaiting what further word might fall from my lips. And for myself; it was my duty to speak, but the grandeur of the moment and the rushing waves of sentiment benumbed my tongue. A burning tear fell from my eyes, a sigh of adoration to the Almighty Lord fluttered on my lips; and, bowing low before the majesty of my people, as I bow now before you, gentlemen, I left the tribunal silently, speechless, mute. [Kossuth here paused for a few moments, overpowered by his emotion—and for this remark, too, we are indebted to the reporter—with which the company deeply sympathized.] Pardon me my emotion—the shadows of our martyrs passed before my eyes; I heard the millions of my native land once more shouting 'liberty or death!'"

Says an English writer who was present: "Deeply sympathizing with him, the whole company cheered responsive to his feelings, and every man, we believe, if he could be questioned, would have declared that never in his life, neither from the pulpit nor the judgment-seat—neither from the bar nor from the hustings—neither in Parliament nor in any public assembly, had he heard such thrilling words as were uttered by Kossuth at Birmingham. We have heard him speak as well as read his speeches; we have listened also to most of the great orators of the last thirty years; and nothing which we ever heard or read

—the most fervent from Dr. Chalmers, the most elaborate from Lord Brougham, the most neat and finished from Lord Lyndhurst, the most pointed and poetical from Canning, the most rounded and impressive from the late Lord Grey, the most terse from Cobden, the most sparkling from W. J. Fox—ever appeared so effectually impressive as the oratory of Kossuth."

He honors justly and gloriously the common soldiery, who are left on the ensanguined field, "uncoffined, unknelled and unknown;" the brave fellows who make their warm hearts the bulwark of their country before the cannon and bayonets of the foe.

"Perhaps there might be some glory in inspiring such a nation, and to such a degree. But I cannot accept the praise. No; it is not I who inspired the Hungarian people—it was the Hungarian people who inspired me. Whatever I thought, and still think—whatever I felt, and still feel—is but a feeble pulsation of that heart which in the breast of my people beats. The glory of battles is ascribed to the leaders in history; theirs are the laurels of immortality. And yet on meeting the danger, they knew that, alive or dead, their name will upon the lips of the people forever live. How different, how much purer, is the light spread on the image of thousands of the people's sons, who, knowing that where they fall they will lay unknown, their names unhonored and unsung, but who, nevertheless, animated by the love of freedom and fatherland, went on calmly, singing national anthems, against the batteries, whose cross-fire vomited death and destruction on them, and took them without firing a shot—they who fell, falling with the shout, 'Hurrah for Hungary!' And so they died by thousands, THE UNNAMED DEMIGODS! Such is the people of Hungary.

"With us, those who beheld the nameless victims of the love

of country, lying on the death-field beneath Buda's walls, met but the impression of a smile on the frozen lips of the dead, and the dying answered those who would console but by the words, 'Never mind, Buda is ours. Hurrah for the fatherland!' So they spoke and died. He who witnessed such scenes, not as exception, but as a constant rule, of thousands of the people's nameless sons; he who saw the adolescent weep when told he was yet too young to die for his land; he who saw the sacrifices of spontaneity; he who heard what a fury spread over the people on hearing of the catastrophe; he who marked his behavior towards the victors after all was lost; he who knows what sort of curse is mixed in the prayers of the Magyar, and knows what sort of sentiment is burning alike in the breast of the old and of the child, of the strong man and of the tender wife, and ever will be burning on, till the hour of national resurrection strikes; he who is aware of all this, will surely bow before this people with respect, and will acknowledge, with me, that such a people wants not to be inspired, but that it is an everlasting source of inspiration itself."

Kossuth is properly regarded as the impersonation of patriotic feeling. It was this unselfish love of country, this willing sacrifice upon her altar, that bound to him in the affection of ardent boyhood, his countrymen. He modestly refers to this trustful fondness of his nation for their chief: "That is the key of the faith and truth my people have in me, their plain unpretending brother—a faith neither troubled by a deluge of calumnies nor broke by adversity. It is that my people take me still for the incarnation of their wishes, their affections, and their hopes."

With the resources of history and literature at his command, and freedom the ruling passion of his soul, he reaches the millions in every realm and in all the walks of life, with accents they cannot forget. The captive eagle hears "the scream of the free bird of sun," from his mountain home, and stirs his drooping plumage. And every weary, struggling spirit, however environed and fettered, listens to the words of the gifted Magyar, who more vividly than human tongue has before conveyed, utters the everlasting principles of right and liberty. Therefore, in kingdoms and republics, and before all classes, he is the same consistent advocate of the essential equality of man, and his two-fold destiny. He reads on the imperishable nature of the humblest being the image and superscription of God, and the heirship of a limitless destiny beyond the passing and visible. He is a deeply religious man; and his eloquence has been styled among his own people, "of the *Psalmist order.*" There is a prophetic fervor in his speeches at times— an undisguised current of devotional feeling, that lends a sacred magic to his oratory.

He shows most distinctly the influence of the discipline he has had in dungeons and in exile, and recognizes God in it all. Stroke after stroke has been laid on his patient heart, and brushing the tear aside, he again lifts his voice for Hungary. That he failed in decision when it might have saved his country is true; but it was not weakness of character. His sensitive sympathy recoiled from inflicting pain, and to sign a death-warrant was impossible. Besides, he was slow to embrace the dreaded issue of open and decisive contest with the monarchy under whose shadow the nation had lain so long. He has learned lessons since of war and civil policy, which shall yet bless his fatherland. He is a good, great and brilliant reformer—the political Luther of Europe.

We have contemplated the history of Hungary, and have grieved over her fall. We leave her bleeding and bound—the heel of the oppressor on her neck, and the iron of avenging tyranny in her heart; but the star of hope shines in her firmament, and forms a rainbow of promise in her tears. There is a future for Hungary. The shadow goes not back on the world's dial, and despotism must die. Its corpse shall soon be wrapped in the robes of royalty and laid with the ashes of the past. There is a glorious goal towards which Humanity is ceaselessly marching. Though disasters thicken, HUMANITY CANNOT BE SHIPWRECKED. The bark may seem lost amid the billows and the storm, but the richly freighted ship, battles with the surges, and again proudly rides the foam.

Around Hungary hover bankrupt Austria, whose national character and aims have been portrayed; and feeble, dependent Prussia; and overshadowing both, with half of Europe besides, Russia, cold, mighty and watchful, waits the possibility of grasping the weaker powers that encircle her vast domain. France has yielded to the arrogant pretensions of "Napoleon the little," and is no more than "a pawn upon the political chess-board of Europe, moved by the iron finger of the Czar." Turkey's crescent pales in the auroral splendor of the throne of the autocrat, and sheds a trembling light upon the path of freedom's exiles, to secure the protection of the free. The masses in all central Europe are murmuring in feverish unrest, and ready to shake the vipers of oppression from their hands, and take the weapons of battle.

The hour of retribution is near. Like the breaking up of a frozen polar sea, the crust of ages is heaving, and shall sink in its rending the glittering thrones of unrighteous authority. The subjects of "His Holiness," the Pope, are smiling at the forsaken altars, and empty pomp of lying miracles, and ripening for another indignant violation of his sacred seclusion. American progress and liberty, have bombarded Europe, and the common mind is fired for action. There is no human might that can roll again the dead-sea wave of passive obedience to King and Priest, over the awakened millions. Despots may combine, and lean upon the armies that girdle them, but the bayonets shall yet impale the royal victims of popular will.

Kossuth beholds the hastening uprising of the masses, and he expects Hungary to lead in the tumult of battling nations, demanding inalienable rights. The intelligence and protestant faith, indispensable to permanent success, are more prevalent there than among her neighbors. Gifted men are imbued with republican sentiments, and could guide well the ship of State amid the tempest and perils of revolution. Her Chief wanders among the wonders of the New World, the Washington of the Old, and shall bind them together in the ties of brotherhood, and in the common glory of free institutions, and a Christianity unfettered by legislation or priestly claim. The GOVERNOR OF HUNGARY is rekindling at our altars, the torch of oppression's funeral pile.

APPENDIX

ADDRESS TO THE PEOPLE OF THE U. STATES

———•◆•◆•◆•———

TWO YEARS ago, by God's providence, I, who would be only an humble citizen, held in my hands the destiny of the reigning house of Austria.

Had I been ambitious, or had I believed that this treacherous family were so basely wicked as they afterward proved themselves to be, the tottering pillars of their throne would have fallen at my command, and buried the crowned traitors beneath their ruins, or would have scattered them like dust before the tempest, homeless exiles, bearing nothing but the remembrance of their perfidy, and that royalty which they deserved to lose through their own wickedness.

I, however, did not take advantage of these favorable circumstances, though the entire freedom of my dear native land was the only wish of my heart. My requests were of that moderate nature which, in the condition of Hungary and Europe, seemed best fitted for my countrymen. I asked of the King, not the complete independence of my beloved country—not even any new rights or privileges—but simply these three things :—

1. That the inalienable rights sanctioned by a thousand years, and by the constitution of my fatherland, should be guaranteed by a national and responsible Administration.

2. That every inhabitant of my country, without regarding language or religion, should be free and equal before the law—all classes having the same privileges and protection from the law.

3. That all the people of the Austrian empire that acknowledged the same person as emperor whom we Hungarians recognized as King, and the same laws of succession, should have restored their ancient constitutional rights, of which they had been unjustly despoiled, modified to suit their wants and the spirit of the age.

The first demand was not for any new grant or concession, but simply a fresh guarantee. In the arrangement made with our ancestors, when, by their free will, they elevated the house of Hapsburg to the throne, a condition was made that the King should preserve the independence and constitution of the country. This independence and this constitution were the very vitality of our national being. During three centuries twelve Kings of the house of Hapsburg had sworn in the presence of the eternal God, before ascending the throne, that they would preserve our independence and the constitution; and their lives are but a history of perpetual and accursed perjury. Yet such conduct did not weaken our fidelity. No nation ever manifested more faithfulness to their rulers; and, though we poor Hungarians made endless sacrifices, often at the expense of our national welfare—though these Kings, in times of peace, drew their support from us, and in times of war or danger relied upon the unconquerable strength of our army—though we ever trusted in their words, they deceived us a thousand times and made our condition worse.

While other nations were able to apply all their energies to promote the general welfare, and to develop their means of happiness, we had to stand on guard, like the watchmen mentioned in Scripture, for three centuries, to prevent our treacherous Kings from destroying entirely the foundation of our national existence—our constitution and independence.

I, as the representative of my countrymen, asked nothing more than a constitutional Ministry, whose responsibility would prevent the King from violating his oath.

The second demand was still less for any political right. We asked for nothing more than a reform in the internal administration of the State; a simple act of justice which the aristocracy owed the people: and in this how much the King would have gained! The strength of his throne would have been increased tenfold by thus winning the affections of his faithful people.

The third demand was prompted by humanity and fraternal feeling. It was the proper and holy mission of our nation as the oldest member of the empire, and possessing a constitutional form of government, to raise its voice in behalf of those sister nations under the same ruler, and who were united to us by so many ties of relationship. Lovers of freedom, we would not ask liberty for ourselves alone; we would not boast of privileges that others did not enjoy, but desired to be free, in fellowship with free nations around us. This motive was inspired by the conviction that two crowns—a constitutional and a despotic crown—could not be worn by the same head, no more than two opposing dispositions can harmonize in the same breast, or than a man can be good and evil at the same time.

The King and Royal family granted these requests, appealing to the sanctity of their oaths as a guarantee of their fulfilment; and I —weak in myself, but strong through the confidence of my countrymen, and the noble sympathy of the Austrian people—proclaimed everywhere, amid the raging storm of revolution, that "the house of Austria should stand; for, by the blessing of the Almighty, it had

begun to move in the right direction, and would be just to its people."
It stood; and stood, too, at a time when, whatever might have been the fate of Hungary, the revolutionary tempest, under my direction, would have blown away this antiquated and helpless dynasty like chaff before the winds of Heaven.

I not only preserved the house of Austria, but placed in its hands the materials of a long and glorious future—the foundation of an indestructible power in the affections of 32,000,000 people. I tendered them the fidelity and assistance of my own heroic Hungary, which alone was able to defend them against the assaults of the world. I afforded them the glorious opportunity—more glorious than had ever been presented before—of establishing an impenetrable barrier to protect freedom, civilization and progess against the Cossack power which now threatens Europe. To attain this honor, this glory, one thing only was necessary—that they should remain faithful to their oaths. But when was it that Austria was not treacherous? We look in vain for as much honor as is found even among robbers, in the Hapsburg family.

On the very day they signed the grant of those moderate demands of the Hungarian people, and solemnly swore before God and the nation to maintain them, they secretly resolved and planned the most cruel conspiracy against us. They determined to break their oaths, to desolate the land with insurrection, conflagration, and blood, till, feeble and exhausted under the burden of a thousand miseries, Hungary might be struck from the roll of living nations. They then hoped, by the power of the bayonet, and, if necessary, by the arms of Russia, to erect a united and consolidated empire, like the Russian, of sixteen various nations; they hoped to realize their long-conceived purpose of making themselves an absolute Power.

Never were so many hellish arts used against a nation before. Not suspecting a counter-revolution or an attack, we were not prepared to defend ourselves when suddenly we were surprised by danger. The perfidious Hapsburg, destitute of all shame, and rejoicing in the anticipation of an easy victory, hesitated not to disclose before the civilized world their horrible plans—to subjugate us by the force of arms, to excite hatred of race, to call in the aid of robbers, incendiaries, and reckless insurgents.

At this crisis of great danger, when many of our ablest men even were ready to yield themselves to this degree of destruction, I stood among those who called the nation to arms; and, confiding in a just God, we cursed the cowards who were preparing to abandon their native land, to submit to a wicked despotism, and to purchase a miserable existence by sacrificing liberty. I called the nation to arms in self-defence. I acted not with blind presumption, and emotions of despair found no place in my breast—for he who despairs is not fit to guide a people. I estimated the valor and power of my country and on the verge of a fearful struggle I had the faith to promise victory, if Hungary would remain true to herself, and fortify her breast with the impulsive fire of a strong will.

To sustain the stern resolution, to combat such an enemy, we were supported, first, above everything, by our unshaken confidence in God, whose ways are past finding out but who supports the right, and blesses the cause of an honest people fighting for freedom; secondly, by a love of country and the holy desire of liberty, which make the child a giant, and increase the strength of the valiant; and, thirdly, by your example, noble Americans! you, the chosen nation of the God of Liberty! My countrymen—a religious, a God-venerating people—in whose hearts burned the all-powerful feeling of patriotism, were inspired by the influence of your sublime example.

Free citizens of America! from your history, as from the star of hope in midnight gloom, we drew our confidence and resolution in the doubtful days of severe trial. Accept, in the name of my countrymen, this declaration as a tribute of gratitude. And you, excellent people, who were worthy to be chosen by the Almighty as an example to show the world how to deserve freedom, how to win it, and how to use it—you will allow that the Hungarians, though weaker and less fortunate than you, through the decaying influences of the old European society, are worthy to be your imitators, and that you would be pleased to see the stars of your glorious flag emblazon the double cross of the Hungarian coat-of-arms. When despotism hurled defiance at us, and began the bloody war, your inspiring example upheaved the nation as one man, and legions, with all the means of war, appeared to rise from nothing as the tender grass shoots up after spring showers.

Though we were inferior in numbers to the enemy, and could not compare with their well-trained forces—though our arms were shorter than theirs—yet the heroic sons of Hungary supplied the want of numbers by indomitable bravery, and lengthened their weapons by a step further in advance.

The world knows how bravely the Hungarians fought. And it is not for me, who was identified with the war—who, obeying the wishes of the nation, stood faithfully at the helm of Government—to extol the heroic deeds of my countrymen. I may mention, however, that while every day it became more evident that the heart of Europe beat to the pulsations of the Hungarian struggle, we maintained the unequal conflict alone. Cut off from the rest of the world and all external aid till a year ago, we laid the haughty power of the tyrant house of Hapsburg in the dust; and, had it not been for the intentional and traitorous disregard of my commands by one of our leaders, who afterwards shamefully betrayed the country, not only would the Imperial family have been driven from Vienna, but the entire Austrian nation would have been liberated; and, though by such treason this base family saved themselves from destruction, they were so far humbled in March, 1849, that, not knowing how to be just, they implored foreign aid, and threw themselves at the feet of the Czar.

The Emperor hoped that the Hungarian people would be terrified by his threatenings, and would prefer slavery to death; but he was deceived. He sold his own liberty to Russia, for aid to enslave his people. The choice of a coward is to purchase a miserable, ephemeral existence, even though at the cost of his honor and independence.

The Austrians fought against us, not only with arms and by the aid of traitors, but with studied and unceasing slander. They never ceased to impeach our motives, falsify our conduct, and vaunt the pretended justice of their own cause before the judgment-seat of public opinion. Efforts were constantly made to weaken among the people of Hungary and among the nations of the world that sympathy and force which spring from a righteous cause.

Free citizens of North America! you have given, in spite of these slanders, the fullest sympathy for the cause of my country. We had no opportunity to explain to you our motives and conduct, and refute the libels against us; but we said, and how truly your noble and magnanimous conduct shows it, that such a nation knows how to defend a just and holy cause, and will give us its sympathy; and this conviction inspired us with more confidence. Oh that you had been a neighboring nation; the Old World would now be free, and would not have to endure again those terrible convulsions and rivers of blood which are inevitable. But the end is with God, and He will choose the means to fulfil His purposes.

Ye great and free people, receive the thanks of my country for your noble sympathy, which was a great moral support in our terrible conflict.

When the house of Austria sold itself to the Autocrat, we, who were fatigued with our hard-earned victory, but not subdued or exhausted, saw with apprehension the spectre of Russian invasion—an invasion which violated the laws of nations, which was openly hostile to the cause of civilization, the rights of man, of order, and even to that principle which the diplomacy of Europe calls "the balance of power." I could not believe that the Governments of Europe would permit this invasion; for I believed they would intervene to effect a treaty of peace, if not so much on our account, yet to prevent Austria becoming the vassal of Russia—to check the growing strength and influence of the latter power in the East.

We desired an honorable peace, and were willing to submit to any reasonable terms. We many times tendered the olive-branch. We asked the constitutional Governments of Europe to interpose. They heard us not. The haughty Imperial family, forgetting that they were the real traitors, rejected every proposition, with the defying expression that they "did not treat with rebels." Ay, more—they threw our ambassadors into prison; and one of them, the noblest of

Hungary's sons, they cowardly and impiously murdered. Still we hesitated to tear asunder forever the bonds that united us. Ten months we fought, and fought victoriously, in defence; and it was only when every attempt to bring about an honorable peace failed; when Francis Joseph, who was never our King, dared, in his manifesto of the 4th of March, 1849, to utter the curse "that Hungary should exist no longer;" when there was no hope of arresting the Russian invasion by diplomacy; when we saw that we must fight to save ourselves from being struck off the earth as a nation; when the house of Austria, by its endless acts of injustice and cruelty, and by calling in the aid of a foreign power, had extinguished in the heart of the Hungarian people every spark of affection—then, and then only, after so much patience, the nation resolved to declare its absolute independence. Then spoke the National Assembly the words which had long been uttered by every patriotic tongue— "Francis Joseph, thou beardless young Nero! thou darest to say Hungary shall exist no more! We, the people, answer, we do and will exist; but you and your treacherous house shall stand no longer! You shall no more be Kings of Hungary! Be forever banished, ye perfidious traitors to the nation!"

We were not only ready to accept any terms that were honorable, but we carefully abstained from doing anything which would give the Czar a pretence, which he had long sought, to meddle with our affairs.

The Hungarian nation loved freedom as the best gift of God, but it never thought of commencing a crusade against Kings in the name of liberty. In Hungary there were none of those propagandists who alarm so much the rulers of the Old World. There were no secret societies plotting conspiracies. My countrymen were not influenced by the theories of Communists or Socialists, nor were they what the Conservatives call anarchists. The nation desired justice, and knew how to be just to all, irrespective of rank, language, or religion. A people so worthy of freedom were generous enough to leave something to time, and to be satisfied with a progressive development. No violence was used; no just right was attacked; and even some of those institutions were left undisturbed which, in their principle and origin, were unjust, but which, having existed for centuries, could not be abolished at once with impunity.

The Hungarian people did not wish to oppress any—not even the aristocracy; they were more ready to make sacrifices than to punish the descendants of nobility for the evils of misgovernment, and of those institutions which emanated from their ancestors; nor would they let the many suffer for the sins of the few.

There was no anarchy among us. Even in the bloodiest conflicts, when the human passions are most excited, there was the most perfect order and security of property and person. How did the conduct of my noble countrymen compare with that of the "order-making" Austria? Whenever the whirlwind of war ceased for awhile, where the social elements were left in chaos, the instinctive moral feeling of this incorruptible people, in the absence of all government, preserved better order and safety than legions of police. A common spirit animated the whole nation—no secret aims, no personal or local attacks, but a bold and open defence in the face of the world. Following the example of your great Washington, we adopted as our policy conciliation, justice, and legality, and scrupulously observed the laws of nations.

The Russians and Austrians made the soil of Wallachia the basis of military operations; and the Turkish Government, which either knew not its own interests, or was unable to defend them, silently permitted this violation of treaties and the rights of nations, thus humbling itself and betraying its own weakness. Several times we drove our enemies across the Wallachian boundaries; for it was only necessary for our victorious army to advance into the countries of the Lower Danube to rouse the inhabitants against the Russians, and to transfer the war to their own soil. But we respected the law of nations, and stopped our conquering forces on the confines of Wallachia. Her soil was sacred to us. Austria left Gallicia almost unprotected, and collected all her forces to attack us. Had we at this time sent a small portion of our army to Poland, it would have caused a general insurrection; and that heroic but unfortunate nation would have revenged herself by throwing the Russian empire into a state of revolution. But we acted in defence only, and we deemed it a sin to precipitate other nations into a terrible and uncertain war, and we checked our sympathies. Besides, we avoided giving the Emperor of Russia a pretence for a war of retaliation against us. Oh it was foolish! for the despotic hypocrite made a pretence; he called our own struggle the Hungarian Polish revolution, though the whole number of Poles in our armies did not exceed four thousand.

We doubted not that the European Powers would negotiate a peace for us, or that they would at least prevent the Russian invasion. They said they pitied us, honored our efforts, and condemned the conduct of Austria; but they could not help us, because Europe required a powerful Austrian empire, and they must support it, in spite of its evils, as a balance against Russia in central and eastern Europe. What a mistake! What diplomacy! Is it not as clear as the sun that the Czar, in aiding Austria, would do it in such a manner as to obtain the greatest advantages for himself? Was it not manifest that Austria, who had always, through the help of Hungary, strength enough to oppose Russia, would, when she destroyed Hungary by Russian bayonets, no longer be an independent Power, but merely the *avant-garde* of the Muscovite? Yet Europe permitted the invasion. It is an indelible mark of blindness and shame. It is ever thus in the imbecile Old World. They treated us just as they treat Turkey. They assert always that the peace of Europe and the balance of power require the preservation of the Turkish empire,—that Turkey must exist to check the advance of the Cossack power. But, notwithstanding this, England and France destroyed the Turkish fleet of Navarino, a fleet which never could have injured them, but might have contended with Russia in the Black Sea.

Always the same worn-out, old, and fatal system of policy, while Russia, ever alert, seizes province after province from Turkey. She has made herself the sovereign of Moldavia and Wallachia, and is sapping the foundations of the Ottoman empire. Already Turkish officials are more dependent on the lowest Russian agents than upon their own Grand Vizier.

Oh that Hungary had received but a slight token of moral support from the European Powers—from those powers whose dreams are troubled with fears of the advance of the Cossack. Had only an English or a French agent come to us during our struggle, what might he not have done! He, too, would have seen and estimated our ability to sustain ourselves; he would have observed the humanity, the love of order, the reverence for liberty, which characterized the Hungarian nation. Had these two Powers permitted a few ships to come to Ossara, laden with arms for the noble patriots who had asked in vain for weapons, the Hungarians would now have stood a more impregnable barrier against Russia than all the arts of a miserable and expensive diplomacy.

There was a time when we, with the neighboring Poles, saved Christianity in Europe. And now I hesitate not to avow before God, that we alone—that my own Hungary—could have saved Europe from Russian domination. As the war in Hungary advanced, its character became changed. In the end, the results it contemplated were higher and far more important; nothing less, in fact, than universal freedom, which was not thought of in the beginning. This was not a choice; it was forced upon us by the policy of the European nations, who, disregarding their own interests, suffered Russia to invade and provoke us. Yes, we were martyrs to the cause of freedom, and this glorious but painful destiny was imposed upon us.

Though my dear native Hungary is trodden down, and the flower of her sons executed, or wandering exiles, and I, her Governor, writing from my prison in this distant Asiatic Turkey, I predict—and the Eternal God hears my prediction—that there can be no freedom for the continent of Europe, and that the Cossacks from the shores of the Don will water their steeds in the Rhine, unless liberty be restored to Hungary. It is only with Hungarian freedom that the European nations can be free; and the smaller nationalities especially can have no future without us.

Nor could the united Russo-Austrian forces have conquered my heroic countrymen had they not found a traitor to aid them in the man whom, believing in his honesty, and on account of his skill, I raised from obscurity. Enjoying my confidence, the confidence of the nation and the army, I placed him at the head of our forces, giving him the most glorious part to perform ever granted to man. What an immortality was within his reach had he been honest! But he betrayed his country. Cursed be his name forever! I will not open my bleeding wounds by the sad remembrance of this event, and will merely mention that the surrender at Vilagos was the crowning act of a long system of treachery secretly practised—by not using the advantages which victories put in his hands—by not fulfilling my commands under cunning pretences—by destroying national feeling in the army—by weakening its confidence, and by the destruction, through unnecessary exposures and dangers, of that portion of the army that he could not corrupt, in his base designs to make himself military dictator. God, in His inscrutable wisdom, knows why the traitor was permitted to be successful. In vain fell the bravest of men in this long war—in vain were the exertions of my countrymen—in vain did the aged father send, with pious heart, his only son, the prop of his declining years, and the bride her bridegroom—in vain did all private interests yield to the loftiest patriotism—in vain arose the prayers of a suffering people—in vain did the ardent wishes of every friend of freedom accompany our efforts—in vain did the genius of liberty hope for success. My country was martyred! Her rulers are hangmen! They have spoken the impious words that the liberty-loving nation "lies at the feet of the Czar!" Instead of the thankful prayers of faith, of hope, and of love, the air of my native land is filled with the cries of despair; and I, her chosen leader, am an exile. The diplomacy of Europe has changed Turkish hospitality to me and my companions into hopeless bondage. It is a painful existence. My youthful children have begun the morning of their life in the hands of my country's destroyer, and I—but no; desponding does not become me, for I am a man. I am not permitted, or I would say, I envy the dead. Who is unfortunate? I am in Broussa, where the great Hannibal once lived an exile, homeless like myself, but rich in services performed for his country, while I can claim only fidelity to mine. The ingratitude of his nation went with him in his banishment, but the sorrowful love of my countrymen follows me to my place of exile. To thee, my God, I offer thanks that thou didst deem me worthy to suffer for dear Hungary. Let me suffer afflictions, but accept them as propitiatory sacrifices for my native land!

And thou, Hungarian nation, yield not to despair! Be patient; hope, and wait thy time! Though all men forget thee, the God of Justice will not. Thy sufferings are recorded, and thy tears remembered. The blood of thy martyrs—thy noble sons—which moistened thy soil, will have its fruits. The victims which daily fall for thee are, like the evergreen cypress over the graves of the dead, the symbol of thy resurrection. The races whom thy destroyer excited against thee by lies and cunning, will be undeceived; they will know that thou didst not fight for pre-eminence, but for the common liberty; that thou wast their brother, and bled for them also. The temporary victory of our enemies will but serve to take the film from the eyes of the deceived people. The sentiment of sympathy for our sufferings will inspire among the smaller states and races the wish for a fraternal confederation—for that which I always urged as the only safe policy and guarantee of freedom for them all.

The realization of this idea will hurl the power of the haughty despots to the abyss of the past; and Hungary, free, surrounded by free nations, will be great, glorious, and independent.

At the moment when I hardly hoped for further consolation on earth, behold the God of Mercy freed my wife, and enabled her, through a thousand dangers, to reach me in my place of exile! Like a hunted deer, she could not for five months find in her own native land a place of rest. The executioners of the beardless Nero placed a reward upon her head; but she has escaped the tyrants. She was to me and to my exiled countrymen like the rainbow to Noah, for she brought intelligence and hope in the unshaken souls of the Hungarian people, and in the affectionate sympathy of the neighboring nations who had fought against us. They had aided the wife of the much-slandered Governor of Hungary.

Although the sympathy of the world often depends upon the result of action, and the successful are applauded, still Hungary, by her noble bearing and trials, has drawn the attention of the world. The sympathy which she has excited in both worlds, and the thundering curse which the lips of millions have pronounced against her destroyers, announce, like the roaring of the wind before the storm, the coming retribution of Heaven.

Among the nations of the world there are two which demand our gratitude and affection. England, no less powerful than she is free and glorious, supported us by her sympathy, and by the approving voice of her noblest sons, and the millions of her people. And that chosen land of freedom beyond the ocean—the all-powerful people of the United States, with their liberal government—inspired us with hope, and gave us courage by their deep interest in our cause and sufferings, and by their condemnation of our executioners.

The President of the United States, whom the confidence of a free people had elevated to the loftiest station in the world, in his message to Congress announced that the American Government would have been the first to recognize the independence of Hungary. And the Senators and Representatives in Congress marked the destroyers of my country's liberty with the stigma of ignominy, and expressed, with indignant feelings, their contempt for the conduct of Austria, and their wish to break the diplomatic intercourse with such a Government. They summoned the despots before the judgment-seat of humanity; they proclaimed that the world would condemn them; they declared that Austria and Russia had been unjust, tyrannical, and barbarous, and deserved to be reprobated by mankind, while Hungary was worthy of universal sympathy.

The Hungarians, more fortunate than I, who were able to reach the shores of the New World, were received by the people and Government of the United States in the most generous manner— yes, like brothers. With one hand they hurled anathemas at the despots, and with the other welcomed the humble exiles to partake of that glorious American liberty, more to be valued than the glitter of crowns. Our hearts are filled with emotions to see how this great nation extends its sympathy and aid to every Hungarian who is so fortunate as to arrive in America. The sympathetic declaration of such a people, under such circumstances, with similar sentiments in England, is not a mere sigh which the wind blows away, but is prophetic of the future. What a blessed sight to see whole nations elevated by such sentiments!

Free citizens of America! you inspired my countrymen to noble deeds; your approval imparted confidence; your sympathy consoled in adversity, gave a ray of hope for the future, and enabled us to bear the weight of our heavy burden. Your fellow-feeling will sustain us till we realize the hope, the faith, "that Hungary is not lost forever." Accept, in the name of my countrymen, the acknowledgment of our warmest gratitude and our high respect.

I, who know Hungary so well, firmly believe she is not lost; and the intelligent citizens of America have decided, not only with impulsive kindness, but with reason and policy, to favor the unfortunate but not subjugate Hungary. The sound of that encouraging voice is not like a funeral dirge, but as the shrill trumpet that will call the world to judgment.

Who does not see that Austria, even in her victory, has given herself a mortal wound? Her weakness is betrayed. The world no longer believes that Europe needs the preservation of this decaying empire. It is evident that its existence is a curse to mankind; it can never promote the welfare of society. The magic of its imagined power is gone; it was a delusion that can deceive no longer. Among all the races of this empire—not excepting the hereditary States—there is none that does not despise the reigning family of Hapsburg. This power has no moral ground of support, its vain dreams of a united empire, for which it has committed the most unheard-of crimes, are proved to be mere ravings, at which the world laughs. No one loves or respects it; and when it falls, not a tear of regret will follow it to the grave. And fall it surely will. That moment Russia withdraws her support, the decayed edifice will crumble to dust. A shot fired by an English or by an American vessel from the Adriatic would be like the trumpet at the city of Jericho. And this impious, foolish Government thinks to control fate by the hangman's cord. How long will Russia be able to assist? This Czar, who boasts that his mission is to be the scourge of all the nations striving for liberty,—will not the Almighty, whose vicegerent he profanely assumes to be, blast the miserable boaster? The very character of his Government is a declaration of war against the rights and interests of humanity, and the existence of other nations. Will the world suffer this long? Not long.

The Hungarian nation, in her war, has not only gained a consciousness of her own strength, but she has forced the conviction into the minds of other nations that she deserves to exist, and to be independent; and she can show justly that her existence and independence are essential to the cause of liberty in Europe. No, no! Hungary is not lost. By her faith, bravery, and by her foresight, which teaches her to abide her time, she will yet be among the foremost in the war of universal liberty.

You, noble Americans, we bless in the name of the God of Liberty! To you who have summoned the murderers of my countrymen before the judgment-seat of the world—to you, who are the first judges of this court, I will bring the complaints of my nation, and before you I will plead her cause. When the house of Hapsburg with the aid of a foreign army, invaded my country, and had destroyed, by their manifesto of the 4th of March, 1849, the foundation upon which the union with Austria rested, there remained for Hungary no alternative than the Declaration of Independence which the National Assembly unanimously voted on the 14th of April, 1849, and which the whole nation solemnly accepted, and sealed with their blood.

I declare to you, in the most solemn manner, that all which has taken place, or that may hereafter take place, proceeding from individuals or Government, contrary to this declaration, which is in perfect accord with the fundamental law of Hungary, is illegal and unjust.

Before you I assert, that the accusation that the Magyar race was unjust to the other races—by means of which a portion of the Servians, Wallachians, Slavonians, and Germans, dwelling in Hungary, was excited against us—is an impious slander, circulated by the house of Hapsburg, which shrinks from no crime to weaken the united forces of our united army, to conquer one race after another, and thus bring them all under the yoke of slavery.

It is true, some of the races in Hungary had reason to complain: but these subjects of complaint were the inevitable consequences of the pre-existing state of things and the Austrian interference. But the Croatians had no reason to complain. This race of half a million, in a separate province, had a National Assembly of its own, and enjoyed greater privileges than even the Hungarians. They contributed proportionally but half as much in taxes. They possessed equal rights with Hungary; whilst the Hungarian Protestants, on account of their religion, were not suffered to hold lands in Croatia. Their grievances and ours were the same, in the perpetual violation of the constitution by the imperial Government. But their own peculiar grievances arose from the evils of former times, and from the Austrian system of government, which forcibly placed the Slavonian, Servian, and Wallachian boundary districts on the German military footing.

The moment, however, our people became free and enjoyed their political rights they became just, and placed all things upon the basis of freedom and perfect equality. But some of these races, blinded by the infernal slanders and suggestions of Austria, took up arms against us. This people, who for centuries had endured slavery, fought against their own freedom! God forgive them! They knew not what they did.

In America, people of different languages dwell, but who says that it is unjust for senators and representatives to use the English language in their debates, and to make it the official language of the Government?

This is what the Magyar race asked in Hungary. There was this difference only, that in America it was not necessary to establish this by law, for the original settlers had stamped their language in the country; but in Hungary a law was necessary to make the Magyar the official language. The use of the Latin language—a bad relic of the Middle Ages, which the clergy and aristocracy preserved as something precious, imitating the ancient despots, who caused the laws to be written in small letters and placed on high towers that the people might not understand their rights—had been retained among us. It was necessary to have a living, spoken, popular language. And what other could we have than the noble Magyar?

How often have I and other leaders with me said to my countrymen, that they must be strictly just, and seek their future greatness not in the predominance of one race, but in the perfect equality of all? My counsel was adopted, and made the basis of the Government. The same freedom, the same privileges, without regard to language or religion, the free development of each race under the protection of the law, were accorded to all. We not only guaranteed the right to use any language in the churches and schools, but we afforded aid for the education and development of each nationality. The principle we announced was, that either the State should protect no religion, no nationality—leaving all to the free action of the people—or that it should protect all alike.

In the general administration, the predominance of our language and, consequently, the race that spoke it, was a necessity; but, in the administration of country affairs, which in some respects resembled that of the individual States of North America, the use of each language was granted. In the courts, in the trial by jury, in the right of petition, in the republication of all laws and ordinances, the various races had the right to use their own language. In one word, nothing was left undone which could tend to place all on a footing of the most perfect equality. True, we did not, as Austria has done for political purposes solely, to enslave all the people, and make the brave Hungarians a subordinate nation, make a territorial division of the land. We respected rights and wished to progress, but were too honest to commence a system of spoliation. And who has been benefited by this policy of the Vienna bureaucracy? Not even those on whom the pretended favors have been conferred.

When those races clamored for national rights, I boldly demanded what was wanting, and what could be granted without injury to the country. No one answered but reckless men, who spoke of territorial divisions. The Servians desired to have the Comitat Bacs, and the three counties of the Banat, as a separate Servian State. The Wallachians wished to have Transylvania. They (the Servians) did not consider that they owned no separate portion of the land of Hungary, and that in Bacs and the Banat were Wallachians, Germans, and Magyars, who could not be made subordinate to the less numerous Servians. So, also, in Transylvania, there were Magyars and Saxons, who would complain of such a connection with Wallachia.

As there were various races, speaking different languages, in Hungary, and divided into as many municipalities, who could blame us for laying the foundation of government in a just equality to all? Croatia alone was a separate territory: and how often have we said to her, that if she would remain in union with us we would give her the hand of brotherhood, but if she wished to separate we would not hinder her? We could not, however, permit such a division of Hungary as would have destroyed her as a nation. It was Austria who sowed the seeds of division and dissolution.

Citizens of America! to you I declare honestly that my aim in the federation of Hungary with the smaller nations was to secure the nationality and independence of each, and the freedom of all; and, had anything been wanting which could have been justly granted to any or all of the races in Hungary, the Magyars had only to know it, and it would have been performed with readiness; for freedom, and not power, was their desire.

Finally, I declare that, by the Declaration of Independence by which I was elected Governor of Hungary, I protest, so long as the people do not by their free will release me from that office, that no one can legally control the affairs of government but myself. This protestation is not made in a feeling of vanity or desire to be conspicuous, but from respect to the inherent rights of my countrymen. I strove not for power. The brilliancy of a crown would not seduce me. The final aim of my life, after having liberated my dear Hungary, was to end my days, as a private citizen and a humble farmer

My country, in the hour of danger, called upon me to assist in the struggle for freedom. I responded to its call. Others, doubtless, were more able, who could have won more fame : but I will yield to none in the purity of my motives. Perhaps it was confidence in my ardent patriotism and honesty of purpose, which induced the people to give me the power. They believed freedom would be safe in my hands. I felt my weakness, and told them I could not promise them liberty unless they were united as one man, and would lay aside all personal, all sectional interests. I foretold that, if the nation was divided, it would fall. As long as they followed my injunctions, and were united, they were unconquerable—they performed miracles of valor. The fall of Hungary commenced the day they began to divide. Not knowing the secret causes of this division, and not suspecting treachery, and wishing to inspire confidence, to give skill and all the elements of success to our army, and caring nothing for my own fame, doing all for the good of my country, I gave command of the forces to another. I was assured by the most solemn engagements, by the man to whom I gave the power, that he would use it for the welfare and independence of the nation, and that he would be responsible to me and the people for the fulfilment of these conditions. He betrayed his country and gave the army to the enemy. Had we succeeded after this terrible blow, he should have met his reward. And even now he is not freed from his accountability to the nation, no more than I, in the moral right and sense, ceased to be the Governor of Hungary. A short time may reverse again the fate of all. The aurora of liberty breaks upon my vision even at Broussa.

I have, therefore, intrusted to Ladislaus Ujhazi, Obergespum of the Saros comitat, and civil governor of Comorn, the mission to be my representative, and through me the representative of the Hungarian nation, to the people and Government of the United States, hoping and believing that so generous a people will not judge the merits of our cause by a temporary defeat, but will recognize Governor Ujhazi and his companions, with the accustomed kindness.

May God bless your country forever! May it have the glorious destiny to share with other nations the blessings of that liberty which constitutes its own happiness and fame! May your great example, noble Americans, be to other nations the source of social virtue; your power be the terror of all tyrants—the protector of the distressed ; and your free country ever continue to be the asylum for the oppressed of all nations.

Written at my place of banishment. Broussa, Asia Minor, March 27, 1850.

LOUIS KOSSUTH,
Governor of Hungary.

SPEECH IN WINCHESTER.

Mr Mayor and Gentlemen,

In rising to thank you most heartily and most sincerely for those noble-minded, generous sentiments which you, Mr. Mayor, were pleased to express, and for the sharing in that expression of those noble sentiments by you all, I cannot forbear a strong emotion, which, however, is not quite subservient to eloquence. Besides, I must say that I am quite unprepared for this opportunity to address such a distinguished assembly of friends and brothers. Though not quite unaccustomed to speak in my own language, still I must feel it now a double difficulty to address you connectedly in English; and, therefore, permit me for a moment to ask your indulgence while I address you. I feel, gentlemen, that the generous sentiments you have expressed I can attribute to nothing else than to the noble sympathy which so well befits the free Englishman for the noble principle of liberty, and to the belief that the cause of Hungary was a just cause, and was a cause intimately connected with the principles of freedom. Now, instead of a vain effort to give you a good speech, perhaps it would be better for me to take the liberty to allow me in a plain common manner—still begging excuses for the faults of my language, which I cannot fail to admit—to give you some information about the true nature of this past struggle in Hungary, because I suppose I can be excused to have this egotism—to be anxious to conserve those generous sentiments, and I believe there can nothing better be done than by a plain common statement of the facts, without any flourish with an attributional pomp, as they passed in Hungary. To understand exactly the Hungarian cause, it is quite necessary to be somewhat acquainted with the true nature of the form of Hungarian institutions. You all know that Hungary was for more than eight hundred years in Europe always a constitutional monarchy, and perhaps this is no small proof of the elements of life, which, in my notion, are to be found when we consider the geographical position of Hungary, and the moral position of the native Magyar race,—an Asiatic people thrust into the midst of European nations, without any kindred, without any affinity, without any resemblance,—and when we consider they were surrounded on all sides by absolute and despotic powers; on one side Turkey, which encroached for centuries, not only upon civilization, but on religion, and where my poor nation was the bulwark of Christianity in Europe; on the other side, the Russian empire, which has, not for the benefit of mankind, grown up prodigiously in the one-and-a-half century; on the third side, the Austrian power—not the Austria of to-day, for that Austrian empire is a very new one—but the government of the house of Hapsburg, which never, if there be told truth by history, gave one friend to political freedom,—though one genius it had, one friend to religious freedom, one friend to the rights of conscience, but even he quite in opposition to the social and political freedom of the people,—the Emperor Joseph II. This then was our position. Turkey, Russia, and Austria, or rather the house of Hapsburg,—by such was Hungary surrounded; and besides, the people, which must ever be considered as the most firm and mighty basis of greatness and welfare of a country, and as the most strong, sure, and powerful safeguard of its liberties—the people in Hungary unhappily were excluded from political rights, they shared not in the constitutional benefits; and still this Magyar race, in such difficulties of circumstance, through eight centuries and more, has conserved, not only its life, but its constitutional liberty and national institutions. There is in such a race, in such a nation, elements of a future; and I believe with some pride I have a right to say, such a nation deserves to have freedom. I told you, a little ago, that the people had not shared in the constitutional rights of the country. The constitution of Hungary was an aristocratic one entirely; but it was an aristocratical constitution which had somewhat a different meaning from that which you attach in England to the word aristocracy. Aristocracy in Hungary was not synonymous with power and with the weight of wealth, but was simply an aristocracy of birth, and was not reduced only to elder brothers; but whoever had a father a nobleman, he and his children, and their children's children remained through all centuries, noblemen always. What was the consequence? The consequence was that, as human fate is subject to many changes of circumstances, the descendants of the old noblemen of Hungary did not remain wealthy, great, and powerful, but became diffused, and, by the course of centuries, descending among them, became almost one part of the people itself; so that the great part of the aristocracy of Hungary remained as poor, ay, poorer, than the people, because the noble had ambition not to work; as if work was not the greatest honor to humanity. So, therefore, we had not only a landed proprietary, but we had these most poor classes of the aristocracy, which were not only in the same condition as the people, but which were still, now and then, in a worse condition, not being so industrious. But one prominent feature was that the old aristocracy was not quite so opposed in its great extension to popular rights and to the popular interest as we find it to be in the middle ages on the Continent and through Europe—because we must confess that the aristocracy of England has known in time to meet the exigencies of the time, to share their privileges with the people, and to take its part in the burdens of the people, and therefore the aristocracy of England remained when those other aristocracies were swept away like dust from the earth. In Hungary the nobility was not in the same position, but the noblemen mixed with all classes of the people—they were not in strong opposition to the people, but they were agriculturists, working not their own soil but the soil of their landlords; but they became manufacturers; they engaged in every trade and every profession, and therefore it was not in such opposition to the people as the word "aristocracy" signifies here; and, though it is no wonder that in Hungary and between the bounds of this aristocratic constitution, where the people had no right to speak for itself, it should not have had its full share of privilege, still, out of the ranks of this aristocracy which I have characterized are always found in the past, and through all their history, generous men who manfully struggled by all legal means to improve the condition of their country, and who strove for the rights of humanity. Now in this struggling for the rights of humanity and the improvement of the condition of the country we had, according to our constitution, in Hungary two principal means. The first was—to call it by a name which is popular and is understood here—the Parliament of Hungary; and the second was by our county and municipal institutions. Those municipal institutions were, still more than in any other part of the world whatever, against the encroachment on the rights of the nation by the Government, because these county institutions were so framed that the Government had no right to convey any order whatever but only through the medium of the county meetings. The county meeting was composed of all noblemen who were residents in that county, and the noble population in a county might number from twenty thousand to twenty-five thousand persons, and in some counties it amounted to thirty thousand. Therefore every one of the nobles had a right to speak in these meetings; not, of course, every one, on every occasion, but according to the importance of the business, and the number of them that appeared in the same way at these meetings. Every noble had a right to be elected a magistrate of the county, who were the only executive power of the orders of the Government; so that when the Government ordered something to be done, the hand of execution was that of the municipal magistrate of the county, who alone had to carry it out; but, the magistrate never coming into contact with the Government, could receive no order but only through the medium of the county meeting, which county meeting met in public assembly had the right to discuss the legality of the Government order, and when the majority of the assembly held an order of Government to be illegal, it did not go into the hands of the magistrate to execute it, but the meeting made a remonstrance against it to the Government, and therefore these municipalities were a very powerful, strong bulwark against the encroachments of Government. And to be sure, no country in the world had greater need of such a barrier than Hungary, because we have been governed for three centuries by the house of Hapsburg, which never, according to the evidence of history, had a single fixed friend to political freedom. I do not know whether I am weary.

Now, the house of Hapsburg ruled Hungary for three hundred years. It ruled Hungary, not by conquest, but by the free choice of the nation; not by the free choice of the nation, without conditions, but on the basis of treaties, the chief feature of which treaties is that the monarch should reign in Hungary by the same lineal succession as in the dominions of the house of Austria; that the Austrian dynasty was recognized, and should remain Kings of Hungary, and thereupon the King took on himself a sacred duty to respect and conserve the Hungarian constitution, and to rule and govern Hungary by its own public institutions, according to its own ancient laws. And that was the duty of the King. I swear to God, I swear to the eternal God, that I hope He will so bless me as I shall keep that word. This is a *résumé* of the facts so far. Well, out of the thirteen kings we had of this house and dynasty, no one who knows anything of history can charge me with exaggeration when I say that their rule was one of continual perjury—of perjury, gentlemen, that is the word—perjury. I am a plain common man; I call things as they are.

Now, when the Hungarian nation elected the house of Hapsburg to the throne of Hungary—of this Hungary which is larger than 400,000 German square miles, which is equal, as I am told, to 100,000 English square miles, with a population of 15,000,000—no small country, gentlemen; no small little patch of land—when she chose the house of Hapsburg, all the other provinces of the Hapsburg were constitutional monarchies. Every other of these states had a constitution, and every one of these afterwards united to her had one too; but by-and-by, through the course of three centuries, the house of Austria has gone on in a straight direction to be an absolute monarchy; and now, before our past struggle, not one place or province in her dominions had a constitution—the ambitious, despotical house of Austria—rather, I should say, the house of Hapsburg, had absorbed every single one of them. The constitutional life of Hungary was not absorbed because it did not belong to the Austrian Empire. Hungary had no other connection with Austria than Hanover had with England, with this difference only, that Hanover had a different line of succession, while the line of succession of Austria and Hungary was the same. But we had laws and coronation oaths and pacifications, which declare that there should be no connection between Hungary and the house of Austria, but this, only to be ruled by the same sovereign; not but that Hungary should have a right to be ruled by its own laws, rights, and institutions; so much so, that should we happen to have a King come to the succession of the sovereignty, being a child in his minority, Hungary should not be governed by the same person as ruled over the Austrian provinces, because there existed in the house of Hapsburg a family treaty by which the eldest of the house must be the tutor (*i. e.* Regent) to the empire, but by the law in Hungary it must be a Palatine who rules as tutor of the King; and therefore there was this possibility, that a Regent might have to govern Austria, while another Regent was governing Hungary. Therefore the constitutional life of Hungary was not absorbed, and chiefly was not absorbed because by the municipal institutions—by that strength which can never be broken, it resisted the encroachments of the crown. I consider these municipal institutions to resemble in a fair instance the siege of Saragossa, where, after Napoleon's army had taken the town they still had to fight single battles in every street. So was it always in Hungary. In my own time, though a young man yet, I remember that there was a time when the house of Hapsburg, without the help of any Parliament, attempted to destroy the constitution, to levy troops, and to raise the taxes to two and a half times their former amount; and that out of the fifty-two counties in Hungary, influenced by every means which Governments—immoral Governments—have at their disposal, only some ten or twelve registered the decrees, but that the others constantly resisted them by lawful grounds, and that this resistance on a constitutional and lawful basis overthrew them. It was, as I said, just like Saragossa, where the town was taken indeed, but where the fight went on from street to street, and house to house. So it was, notwithstanding these encroachments, we conserved some shadow of constitutional liberty; but the house of Hapsburg, after having absorbed all constitutional life in its dominions, came to this, that there was only Hungary, which is so bold as to oppose it in its aim to be entirely an absolute monarchy, and, seeing that its head availed himself of every means in his power, of open violence, of all kinds of intrigues, to destroy and overthrow our constitution; he fomented our discords, he undermined our national character, he impoverished us, he corrupted us, he oppressed, and, by-and-by, our rights were taken away, and by-and-by we became aware our municipal institutions and our Parliament, which should have been convoked every three years, and was not convoked once in twenty years, though taxation went on, and an arbitrary Government went on—were not enough; and we became aware that some two hundred or three hundred or four hundred or five hundred nobles by birth, meeting by right in their county meetings, were not sufficient to defend the constitution of the country against the predominant direction of the head of the Austrian absolutism; and that was the origin of our endeavors, which are as old as twenty-eight years; that men influenced by justice and pure patriotism took for aim to go on, degree by degree, and step by step, to make the people participate in constitutional right and liberties. That was the aim and direction of the public life of Hungary from 1825.

The more Hungary has felt this necessity because she had a Board of Government, a Commission or Council of Government, which, by law, was made responsible not only not to do anything contrary to the law, but not to carry into execution any order of the sovereign himself, contrary to the law; but still we saw there was no responsibility in that Council, because no corporate body can be made responsible. Individuals can be made responsible, but where the Government is collective, responsibility is a folly, and vanishes like a dream.

We saw that our national independence and the lawful rights of our nation were entirely absorbed by the Austrian Government, and in our times chiefly by Prince Metternich, who was all in all in Austria. We were conscious that the Austrian Ministry had nothing to do with the affairs of Hungary, that the Emperor of Austria, as King of Hungary, was obliged to govern Hungary by its own laws, and not as he liked. We did not like these Austrian influences, and we took, as the direction of our efforts, to give the people their national share in the constitution, in order that they might be the safeguard of the constitutional life which 400,000 or 500,000 were not able to defend, but which a people of 15,000,000, united in the great principle of common duties, and equal, may have good reason to defend. In the peasantry in every country, to be sure, the agricultural classes are of important consideration, but they are chiefly so in Hungary, which is almost entirely, with few exceptions, an agricultural country. Of course the condition of this peasantry was the first topic of any design to reform; and, seeing that the country, in all material respects so highly gifted by nature, could never be converted into an earthly paradise, such as you have made this land, but by free work, where every one enjoys the fruits of labor, we saw also that the agriculturist had to work for his landlord, one hundred and four days in the year. If you take off the Sundays, the festival days and the winter, why what remains to him? And still he had to give one ninth to his seigneur, and one tenth, or the tithes, to his bishop. That was a condition quite contrary to justice, contrary to the inborn dignity of the people, to the future of Hungary, and to the rights of human nature. Therefore the first step we took was to emancipate the peasantry; but being, as I have briefly stated, under very arduous circumstances, and as the legislative power was in the hands of the nobles, these reforms went on but by slow degrees. In the Long Parliament, as I may call it, which sat from 1832 to 1836, the Lower House, that is, the House of the members elected

by the county meeting, it was proposed that every peasant—I do not
know what to call them (*a voice*,—" Serfs"),—that every peasant
should have a right to make himself free of his seignorial and feudal
burdens by paying off the capital to which the amount of these burdens came. Do you understand me ? We wished, then, that this
should not be dependent on the will of the landlord to accord it to
him, but that an estimate should be made of what was the worth of
those duties and burdens, and that if the peasant should pay the capital estimated at the rate of 5*l.* or 8*l.* per cent., he should be free.
This was opposed by the House of Lords, and then, by the influence
of the Government, it was reduced to this,—that, when the landlord
should give his consent to it, every peasant, as also every corporation of peasantry together, should have the right to be free. This
proposition I have stated was agreed to by the common consent of
the House of Lords and House of Commons, but it was rejected by
the Government,—that is, the Austrians rejected that reform. That
was the issue of the reform question in 1836. I mention it as a
fact. And here I must explain—whatever your opinion may be as to
pledges I know not—that the members of the House of Commons
were not entirely plenipotentiary, but received their instructions from
the county meetings, which were sitting four or six, or even ten
times a year, and which controlled their representatives, and instructed them how to vote. The intrigues of the Government, therefore,
were chiefly directed to the county meetings in order to carry bad instructions, and then we perceived, for the first time, the very dangerous direction of the movement of the Government with respect to
these institutions, to endeavor to influence, to ruin, to weaken, to corrupt our public meetings and municipalities. Still, with respect to our
Legislature, there was, fortunately, some independence left in these
public meetings, for though our Supreme Court, who is something
like your Lord-Lieutenant of Counties, was named by the King, yet
being a member of the House of Lords, and being present in Parliament, he could not continually influence the meeting when the instructions were framed, and therefore Government had no one present
fit by his influence and station to carry out its views, and its means
of corruption were few. They therefore adopted the new rule,
which was leaving nominally the Lord-Lieutenant to appoint besides
an administrator in his place, who had orders to be present at every
meeting, to control every step they took, and never to leave his
county, and everything being in the hands of the Lord-Lieutenant,
such as gifts of offices, so to make the votes of county meetings a
mere nonsense, or to make them rather a tool of the Government.
Therefore, we opposed it with all our possible strength, but we
opposed it, not in any privilegiary view, but because we wished for
the independence of the municipal institutions in order to carry out
reforms in this direction—not to make the condition of Hungary such
that there should be there no close privileges for a few, but to erect

a temple of liberty there for all the people. But the more we developed our progress in a view to reforms, the more the Government insisted on the progress to demoralize the people. That was our condition when the Diet met in November or October, 1847, just before the French Revolution. You see, then, that we in Hungary were not planning revolution. Hungary was not the soul of secret conspiracy, but we in public meeting struggled, fairly and openly, for the rights of the people. I myself had the honor to be elected member of Parliament in 1847 as a deputy for the chief department, in fact, by its geographical position, the metropolitan county, of Pesth, where the Austrian Government did everything possible to oppose my election; but the good sense of the people carried it out to a triumphant success. When we came to the Diet, the first question I proposed, according to the instructions of my constituents, was that the municipal institutions of the country should be upheld in their natural purity, and that the system of administrators should be put aside, and that if this motion was not carried, no taxes should be voted.

On this motion the House of Commons and the House of Lords did not agree for two months, because it was necessary both should agree to carry a bill before it could be laid before the King; but there is no limit to the number of communications which passed between the two houses, so that they might go on to the number of one hundred or three hundred till the question is settled or abandoned. This measure did not meet the approbation of the House of Lords, because it was composed for the most part of functionaries named by the Government, or of those who aspired to be the nominees of Government. Still, we were happy to have the most important part of the Lords of Hungary with us, at the head of whom was the unfortunate, the worthy of a better fate, Louis Batthyany. These supported the House of Commons. Still the commission and Government went on to corrupt the county meetings, and I, seeing that we should get the worst in the end, and that the Government were carrying one after the other by violence and fraud, I proposed in the House of Commons that we should meet the continual encroachments of the Government by having recourse to the chief source of them. We saw that on the head of the King of Hungary, who is Emperor of Austria, two crowns are laid; the one was a constitutional crown, the other an absolute crown. These two opposite directions never could agree, they never could be united. Which of them was to prevail, history will show; but as we felt that the Austrian crown was the source of all encroachments on the rights of Hungary, and that so long as the two were united there would be no solidarity for the fate of nations in the future—so long as the house of Hapsburg does not restore their rights to the people of Hungary—so long will you see a rebellion ready to break out against Austria; and Hungary, having freedom, it was her duty, as elder brother, to seek to restore freedom to those other countries of which the house of Austria had deprived them. Seeing this, I proposed that it was our duty, as the elder brother of Austria, to go to the King and ask him to restore the constitutional liberties of the other portions of his dominions, and so by this means to put away the enchainment placed on the constitutional rights of Hungary. That was what I proposed. No just man can me charge that, by proposing this measure that was universally accepted by Parliament, I was planning a revolution. No one will say I was a Red Republican—the words of a true man, faithful to the rights of humanity, ever meet an echo in the breasts of generous Englishmen. My speech was translated into German, it was published in Vienna, it was read in the coffee-houses, in the public resorts. And now the news of the French Revolution came upon us, and Vienna rose up in revolt; that was the Austrian Revolution. I myself, with a knowledge of all the circumstances of Europe before me, frankly own I decided not to be carried away by the elements, but to take the reins of the elements into my own hands, to avail myself to the utmost of the opportunity which God had given—not Hungary made.

Our first proposition now was for the emancipation of the peasantry, which was carried unanimously by both Houses. But I was anxious not to hurt the interest of any class, but rather to spare those which, though not just in their origin, by time, circumstance, age, had got interlaced with the private fortunes of the people; and I therefore proposed, and it was agreed to unanimously, that the people should be free of all its duties—free without paying anything for it. Liberty must not be paid for; but, at the same time, there should be an indemnity, not by the peasantry, but for the landlords. Hungary is rich enough to give compensation and indemnity to the nobles, and by good financial operations might be made to pay more than two or three times what it does now. I engaged my honor and my word that a full indemnity should be given, and the measure was carried unanimously; the second measure I proposed was that, whereas before the people had every duty but no right, there should be an equality in duty and in rights, and that every man, according to his fortune, should contribute to the public necessities—this was also carried; the third proposition was, that the people should be admitted to the right of electing not only members of Parliament, but the magistrates who administer the laws; but, of course, half a million of people could not be convoked together in one room, and therefore the personal was transferred to a representative basis, and every community was ordered to elect men to represent them in the county meetings. That being my chief directive principle—that I recognized the rights of men, the rights of families, the rights of communities, which I considered as not to be subjected to Parliamentary interference—Parliament has no right to direct me how I shall rule my own family if I do not interfere with the rights of other families, and the same is true of communities in matters which affect a kingdom. Government should have sufficient power to provide for the public necessities of the whole country, to uphold and enforce obedience to the laws; but it ought to have no power at all to encroach upon the rights of men, the rights of communities, or of municipalities in their own domestic matters; that was my ruling principle. We ordered the Government to prepare bills for the representation of the parishes, but it was not enough for me and for my friends to establish municipalities as a barrier against the Government. Seeing the evil effects of the Administrative College, which, as a commission, could not be made responsible, we determined that as, as had often happened, part of these councils had been modified according to circumstances, we resolved to modify it so that the responsibility which was provided in the charter, but which was not a reality in effect, should be made real; and that could only be done by substituting individuals for collective and general bodies. There were some other measures, with the details of which I shall not abuse your attention. Thus we had participation of the nobles in all public duties and taxation; of the people in their general rights and responsibility in government. A deputation, of which I was a member, headed by the Archduke Palatine, was sent to Vienna, in the name of the future of Hungary and of Austria, and of the peace and happiness and tranquillity of Hungary, to ask the sanction of the King to these propositions. We were also instructed to ask the Emperor to restore to our friends in the other nations, and to our fettered brothers in Austria, their constitutional rights, and to interpose the word of Hungary in their favor. The agitation was then great in Vienna, as almost it was in every other country in Europe, save this England only, which, having once established its peace by revolution, can enjoy its public liberties without any desire for another. Here all was quiet—on the continent all was movement. The Government of Austria still hesitated to give us our rights. I went up to the Imperial palace, and I told them there that if the deputation was kept long waiting I would not guarantee on myself what the consequences would be, or that the movement that was taking place would not reach Hungary if we were discomfited and disappointed in our just expectations, and I therefore entreated them to do us justice. They promised they would do so, if only Vienna was quiet, but that they did not wish it to appear that the house of Hapsburg was compelled, by its fears, to be just and generous.

This was one of the moments in which I, in my own humble person, was a strange example of the various changes of human life. Myself, an numble, unpretending son of modest Hungary, was in the condition that I had the existence of the house of Hapsburg and all its crowns here in my hand. [M. Kossuth here stretched out his arm with clenched fist across the table.] I told them, "Be just to

my fatherland, and I will give you peace and tranquillity in Vienna."
They promised me to be just, and I gave them peace and tranquillity
in Vienna in twenty-four hours; and before the eternal God, who will
make responsible to Him my soul—before history, the independent
judge of men and events, I have a right to say the house of Hapsburg has to thank its existence to me. At last sanction was given;
but while we received the promise of the king in one room, in the
other room the Duchess Sophia, mother of the present king, and
sister of Francis Joseph, was plotting with Metternich how to get rid
of this word and sanction. In a few days afterwards, the king, who
was afterwards deposed, came to Presburg, and sanctioned publicly
our laws. I was there as a member of the ministry, in which I was
what you call first Lord of the Treasury, which I was forced to accept. I say so, because I can call the public knowledge of my
nation—my enemies in my nation as well as my friends—that I
always considered office and power as a burden, and as no glory; but
that it was myself who, before going up to Vienna with the laws for
sanction, said to the people of Presburg (assembled below) from the
balcony, taking Louis Batthyany, my poor friend, by the hand,—
"Don't cheer myself. Here is the man who shall be—who must
be, first minister, President of Hungary;" but Batthyany refused to
accept it, so I was forced to accept it; and I state this because I see
it is said in some papers that I made myself minister. We came
down to Pesth, and in a few days after the Serbs revolted—stirred up,
as it was quite clearly proved afterwards, by the intrigues of the Camarilla of Vienna. They took for pretext, that in the diplomes there was
a treaty that a part of Hungary, containing about 200,000 people, was
given to them; which nobody denied; but their design was, as is
now quite clear, to separate that part of Hungary, and to form in
separate provinces the Banat and Buchna, though they contain
2,000,000 inhabitants, out of which only about 300,000 or 400,000
are Serbs; some are Wallachians, some speak the German tongue;
but the Hungarian government seeing there must be some plot by
which the poor people were misled, did not employ all the necessary
strength to suppress it; besides, I must also state that one of the
chief political manœuvres of Metternich was ever and ever to oppress one nation by another; but our army was drawn out of the
land—one part in Bohemia, one in Italy—and we had German, Polish,
and Wallachian troops in Hungary. Without entering into details,
I will only state that the revolt spread itself over Croatia, which declared it was independent of Hungary, without any reason at all.
And I will state that the head of this revolt of the Serbs and Croats was
the Ban Jellachich. We entreated the King to give his command to
convoke Parliament, in order to take measures against these internal
disturbers. The King gave his consent, and I, as Minister of State,
stood by the side of the Archduke Palatine when he received the order
of the King, who had fled from Vienna to Innspruck, where he had been

visited by a deputation from Pesth, sent by the Diet, inviting him to come to Buda, to rely on them, and that they would defend him against half the world; and it has been proved that the Hungarians can defend the Crown. I stood by the side of the Archduke Palatine when he read the declaration of the King, that he solemnly condemned the damnable efforts of Jellachich, and of the Serbs, and Croats, and Wallachians, who had rebelled against the common liberty of the land, which they enjoyed, without any distinction of the language they might use, or the church to which they belonged. At that very time that the orders were given by the Ministers of Hungary to put down this revolt against the law, and that the King had convoked his faithful Parliament of Hungary, to provide as well for the army as for the financial means to defend and protect the realm; that was done; and in the convocation of the kingdom I saw one of the grandest sights of my life, when nearly four hundred representatives rose as one man, and stopping me in the address which I was making, declared, "You shall have it—you shall have all you want."

While we were engaged in making these legislative provisions, the battle of Novarro, or rather the battle of Costlanga, was won by the armies of Austria, and the house of Hapsburg was saved. Now was the moment to crush Hungary. The King issued a proclamation in which Jellachich, who had been proclaimed a traitor to his country, was lauded as his most faithful servant, and thanks were given to him for his services, and in which the King begged him to go on against the Hungarians. There was not an honest man in the world who would not pronounce against such an act as that. We had no army—not more than 5000 men—he came down upon us with 30,000 men. We met him. We took with our army, two generals, 12,000 men, and their artillery; and this we did with people armed with scythes and without discipline. Jellachich himself, seeking for a truce of two days only, obtained it; and in the meantime breaking his word of honor and his faith, he made his escape. We followed him. I was President of the Council, because at the time there was no Ministry, for the ministers had resigned as soon as the King issued his proclamation. How could they continue to act as ministers with such an order from the King.

Now came an order that Parliament should be dissolved, which was forbidden by the constitution and by the laws, as the budget was not fixed; and further, the order stated that the King, superseding all constitutional rights, gave, as to his *alter ego*, Jellachich power to govern Hungary as Dictator—that very Jellachich whom he had declared to be a traitor. We said, when we received this order—this is no order at all, it is not signed by a responsible Minister—Parliament cannot be dissolved, because the budget is not yet fixed, and the Ministry having resigned steps must be taken to conduct our defence. Jellachich escaped towards Vienna—I ordered to follow him. When he came to the frontier of Austria, I sent up instructions to the officer in command of the army to send to the commander of the Austrian army that he might be asked to respect the law of neutrality, and not to give any shelter to those who had revolted against us; but the Austrians not only protected him, but his troops joined the Austrian army. The Austrian army joined him — the siege of Vienna was made, and after that these two armies came into Hungary under the command of Windischgrätz, calling us, and especially my humble self, rebels. We opposed; we struggled; we fought battles; history will tell how; but still I must add one single thing, and that is, that though we had been victorious, defeated the Imperial armies in repeated battles, though the Emperor of Austria issued a proclamation, dated the 4th of March, 1849, when he, relying on the false report of the Camarilla of a victory in a battle that never was won, declared, by one scratch of his pen, that he blotted out Hungary from the list of nations, that that kingdom no more existed, that its constitution was torn up, and that Hungary was declared to be incorporated in the Austrian empire and ruled according to the laws which his good pleasure would give—notwithstanding we had beaten our enemies—notwithstanding this proclamation which severed all ties between Austria and Hungary—still we did not even proclaim a rupture with the house of Hapsburg. When did I make the proposal no more to acknowledge the house of Hapsburg? When I got true and exact intelligence that the Russian intervention was decided on, and had been accepted; and when I had got, I am sorry to say, the intelligence that, in order to avoid this Russian intervention, we had no help in the world—from nobody—no, not one.—[Here, overcome by irrepressible emotion, the voice of M. Kossuth faltered; he burst into tears, and for some moments was incapable of proceeding, while a burst of sympathy broke from the assembly. As soon as he had recovered, he proceeded, still agitated.]—Then I considered matters in my conscience, and I came to the resolution that either my nation must submit to the deadly stroke aimed at her life, or, if we were not cowards enough, not base enough to accept this suicide, it would not be amiss to put as the reward of our struggles—our fatal struggles—that which should have the merit of being worthy the sacrifice of the people; and if we had to contest with two great empires, if we had no one to help us, if we had no friend, and to contest in our truggles for the liberties of Europe, because now the Hungarian question rose Europe high; it assumed the dignity of an European question—if it was our fate to struggle for the liberties of Europe, as once we had struggled for her Christianity, and if God should bless us, I proposed as a reward the independence of Hungary, and it was accepted. That is the statement, the brief—no, not the brief, but the true statement of the relations between Hungary and Austria. What was the result? How we fell—let me not speak about it (after a pause)—that is a matter of too deep sorrow to dwell on.

So much I can say, that, though forsaken by the whole world, I am to-day confident we would have been a match for the combined forces of these two despotical empires, but that it was my fault and my debility, that I, the Governor of Hungary, who had the lead of this great cause, had not faculties enough to match Russian diplomacy, which knew how to introduce treason into our camp but had I been capable even to imagine all these intrigues, we should not have fallen. As it is, you know the house of Hapsburg as a dynasty, is gone; it exists no more—it merely vegetates. The Emperor can only act by the whim and will of his master, the Czar. If only the Czar would not threaten every portion of the world where the prayers for liberty rise up from the nation to Almighty God—if the people of England would only decide that the Russian should not put his foot on the nations of Europe—it England would but only say, Stop—and nothing more—the boast of Paskievitch, that he would put his foot on the neck of Hungary, would never be realized, and Hungary, I am sure, would have knowledge enough, truth enough, and courage enough, to dispose of its own domestic matters, as it is the sovereign right of every nation in the world, and to put down any aggression on her liberty. Excuse me, gentlemen, if I have not answered your expectations; I fear I have tired you. My intention was to show you the past of my country was worthy of your generous sympathies, because it has struggled in a fair cause, it has struggled valiantly for its national existence, which, once lost, there is no resurrection more for the people. That is the case of my country. I wish to secure for her your generous sympathy for this plain expositionof facts. The principle involved is one which you honor; the cause has been honored in my undeserving person. When landing on your shores, I was received by my kind friend the mayor, the father of the unfortunate, brother to the oppressed. Happy is the nation where such men as herise from the people, for I have heard that it is one of his glories that he has risen by his own energy, by his own perseverance, by his own integrity, from the people; and it is the glory of England, that such men rising from the people gain the love and the confidence of their countrymen. Let me, in returning my best thanks, my heartfelt acknowledgments for the reception you have given me, propose, with the deepest affection and respect, "The health of the Mayor of Southampton."

SPEECH IN SOUTHAMPTON.

This is the second festive occasion on which I have had the honor to express my most sincere thanks to the Mayor and Corporation of Southampton, for the generous welcome with which they favor me, and to all the gentlemen for the sympathy with which they join this demonstration. God has awarded two blessings to those whom He has elected—bliss in heaven, and freedom on earth. May you all —may your nation be blessed by both these blessings.

No man, aware of the value of his destiny, can live satisfied without freedom; but he to whom God has granted freedom, he has got all, if he has got the mind and the will to use his freedom for the development of his happiness with so consistent an exertion as the English people do. This is the basis upon which England has grown a paradise on earth, on which the eye and the heart rest with joy, and which must strengthen the desire in every foreigner to become likewise free, and, by becoming such, to be endowed with the possibility of converting other parts of the world into a paradise such as England is. During all my life I had but one leading idea—liberty. It was the aim of my life—the aim of my existence—to secure its blessings to my people, though I knew these blessings but instinctively. Now that I behold England, I see how liberty ennobles men and beautifies nature.

How should I, then, not be doubly determined—in spite of all danger, in spite of all difficulties—to endure, to act, to struggle, and, if it must be, to die, that my people should become free—my people, of which I can say, with deeply felt satisfaction, that there is no people on earth which deserves better to be free? But besides the bliss of liberty, gentlemen, there is also a glory allotted to you; this is the proud position, which the English hold, not only to bear good-will to those who do not enjoy their happiness, but also to offer their hand to their less fortunate brethren.

Gentlemen, this is a great glory, it raises the dignity of men. Being in that position, you, in your national capacity, carry into life, even in your relations and feelings towards other countries, the divine doctrine of our Saviour—" Thou shalt love thy neighbor as thyself." It is only thus that I can explain the grand phenomenon, that so many noble-minded men, different in rank and station, but united all in the love and enjoyment of freedom, that they all join in the expression of their sympathy for the principles of freedom of which they choose to consider me an humble representative. Yes, it is so, I can explain that even those honorable classes, whose only capital is their honest labor and their time, they stop their work and sacrifice their time to express with that noble instinct of the people before which every individual grandeur bows, that the great principles of liberty can reckon on the sympathies of the people of England.

And there is a reason why they can justly reckon on the sympathies of the working classes, for without liberty there can exist no lasting social order, so indispensable that everybody may enjoy in full security the fruits of his labor. Without liberty there is no field for productive labor, such as benefits those who work. Without liberty there is no personal security, and no security for property. And if it is not the aim of society to open a field for productive labor, to grant security to the person and property, and by this to develop man's mind, and to ennoble man's heart—if this be not the aim of human society, then I do not know what aim it can have. But it is also not without reason that all the classes of England are united in sympathy, in order that that liberty, which, under different forms of government but similar institutions, is the bliss and the pride of the English race in both hemispheres, should likewise be allotted to other nations, to enjoy it under a government which best suits their wishes and their wants. It is not without reason this sympathy, not only because there is a moral solidarity in the destinies of the nations, but also because where the productive powers of a people bring forth more than they can consume—as is the case in England—such a country must have free intercourse and an uninterrupted interchange of communication with the world, in order to secure the benefits of its labor, that by the stoppage of one channel there should not arise plethora no less dangerous than consumption.

Now, without the liberty of Europe there is no liberty of trade. All despots fear free trade, because the liberty of commerce is the great vehicle of political liberty. Free trade is only possible with free Europe. I hope I am not wrong in touching likewise on this material side of the question. I feel that it is fortunate as well as glorious when the material interests of a great nation are identical with the interests of the freedom of the world. This is a providential law. Even a single community can but enjoy welfare and security when the interests of the whole are in harmony with the interests of the individuals. Your sound judgment, gentlemen, and your comprehensive views make it unnecessary for me to develop all I could say about the connection of the material interests of England with the liberty of the continent. Be it sufficient to express my views in a few dry but truthful words.

The principle of all evil on the continent is the despotic and encroaching spirit of the Russian power. There is the pillar which supports every one who wishes to establish his ambitious sway on the sufferings of nations, raising himself on the ruins of their liberty. Russia is the rock which breaks every sigh for freedom, and this Russian power is the same which England encounters in her way, on every point—in Pekin and in Herat, at the Bosphorus and on the Sound, on the Nile and on the Danube, and all over the continent of Europe. Even Jesuitism, which in latter times has again begun to raise its head, is employed in support of Russia. We are in the neighborhood of a great country which unfortunately does not enjoy the fruits of sorrowful times and great sufferings. The Jesuit party in France threaten that country with the Cossacks. Even here, in this glorious country, a question connected with this not long ago was agitated, as well in the public opinion as in Parliament. I know what is convenient to myself and due to you. I will not enter into that question. I will only state one curious coincidence—I am a Protestant. I am a Protestant not only by birth but by conviction. I am a humble member of a nation, the majority of which is composed of Catholics, and it is not the least glory of my nation that in all times we have fought and bled for religious liberty—Catholics as devotedly as Protestants. The rights and freedom of the Protestants were always strongly opposed by the house of Hapsburg. That house had always in history been closely united with the spirit of Jesuitism; but the freedom of Protestantism had been established by treaties gained by the swords of victorious Hungary.

Scarcely had Russia restored the house of Hapsburg by putting its foot on the neck of Hungary, when the first act of that house was to spill noble blood by the hands of the hangman, and its second was to destroy the rights of the Protestant religion in Hungary. The kings of Hungary in former times were always anxious not to allow any meddling of the Court of Rome in the temporal affairs of the Catholic Church, and a glorious king, Mathias Corvinus, a Hungarian by birth, once used these words to the Pope—" Your Holiness must remember that we bear two crosses on our ensign, and we will make our crosses pikes before we allow you to mix yourself up with the affairs of our church." Since Russia had restored the house of Hapsburg, for a brief time the Jesuits have obtained full power to act. The encroaching spirit of Russia is that which every man in Europe relies on who wishes to do wrong. The identity of the interests of England with the interests of the liberty of Europe, gives me the hope that the generous sympathy which I have the honor to meet with will not remain an empty sound, that it will not remain without practical results for my poor country—for humanity. There is no party in England which can deny it, that the armed intervention of Russia in the affairs of Hungary has increased beyond measure the preponderance of Russia on the continent, while at the same time it has violated the sacred principle of the independent right of nations to dispose of their domestic concerns. It can, therefore, hardly be denied that, as long as Hungary is not restored to liberty and to independence, the weight of Russian preponderance over Europe will not subside, but will increase.

And what is it which I request in the name of my poor country, and in the interest of the oppressed people of Europe, from the great, free, and powerful English nation? Is it that England should take up arms for the restoration of Hungary? Oh no! All I request, and all I hope, is only that England should not abandon the weight which in Europe is due to her; that England should not grant a charter to the Czar to dispose of the destinies of the world. Public opinion in England can establish it as a leading principle in acknowledging the fundamental right of every nation to dispose of itself, not to allow the Czar to interfere with the domestic affairs of the nations of Europe. People of mighty Albion! this it is, and nothing more, which oppressed humanity expects, entreats, and hopes for. As to the rest, leave it to the nations of Europe themselves.

Austria—but no, I can't say Austria—I love, I esteem the people of Austria as my own brethren; I feel their griefs as keenly as those of my own people, and I have wishes and hopes for their future as fervent as those for my own nation. I have the right to say so. My life is an open book, and the judgment on it will be pronounced by disinterested history, and neither by the hirelings of the house of Austria, nor by party spirit, nor by blind passion, as also not by those base, absurd calumnies, which in my position could not naturally fail to be launched against me, but still which I regret, not for myself, because they can but enhance the affection of every generous man, it being so natural to feel revolted at such mean, base work; but I regret them because it is no consolatory view to see our fellow-creatures so delight in such foul calumnies which must offend the self-esteem of my people which chose me to be its chief. I am surprised to find these calumnies, even in places where I had not expected them. It may be, that relying on the affection that my people has for me—and they are a moral people, that never can be said in any instance to have given their confidence and love to a man who is not an honest man—it may be that for this reason it is supposed I will not entreat the protection of the law of England. I will, however, consider the matter as soon as my duties to my fatherland leave me a single moment to myself. Still, as I said, it is history will pass a verdict on me; and so I have the right to say before God and mankind, that the people of Austria never had nor have a warmer friend than myself.

It is, therefore, not in regard to Austria, but to the house of Hapsburg, that I wish to say some few words; and all I will say of it is, that its perjury, with which it has violated the rights of all its nations, ha doomed it to destruction. There is a God in heaven, and therefore there must be justice on earth. The house of Austria, having forfeited even the possibility of the love of the nations it rules, has lost the basis for its existence. Bayonets alone are no basis, for the soldier belongs also to the people, and the soldier thinks likewise. The continued loans are no basis; they lead rather to bankruptcy. What is it, then, upon which rests the house of Austria? It is on nothing else than its master the Czar, around whom the house of Austria moves as an obedient satellite. But while the Hapsburg dynasty can have no future, the people of Hungary has a future yet, because it deserves to live; it has a future, because it has vitality; it has a future, because its independence is a necessity to the freedom of Europe.

To me every occasion is valuable in which I can, by feeble words, and not by the power of eloquence—for you see I designedly employ no eloquence, but only a simple statement of facts, and the sound logic of a common understanding—discuss the matters of my poor native land; and your generosity would enable me to do so still longer, but I suffer from a sick chest, and am not much capable of speaking without bad consequences, and therefore I beg leave to ask you to charge your glasses. It is to the future of my country that I devote the activity which I have regained by my liberty from the bondage in Asia; and this my liberation is, in the first place, due to the noble feelings of the Sultan, who, in spite of the arrogant threats of Russia and Austria, has protected my life and the life of my companions—who later yielded, but with sorrow, to the pressure of the circumstances which had forced him to surround his hospitality by detention—and who, at last, raising himself by the magnanimity of his inspirations, and his respect for the rights of humanity, above all threats, restored me to liberty in the most dignified manner. But, expressing my grateful acknowledgments to Turkey, I may also return my deeply felt thanks for the magnanimous interference of the Governments of Great Britain and the United States of America in such a high and generous manner, supported by the public spirit of the people in both countries, and even sanctioned by the magnanimous resolution of Congress, in obtaining the liberation of myself and of my associates. It is, therefore, with the warmest feelings of a grateful heart I propose the toast—" England, the United States, and Turkey."

SPEECH IN LONDON.

My Lord Mayor, Aldermen, and Commons of the great and glorious city of London in Common Council assembled, I step into these halls overpowered with sentiments in respect to that honor which I was aware that it (the corporation) advanced me here, and overpowered by what I had seen in the streets of the great and glorious city of London, coming forth thousands and thousands after me, by no other motive but only to manifest the sympathy of the people of England for the principle of liberty. That is a view, my Lord and Gentlemen, full of hope for the oppressed—full of consolation for our down-trodden nation. After having seen these manifestations here, I may be allowed to ask—who are those oppressors of the world that believe that the sympathy of the people of England will melt away in the breeze like the sigh of a girl? I hope, from the manly sense of the people of England, that this sympathy will be the trumpet call for the liberation of the world. It is a proud moment of my life to have the high honor and the most important benefit to have this generous address, by which you, my Lord Mayor, Aldermen, and Commons of the city of London, in Common Council assembled, have pleased in such solemn manner, and in such generous words, to assure me that you have watched the past struggles of Hungary for freedom and independence which it was my destiny to lead—that you have watched those struggles with deep interest—that you entertain warm wishes for the future of that noble cause which it was the object of those struggles to secure to my native land, and that you heartily congratulate me on my liberation from captivity, which heartfelt congratulation and accompanying generous welcome can of course only have reference to my regained activity, to be devoted to that noble cause, the past of which you honored by your lively interest, and the future of which you insure by your wishes and sympathy.

That being the character of the present solemnity, while I express my most sincere, my most fervent thanks, in the name of my nation, for my country as well as for myself, I beg leave to state that even were I ambitious to be willing to have a personal share out of the high honor of this solemn occasion (which I am not, having the only ambition not to know and not to feel any ambition whatever), still, were I ambitious, the character of this solemnity is so distinguished, that I must feel it my duty at once to abandon any personal sigh, and to entreat you to give me generous permission in expressing my gratitude at once to enter into that which I consider the real meaning of these demonstrations to be. Of course, I must again entreat and beg pardon for my bad language, as well as also that I will be in no way able to answer your expectations. My past days have been very much occupied; my brains are filled with ideas, but I do not know how I can, how I will succeed to find words for them.

Now, as to the true meaning of the present demonstration—my opinion is that the corporation of the city of London, lawfully represented by its municipal authorities, could not have intended to bestow these words of honor to a man, but to a principle. Every side of the present demonstration is a principle. The corporation of the city of London is not an aggregation, on the present occasion, of men; but the corporation is a principle. Even the place where I have now the honor to bow before you, my Lord Mayor and Gentlemen, even the place is a principle; and myself as well as my countrymen who surround me, faithful associates in our past struggles, present sufferings, and future hopes—even we are no men here; we are a principle. This being the true nature of the case, I beg leave humbly to consider what is the place where I stand, who are those who bestow upon me the honor of this day, and what is the object of this demonstration. My Lord and Gentlemen, I have put the question to myself—what is the place where I have the honor to be? London—the metropolis of England; London—the metropolis of the world. That is no compliment, but the most serious truth; London is the metropolis of the world, because there is no place, no city in the world, which is so strongly and so intimately connected, in many respects, with the whole world as London is. There is scarcely any place—no country of course—the movement and the tranquillity, the present and the future of which, would not meet some interest here in London connected with it. London is the heart of the world, which, like that metropolis of the human constitution, cannot fail to partake a feeling of the least impediment in the circulation at the remotest parts of the world. It is the place to whose vibrating centre the most distant links carry back the tide of life. I believe no man in the world can charge me with the intention of making a compliment when I say London is the metropolis of the world. London being the metropolis of the world, there is no place, no other city in the earth, which has such strong motives to feel extremely interested in the condition of foreign nations and the foreign affairs of this country. Having a due sentiment of what is due to England from me here, and what is convenient to me so long as I have the honor to enjoy the protection of English laws, which make the Hungarian free in touching the English soil—so long as I am upon the English soil, I will never interfere in the interior affairs of England.

The fate of my country making one part of the foreign relations of England, perhaps I may be excused when I venture a single remark—that I believe every age has its necessities, and every position ts conditions. At the present moment I confidently state that among all the interior questions of England, there is not a single one which could outweigh in importance this question to the whole of England; and in regard to London, the metropolis of the world—to London, foreign affairs constitute a very question of life. The city of London, aware of this position of being the metropolis of the world, and consequently aware of the necessity to watch attentively foreign affairs, and the condition of foreign countries, has bestowed the benefit and the honor to be attentive to the cause of freedom. In consequence of this attention, you bestowed your interest upon the past struggles of Hungary, because you saw our cause to be just, righteous, and in harmony with those mighty interests which are embodied in the city of London; and, therefore, you united with your interest for the past your wishes for the future. And here, my Lord Mayor and Gentlemen, you meet my first request. Let not these wishes, this sympathy, remain a barren word. You have the power to do so—give to oppressed humanity your helping hand.

I cannot forbear, having spoken some words on the importance of foreign affairs, and especially in respect to the city of London, stating that I believe the time draws near when, for the whole world in the management of diplomacy, a radical change must take place. The basis of diplomacy has been secresy; and there is the triumph of absolutism and the misfortune of a free people. I hope soon this will cease, and foreign affairs will be conducted by that power which must be the ruling one in a constitutional government—public opinion. I scarcely can see how it is possible that this principle of the secresy of diplomacy got ground, not in England only, but throughout the whole world, when a question of a single penny of the national property could not be disposed of without the consent of the people. How are the interests of the country guarded and carried out in respect of these foreign affairs? There is a secresy which would be dangerous to the interests of the country and to constitutional liberty to develop. Not only that the people should not know how its interests are treated, but even after the time is past they should be told, "The dinner has been prepared and eaten, and the people has nothing to do but to digest the consequences." What is the principle of all evil in Europe? The encroaching spirit of Russia. And by what power has Russia become so mighty? By its arms? No; the arms of Russia are below those of many Powers. It has become almost omnipotent—at least very dangerous to liberty

—by diplomatic intrigues. Now, against the secret intrigues of diplomacy there is no surer safeguard, or more powerful counteraction, than public opinion. This must be opposed to intrigues, and intrigues are then of no weight in the destinies of humanity. You will excuse me, my Lord and Gentlemen, for these hints. I hope the English people will feel the truth of these humble remarks, and that they will not be quite forgotten.

Besides, London being the metropolis of the world, I know London to be the seat of the constitutional Government and of the Parliament. Here again I meet a principle. I believe that London, being the seat of the constitutional Government and the free Legislature of Great Britain and Ireland, is more strongly than whatever other place in the world identified with the principle of free legislation, emancipating the whole world from arbitrary power; no place in the world can be so much interested in freedom as London. As in one family, as in one community, as in one country, things and affairs cannot be ruled in two different divergent directions—that is the destiny of mankind—so, ere long, one of the two ruling principles of the world must prevail, and one only; liberty and absolutism cannot much longer subsist together in the present state of development of the human mind and heart; it cannot remain so—one or other must vanish from the earth, and unity be brought to the destinies of the world. Now, this principle of freedom can be established in different countries and different governments, according to the wants and wishes of different peoples and different nations; but the principle which can be the only basis of the moral dignity and material welfare—of the contentment and happiness of the world—is, under different forms of government, only the principle of freedom. That principle you have in the United States and in this country. Now permit me, my Lord and Gentlemen, to draw one consequence out of this principle. London, the metropolis of the world, the seat of constitutional government and free legislation—with which principle will it side? With absolutism or with freedom? You gave your sympathy, you watched with liveliest interest the cause of Hungary in the past; if you thought it worthy to feel a lively interest in the cause of Hungary in the past, you gave your wishes for its future; now let me again ask, do not permit this lively interest and these wishes to be a barren sound. You have the power to help :—help !

A principle which I meet here in this place is a principle of social order. Many people when they hear this word " social order," get almost nervous and excited. There are many that misuse this sacred word as blasphemy. They call social order absolutism; they call social order when humanity is put into a prison; they call social order the silence of the grave. This 30th of October has presented to the world a spectacle which, once seen, I proudly proclaim that no Czars and Emperors of Austria have the right or can have the pretensions to speak more of social order. Here is social order in London ; and by whom watched? I had my thousands and thousands of the people rushing forward, not with effusion of blood, but with the warm enthusiasm of noble hearts to cheer liberty and the principle of freedom in my poor humble self. And what is the safeguard of social order in this meeting of the people? I asked the attention of Lord Dudley Stuart: " Let us look how many policemen are present. I have seen four." Such a scene, my Lord, for the Czars and the Emperors, and all men ambitious, who may be called Presidents, for they are all the same thing, no matter how called ! They would have had their twenty thousand bayonets, and I do not know how many open and secret spies; they would have safeguarded by arms and cannon, what? Social order ? No. Against whom ? Against foes and enemies of social order ? No; against their own people. The people are never averse to social order; it is the basis of security of person and property. It is blasphemy to say that the people love disorder ; but neither a single man, nor thousands, wish to be the tools of ambition.

Now, having met here the principle of social order, permit me the question—What is, in the opinion of this illustrious corporation, the surest safeguard of social order ? I believe the surest safeguard of it is that which this illustrious corporation have seen, have experienced to be successful in maintaining social order here in this mighty, immense city, which is an empire—mightier than an empire or a nation. And what is the safeguard of social order ?—Liberty. I was not so happy as to arrive in London soon enough to see that great meeting which London appointed to humanity—the Great Exhibition ; but London is the greatest exhibition of all, and, should I need yet one spur to devote all my life and all my activity to that liberty which is capable to preserve, in so magnificent a manner, social order, in such an immense city as London, the contemplation of your social order, of your liberty, your demonstration to-day, would have given me the spur. I thank you for it. You have marked, my Lord and Gentlemen, that we in Hungary have struggled for that very freedom which experience here in England has shown to be the surest safeguard of social order ; therefore you gave your sympathy to our past—you give your sympathy to the present—you entertain wishes for the future of that cause, let me again entreat you in the name of the principle of social order, let not be barren this sympathy for Hungary—you have the power—help—help !

A principle I meet is the principle of municipal institutions. London is almost the oldest, to be sure one of the oldest, municipal institutions on the earth; in every case it is older than the great glorious nation of England itself, because it derives its municipal institutions from the Roman times. Nations, empires have fallen ; mighty people have vanished from the surface of the earth ; a new world arose ; even here in England, dynasties passed ; religion, governments changed; a revolution swept over England as a mighty storm; a restoration came, which never in history lasts long; and, after that had passed, the establishment of social order upon the principle of liberty for the people; and, during all these immense changes, London stands! Stands?—no, it does not stand; it has grown, during those changes, a giant; itself an empire—more than an empire; itself a nation—mightier than a nation. Now, what is the keystone of all this? The keystone is, in my opinion, that the existence of London is founded upon municipal institutions. The principle of municipal institutions is crushed down on the continent of Europe everywhere; it is swept away by the disease of centralization. This centralization is so propitious—to what? To ambition, but not to liberty. But chiefly on the continent of Europe the principle of municipal institutions is swept away by the principle of absolutism—by the propensity to centralization and absolutism, for the two words are identical. What is absolutism? It is the centralization of power. That is the banner to the perjury of the house of Austria, and which banner it has obtained in so sacrilegious a manner through Hungary. That is the basis of Russia having assisted it. As long as Hungary was free, though continually encroached upon by the absolutist direction of the Austrian Government, still it continued to be for the existence of the house of Austria an immense benefit, because the very idea that Hungary has had municipal institutions was a check to Russia, that it could not get the Austrian dynasty into its hands. Hungary fallen, the power of Austria centralized, and Austria is no more than a mere tool of Russia. See the consequence of the crushing down of municipal institutions and centralization. The house of Austria became a traitor to God, a traitor to humanity, only out of the wish to get rid of the check which the municipal institutions of Hungary had put before its absolutist direction. What is the consequence of centralization? That Austria is in bondage, forced to be obedient to the Czar. You, the metropolis of the world, strong in your municipal institutions, remembering to be attentive to the condition of foreign nations, have given your attention to the cause of Hungary. You have marked us to struggle for freedom and municipal institutions; finding this in the struggle of Hungary, you have given your sympathy to our past, your wishes for our future; then excuse me again for repeating the request that these wishes be not barren; you have the power to help,—then help!

For the cause of Hungary I could go on for weeks to show how united, or at least in harmony, it is with those principles which you cherish and love, and which make your glory. The next principle which I meet here is that of industry and trade. Nothing in the world can be in closer connection with freedom than the development of industry and trade. Absolutism has in its train, and must have in its train, everything contrary to liberty; therefore it must always be opposed to the free intercourse of nations. It must be opposite even to the moderate protection of home industry, which some in other parts of the world consider to be a mere question of political economy. Absolutism is prohibitory; it must be so, because it fears free trade and free commerce from political motives, because free trade and free commerce are founded upon the development of freedom, and are the most powerful lever of political rights. Now, let me ask what is the market which Austria gave to the industry of England? No market at all. Hungary, even before our past struggles, has consumed cotton manufactures—not home fabrication, foreign fabrication—Austrian fabrication—at an average from 67,000,000f. to 70,000,000f. a year—about 2,600,000*l.* How much place occupied in this important consumption the industry of England? Not 5*s*. And why not? Because the principle of absolutism of Austria, of course in strong harmony with the prohibitory principle, managed matters so as to oblige Hungary to buy these manufactured articles, not there where she could get them for the cheapest price and in the best manner, but in Austria, in order to drain millions out of Hungary for the benefit of Austria—an absolutist Power; for Hungary was obliged to pay for cotton manufactures, which here in England can be bought for 8*l*. or 9*l*., 20*l*. or 22*l*., because of the importation taxes. Therefore in this great market England almost, if not quite, in an open loyal manner, has not partaken 5*s*.; not to speak of smuggling. What is the market of Russia for English manufactures? If not by smuggling, very small, very insignificant. Here you see the direction of absolutism.

Now see the direction of freedom, of liberty, which I have the honor to represent for my country. The very day when Hungary proclaimed its independence, and intrusted me to be the chief, the Governor of my ill-fated country, my first deed was to send instructions to my representatives in England to make known to the English Government that the barriers of Hungary had fallen, and that Hungary was open to the industry of England. It is not my fault that very little profit was made out of it. I have proved the direction of freedom in respect to industry and trade. Now, my Lord and Gentlemen, only to think for a single moment that as the Russian principle triumphs over the continent, and it is said the Cza has put his foot upon Hungary's neck, and this step was only a degree to that immense preponderance it has on the continent—only think for a single moment, as the Russian and Austrian principle of absolutism triumphs on the continent, what must the consequence be for the industry and trade of England? A new continent like that of Bonaparte, on absolutist, because prohibitory principles. It will stop, it must stop, as, through the liberty of English commerce, the triumph of absolutism would meet again and again a principle, the shock of which absolutism cannot stand. Only think of such a triumph of absolutism, of such a stoppage on the continent to the trade and industry of England! Look at the terrible consequences of such a triumph of absolutist principles, to stop the trade of England, only for a short period. You would have to go to war against the world; you must. You must send your fleets, as your forefathers did, to protect the interests of England. You would spend millions, and torrents of blood, to get freedom for the trade, for the industry of England; or else England, or else London, now the fairest spot on earth, now the place where only exists social order, not by terrorism, but by liberty, this glorious place would inevitably decline.

But you have not to spend money, blood, to insure this harmony, this connection of the welfare of the world with the industry of England; there is an open, an immense market, for the industry of England at your very doors, with Europe free. We have struggled in Hungary for that freedom; for the principle connected with freedom, of free trade, and the free intercourse of nations. Hungary, restored to its independence and its liberty, is equal to proclaiming to the world that the principle of absolutism is crushed on the continent; and, were this principle crushed, there is no impediment any more to the free intercourse of nations. You have seen we struggled for that principle; you have given your sympathy for the past, your wishes for the future; let me repeat, let them not remain barren.

The sixth principle which I meet here, in this place, is the financial. My Lord and Gentlemen, London is the regulator of the public credit and of the money-market of the world. These few words spoken to you suffice to state the immense importance of this principle. Well, if London is the regulator of the public credit of the world, and if a very considerable quantity of the loan shares of every Government in the world are concentrated here in London, let me ask where is the security of those loans?—where is the possibility to see paid the money under the Governments of the world? Is the security in the victory of absolutist principle, or is it in the victory of the principle of freedom? Take despotic Governments: what is their basis of existence? Is it the love of the nations? Oh, how could the principle of despotism be love? Love in such case is a contradiction to our nature. Is perhaps the basis of the absolutist Governments contentment of the nations? How can men be contented without freedom? What is the complexion of the principle of absolutism? It can be marked out in a few plain words,— "People, pay; because I want soldiers and spies, and to be your illimitable master." How could the principle of these nations be contentment? Therefore, what is the basis of their existence? Immense costly armies, and not less costly diplomatic intrigues. The sweat of the people cannot suffice to provide for all these necessities; not for the welfare, not for the happiness of the nations, but to keep them in servitude. Therefore, the absolutist Governments must come again and again to the money-markets to get some loans. Every new loan, in whatever unproductive manner applied, diminishes the resources out of which it should be paid; and when the same goes on again and again, who could take the guarantee upon himself for the nations of the world with these eternal loans, employed, not for their benefit, but against their benefit, and against their liberty?—who could take the guarantee upon him that, once these nations groaning under their material sufferings, will not say, "Let him pay who has made the debt; we made it not!" Here is the prospect which absolutist principles point out in that respect. But there is a prospect, especially to the house of Austria. That prospect is inevitable bankruptcy! You know how it is where a Government has often need to make loans, and where it is in necessity to make, for instance, now a new loan of 8,000,000*l*., for the purpose of restoring the balance of the financial system in Austria. Oh, no; only to get through three or four months, and then to get a new loan; the interest of these new loans has to be added to the expenditure of the Government. Men without any enthusiasm, earnestly pondering this state of the house of Austria, must confess that the very early prospect, unless averted by restored liberty, is bankruptcy.

Now I will beg leave to state to you, in a very few words, what prospect is presented to the financial principle by the freedom and liberty of the world. Since I left Kutayah, I had occasion to stop for a short time in different parts of Europe, on the shores of Italy, in France, in Lisbon. I had the honor to meet the free offerings of a most noble sympathy; the most cheering welcome everywhere. Why? Because I am taken for the humble representative of the principle of freedom. And why am I so taken? Is it perhaps to make a compliment to this my miserable frame, broken by labor and anxieties? No; I am taken as the representative of the principle of freedom for my past. And what is my past? My past is, that I have undertaken to give political and social freedom to the whole people; to make free their soil, free their labor, free their trade, but in the same time to spare, and not to hurt, but to protect every existing material interest of every class. Here you have, my Lord and Gentlemen, the key of that confidence and of that love which my people bore, and bear still, to me. Here is the key to the unity of Hungary, in the principle which I have the honor to represent,—freedom to all, but no injury to the material interests of any. Therefore I met sympathy everywhere, because I have imparted this direction to the struggles of Hungary; I got not only the confidence of my people, but the sympathy of the world. I pledged my honor and my word to be faithful to this direction all my life; and so may God bless me as I will, if only those whose material interests I undertook to protect and to spare will not deprive me themselves of the possibility to do so.

Now, when the nations of Europe see that whenever a despot wants means to oppress humanity he finds ever and again money, what must be the consequence? I am no capitalist; I never was, and never shall be; I am a poor man, and content with my station; but, were I capitalist, I would very much consider these circumstances—I would very much consider if there is possibility to the lasting triumph to absolutism, or if freedom must not have a future; and, considering these circumstances, I would rather give confidence to that principle which is pointed out to be the destiny of mankind by God himself. I would bend with my sympathy towards that class which, by that sentiment to spare every material interest, will, of course, seeing the *rapprochement* of the material interests of the world to the principle of freedom, give full security to it to pay the debts the Governments have made. But when the nations of the world see that the money of the world is lent to oppressors, and identified again and again with the principles of absolutism, I do not know what the consequence will be. I believe, with these few words, I have proved that the principle of security to financial interests is not in absolutism, but in the victory of the principle of liberty in Europe. This you have seen in Hungary, having bestowed your attention to our struggles. You have seen Hungary struggling under me for liberty—struggles not to injure any one; to have the blessing of all, but not the curse of a single man. You have given your interest to our past, your wishes for our future; let me again entreat you, let not the sentiment of London pass as a barren sound; you have the power—help!

The seventh principle which I meet is the consolidated peace of Europe. Such a city as London, with such immense industry and trade, wants the consolidated peace of Europe. Now, I think you will see the peace of the world is only possible when the nations of the world will be contented. The contentment of the nations is such a tree as only in the garden of liberty grows. So long as the nations of Europe shall not be free, so long there cannot be peace in Europe, because that would not be peace, but a prison, and this fair world was not created by God to be a prison to humanity, neither is it created for the gaoler's sake. It is not long ago that a great association—the Peace Society—had a meeting here in London; humanity greets the existence of that Society with hope. We will have peace, but a lasting and true peace, and not oppression, slavery. Now, this association has proclaimed the principle of non-intervention. Could there be found a single man in the world to give such an interpretation to this principle of non-interference, that whatever the Czar of Russia, or his satellite Hapsburg, should do with mankind and humanity, England would not care for it? This is not non-interference; this is a letter of marque given to the Czar to become the master of the world. The principle of non-interference proclaimed even by the Peace Association has this meaning:—Every nation is free to dispose of its domestic concerns according as it is willing, and England should not interfere, and no foreign Power should dare to interfere, with this sovereign right of the nation. Oppressed humanity expects England to execute and safeguard this divine principle. Oppressed humanity expects, in the name of all those mighty principles I have had the honor to mention, London to take a lead in the direction of public opinion. And so, my Lord and Gentlemen, I could go on in the enumeration of the principles which I meet here, were I not even so exhausted as you are tired.

Still, one more permit me to mention; it is the principle of generous humanity. England is the only spot in Europe which is an asylum to those who are oppressed; London ever generously partakes in that glory of England, and you, my Lord, and the corporation of the city of London, even now gloriously represented the allotting to the generous undertaking of the noble Lord (Lord D. Stuart), whom I long ago already am accustomed to call the father of the unfortunate,—allotting to his undertaking in behalf of homeless exiles these noble apartments, these glorious halls. Permit me to express for this token of your generous sympathy my warmest thanks. May the freedom of the world soon release you from those cares! I hope it soon will. But, in the meantime, I wish may never an Englishman be found adding the thorn of humiliation to the bitterness of the bread of the poor unfortunate exile.

My Lord and Gentlemen, in stating the principles of the place where I have the honor to stand, I stated at the same time the principles which you represent. I see spreading before my eyes the immense history of the municipality of London—the most glorious, the most instructive topic to men like me. But this you know, being the inheritors of this glory and of this history. So I will only state that you, my Lord Mayor, Aldermen, and Commons of the city of London, in Common Council assembled, being the lawful representation of the city of London, are altogether the incorporation, the lawful incorporation, of all those principles which I had the honor to enumerate. Such are you, before whom I in my humble quality represent that noble cause of Hungary, the past struggles of which you honored by your sympathy, and for the future of which you express your generous wishes. I have often repeated during my tiresome speech the humble request, let your sympathies and your wishes not remain barren. Now, again, I repeat it the more, because this practical direction which I wish to see imparted to the noble sentiments of the people of England is in the most intimate connection with the principle of freedom, the principle of lasting social order, the principle of municipal institutions, with the principle of industry and trade, with the principle of public credit, with the principle of the possibility of the peace of the world, and with the principle of humanity.

As to the practical result to which oppressed humanity, and especially my poor country, looks forward with manly resolution, with unshaken courage, and with hope, I will but repeat that which I elsewhere already have said. When I declared—" Let not remain barren your sympathy ; help us to carry that noble cause to a happy issue ; you have the power to help,"—when I spoke that, I intended not to ask England to take up arms for the restoration of Hungary to its independence and liberties. No, gentlemen, that is the affair of Hungary itself; we will provide for our own freedom. All I wish is, that the public opinion of England may establish it to be a ruling principle of the politics of Europe to acknowledge the right of every nation to dispose of its own internal concerns, and not to give a charter to the Czar to dispose of the fate of nations, and so not to allow the interference of Russia in the domestic concerns either of Hungary, or of whatever other nations on the continent, because the principles of freedom are in harmony, and I love—I am interested in—the freedom of all other countries as well as of my own.

My Lord and Gentlemen, these are the words which I again and again will repeat here in England, and there in the United States, from a most honored member of which I have had the honor to hear principles which, quite once carried into effect, would and will give liberty to the world. I have heard it proclaimed from an honored citizen of the United States, the honored object of the sympathy and confidence of a great part of his countrymen, even a candidate to become the chief magistrate of the United States—I have heard, in answer to my appeal, declare that he believes the younger brother of the English race very heartily will give his hand to England to protect oppressed nations, not admitting interference with their domestic affairs. Gentlemen, I will again and again repeat to you these words ; I will repeat them with the faith of those martyrs of old, which has moved the hills and the mountains ; I will concentrate all the fire of my sentiments, all the blood of my heart, all the energy of my mind, to raise these words high and loud, deep and solemn, till the almighty echo of the public opinion in repeating it becomes like the thundering trumpet before the sound of which the " Jericho" of human oppression falls ;—and, should this feeble frame succumb sooner, should it succumb to the longing of my heart to see my fatherland independent and free, which longing beats everlasting in my feebl frame, as the captive lion beats his iron cage—even the grass which will grow out of my grave will cry out to Heaven and to man, " England and America ! do not forget in your proud security those who are oppressed. Do not grant a charter to the Czar to dispose of humanity. Do not grant a charter to the despots to drown liberty in Europe's blood. Save the myriads who else would, and will bleed ; and, by not granting this charter, be the liberators of the world !"

SPEECH IN MANCHESTER.

If you expected to hear from me an eloquent speech I very much fear you will be disappointed. Disappointed, because since my arrival, God, the mighty protector of mankind's destinies, has caused me to be so much occupied with the sympathies of the people of England, I could not find time to prepare an eloquent speech—at all events not couched in words which in England, where every word is caught by the press (that mother and guardian of all progress), you would expect from me. You would be disappointed in the second place, because I have to answer an eloquent speech, and because when I would be eloquent in my own language, and when I want to give inspiration to those who hear me, I feel at a loss to utter my sentiments in a language to which I am a stranger. I have therefore to crave your indulgence, while I attempt to address you.

Mr. Chairman, there was once a king of Epirus, sent once a man, though I do not remember his name, to Rome. On his return it was reported by him to his master that he had seen a city of kings, where every man had as much happiness as the king himself holds. I have seen more in England under your Government. I have seen the public opinion of the English people pronounced in such a voice as that of which Lord Brougham once said: that now and then the voice of the people as the thunder of the Almighty is heard. I saw the crowding of the people, which went to my heart; and I have received addresses from all parts of Great Britain, equally as numerous as generous; and I have had some idea of the public opinion of England. But I saw that public opinion incarnated in the great demonstrations of London, Birmingham, and Manchester; and after I have seen those demonstrations, I loudly proclaim, Ye oppressed nations of Europe, be of good cheer and courage! I have experienced enough in my public life to know that public opinion, as that pronounced by the people of England on that class of which I am one of the humble representatives, may be dissimulated for a while; it may be perhaps jeered at hardily; but at last obeyed it must be—because

England is a constitutional country, and in a constitutional country the public opinion is by right and by the constitution to give directions to Government and to the Parliament. I know what power public opinion has a lawful right to claim in this glorious land; and because I know that it must be very much, I say that I thank the people of England, I thank the people of Manchester, for their great aid to the cause of humanity, not in my name, but in the name of the oppressed nations.

Since my arrival on England's happy shores, I have seen a continual opportunity for the pronunciation of that public opinion on that question the solution of which is ostensibly (apparently) looked to by Providence to be the task of our times—the question which will decide the fate of mankind for centuries. This question is none of scanty or partial interests. It is none of a noble commiseration for the misfortunes of an individual, or of one country. It is a question of universal interest, in which every country, every people are equally interested—I say equally interested. There may be a difference as to the succession of times, in which one or other nation will be affected by the unavoidable consequences of this question; but affected they really are—one a day sooner, or one a day later than another—it is a mere question of time. No country, however proud its position, but chiefly, none within the boundary of the Christian family, and of European civilization, can avoid that share of the consequences of this all-comprehensive question, which will decide the approximate fate of humanity.

I scarcely want to say that this comprehensive question is, whether Europe shall be ruled by the principle of freedom or by the principle of despotism—or to bring more home in a practical way to your generous heart that idea of freedom—the question is, whether Europe shall be ruled by the principle of centralization or by the principle of self-government—because self-government is freedom, and centralization is absolutism. Shall freedom die away for centuries, and mankind become nothing more than the blind instrument of ambition, of some few, or shall the print of servitude be wiped out from the brow of humanity, and mankind become noble in itself, and a noble instrument to its own forward progress? Woe, a hundredfold woe, to every nation which, confident in its proud position of to-day, would carelessly regard the comprehensive struggle of those great principles! It is the mythical struggle between heaven and hell. To be blessed or to be damned is the fate of all—this may reach us one day, sooner or later; but to be blessed or to be damned is the fate of all; there is no transaction between heaven and hell. Woe, a thousandfold woe to every nation which would not embrace within its sorrows and its cares the future, but only the passing moments of the present time. In the flashing of a moment, the future becomes present, and the objects of our present labors have passed away. As the sun throws a mist before the sun rises, so the spirit of the future is seen in the events of the present day.

There are some, who endeavor to contract the demonstrations of sympathy which I have had the honor to meet, to the narrow scale of personality. They would fain make believe, that there is nothing more in these demonstrations than a matter of fashion, a transitory ebullition of public feeling, passing without a trace like the momentary bubble ; or, at the utmost, a tribute of approbation to the bravery of a gallant people in a just cause, and of consolation to their unmerited misfortunes. But I say it is not so. I say, may no nation on earth have reason once to repent of having contemptuously disregarded these my words, only because it was I who said them. I say that the very source of these demonstrations is, the instinctive feeling of the people—that the destiny of mankind has come to the turning point of centuries ; it is the cry of alarm on the ostensible approach of universal danger ; it is the manifestation of the instinct of self-preservation, roused by the instinctive knowledge of the fact, that the decisive struggle, the destiny of Europe, was near, and that no people, no country, can remain unaffected by the issue of this great struggle of principles. The despotic governments of Europe feel their approaching death, and therefore they will come to the death-struggle. And I hope this struggle is unavoidable, and because it is called forth by them, it will be the last in mankind's history.

That is the state of the case, as I conceive it, gentlemen. It is not my individuality—it is not my presence, which has aroused any feeling or sentiment ; I am nothing, but the opportunity which elicited the hidden spark—the opportunity at which the existing instinctive appreciation of approaching danger caused in every nation the cry to burst forth—the loud cry of horror. Or else, how could even the most skilful sophist explain the fact of the universality of these demonstrations, not restricted to where I am at present—not restricted to any climate—not restricted to the peculiar character of a people—not restricted to a state organization—but spreading through the world like the pulsation of one heart—like the spark of heaven's lightning ! The addresses, full of the most generous sentiments, which I am honored with in England, are the effects of my presence ; but I am but the spark which kindles a feeling which has long existed, from the people of the metropolis, down to the solitary hamlets hidden by neighboring mountains from the business of public life.

And I humbly entreat you to consider that this feeling is not restricted even to England : there is the public of the United States—Italy, France, the noble English garrison of Gibraltar, the warm-hearted Portuguese, have all joined in these views ; and on the very day when a deputation came over to England to honor me with the greeting of Belgium, that lofty monument of the love of freedom, and of its indomitable force—even on that very day I got the knowledge of a similar demonstration in Sweden—the future left wing of the forces of freedom. Now, gentlemen, is this an accident ? Is this fashion ? Is this personal ? What have I in my person, in my present, in my future, not to justify, but even to explain this universality of demonstration? Nothing—entirely nothing; only the knowledge that I am a friend of freedom—though I am nothing but the opportunity for the manifestation of the instinctive feeling of so many nations, and at which the St. George of England is ready to wave the red flag. How can I say that this struggle is so near? Why, ladies and gentlemen, I state it because it is. Every man knows it; every man feels, every man sees it.

A philosopher was once questioned, how he could prove the existence of God? "Why," replied he, "by opening my eyes. God is seen everywhere; in the growth of the grass, and in the movement of the stars; in the warbling of the lark, and in the thunder of heaven." Even so I prove the decisive struggle in mankind's destiny draws near. I appeal to the sight of your eyes; I appeal to the pulsations of your hearts, and to the judgments of your minds. You know, you see, you feel that the judgment is drawing near. How blind are those men who have the affectation to assert that it is only certain men who push to revolution the continent of Europe, which, but for their revolutionary plots, would be quiet and contented? Contented! With what? With oppression and servitude? France contented, with its constitution subverted? Germany contented—with being but a fold of sheep, pent up to be shorn by some thirty petty tyrants? Switzerland contented, with the threatening ambition of encroaching despots? Italy contented, with the King of Naples? or with the priestly government of Rome—the worst of human inventions? Austria, Rome, Prussia, Dalmatia contented, with having been driven to butchery, and after having been deceived, plundered, oppressed, and laughed at as fools? Poland contented with being murdered? Hungary, my poor Hungary, contented with being more than murdered—buried alive—for it is alive. What I feel is but a weak pulsation of that feeling which pervades the breasts of the people of my country. Russia contented with slavery! Vienna contented! Lombardy, Pesth, Milan, Venice, Russia, contented! Contented with having been ignominiously branded, burned, plundered, sacked, and its population butchered, and half of the European continent contented with the scaffold, with the hangman, with the prison, with having no political rights at all, but having to pay innumerable millions for the highly beneficial purpose of being kept in serfdom.

That is the condition of the continent of Europe—and is it not ridiculous and absurd in men to prate about individuals disturbing the peace and tranquillity of Europe? How is it that there are no revolutionizing movements in England? Why no attempt to disturb the peace and tranquillity of England? Because you want no revolution. Because you are ensured by your constitution, and by your public spirit, that whatever you request to be done—because no human things are perfect—it will be done, and done peaceably. I would like to see the man who would stand up here in England for the purpose of making a revolution. But there, on the continent of Europe, in its greatest part at least, tyrants of the world, you have disturbed peace and tranquillity, you have checked the growth of freedom on the continent, and it cannot be restored until the lovers of freedom contend successively against you, the sworn enemies of mankind, freedom, peace, and tranquillity.

Let us look back, and see what has been done in the past. The gigantic contest against Napoleon was fought under the promise of freedom—the promise of freedom was the bait which brought the nations to fight. Then came the Congress of Vienna, which was attended by some of the most ambitious men of the world; but even there the interference of England in the settlement then to be made was a guarantee to mankind for some constitutional life at least. And even your Castlereaghs were unable to bind Europe in oppression—to Poland, Sicily, and many other nations liberty was guaranteed; but where is Poland now, where is its constitution? And here I would appeal to the public opinion of the world. And I would appeal to those very statesmen of England who belong to the very retrograde school—to them I would appeal as to those who had made terms without the sanction or consent of nations. And I would put to them the question, " Is the present condition of Europe that for which the people of England shed their blood in torrents—is it that for which England spent its innumerable millions, the interest of which you have to pay now, and will have to pay hereafter—I ask the question, is the condition of Europe that which the people of England were willing to guarantee, and which God purposed should be the case?"

Let oppression go on, and the spread of freedom will be the result. France had aroused herself, and the despots trembled. Despots had always tried to crush the nations of the world. But oh, how trembling despots are in these days! I have seen some of them—I have weighed them in the very hands of mine. Formerly, they broke only their words, now we are subjected to the consequences of a breach of their sworn oaths—and every tie is broken, every sentiment revolted, every interest hurt. The praises of God are mingled with curses against despots, and oppressed European nations shake their chains, and bleeding nations feel their degradation. This is the present state of the European continent, at least for the greatest part. And still there are men who have regard for despots, but who are silent in regard to the duties due towards humanity. They speak of regard to tyrants, but they are silent about the dangers of mankind. In regard to the condition of mankind, the people of England have instinctively felt that we are on the eve of the day when liberty or despotism must be crushed down. The people of England felt that their freedom was in intimate connection with the principle of freedom on the European continent.

I feel most anxious to have this view shared by you, that Hungary is not so much an object of commiseration as it is a European question, and in this view I am supported by a gentleman whose opinion is as disinterested as it is important. He is a candidate for the high office of President of the United States, and therefore his opinion may be taken as that of the great Democratic party to which he belongs: I quote some lines from the speeches made by Mr. Walker at Southampton. He says that an alliance of despotic powers to submit to them free governments less powerful than themselves, can have no aim but to sweep all free governments from the face of the earth. Poland was thus swept away by despotic powers, and Hungary, which had secured its freedom, and overthrown the forces of Austria, was overwhelmed by Russia, the very incarnation of despotism. Now, when this was done, England could not expect long to enjoy her own institutions. Would free government and a free House of Commons be permitted, with trial by jury, freedom of speech, and freedom of the press, if despotism ruled on the continent? Despotism could not long flourish there while there was freedom of speech and of the press in England. Such a moral artillery would overwhelm the despots, and, therefore, they would ultimately conspire to ruin the free institutions of England.

This is not the humble opinion of a poor individual like myself, the representative of an oppressed country, but of a man who is the representative of a large party, and a candidate for the government of a free people. I will only add that this alliance of despots is a fact. The case of Hungary shows it; and as I have faith in the rights of nations, I can with all confidence ask what is, and what will be, the practical issue of the thing that is here to be seen beginning?

I have every reason to look with particular hope, in respect to the solution of this question, to Manchester. Firstly, because Manchester is a young city. In 1720 it was a village of 24,000 men, and now it is the first manufacturing city of the world, with nearly half a million. It is a glory to a city to have endured to old age, to have lived through the vicissitudes of centuries, but it is no small glory to have grown up to a giant in a short period. That people which has grown up in a short time is a practical people, and therefore I look for a practical result from it. I, secondly, have much faith in this, because Manchester, with Liverpool, is the most powerful link between Europe and the United States. Commerce is the locomotive of principles. Your glorious destiny is to offer by your hand the support of the public opinion of England to the United States, for the purpose of union in the policy of both countries in respect to Europe. That union, I say with a perfect conviction, would be the turning point in the destinies of Europe and mankind; it would be the victory of the principle of freedom, because the United States and England united, they will not, and they cannot, side but with freedom. That is to be one point, gentlemen, for which I must humbly ask the support of Manchester, in the councils of this city, which is in all respects in the most intimate connection with the United States.

When I go to the United States in some few days, it will be—I will consider it to be—one of my duties to try if there I cannot be a humble opportunity for this union, as I was a humble opportunity for the promulgation of the solidarity sentiment of nations for the principles of liberty; and I have some hope, with your generous aid, to succeed: firstly, because there is in the United States already a great party which professes an inclination and a propensity to unite with England in its policy towards the world. Secondly, because the fate of Hungary has already somewhat contributed to change the old rivalries between the two brothers into the most brotherly feeling. Both countries have united in rescuing me from captivity. I say—I may state as a matter of fact—that the first link to this union in policy is already made. Thirdly, because all depends on a true and exact definition, how it is thought that in the United States there is a ruling principle of non-intervention in European matters. I say very wise were those men that established that principle, and very wise were those who followed it. But neither those who established that principle nor those who followed it, were of the meaning that the United States should have nothing to do and nothing to regard, whatever fate attends humanity.

The principle of non-intervention is the recognition and the acknowledgment of the several right of every nation to dispose of its own domestic concerns; and so I take it as a principle, that though we have not the right to interfere with the domestic affairs of another country, whether it chooses to be a republic or a monarchy, or chooses to be even a despotism, so as it depends on its own will, that is what I assume to be the principle of non-intervention—the acknowledgment of the several right of every nation to dispose of themselves. But that is not non-intervention which would be manifested if I use the words "that I don't care whatever be the fate of humanity—I don't care whatever the despots of the world may do with Europe, with mankind, and with liberty." Because that is not non-intervention, but it is an encouragement even to despotism, to carry their victory of absolutism, which has gone so much too far already, I suppose there is no doubt that it is the policy of England and the United States to unite.

And I look with peculiar hope to Manchester, because—and I bow with deep respect to it—Manchester carried the principle of free-trade. What Manchester undertakes, it will carry. Now, excuse me, ladies and gentlemen, it may perhaps appear strange what I say, but I am deeply convinced of it. I say that free-trade is not carried. Cheaper bread is carried, but free-trade is not carried. Free-trade will be carried when the produce of England's industry will have a free accession to the markets of Europe, from which by the absolutist principle they are now excluded. When I came to England I took it for the rule of my behavior not to mix with the internal affairs of England, because I wished to show that very respect for a nation's domestic affairs which I asked for my own country. But I may be excused when I find in England a fact largely established as the law of the land which has a connection with the laws of my own country, if I mention it. And still even in that respect I say that the freedom of Europe is connected not only with the free-trade party—it is also connected with the interest of the protectionist party in England, though I consider that the victory of the principle of freedom in Europe is such a question which, if duly considered, can be no party question in England itself; because if I take the principle of free-trade, it is carried in respect to the importation of corn.

Now, if I were a protectionist, would I endeavor to overthrow that law? No; that were to try what is morally and materially impossible. It would scarcely be done without many misfortunes to the country. What would I do? I would carry on as a protectionist—if the definition of protectionist is to take guard of the agricultural interest of this country—I would carry on the principle to free exportation to other countries, that by this re-exportation the industry of England should have a greater market, more employment, better wages, surer and more efficient labor for the industrialist or the manufacturer; and by this they would, and in the best manner, promote the interest of agriculture. Because, where is better trade, where is more money, where is money hard to buy back that is bought by a country's produce? That would be the way to carry on, to protect the interests of agriculture—which, of course, are very important in every country—but that carrying on of the free-trade principle to free exportation to other countries, is strongly connected with the great principle of freedom. Without that it is entirely impossible. Let me especially honor the people of Manchester, for having so far carried out the principle.

My poor nation, Hungary, even now, when groaning under the weight of despotism, consumes cotton manufactures of the value of two millions and a half pounds sterling yearly. In that consumption, which is a very great one, not a single yard of Manchester industry appears. Why? Because the governments of every people are the greatest locomotives of principles. An alliance between the absolutist principle and free governments and free opinions is impossible and unheard of. And what would be the consequence in the future, if Hungary had a free government on the basis of liberty! Of course, the Hungarians would undertake—will undertake—new developments of industry themselves. But the cotton manufacture they could never think of, because it would not be natural to them. British exports during the last three years—that is to say, from the beginning of 1847 up to the end of 1849, that is the last year for which the returns have been made up by your Board of Trade—give an average of a fraction under 6¼d. for each individual of the Russian population. To Austria British exports are still lower, averaging for every individual a fraction over 4¼d. per head during the same period. Yet, during these three years, British exports to the United States have amounted on the average to more than 10s. for each individual. Great as is this difference, the difference is daily increasing. The despotically governed countries are taking gradually less, and the United States gradually more, of your progress. In the three preceding years, 1844, 1845, and 1846, your exports to Russia averaged 7¼d. They have fallen off, as I have had the honor to state, to 6¼d. During the same three years, your exports to the United States averaged 7s. 6d. They have increased by one quarter—that is to say, up to 10s.; so that not only is your market increased with the increase of the United States' population, but every individual of the United States' population consumes more of your products, while in Austria and Russia the reverse has taken place.

You will remark that though you ought proportionately to their respective populations to have five times more commerce with Russia and Austria than the United States, you have in fact nearly five times more commerce with the United States than with Russia and Austria; whence it may be inferred that, under a free Government, your commerce with those countries would be at least five-and-twenty times its amount at present. If 125 or 130 millions of Russia, Austria, and Italy were in the same condition as the highly manufacturing United States, those millions would consume as much at least as 50 or 60 millions more than the amount of the whole taxation of England and Ireland, who wish naturally to reduce taxation by cutting down those articles whose very existence tends to the disturbance of peace. But how can you reduce your armaments whilst France has got her armaments on foot ready to the hand of Changarnier; and how can you expect France disarmed whilst the armed despotisms are existing? Therefore, I venture to say, that in entreating your aid for the victory of the principle of liberty of Europe's continent, it is more than a dispensable compliment to your free trade school, of which I see the most able leaders and most energetic promoters around me. To be sure they are not men to do things by halves.

Before my coming to you, ladies and gentlemen, I was asked by many what can I have to do here when many of your most influential individuals are intimately connected with the Peace Society, whereas I of course must be aware that what Austria, by Russian armaments, has taken away from Hungary, it will not restore by peaceable means. Francis Joseph, though a Jesuit, surely has not the intention to exchange his purple for the monk's garb of Charles the Fifth; neither does the Czar Nicholas intend to abandon his trade of tyranny. But this is true, and I will look confidently to several great associations of England. I hope they will support the great cause of which I am one of the humble representatives. I hope that it will be supported by the religious associations, because in Hungary freedom of conscience is put down by despotism. Even in these very times the Protestants of Hungary shut their schools because they were forced by the Government to surrender their system of education and give it into the hands of the Austrian Jesuitical government. Therefore they shut up their schools, and I suppose they will not want for their support the religious protection societies. I look to the protection of the Reform Society, to the Free Trade Society, to the Association of the Friends of Italy, as, of course, the cause of Hungary and Italy must be identical. I openly declare that to none of these associations I look with more hope for a generous support than precisely to the Peace Association. And should I not have entertained this expectation, the generous speech of one of your most eloquent and kind-hearted men, one of your most decided artisans, upholders and champions of freedom, would have convinced me I did not plead in vain for the support of that association of peace.

Too truly other associations can perhaps oppose the cause of Hungary. The Peace Society is morally obliged to support it. If it is logical, certainly it is. If it is willing to fulfil the necessary conditions of its success, certainly it is. Everything depends on a good definition, and none of the continent of Europe represents the true meaning of the word " peace." Let us take first, in a private aspect, the word " peace." A man, for instance, is kicked out of his house. What shall he do ? Shall he act according to the principles of the Peace Association—try to convince by reasoning ? Shall he require the protection of the law ? But what shall he do where there is no law—where he is out of the law ? I believe that to surrender so much, then, would be to surrender the principle of the security of property, on which a certain one pillar or two, of social order repose. It would be contrary to the instinct of self-preservation, which God himself has given us. Though I must consider the principle of peace which is taken up to be agitated, carried out by the Peace Association, a principle for legislative adoption, the principle of non-resistance is a different principle to that of peace. That is precisely the case in Europe now. The nations are oppressed by the armed force of military governments. Despots will not give way—at least they will not without a struggle. Now, what should do the aggressed nation ? Should they rely upon the principle of capitulation to the Czar, or the other military powers ? Capitulation is no ground that they should rely upon—that they will themselves abandon their power, never.

If we look to history, where is there a single free country which was not forced to win its institutions ? In the first progression and development of opinion, where is a single nation which was not forced to win these institutions by a legitimate defence of arms against arms? There is not a single case in history. Of course, when a nation is in the happy condition of the people of England, it is an example of freedom to the world, which has its parliament, its free institutions, its responsibility of ministers, its public spirit, and its position in the world. Such a country, of course, will never need to have recourse to arms as material forces. But how in England are these materials acquired? If you had not had the revolution of 1665, what then would have become of your parliaments? Therefore I confidently know that it is not possible for the glorious association of peace to have the intention to condemn the nations of Europe to a weak and artificial feeling of despotism. The first principle of that great society is the Christian principle. No one can subscribe more heartily than myself to that principle. What is there in the Christian religion? There is your glorious, great, angelic aspiration, " Glory to God in Heaven, peace and good-will amongst men." But peace to tyrants—that is impossible. Peace to murderers— that is suicide, that is not part of the Christian religion. The second rule is, " Thou shalt love thy neighbor as thyself, and thou shalt not do to others that which thou wouldst not have done to thyself."

Now, if somebody is in need because he is assailed by a murderer, who burns his house down, and who will slay him, would it not be contrary to the command for me to say, that I never would come to help him? I assume that every member of whatever society— Peace Society, or whatever else—remembers the great rule, " Thou shalt do to thy neighbor as thou wilt that thy neighbor shall do unto thee." I find in the Christian religion there is given to the emperor what belongs to him, but it is not taught by the Christian religion to give him what does not belong to him. The freedom of opinion is not the property of emperors. The second principle of this glorious society is the principle of non-intervention in foreign matters. That is precisely what I ask for: I am not come to England to ask your armed interference—to entreat England to take part in an armed restoration of Hungary. I only entreat England to respect, and make respected, the principle of the sacred right of every nation to dispose of its own affairs. That glorious association I consider not an English society alone, but an association of the world. It is not for England alone. It has proclaimed to the world the principle of non-interference, and, therefore, I confidently trust there is not a single member of the Peace Society who would give this definition of the word non-interference as to say, " Some of these despots wish to dispose of mankind, England will not care about it." That is not the principle of this society. It cannot be its principle, we have heard so to-night from one of its most worthy members. It is true public opinion is almighty, where it can act. In what reposes the omnipotence of public opinion? It reposes in the belief that where it is respected by power there public opinion will make itself respected. This belief gives omnipotence to public opinion. This gives a force to it by which it carries things morally. That being my opinion I declare that myself, although I would have peace to all nations of Europe, I would have peace and not prisons, because if they have prisons they will have armies; nations cannot be free so long as the moral conduct continues to be sacrificed to the interest of certain families—so long as the entire system of the affairs of the greatest part of Europe can be summed up in these few words, "The people pay because I want soldiers and spies to keep up my power." That is not peace. They are chains which God has not created for the world.

Absolutism can only be defended by the contentment of nations. It is calumny and almost perjury, to charge people for soldiery and spies. While there is freedom there is order. I view these thousands here—I view the thousands at Birmingham—without a single man to keep order, and I have never seen greater order than here. It is not true that nations like despotism and look for it. There is no such people; but there is many a people which feels less death than oppression; and I am one of them. So I am entitled to say I feel with confidence the identity of my principles with the principles of the association, and the identity of their principles with my wishes and my wants; and it is, therefore, that I was confident that Manchester, being one of the most glorious workshops of the Peace Association, would prove to be a supporter of the cause of liberty; and this my presentiment and expectation is closely fulfilled here.

So, gentlemen, let me now, in a few words, say what are the practical results which I, in the name of my good country and in the interest of humanity, would entreat the practical and glorious people of Manchester to give a generous sympathy towards my cause. It may be that in these principles substantial aid may enter. I feel, gentlemen, that never in my life, from no one, would I accept anything. My life is a proof of it. I would rather starve. It may be my fault; I feel it is my nature; but for the triumph of liberty—for my dearest country, I would not be ashamed to go begging from door to door like a poor mendicant. But there are yet other things to which I look for a practical result. Firstly, public opinion has declared itself freely; but, to have force, this public opinion must go on pronouncing itself. Only I hope that the words of *Falstaff*, " I would it were bedtime, and all were well," may never be taken for a motto by the people of England; but that public opinion may go on to pronounce itself. But, to be sure, there are many respects in which this pronunciation will tend to a happy result for humanity and for England also.

Firstly, it would be a benefit to the cause of Hungary if public opinion is directed to what we are told about the secrecy of diplomacy. I confidently declare, I believe that every interior question of great importance in England is now resumed in the foreign-office. The principle of free-trade is much resumed. It depends entirely upon how the foreign relations will be adjusted, whether England shall or shall not have free-trade in Europe. And so every other question. Our reform questions depend on the progress of despotic principles in Europe, or upon the progress of liberty in Europe. Every interior question is resumed there; and I humbly entreat the people of England to bestow more attention and sympathy to the foreign relations, and that the people of England, feeling themselves to be a constitutional nation, has a conviction that it is right to give a direction to the foreign affairs in accordance with the public opinion of this country, as pronounced by those organs which by the constitution are established. If the secrecy of diplomacy is turned out, I confidently hope that will give to the public of England such a weight in the destinies of mankind, that it shall not need to speak of moral or material forces, but only to go on with the pronunciation of that public opinion, and it will carry into effect the principle of liberty. Therefore, these are my wishes—meetings, petitions—a press to throw out the secrecy of diplomacy, and pronounce the will of the people of England, that all may be considered a right when the great day of decision comes. I humbly ask this pronunciation of the public opinion of the people of England for a full acknowledgment of the several rights of every nation to dispose of its domestic affairs.

And by the principle of non-interference, I understand not to permit the interference of one nation with another. Here I take the opportunity to declare, that it is true I for my own country, and for myself, have convictions; I consider that after what has happened in Hungary, if it were the most monarchical country in Europe, still the mere establishment of it is impossible, because the treachery of the house of Hapsburg has blotted out every hope of it. But it never came to my mind to have the pretension to go round through the world to preach government principles. Wherever I go, I acknowledge the right of every nation to govern itself as it pleases, and I will say that I believe freedom can dwell under different forms of government. This I say, because gentlemen whom I have had the honor to answer, upon an address presented to me—of course, not having quite well understood my words—have given such a report as that I should have said, I considered in Europe there was no other form of government possible—no other really constitutional form of government than a republic. That was a misunderstanding. I never said so. I consider that a form of government may be different, according to the peculiar circumstances of a nation. Freedom exists in England under monarchical government as under republican government. There social order is established. Combine my republican convictions with the principle of respect for the security of persons and property.

Here, gentlemen, I will end. The generous attention I meet with in England makes me believe you expected to find in me something worthy of your attention. Now the spell is broken which distance had imparted to my name. The halo of expectation has died away, and here I sit, as a plain common man, as thousands and thousands are in your own country. But, ladies and gentlemen, however deep I may have fallen in your estimation, as to myself, let me most certainly believe that the present day will not vanish without some benefit to the cause of my unhappy land, and without some benefit to the cause of humanity. And, therefore, I end with these words: People of Manchester! let not the world, let not history say, that on the eve of the last struggle between despotism and liberty, you had nothing better to give to the principle of freedom than the compassion of tender hearts. People of England! shout out with manly resolution to the despots of the world, like the people of old, that the world shall be free—and you have given freedom to the world!

SPEECH IN BIRMINGHAM.

LADIES AND GENTLEMEN,—

Three years ago, yonder house of Austria, which had chiefly me to thank for not having been swept away by the revolution of Vienna in March, 1848, having in return answered by the most foul, most sacrilegious conspiracy against the chartered rights, freedom, and national existence of my native land—it became my share, being then member of the ministry, with undisguised truth to lay before the Parliament of Hungary the immense danger of our bleeding father-land. Having made the sketch, which, however dreadful, could be but a faint shadow of the horrible reality, I proceeded to explain the alternations which our terrible destiny left to us, after the failure of all our attempts to avert the evil. Reluctant to present the neck of the realm to the deadly snake which aimed at its very life, and anxious to bear up against the horrors of fate, and manfully to fight the battle of legitimate defence, scarcely had I spoken the word—scarcely had I added the words that the defence would require 200,000 men and 80,000,000 of florins, when the spirit of freedom moved through the hall, and nearly 400 representatives rose as one man, and lifting their right arms towards God, solemnly said, "We grant it—freedom or death!"

Thus they spoke, and there they swore, in a calm and silent majesty, awaiting what further word might fall from my lips. And for myself: it was my duty to speak, but the grandeur of the moment, and the rushing waves of sentiment benumbed my tongue. A burning tear fell from my eyes, a sigh of adoration to the Almighty Lord fluttered on my lips; and, bowing before the majority of my people, as I bow now before you, gentlemen, I left the tribunal silently, speechless, mute. Pardon me my emotion—the shadows of our martyrs passed before my eyes; I heard the millions of my native land once more shouting liberty or death! As I was then, sirs, so am I now. I would thank you, gentlemen, for the generous sympathy with which, in my undeserving person, you have honored the bleeding, the oppressed, but not broken, Hungary. I would thank you for the ray of hope, which the sympathy of the English people casts on the night of our fate. I would thank you, gentlemen, warmly as I feel, and as becomes the dignity of your glorious land. But the words fail me; they fail me not only from want of knowledge of your language, but chiefly because my sentiments are deep, and fervent, and true. The tongue of man is powerful enough to render the ideas which the human intellect conceives; but in the realm of true and deep sentiments it is but a weak interpreter. These are inexpressible, like the endless glory of the Omnipotent!

But could I dare to say something about my humble self without becoming presumptuous, I would beg leave to state that it is not only from to-day, but from my early youth, I have been spiritually connected with Britannia. I was yet young, sir, under rigorous circumstances, almost anti-didactically, preparing my soul for the future, which is a common one to us all—to be useful so far as possible to Fatherland and to humanity. The great things that have occurred I could not then anticipate. I could not anticipate that it was I who would have, by my sufferings, to break way to the freedom of thought in my native land—that it was I who, by applying to several special objects of association which has produced so many wonders in this glorious country—should have unprecedented influence on my nation's life, capable of leading from the indifference of despondency to the cheerfulness of activity, and by activity to self-confidence—that the liberation of my people from those hereditary burthens that have weighed them down for 500 years; that the political emancipation which transformed the close hall of privileges into an open temple of common liberty, that the sanction of the great principle of equality in duties and rights, should ever be associated with the recollection of my humble name; or that it should be my lot to reconcile the stubbornness of past ages with present necessities and the exigencies of modern times. I could not anticipate that it was I who should at one time of my life be the shield of protection to the head of the proud house of Hapsburg in his own imperial residence, and that, seeing this service returned by a war of extermination to my native land, it should be my destiny to lead on Hungary in such a gigantic struggle for independence—that struggle which but for a moment— yes, with an unshaken trust in the justice of God, I swear—for a moment only, even the combined powers of the despots of two large empires were able to overcome by getting for an ally a traitor in our own ranks—that it should be my destiny to lead on Hungary in such a contest, which, spite of its momentary misfortunes, will still prove the death-blow to the bondage of feudality, the turning-point in the future of at least one half the European continent, a cry of alarm to all nations to unite in the cause of freedom against the union of absolutism, and to raise my nation out of the narrow proportion of a provincial vegetation to such a rank as would make her an element indispensable to the triumph of civilization and liberty; and, at last, that I, the insignificant son of modest Hungary, should be honored with so much notice from this glorious land, that such as, since Hungary was a nation, no Hungarian, or perhaps any other stranger, was ever honored with.

These and many similar things could never have entered into my early dreams. The sphere of activity which was then open to me was narrow as my faculties, and modest as my condition. Ambition never troubled the peace of my mind. I knew that it is not given to man to choose his position in the world, but I knew it is given to him honestly to fill the place which Providence has assigned to him. So I rested contented with the idea that the great architect above knows best what use to make of the meanest nail, and endeavored to prepare myself to become a feeble instrument in the hands of Providence to do some little good work. In this endeavor I had for my teacher that book of life, history. It was the great examples of the classical past that warmed the susceptible young heart to noble aims and instincts; but the thirst of scrutiny pushed on the mind to look around for some other master than the ruins of vanished greatness, or those mournful monuments of the fragility of human things. I looked round not for ruins, but for life, and to be able to teach my nation how to live.

It was then that my regards turned with admiration upon the Anglo-Saxon race, this living wonder of both hemispheres, the glorious Albion. Hither my attention was drawn by the striking resemblance and coincidence of institutions which the observer cannot fail to mark in the histories of our past; hither my attention was drawn by the fact that the fatal sickness of European statesmanship, inherited from ambitious conquerors—the propensity to centralize every power, and to govern the people like imbeciles, even in their domestic concerns, is here. It has not yet extirpated the germ of municipal public life, without which—I repeat the word, which my bad pronunciation made not quite well understood on another occasion—I mean that without a municipal public life, I believe no practical freedom can exist; and for the loss of it all ministerial responsibilities, all parliamentary omnipotencies, are but a pitiful equivalent. But above all, hither was my attention forcibly drawn by the wonderful great ness of your country. And I was searching the source of it, and I found it, not alone in your institutions, because these, as every human thing, can nowhere be entirely perfect, but I found them, together with your institutions, in that public spirit which pervades every fibre of your nation.

Sir, like the spirit of God, which, on creation's day, spread over the waves, I found it in the freedom you enjoy Yes, sir, I found England not free because mighty, glorious, and great; but I found her mighty, great and glorious, because free. So was England to me the book of life, which led me out of the fluctuation of wavering thoughts to unshakable principles. It was to me the fire which steeled my feeble strength with that iron perseverance which the adversaries of fate can break but never bend. My heart and my soul will as long as I live bear on itself the seal of this book of life. And so has England long ago become the honored object of my admiration and respect; and so great was the image of Britannia which I cherished in my bosom that, lately, when the strange play of fate led me to your shores, I could scarcely overcome some awe in approaching them, because I remembered that the harmony of great objects wants the perspective of distance, and my breast panted at the idea that the halo of glory with which England was surrounded in my thoughts would perhaps not stand to the touch of reality, the more because I am well aware all that is human, and every age, has its own fragilities. I know that every society, which is not a new one, has, besides its own fragilities, to bear also the burdens of the sins of the past, and I know it to be almost a fantastical law in mankind's history, that the past throws over so large a shadow in the present and in the future, that to dispel it entirely the sun must be mounted very high. But so much I must state with fervent joy—that on the whole the image which reality in England presents bears at every step such a seal of greatness, teeming with rich life, and so solid in foundation, that it far surpasses even such expectations as were mine.

And the thing which in the midst of your great nation strikes most the mind of the observer, is that he meets in moral, material, and social respects such elements of a continual progress towards perfection; and these elements display such a mighty, free, and cheerful activity, and this activity is so lively pervaded by the public spirit of the people, that however gigantic those triumphs of civilization may be which England has already proudly to show to the astonished world, and great they are—they are things called wonders by history which shrink to pigmies before them. Nevertheless, one feels by instinct all this to be but a degree—a gigantic one to be sure, but still only a degree to what posterity will have the lot to admire here. But, having the honor to dine in Birmingham, surrounded by you here in the Town-hall, which, like your free schools, your Market-hall, and several of your hospitals, all raised without any external assistance, are so many proofs of the lofty public spirit, self-confident force, and perseverance of Birmingham, you will allow me, gentlemen, to state, that in no place of England have I met the elements of your country's greatness on more solid basis displaying their activity; in no place I more confidently hoped to see that sympathy which I meet, to have a practical result, than here in Birmingham.

I have not the pretension to tell your own history to you. It is one of your particular glories to call men like William Hutton your own, and I like to prove what I say, so you will allow me briefly to state the motives which make me look to your city with that trust and that hope. Industry is a chief element of greatness, welfare, power and might. It is industry which gives practical value to science. In other branches of employment, human faculty appears to be a developing power, but industry is a creating power; and being so, it is the most efficient locomotive of progress. But industry, highly beneficial in itself, becomes a pedestal to the public order of a country, and a lasting source of public and private welfare, when it is not only largely diffused, but also connected with an independent condition of the manufacturers, which independence, securing a substantial condition to entire classes, cannot fail to impart to the manufacturing man that self-esteem, that noble pride, and that sentiment of proved dignity, which is the mark of a free man, and the richest source of private and public virtues. It is so that we see in the historical period of the middle age, the cities to be the last stronghold of liberty, when all around them was feudal bondage. And what were the cities of old? Almost nothing else but corporations of manufacturers, independent in their situation, working at the fire of their own domestic hearth, working for themselves—men whom we might characterize as small masters, not overwhelming in wealth, but independent in their position. So became industry the last stronghold of political freedom, as it was precisely the means of personal independence. The development of science and wealth must have led, of course, to large, mighty industrious establishments, where the secret powers of nature are made subservient to the creating power of industry; and these mighty establishments are even as beneficial to every country, where a large population works for employment, as they are glorious in the history of the development of man's faculties, but requiring large capital, and therefore more subjected to the fluctuations of commerce. Being exposed to great losses, as well as to great gains, they have more of a personal character, whereas industry largely diffused, and founded on a substantial, independent situation of those who work, has a more public and political character, and constitutes a lasting public element of the condition of the country.

Now, this is precisely the happy condition and the glory of Birmingham. It is this basis upon which Birmingham rose from the time of Julius Cæsar. Always a seat of industry, it became the centre and the heart of a large manufacturing district, bringing the combination of the lime, iron, and coal of that district in suitable forms to become the common benefit of the world; giving arms to those who had the lot to fight for their liberation, the pen to fix the idea of thinking men, the cable to the wandering sailor, as also the fine neck-chain to the fair beauties of the world. I saw with admiration the Crystal Palace, that magnificent meeting-hall to humanity. The meeting was in London, but I was lost in a wonderment at Birmingham's astonishing industrious energy. I saw and admired the crystal fountain, the most magnificent work in glass industry. I know Birmingham to be the metropolis of the great railway system. I know that it was Birmingham which preceded, by its local exhibition, the idea of the World's Exhibition. I know that it is Birmingham which gave, by the genius of its Elkington, the electrotype to us. I know that machine-weaving was here used before the power-loom was introduced elsewhere. I know that here was the workshop of Watt, whose steam-engines blotted the word "distance" out of the dictionary. But what I the most admire is that you have even made the steam—this omniferous power of our times—subservient to the peculiar domestic and independent character of your largely-diffused industry, so as to be almost an article of domestic use.

The character of your industry makes me consider Birmingham as a real seat of that strongly-felt spirit of independence and freedom which makes your glory and my hope. Myself, the wandering son of a bleeding nation, feels, after two hard years, for the first time, my heart flushed with joy, because on seeing the English people, and on inhaling their public spirit to my vexed soul, I can't forbear to believe that the freedom of such a nation must be the pulsation of mankind's approaching liberty, and that the part of the world where such a pyramid of civilization stands, cannot be doomed to be the prey of Russian or Austrian despots. You remember Paulus Amilius, whose triumph by a whim of fate was placed between the tombs of his two sons. You remember his quite Roman words— "*Cladem domûs meæ vestra felicitas consolatur.*" Were there anything in the world able to console a Magyar for the misfortunes of his fatherland, here is the place where I would repeat the words of yonder Roman son! But alas! (and who would blame me for it?) even here where I am, and so surrounded as I am, still I feel myself a homeless exile—and all that I see carries back my memory to my down-trodden land. Sorrow takes deeper root in human breasts than joys; one must be an exile, and the home of the poor exile must be suffering as mine is, that the heart of man can feel the boundless intensity of the love of home.

And, however strange it may appear to you, the roots of my life are not within myself, my individuality is absorbed in this thought, "Freedom and Fatherland!" What is the key of that boundless faith and trust my people bear to me, their plain unpretending brother—a faith and confidence seldom to be met in like manner in his way. What is the key of it—that this faith, this confidence, stands still fast, neither troubled by the deluge of calumnies, nor broken by adversities? It is that my people took, and take me still, for the incarnated personification of their wishes, their sentiments, their affections, and their hopes. Is it not then quite natural that the woes of my people also should be embodied in myself? I have the concentrated woes of millions of Magyars in my breast. And allow me, gentlemen, a sort of national self-esteem in that respect. The people—that mighty basis of the pyramid of mankind—the people is everywhere highly honorable, noble, and good. Some few may be selected to be the honored of humanity; they may, by the powerful soar of their genius, rise to the very height whence, as Halley or your Newton said, "Man is forbidden nearer to approach God." But they are exceptions, and, because so, they are not the manifestation of the eternal law. And you know the development to which mankind is called in going on according to steady eternal laws. Those selected few stand on the top of humanity, so they are not the basis of it. The basis is the people; they are steady and lasting. My belief, therefore, is, that it is the instinct of the people which is the true revelation of mankind's divine origin. It is, therefore, I was saying, that the people is everywhere highly honorable, noble, and good.

But, though to me, as to a Hungarian, that sort of sentiment may not be becoming which befits a British man, who, whatever be his personal merits, puts—and with right—his greatest pride in the idea to be a citizen of Great Britain; still allow me to prostrate myself in spirit, before the memory of my suffering people; allow me to bear witness before you, that the people of Magyars can take with noble self-esteem a place in the great family of nations; allow me, even in view of your greatness, to proclaim that I feel proud to be a Maggar. While, during our holy struggle, we were secluded from the world, our enemies, wanting to cover their crimes by lies, told you the tale that we are in Hungary but an insignificant party, and this party fanaticized by myself. Well, I feel proud at my country's strength. They stirred up by foul delusions to the fury of civil war our Croat, Wallach, Serb, and Slovack brethren against us. It did not suffice. The house of Austria poured all his forces upon us; still it would not do. We beat them down. The proud dynasty was to stoop at the foot of the Czar. He thrust his legions upon us, and still we could have been a match for him. One thing there was which we, the plain children of straight uprightness, could not match—that is, the intrigues of Russian diplomacy, which knew how to introduce treason into our ranks. This caused us to fall, combined with Russian arms. But still we were styled to be only a party fanaticized by me.

Well, "I thank them for the word." You may judge by this what will then be, when not a mere party but together all the Magyars, also all the Croats, Wallachs, Serbs, and Slovacks, melted in one body, will range under the standard of freedom and right. And be sure they will. Humanity, with its childish faith, can be deluded for a moment, but the bandage soon falls from its eyes, and it will be cheated no more. And yet, though we are oppressed, they are oppressed and deceived. Afterwards, the scorned party turned out to be a nation, and a valiant one; but still they said it is I who inspired it. Perhaps there might be some glory in inspiring such a nation, and to such a degree. But I cannot accept the praise. No, it is not I who inspired the Hungarian people—it was the Hungarian people who inspired me. Whatever I thought, and still think—whatever I felt, and still feel—is but a feeble pulsation of that heart which in the breast of my people beats. The glory of battle is ascribed to the leaders, in history—theirs are the laurels of immortality. And yet on meeting the danger they knew that, alive or dead, their name will upon the lips of the people forever live. How different, how purer, is the light spread on the image of thousands of the people's sons, who, knowing that where they fall they will lie unknown, their names unhonored and unsung, but who, nevertheless, animated by the love of freedom and fatherland, went on calmly, singing national anthems, against the batteries whose cross-fires vomited death and destruction on them, and took them without firing a shot—they who fell falling with the shout, " Hurrah for Hungary !"

And so they died by thousands, the unnamed demigods. Such is the people of Hungary. Still, they say it is I who have inspired them. No; a thousand times, no! It is they who have inspired me. The moment of death, gentlemen, is a dreary one. Even the features of Cato partook of the impression of this dreariness. A shadow passed over the brow of Socrates on drinking the hemlock cup. With us, those who beheld the nameless victims of the love of country, lying on the death-field beneath Buda's walls, met but the impression of a smile on the frozen lips of the dead, and the dying answered those who would console, but by the words, "Never mind; Buda is ours. Hurrah for the fatherland!" So they spoke and died. He who witnessed such scenes, not as an exception, but as a constant rule,—he who saw the adolescent weep when told he was yet too young to die for his land; he who saw the sacrifices of spontaneity; he who heard what a fury spread over the people on hearing of the catastrophe; he who marked his behavior towards the victors, after all was lost; he who knows what sort of curse is mixed in the prayers of the Magyar, and knows what sort of sentiment is burning alike in the breast of the old and of the young, of the strong man and of the tender wife—and ever will be burning on till the hour of national resurrection strikes—he who is aware of all this, will surely bow before this people with respect, and will acknowledge with me, that such a people wants not to be inspired, but that it is an everlasting source of inspiration itself. This is the people of Hungary. And for me, my only glory is, that this people found in myself the personification of their own sentiments. This is all he can tell of himself, whom you are honoring with so many tokens of your sympathy. Let me therefore hold the consoling faith that, in honoring me by your sympathy, you were willing to give your sympathy to the people of the Magyars.

But let me ask what can be the meaning of the sympathy of the English people? Is it but a funeral feast offered to the memory of a noble dead? God forbid! The people of England are the people of life; their sympathy belongs to the life. The hurrah which greeted me on your shores—the warm, sincere cheering of the hundred thousands in your streets, so generous and still so modest, so loud and so sincere, so free and still so orderly—I take for the trumpet-sound of the triumph of freedom, justice, and popular rights. To be sure, deep is the sorrow which weighs on me: it is, as I have said, the concentrated woe of millions; but do not think, I pray, this sorrow to be that of despondency, which knows nothing better than hopeless complaint. No; this sorrow is such a one as enlarges the horizon of hope and perseverance, getting, like the Antæus of the fable, new strength from every fall. Let me, therefore, assure you, gentlemen, that the people of Hungary has a future yet; let me confidently state that the people of England have not spent their sympathy to a corpse. But, well may you ask, "What are the motives of this hope?" The first basis of my hope is the Almighty himself —the God of Justice who cannot grant a lasting victory to wickedness. History has to be sure recorded the downfall of mighty empires, of nations, to whom compared, the Magyars can scarcely claim a name. But the fall of those nations was precisely the revelation of the eternal justice of God. They fell by their own crimes. Nations die, but by suicide. That is not our case. Hungary is not the sacrifice of its own crimes. An ambitious woman had in the palace of Vienna the sacrilegious dream to raise a child to the seat of power upon the ruins of liberty. Well she knew that God would not be with her, but she knew that the Czar would be with her; and what do they care for God if only the Czar be with them?—the Czar who dared to boast that he has the calling to put his foot upon mankind's neck. Arrogant mortal! thou dust before God! No, gentlemen, by such an act a nation may suffer, but not die. The God of humanity cannot admit this. And do you not already his judgment mark? They said, "Down with Hungary, that Hapsburgs may rule as they please." And look! they had already in the first act of their sacrilegious plot to mendicate the helm of him whose aid gave them dishonorable bondage instead of the coveted might. They longed to be the sun, and have nations like moons to revolve around them in obedience; and they themselves became the obedient moon of a frail mortal. Let them not rely on their Czar; his hour also will come. The millions of Russia cannot be doomed to be nothing else than blind instruments of a single mortal's despotic whims. Humanity has a nobler destiny than to be the footstool to the ambition of some families. The destiny of mankind is freedom, sir, and the sun of freedom will rise over Russia also; and in the number of liberated nations who will raise the song of thanksgiving to God, not even the Russians will fail. So let the house of Austria trust to his Czar. The people of Hungary and myself we trust to God!

The second anchor of my hope is my untowering faith in the destiny of humanity. The realization of this destiny can have no other basis than the people itself. However arrogant may therefore be those potentates of the continent, who, unlike to the gracious Queen of these isles, take themselves for the aim, and the people but for a mere tool, I have the firm conviction that every state's organization is perverted, perverse, and doomed to be turned up, where single individuals or single classes have the pretension to constitute the basis of the society. Mankind has but one single aim, and that is mankind itself. And this aim has but a single instrument, mankind again. They are rebels against God who believe their calling to be—to form the Atlas, and to bear upon their shoulders the vault of humanity. One single pressure of the vault and they are crushed to dust. They are rebels against God who believe the great pyramid of mankind but for the purpose to exist that they may proudly stand on its top, having the pretension to doom the pyramid to immobility, only to serve as a pedestal to them to look down haughtily from the height. One shivering only, and they are shaked off, and hurled down to the dust. There let them lie!

Truly on throwing one unpreoccupied regard on the greatest part of our continent, sir, on looking to Germany, to Austria, to Hungary—on looking to the indignities of Rome, or to that of Naples, the horrors of which Mr. Gladstone has lately with generous indignation shown—on looking in general to that Italy which cannot forbear to become furious when with its glorious remembrances it casts but one look into the mirror of its present horrible state—on casting a glance even over the great French nation, which the fairest fruits of three great revolutions, the glory outside and the freedom within, one by one beholds absorbed by centralizing omnipotence—upon seeing all this, it is not possible, sir, that the unpreoccupied observer, to whatever party he may belong, should not be convinced this situation to be so unnatural, so much in contradiction with the laws of nature and the destinies of humanity,—it is in such striking opposition to the most sacred interests of millions, that it is entirely impossible to endure. And, besides, when we see the great and the petty tyrants, how they have paid their people for having been merciful to them, when the people might have been but just; and when we see how they are incorrigible, how they have nothing forgotten, nothing learnt; when we see, on the other side, how nations have by common suffering learnt that their fate is bound one for another in perfect solidarity; and out of this conviction what Christian brotherly love sprung up instead—the unhappy rivalries of old which formed the sole strength of the oppressors—sir, it is quite impossible not to feel that we are already on the eve of those days when the oppressed nations will hold the greatest court-day ever seen, before the verdict of which all artificial buildings of mankind's oppression will fall to dust.

The third anchor of my hope is the history of my nation. Our country has seen already many a storm, and still the Magyar lives, and still Buda stands. There was a time when one half of Hungary was under Turkish dominion, the other half under the iron rule of the Bastas or the Canatas, the model after which the Haynaus of the day—or I should rather say their masters—were formed. The horrors of Arad are not the first bloody leaf in the house of Hapsburg's history; and still the Magyar is alive. The house of Hapsburg has during more than three dreary centuries exhausted against us open force as well as all sorts of craft. It has fomented our discords, poisoned our habits, undermined our national character, lopped our freedom, robbed us of our rights. It has impoverished, weakened, oppressed us; and my nation has not perished yet. The single genius which has to be found in the house of Hapsburg—Joseph (but he of old, and not the modern Francis Joseph)—bent his powerful mind to the design of Germanizing Hungary, and of melting it into his empire; and our country, and our nationality, already by the preparative cunning of ungrateful Maria Theresa, cast back to the huts of the poor, did but with renewed strength out of the ordeal arise. And even we, three years ago, the feeble offspring of mightier times, there we stood desiring nothing but peace, in order that the ant-like industry of the people may change into a paradise our country, stopped in its progress by long sufferings. There we stood, not only not suspecting treachery and royal perjury, but even then not willing to believe it, when it ought to have been believed; and, because not believing, there we stood unprepared to meet the danger which gathered in a frightful manner over us, and so we were attacked—and you know, gentlemen, how we were attacked, and we, secluded from the whole world—alas! forsaken by the whole world —without friends, without an army—four scanty ranks filled with treacherous elements, who delivered our fortresses—without money, without arms, without ammunitions—still we beat back the unjust assailant, yea, beat him down, that he flew to the foot of the Czar, mendicating his assistance to his impious design; which he obtained it is true, but had to pay for it all his hopes, all his future honor, independence and dignity!

Who could think this Hungarian nation not to have yet a future, sir? Even the means by which it was oppressed did this future but assure. While the house of Austria, by the manner of its victory, and the manner of making use of that victory in Hungary, in Vienna, in Prague, in Italy, has doomed itself to certain fall—while the house of Austria, precisely by its victory, revealed its power to have no natural basis at all—meanwhile has my nation, precisely by its fall, to Europe revealed that she is necessary to Europe's security, as also by her glorious defence, she revealed her vitality. While the house of Austria, on the faith of his own crimes, is still sliding down, so as slide must he who came upon the bridge painted by Milton's master hand, my nation stands fast amidst all adversities, unshaken in courage, steady in resolution, firm in confidence. While the house of Austria, sliding along yonder fatal bridge, estranged from itself every people, hunted every race, every interest, and revolted against itself every sentiment from Schleswig-Holstein to Rome, from Hessen to Constantinople; meanwhile my nation has had to contend with millions of those who, stirred up by foul delusion, fought with the fury of extermination against us: now they all have learnt that their own freedom also is dwelling with us, that our oppression is but the tool of their own servitude; and they all look as fervently for the day of retribution as we ourselves. Could anybody earnestly think that these Magyars and all their fellow-people, hunted to their very heart, the Bohemian, the Pole, the Croat, the Slavon, the Dalmatian, the Wallach, the Serb; yea, even the Lombard, and the Venetian also—the Lombard which Austria even now but with an iron glove dares to touch, and where Radetzky during three short years has immolated 3742 human lives on the scaffold; and yonder Venetian, who cannot forbear to weep tears of blood, when he chances to look along from the Rialto—could anybody think that all these offended bleeding nations can lightly be melted together by the alchemists of Vienna in the crucible of united slavery?

With us, Hungarians, there have been alchemists of other stamp to make the same trial. Sir, men like Joseph the Second. But all in vain. Though Joseph has had what, to give in, makes amends to the people of Hungary—abolition of slavery, add liberty to conscience and to thought—still the trial failed. But Francis Joseph, what has he, the blood-stained child, to give to the down-trodden nations? Oppression at home, shame and curses abroad; one-and-a-half milliards of debts; an approaching bankruptcy; the monopoly of tobacco; heavy stamp duties; consumption taxes (the very name tells the nature of it); and all his other glorious inventions to drain the life-sweat of the people. These are his gifts. And when the blunt murmurs of groans raised by these gifts, in spite of martial law, the hangman, and the state of siege, rises so high as to reach even the imperial palaces, do you know, gentlemen, what the consoling answer is? I will tell you with the very words of the most decided organ of Viennese politics: "It is told the Magyars are discontented. We know it well; but it was not our design to see them contented, but to see them pay." Horrible! This word gives the key of the unavoidable future in your hands, gentlemen. The house of Austria will not be loved, but paid. Well, Hungary will pay off all it owes to them. It will pay them, I swear in the name of the honor of my native land. There are some nations, sir, the situation of which, though very painful upon the whole, promise still some duration to the power; because at least some classes there are, the interests of whom are not hurt. In Hungary, sir, except some hundred foreign functionaries, there is not a single man, still less a single class, whose interests were not mortally hurt. Wounded is the nation's heart, conscience, religion, honor, nationality, freedom, memory—wounded in all that it held sacred and dear. Besides, wounded is the material interest of every class. The landlord and the agriculturist, the citizen and the soldier, the artist and the scholar, the workman, the merchant, the professionist—all cut down to that poor Wallachian who lived upon some plum-trees, which he now cuts down to free himself from the heavy duties laid upon him. Elsewhere whole classes may be found who dread every change. In Hungary there is not a single class which the wise and honest Austrian government, by his paternal cares, had not driven to the point, to be forced to desire the most complete change, however desirable it may be.

And we have yet one thing not to forget. The people are merciful and generous. They can forgive those who govern many a fault, as long as the faith to the rulers is not plucked out from their heart. But where there is no more such faith, there is no power on earth again to knit a lasting tie between the rulers and the ruled Now that is the very case with Hungary. It experienced such faithlessness, such an injury from the dynasty, that the faith in the morality of this dynasty is to the last root plucked out from his heart; so much so, that the nation holds the reign of right, law, and justice, impossible under the Hapsburgs. How should it not? Every day even now brings new falsehood, new treachery; every promise has turned out to be a lie, the Imperial word has become equivalent to perjury, and in addition, the people have been told that the Hapsburgs will have money and not love. As the Czar has brought the Hapsburgs to us, so Monk once brought the Stuarts back to you; but the faith was lost in their morality, and where are they now? Forsooth, I say, there is much likeness in our histories. We are now where you were after 1665. Only time went on. It will not last so long. Look to history. Restored dynasties have no future, sir; and in Hungary, after what it experienced, no monarchical combination has a future. But the house of Austria can have no future even beyond Hungary, because it has lost every natural basis of its existence, and that is a bad reason to claim further life. Had the house of Austria in 1848 been just towards the nations it rules, or wise towards the great German national family, it might have had a future yet; but while it deceived every one of its own nations, to Germany it rendered itself. Where will at last subside the fluctuations of great Germany's fate it is not for me to tell; but sure as it is that they will somewhere subside, even so sure it is that the wedge-stone of it can never become yonder house of Austria, which threw itself away, to be a mere tool of Russian preponderance, which being a foreign one is also even as ambitious as despotic.

The rule of the house of Austria in Germany would therefore equally hurt as well the national feeling, as the sentiment of liberty in Germany (as even the intrigues for supremacy already show) without having even any glory to offer in exchange. The historical basis of taxation it has lost; the basis of the new era it refused to accept, how then should it continue to live? It had yet one artificial fancy of its existence, the idea of being necessary to Europe against Russian omnipotence, that Europe might not become Cossack, as Napoleon said. The idea was idle and false; because the guarantee of Europe could never be sought in one family, but in nations. The idea was a false one, but still it was. Where is it now? Since by asking and accepting Russian armed interference against Hungary, the house of Austria became a mere vanguard to Russian preponderance. Its existence not only cannot be necessary to Europe, but it turned to be rather dangerous to it, since it is precisely Austria that has thrown up in Europe the conventional public law and so-called system of equilibrium. So the house of Austria, bare of all natural elements of life, has but three things to vegetate upon—loans, bayonets, and the Czar. Its eternal wars lead to bankruptcy—its armies are composed out of the sons of those nations which hate it as man nates the hand which the blood of his mother has spilt; and as to the Czar, Europe will not, cannot, admit him to rule on the banks of the Rhine, of the Danube, and of the Po.

Let, therefore, the house of Austria, proudly relying on its bayonets and its Czar, trample upon oppressed nations. I know the armies of to-day are not the condottieris of old—I know that the light has spread, and even bayonets think—I know that all the Czars in the world are but mean dust in the hands of God—and so I firmly hope, nay I am certain, I shall yet see Hungary independent and free. You have to judge, gentlemen, by what I have had the honor to expose, if there be serious motives for that hope. But still one I have to add. The last not least of all. It is the sympathy not only of every oppressed, but also of every free nation; it is the sympathy of the mighty English race, called to be the pillar of oppressed humanity, the younger offspring of which glorious race, those in the mighty republic of the new world, has put under the ban of mankind the oppressors of Hungary and sent a war-ship to conduct me out of prison, while the elder brothers of that mighty race here in these glorious isles raised its powerful voice to break the chains which fettered my activity; and, upon my arrival on its happy shores, honors me with an attention almost unparalleled in history, and this too in the very moment when the blood-stained Hapsburgs, raging like an impotent furious child, let nail my name to the gallows. I feel not offended, sir! My honor is not dependent on Hapsburgian folly, Hapsburgian rage. There may be rather some glory in the idea to be hated and feared by bloody despots whom nations curse. I vow to do all where I can to merit this hatred, this fear. I have the honor to represent a principle, sir! The English race, in honoring me with its generous sympathy, has pronounced in favor of this principle. The Hapsburgs nail it to the gallows by a hangman's hand. It is a defy, it is a challenge of an arrogant tyrant, to the public opinion of the world; a defy to your sympathy, gentlemen; a defy to the generous sympathy the fate of my country is honored with in this glorious land.

I fear not to be contradicted when I say, that it were a want of appreciation almost like an offence to the people of England, were I capable to think this sympathy to be nothing more than the passing emotion of noble hearts. No, sir! full well do I know that the sympathy of the people of England is no idle thing. If the people of England has once taken a direction, has once bestowed its sympathy, has bent its mind to anything, it will carry it—it will have out of it some practical result. This firmness of character, this untirable perseverance in every great and noble aim, is the true key of your country's greatness, gentlemen. So I rely upon it confidently, sir. What is it I could dare to look to as for a practical result of the people of England's generous sympathy for my native land? That is a matter which myself, an unpretending stranger, could but slightly dare to touch. But would I not too much tire you, I would beg leave, sir, briefly to state some few particulars out of the past, for future's sake. Before all, I have to insist upon the point, that the manner of taking such a view of the Hungarian revolution—as if in making it, anybody in the world could have had his hand in it—is an entirely false one. Let the word—Hungarian revolution—be a praise or a reproach, it is a matter of fact that we have made no revolution, sir.

Take a man who, confident in the protection of law, rests quietly in his house; and the night-watch, instead of taking care that his tranquillity may be not disturbed, gives himself the incendiary torch to some fellow-lodgers of his house, and persuades them, by falsehood and promises, to burn his house and to murder him; and he, starting from his quiet rest, rushes from his room to put out the fire and to preserve his life; and he cries out for the very night-watch to help him in his legitimate defence; and this very night-watch brings an armed guard with himself, and instead of defending the injured man, calls him a traitor and a conspirator for daring to oppose the honest incendiary, the faithful murderer—yea, more, he joins the incendiary, and rushes on the injured man with his armed guard; and he, the poor injured man, calls together his brethren and his sons, beats down the incendiary, the murderer, the night-watch, and his guard. Is there any honest, any just man in the world who could charge the man with having committed an assault on the legitimate authority of the night-watch, sir? I have given you in this popular sketch the history of the past Hungarian war.

I beg not to be misunderstood. Sir, it is not the fear of the revolutionary question which makes me say this. I am a man of justice, right and liberty, sir, and will be so my whole lifetime. Little do I care for, how the sworn enemies of justice, right, and liberty may call me, sir. Your Hampdens, your Russells, and Sidneys, were also called revolutionists in their turn; and so, may God bless me, I wil never be longing for a brighter fame than theirs; still less would ı see this disavowal applied to the future, sir. To be sure, I take a revolution for a very great misfortune, sir; but also highly I own that an oppressed people, seeing every other means of preservation fail, has a right to make a revolution. The people of England must acknowledge this truth, because the freedom and greatness of England derives from the practical success of this truth. Highly I own that my oppressed people is in this very case. But I look, sir, for a lively interest to verify a matter of fact, and to reduce the misrepresentations of tyrants and their satellites to their just value. All the like gossip about anarchy, about our having been most licentious demagogues, who were forming incendiary plots against the tranquillity of neighboring states; about my despotic government carrying on Hungary with me by terrorism; and all other trivial phrases, in which soul-oppression of mankind excels, are entirely to be put on the same scale. Though the reign of the house of Austria over Hungary was three centuries ago but a continual series of perjury, and though it encroached immensely upon our rights, still we conserved some shadow of constitutional liberty. We enjoyed no freedom of the press, this mother as well as the chief guarantee of all progress; but still our municipal institutions afforded us a certain degree of self-government, and our county meetings and their publicity conserved to us the power of words. We were persecuted for its use, till it became almost "treason to love the country, and death to defend." But still we spoke; the people, though excluded from any share in these constitutional rights, and reduced to the scanty role of mere spectators, but seeing still there were men struggling manfully for them and the rights of humanity—even the people were generous patiently to endure and confidently to wait.

And so the Hungarian soil was not the soil of conspiracy, sir. My nation had, and has still, neither the will nor occasion to share in the movement of those new doctrines which disturb the sleep of the mighty of the earth. We have struggled fairly and openly, by the arms of truth and justice, for the social and political freedom of the people, as you have struggled for all those mighty reforms which helped to preserve your country from all dreadful concussions which never fail to arrive, wherever progress and reform have no fair course; we carried our reforms peacefully, availing ourselves of the opportunity which God has given, and which we made; we knew how to be just to the people, without regarding to what tongue he speaks, or in what church he prays; but the Hungarian people becoming master of his fate, was moderate enough to reserve his part to time, contented with gradual progress. With us there was nothing done by violent commotion; no equitable interests trodden down; and generously spared even those which though insignificant their origin were interlaced with the private fortune of a whole class. The peo-

ple of Hungary was rather inclined to undergo many sacrifices, than
to punish the sins of former ages in the present generation, or the
crimes of some few by the sufferings of whole classes. There was
with us no trace of anarchy. In the midst of our war, in every part
of Hungary which our victories brought back under our rule, order
and security of person and property was far greater than that of
which the " undermining" Austria can boast even now. And this
was not my merit, sir, but the people's. Struggling on nine different sides, after the storm of battles passed from our region, and still
it was for weeks not within the reach of my government; but the
moral sense of the people, and his noble instinct, safeguarded order
and security. Very seldom I was in the case to use the authority
of command ; and when so, it was not the people but others who required it. To the people a word of advice, pointing out the necessity of the country, sufficed. The greatest force of our army was
composed of volunteers ; the stock of my financial operation was
made out of free sufferings ; our cannons were cast out of bells,
which were offered in an embarrassing quantity. We defended ourselves but attacked nobody ; and secret designers were far from the
straight spirit of my land. Austria and Russia took the neighboring
Turkish provinces for a basis of aggression against us. Whole
armies of theirs have we thrown back of these frontiers ; we had but
to follow—and we had a right to do so, because the duties of neutrality had not been maintained—and the theatre of war would have
been changed, yea, brought home to Russia itself; and yet we
stopped ; we respected the international rights, though towards ourselves nobody respected them. Austria concentrated all her dispos-
able forces against us. Gallicia was entirely denuded. Had I but
a feeble force thrown in, the flame of revolution might have been
blown up amidst that heroic unhappy nation—the noble sacrifice of
the morality of kings, as Johannes Müller has stated, which looks so
fervently, and with so much right, for the day of retribution—and the
flame of that revolution might have spread over Russia itself; but I
took it for a crime to play with the blood of nations, and I refrained
the sympathy of my heart, and scrupulously avoided to afford the
slightest pretext to the ambitious views of the autocrator of the
north.

Vain to count on morality in those quarters ! Sir, they knew full
well that the heroic Polanders desired to flock in thousands to join
us ; but I did not accept them. I told them that we had a thousand
times more hands than arms. The Czar knew very well that the
heroes of Poland, who fought so valiantly in our ranks, scarcely
amounted to four thousand men; but still he styled the Hungarian
struggle a Polish conspiracy, and charged us with plotting against
the security of his empire. Well, he was enraged at the idea that it
was a Polish hero, now lying in the cold grave of far Alepp, who
beat down his bands in Transylvania. He wanted a pretence to set

his impious foot on Europe's neck; and not finding a pretence, he took it, sir. So was that Hungary, gentlemen, which the despots of Austria and Russia, and their numerous satellites, calumniated as the focus of disorder and anarchy. But, why were I dwelling upon these particulars, sir? The reason is, that I have to attribute to these calumnies and misrepresentations, that during our past struggles we were not happy enough to meet that assistance in England which, I readily confess, I hoped to meet, and considering the interests, as well as the position, which your country so gloriously holds in the world, as also considering the known public spirit of the people of England, I claimed to be entitled to hope.

Unhappily, the people, as well as the government of England, has not been well informed, at the period of our greatest need, about the true nature of the Hungarian war; about its high importance to Europe; its importance to that Orient, which in so many respects enters into the dearest interests of Britannia, so as to be nearly its Achilles' heel. We were hermetically secluded, and chiefly at the very time when our struggle rose to European height. So either we were not in the case to afford the wanted explications, or the effect of those we could give was paralyzed by adopted rules of diplomatical formalities. And have the kindness to excuse my poor country daring to make one humble remark: The people of England—the public opinion in England, was not very wont to be occupied with foreign affairs till now. Surely there might have been sufficient reasons to do so. The people of England has grown up from within. But already it has fully grown. This great empire has no more to fear any danger from within; not as if there would be nothing more to do, but because by the freedom you enjoy, by your institutions, and by your public spirit, you are positively insured that whatever you may have yet to do, not only will be done, but also will peaceably be done within. Your fate is not depending upon any mortals' whims. Here you are, the only masters of your fate. But in respect to foreign relations, things are somewhat different; every position in the world has its own conditions; every time has its own wants. According as things actually stand, I dare confidently affirm, that amongst all your interior questions, there is not a single one which could outweigh in importance the external. Nay, more, I am persuaded that all your great interior questions themselves are independent of your foreign-office. Danger can gather over England, not from within, but only from abroad.

Do not doubt me, gentlemen, that Albion, in its insular position, and with the self-confident knowledge of its immense power, does but laugh at the ambition of all conquerors of the earth. I know it, sir. Full well I know that Britannia, with the mighty trident in her powerful hands, is fully entitled—even more entitled than of yore—to proclaim with your great Shakspeare—

> "This England never did, nor ever shall,
> Lie at the proud feet of a conqueror."

I know this very well. But give me permission to ask yonder glorious thing, which we call the greatness of Britannia, is it but embodied within the material shores of these isles? Freedom, civilization, your parliament, being the senate of whole parts of the earth—the principle of free-trade—your due influence on the condition of Europe—your India, and many other considerations, are they not so many life arteries to Britannia? Let but one of these arteries be cut, and Britannia will not only no more be what it is, but these foreign questions will also powerfully re-act upon your interior. The catastrophe of freedom and civilization abroad cannot fail to bring concussions home to you. Yea, these only things can call forth such concussions within which might endanger your own tranquillity, your own welfare, your own happiness. To break Britannia, it is not necessary to conquer these glorious isles. The very moment that Britannia should not weigh so much in the balance of the world as it must weigh, Britannia will be broken. The greater a body, the more vulnerable points it has. However you may trust to the present or any future government, or to the vigilance of your Parliament, I know the most efficient axle-point of your history to be that principle—that your Parliament and your Government receive direction from the public opinion, instead of giving direction to it. And I am fully confident, gentlemen, that your gracious Queen, as well as all constituted authorities, can but be glad to see the people pronounce in time their will which might compass them in the storm of those grand *événements*, the scent of which is already felt in the air.

The finger of God is over Europe stretched out. There are but two cases possible—the one is, that the crisis of approaching events will place the established governments one against another on Europe's continent. In this case England cannot rest indifferent. Should the fate of Europe happen to be decided without England's vote, England would be a European power no more. And should, in this crisis, reaction and despotism be the victors on the continent, it were not necessary to see the Cossacks watering their horses in the Thames in order that England should no more be great, glorious, and free. You are aware, I trust, that there is a solidarity in freedom now-a-days, because that struggle will not turn about particular points. The question will be, what principle shall rule over Europe —liberty or despotism? I know that in that case the people of England will not side with despotism, but that it will side with liberty. But then the people of England, I humbly trust, will pronounce their will in time, that her silence might not be taken for irresolution or indifference. The second case is, that in the approaching crisis there will not stand states against states, nations against nations; but that the nations will make up accounts with their own rulers, and settle their own domestic affairs. What is it humanity expects in that case from Britannia ? It expects that the people of England may not only respect (that is out of doubt), but shall make respected, the natural rights of nations; and should the Czar—requested or not requested, that cannot alter the matter—should the Czar once more threaten oppressed humanity, should he once more be willing to violate the sovereign independence of nations—should he once more be willing to take any pretence to put his foot on whatever people in the world he chooses and to drown Europe's liberty in blood—humanity expects from the people of England that it will shake its mighty trident, and shout out a powerful "Stop!" like yonder Perfilius of old. Be sure, gentlemen, this single word—spoken with the resolution to be as good as your word—this single word will suffice. It will cost you neither money nor blood. Yea, by that single word, by the will to speak so, made known in time, you will have saved the lives of myriads, averted much bloodshed, and given liberty to the world. A glorious power! A glorious calling!—nearly divine!

The short moral of my long speech, gentlemen—there it is. The Russian intervention in Hungary has put the foot of the Czar upon Europe. As long as Hungary shall not be restored to its sovereign liberty and independence, as long as Italy shall not become free, that foot of Russia will rest on Europe's neck—yea, it will step from the neck upon the head, and there will be in Europe neither peace nor tranquillity, but a continual boiling-up volcano, and Europe a great barrack and a great bloodfield. The cause of Hungary is the cause of civil and religious liberty. I say of religious liberty, and therefore not religious exclusion or sectarianism, but free liberty to all—common liberty and protection to every religion alike. I, as you know, am a Protestant; and not only a Protestant by birth and education, but a Protestant by conviction: but I here declare that I would struggle with equal enthusiasm to obtain religious liberty for Catholics as for Protestants, and for the protection of all men in the exercise of their religious convictions. My opinion is that the Church should not meddle with politics, and that government should not meddle with religion. That is my creed. I wish not to be misunderstood. It is possible that, with my inadequate command of the English language, I may so express myself as to convey an impression different from that I intend. Yesterday, and on previous occasions, I have said that the papal priestly government of Rome is the worst of human institutions, and I am led to fear that I may have given some offence to some well-meaning persons, who may have understood these words in a different sense from that in which they were intended. What I meant to say was, that the Church should not meddle with politics, and that as a political government, a government for secular purposes, a priestly government was the worst government ever invented. But I say, on the subject of religion, I object to any one interfering with mine, and I wish not to interfere with that of any other man.

I differ in my view with many as to Church property. To me the principle of property is sacred. When I was in power in Hungary there was no confiscation, no meddling with Church property, but an anatomy of the whole Church. I would have the Church dispose of its own property by means of its own dignitaries and its own offices, but I would have them dispose of it so as to promote the efficiency of the Church, and not to leave the working curates on 30*l*., which it is clear no man can live on, while bishops were receiving thousands.

Some have questioned the capabilities of Hungary to maintain herself as an independent nation. But she has all the elements of independence. She has 4000 German square miles. She has a population brave and industrious. She has no debt of her own—and Hungary is not liable for the debts of Austria. True, we created a debt during our recent struggle, but the house of Austria burnt the greater part of it, so (thanks to them) we are free from that. Then Hungary is, in consequence of her municipal institutions, accustomed to cheap government. Municipal government is always cheap, while centralized governments are always dear. Again, she has great resources; she is rich in mines, so much so that she could supply the whole world with the purest salt for ten thousand years. Then she has large national estates which might be distributed so as to increase the revenues materially. The principle of self-government is so strongly implanted in the Hungarian that nothing will eradicate it. I would impress on Englishmen that the freedom of Hungary is intimately connected with the question of freedom in Europe and the principle of self-government, and I hope that Englishmen, while they will not interfere in the self-government of foreign nations, will determine not to allow other countries to interfere. To this extent I wish to see the people of this country turn their attention to foreign affairs, and that they may exercise their influence to spread the principles of freedom and self-government. Mind that with every downbeaten nation one rampart of liberty falls. The people of Birmingham have ever been the champions of freedom. In Birmingham the political union which carried the Reform Bill emanated; and in olden time, when the principle of liberty was threatened by Charles I., Birmingham made a successful stand against Prince Rupert.

I rely, then, on the sympathy—the active sympathy—of the men of Birmingham. I rely upon it confidently. I rely upon it in the name of all who suffer oppression, and languish for freedom, like my people and myself. All they are my brethren whatever tongue they speak, whatever country they call their home. Members of the great family of mankind, the tie of blood is strengthened between us by common sufferings. To be sure I have not the pretension to play the part of Anacharsis Klotz before the convent of France.

You are not the convent of France, and myself also, humble as I am, still I am no Anacharsis Klotz; but my sufferings, sir, and the nameless woes of my native land, as well as the general reception I enjoy, may perhaps entitle me to entreat you, gentlemen, to take the feeble words I raise to you out of the bottom of my own desolation, —take it for the cry of oppressed humanity crying out to you by my stuttering tongue. People of England! do not forget in thy happiness our sufferings; mind in thy freedom those who are oppressed; mind in thy proud security the indignity we endure; remember the fickleness of human fate—remember that those wounds with which our nations bleed, they are so many wounds inflicted to that principle of liberty which makes thy glory and thy happiness; mind that there is a tie in mankind's destiny; be thanked for the tear of compassion thou honorest with our mournful past, but have something more than a tear, have a brother's hand to our pressure to give!

BANQUET SPEECH,

BEFORE THE CORPORATION OF NEW YORK.

Sir: In returning you my most humble thanks for the honor you did me by your toast, and by the benefit of coupling my humble name with that cause which is the sacred aim of my life, I confess to be so overwhelmed with emotion by all it was my prodigious lot to experience since I am on your glorious shores, that unable to find words to express my feelings, and knowing that all the honor I meet with has the higher meaning of principles, I at once beg leave to fall back to my duties, which are the lasting topics of my reflections, my sorrows, and my hopes. I take the present occasion for a highly important opportunity. I take it for such as will probably decide about the success or failure of my visiting the United States. I must therefore humbly embrace your indulgence for a pretty long, plain, and in no case eloquent development of my humble views, to the benefit of that cause which the citizens of New York, and you particularly, gentlemen, honor with generous sympathy.

When I consider the sympathy of the people of the United States for the cause of Hungary, so generally diffused as to be almost universal, and so resolutely pronounced as men pronounce those feelings which are intended to be followed by noble and great deeds, I would feel inclined to take your generous aid for the restoration of my native land to its sovereign independence already as granted in principle, and for me nothing left to do but to enter into a negotiation about the arrangement of the details, were my confident hopes not checked by that idea of non-Interference in foreign, chiefly European, affairs, which, according to the numerous testimonials of your most distinguished politicians, we are told to be one of the ruling and lasting principles of the policy of the United States.

I highly respect the source of this conviction, gentlemen. This source is your religious attachment to the doctrines of those great men, who highly proved to all posterity their wisdom by bequeathing to you the immortal work of that Constitution which, aided by the unparalleled benefits of nature, has raised you, in the short period of seventy-five years, from the precarious position of an infant people to the prodigious strength of a giant nation. The beneficial results of the wisdom of the founders of your great Republic you see in a happy reality. What would be the consequences of the departure from that wisdom you are not sure of. It is, therefore, natural that you feel an instinctive fear to touch, even with improving hands, the dear legacy of those great men.

And as to your glorious Constitution, all humanity can only wish, in the common interest of mankind, that you and your posterity may yet long conserve this religious attachment to its fundamental principles, which by no means exclude development and progress; and that every citizen of your great Union, thankfully acknowledging the immense benefits of this Constitution may, even in the moments of the most passionate irritation, never forget to love that Constitution more than the momentary passion of his heart, or the egotistical interest of the passing hour. May every citizen of your glorious country forever remember that a partial discomfort of a corner in a large, sure, and comfortable house, may be well amended without breaking the foundation of it; and that among all possible means of getting rid of that corner's partial discomfort, the worst would be to burn down the house with our own hands.

But while I thus acknowledge the wisdom of your attachment to the fundamental doctrines of the founders of your United Republic, I beg leave with equal frankness to state that, in my opinion, there can be scarcely anything more dangerous to the progressive development of whatever nation, than to take for a *basis* that which is none—to take for a principle that which is but the convenience of the passing situation—to take for substantial that which is but accidental, or take for a constitutional doctrine that which was but the momentary exigency of administrative policy. Such a course of action would be like to that, when a healthy man refuses to take substantial food, because when he was once laboring under weakness of stomach his physician ordered him a severe diet to keep. The consequence would be consumption—death.

Let me suppose, gentlemen, that yonder doctrine of non-interference was really bequeathed to you by your Washington—and that it was not I will prove to you afterward—and let me even suppose that your Washington imparted such a meaning to yonder supposed doctrine—which were equivalent to the words of Cain, "Am I my brother's keeper?"—which supposition would be of course a sacrilege. But suppose all this. And I believe that, even under such suppositions, I may be entitled to ask—is the dress which well suited the child still convenient to the full grown man—nay, to a *giant*, which you are? Would it not be ridiculous to lay the giant in the child's cradle, and to sing him to sleep by a lullaby?

In those times of the foundation of the United States, you were an infant people, and the large dress of your then comparatively not large territory, hung loose on your puerile limbs. In those times, you had, of course, no wiser thing to do, but to grow—to grow and to grow!

But now you are so far grown that there is no foreign power on earth from which you have anything to fear for your own existence, —for your own security. This being your present condition, you have entered into the second *stadium* of political existence, the destination of which is not only to exist for yourself exclusively, but to exist as a member of the great human family of nations, having the right to all claims, which are due from that family toward every one of its full grown members, but also engaged to every duty which that great family has the right to claim from every one of its full grown members.

A nation may be in the situation, either by a comparative weakness or by choice and policy, as Japan and China, or by both these motives, as Paraguay, under Dr. Francia, to live a life secluded from the world, indifferent to the doctrines of mankind, in which it cannot, or will not, have any share ; but then it must be prepared to become also excluded from the benefits of progress, civilization, and national intercourse. Such a nation may well say, " I don't care about the fate of whatever other nations in the world."

But I am sure no citizen of the United States had, has, or ever will have, the wish to see this country degraded to the rotting vegetation of a Paraguay, or the mummy existence of Japan and China ! The feeling of self-dignity, and the expansive quality of that enterprising spirit, which are congenial to free men, would revolt against the very idea of such a degrading national captivity. But, if there were even a *will* to live such a mummy life, there were no possibility to do so!

The very existence of your great country, the principles upon which it is founded, its geographical position, its present state of civilization, and all its moral and material interests, would lead on your people not only to maintain, but incessantly more and more to develop your intercourse with the world.

Then, of course, being in so many respects linked with the world —connected with the world, you can have neither the will, nor be in the possibility, to remain indifferent to the condition of that outward world you are in so many respects connected with. And if you cannot remain indifferent, so you must be resolved to put your own self-consistent weight into that balance, in which the fate and condition of the world is weighed.

In a word, the glorious Republic of the United States must feel resolved to be a *power* on earth—a power among the nations ; or else itself would be doomed to continual decay, and soon cease to be great, glorious, and free.

You are a power on earth. You must be a power on earth. So, of course, you must also unhesitatingly accept all the natural consequence of this situation. You cannot allow that any power whatever should dispose of the fate of that great family of mankind of which you are such a pre-eminent member; or else you would resign your proud position, and resign your still prouder future, and be a power on earth no more.

Thus, I hope, I have sufficiently shown, that, should even that doctrine of non-interference have been established by the founders of your Republic, that which would have been very convenient to your infancy would not be convenient to your manhood.

It is a beautiful word of Montesquieu, that Republics are to be founded on virtue. And you know that virtue, as sanctioned by our Christian religion, is but the effective exercise of a principle—" Thou shalt do to others as thou desirest others to do to thee." So, I am confident, that it were sufficient for me to rely simply—for the decision of the question I have the honor now to treat—upon the virtuous feelings of your generous republican hearts, and the consistency of principles. But still I beg leave to mention also, in material respects, some essential differences between your present condition and that of yore.

Then your infant Republic, composed of thirteen States, was restricted to the borders of the Atlantic. Now your giant Republic spreads to the Gulf of Mexico, the Pacific, and your territory is a world. Your right hand reaches Europe over the waves, while your left hand reaches over the Pacific, the East of Asia; and then, in the midst of two great continents, there you stand, in proud immensity, a world yourself!

Then you were a small people of three and a half millions. Now you are a mighty nation of twenty-four millions. And more than nineteen millions out of these twenty-four, are over yonder immense territory, the richest in the world, employed in the cultivation of the soil—that honorable occupation, which in every age, has proved to be the most inexhaustible, the most unfaltering source of public welfare and of private happiness—as also the most unwavering ally of the love of freedom, the most faithful preserver of all those straight, noble and generous sentiments which the constant occupation with ever-young, ever-great, ever-beneficial Nature imparts to man. Add to this consideration, that this immense agricultural interest, which deriving large markets and affording at the same time a most solid basis, also to your manufactural industry and to your commerce, has developed in such an immense proportion, makes such a boundless difference between the infant Republic of the time of Washington and your present giant Republic; that though you may very well be attached to your original constitutional principles, because the principles of liberty are everlastingly the same; but in respect to the exigencies of your policy, it is impossible not to feel that, if you are to be regulated in your policy by interest, then your country has other interests to-day than it had then; and if ever you are to be regulated in your policy by the higher consideration of principles, then you are already strong enough to feel that the time has come to do so. And I, standing here before you to plead the cause of oppressed humanity—I resolutely declare that there may perhaps never again come a time when the elevation of your policy to the high level of principles identified with liberty, could prove either more glorious to you, or beneficial to humanity; because we in Europe are apparently on the eve of that day when either the hopes or the fears of oppressed nations will be crushed for a long time.

Having stated so far the difference of the situation, I beg leave now to state that it is entirely an unfounded supposition, that the doctrine of non-interference in foreign matters had been, to the people of the United States, by your great Washington, bequeathed to be a constitutional principle to you.

No! that is not the case.

Firstly: Washington never even recommended non-interference, or indifference to the fate of other nations, to you. He has only recommended *neutrality*. And there is a mighty difference between these two ideas.

Neutrality is an idea which has reference to a state of war between two belligerent powers, and it is this case which Washington contemplated when he, in his Farewell Address, advised the people of the United States not to enter into entangling alliances. Let quarrelling powers—let quarrelling nations war; you consider your own concerns, and let foreign powers quarrel about ambitious topics, or scanty, particular interests. Neutrality is a matter of convenience—not of principle.

But even as neutrality has reference to a state of war between belligerent powers, the principle of non-interference has, on the contrary, reference to the sovereign right of nations to dispose of their own domestic concerns.

Therefore these two ideas of neutrality and non-interference are two entirely different ideas, having reference to two entirely different matters.

The sovereign right of whatever nation to dispose of itself, to alter its institutions, to change the form of its own government, is a common public law of nations, common to all, and, therefore, put under the common guarantee of all.

This sovereign right of every nation to dispose of itself, you, the people of the United States, must recognize, because it is a common law of mankind, in which, being a common law of mankind, every nation is equally interested. You must recognize it, secondly, because the very existence of your great republic, as also the independence of every nation, rest upon this basis—rest upon this ground If that sovereign right of nations were no common public law of

2

mankind, then your own independent existence would be no matter of right, but only a matter of fact, which might be subject to whatever time, to whatever chances of power and of violence.

And where is the citizen of the United States who would not feel revolted against the idea that the existence of this great Republic is not a righteous, nor a lawful one, but only a mere accident, a mere matter of fact?

If it were so, you were not entitled to invoke the protection of God for your great country; because the protection of God cannot, without sacrilege, be invoked but in behalf of justice and right. You had no right to look to the sympathy of mankind for yourself, because you would profess an abrogation of the laws of humanity, upon which is founded your own independence, your own existence.

Now, gentlemen, if these be principles of common law, of that law which God has given to all, and to every nation of humanity,—if the faculty to dispose of itself is the common, lawful right of every nation, then the interference with this common law of all humanity, the violent act of hindering, by armed forces, a nation from exercising that sovereign right, must be considered as a violation of that common public law upon which your very existence rests, and which, being a common law of all humanity, is by God himself placed under the safeguard of all humanity; because it is God himself who commands us to love our neighbor as we love ourselves, and to do toward others as we desire others to do toward ourselves.

Upon this point you cannot remain indifferent. You may well remain *neutral* to every war between two belligerent nations, but you cannot remain indifferent to the violation of the common law of humanity. That indifference WASHINGTON has never taught you. I defy every man to show me out of the eleven volumes of Washington's writings, a single word to that effect. He recommended *neutrality* in the case of foreign wars; but he never recommended indifference to the violation of the common laws of humanity, by interference of foreign powers with the sovereign right of nations to dispose of themselves.

And he could not have recommended this indifference without ceasing to be wise as he was, because there is, without justice, no wisdom on earth. He could not have recommended it without becoming inconsistent, because it was this common law of mankind which your forefathers invoked before God and mankind, when they proclaimed your independence. It was he himself, your great Washington, who not only accepted, but asked again and again foreign aid,—foreign help for the support of that common law of mankind, in respect to your own independence.

Knowledge and instruction are so universally spread among the enlightened people of the United States—the history of your country is such a household science at the most lonely hearths of your remotest settlements, that it may be sufficient for me to refer, in that respect, to the instructions and correspondence between Washington and the Minister at Paris,—the equally immortal FRANKLIN,—the modest man, with the proud epitaph which tells the world that he wrested the lightning from Heaven, and the sceptre from the tyrant's hands.

Thus I have proved, I believe, that Washington never bequeathed to you the principle of non-interference against the violation of the sovereign right of nations to dispose of themselves, and to regulate their own institutions; but he taught you only neutrality in respect to the wars of foreign nations.

I will go further. And I state that even that doctrine of neutrality he taught and bequeathed to you, not as a constitutional principle—a lasting regulation for all future time, but only as a matter of temporary policy. I refer in that respect to the very words of his Farewell Address. There he states explicitly, that "*It is your policy to steer clear of permanent alliances with any portion of the foreign world.*" These are his very words. *Policy* is the word, and you know policy is not the science of principles, but of exigencies; and that principles are of course, by a free and powerful nation, never to be sacrificed to exigencies. The exigencies are passing away, like the bubbles of a rain; but the nation is immortal; it must consider the future also, and not only the egotistical comfort of the passing hour. It must be aware that to an immortal nation, nothing can be of higher importance than immortal principles.

I will go yet further, and state that even this *policy* of neutrality Washington taught you, not as a permanent rule, but as a temporary convenience. I prove it again by referring to the very words of his Farewell Address, when he, in reference to his policy of neutrality, explicitly says that "*with him* (Washington) *a predominant motive has been to endeavor to gain time to your country to settle and mature its institutions, and to progress, without interruption, to that degree of strength and consistency which is necessary to give it the command of its own fortunes.*" These are highly memorable words, gentlemen. Here I take my ground, and casting a glance of admiration over your glorious land, I confidently ask you, gentlemen, are your institutions settled and matured, or are they not? Are you, or are you not, come to that degree of strength and consistency to be the masters of your own fortunes?

Oh, my God! how I thank thee for having given me the glorious view of this country's greatness, which answers this question for me!

Yes! you have attained that degree of strength and consistency when your less fortunate brethren in mankind may well claim your brotherly, protecting hand.

And here I stand before you, to plead the cause of these, your less fortunate brethren—the cause of humanity. I may succeed, or I may fail. But I will go on, pleading with that faith of martyrs, by which mountains were moved; and I may displease you, perhaps;

still I will say with Luther, "*May God help me—I can do no otherwise!*"

One word more to prove that Washington never attached to his doctrine of neutrality more than the sense of *temporary* policy. I refer to one of his letters, written to La Fayette, wherein he says :— " Let us only have *twenty years* of peace, and our country will come to such a degree of power and wealth that we will be able in a *just cause*, to defy whatever power on earth !"

" In a just cause !" Now in the name of eternal truth, and by all that is sacred and dear to man ; since the history of mankind is recorded, there has been no cause more just than the cause of Hungary ! Never was there a people without the slightest reason, more sacrilegiously, more treacherously, and by fouler means, attacked, than Hungary ! Never has crime, cursed ambition, despotism, and violence, in a more wicked manner, united to crush down freedom, and the very life, than against Hungary ! Never was a country more mortally offended than Hungary is. All your sufferings, all your complaints, which, with so much right drove your forefathers to take up arms, are but slight grievances in comparison with those immense, deep wounds, out of which the heart of Hungary bleeds ! If the cause of my people is not sufficiently just to insure the protection of God, and the support of good willing men, then there is no just cause and no justice on earth. Then the blood of no new Abel will move toward Heaven. The genius of charity, Christian love and justice will mourningly fly the earth ; a heavy curse will upon morality fall— oppressed men despair, and only the Cains of humanity walk proudly with impious brow, about the ruins of Liberty on earth !

I have shown, gentlemen, that Washington has never bequeathed to his country the doctrine of not caring about the violation of international law,—has not bequeathed the doctrine of indifferentism to his countrymen, but only neutrality. I have shown that these two ideas are essentially different. I have shown that even the doctrine of neutrality he never intended to recommend to his countrymen as a lasting constitutional principle, but only as a measure of temporary policy, advisable until the United States should progress in strength and consistency, to which end he judged twenty years to be sufficient,—after which he himself declared to be resolved to espouse any just cause. Now allow me briefly to consider how your policy has been developed in the course of time, with respect to the principle of non-intervention in foreign concerns.

I will only recall to your memory the message of President Monroe, when he clearly stated that the United States would take up arms to protect the American Spanish Colonies, now free Republics, should the so-called Holy (rather unholy) Alliance make an attempt either to aid Spain to reduce the new American Republics to their ancient colonial state, or to compel them to adopt political systems more conformable to the policy and views of that Alliance. I entreat you to mark well, gentlemen, not only the forced introduction of Monarchical Governments, but in general the interference of foreign powers in the contest for independence of the Spanish Colonies, was declared sufficient motive for the United States to protect the natural right of those nations to dispose of themselves.

I beg leave to desire to remember that this declaration of President Monroe was not only approved and confirmed by the people of the United States, but that *Great Britain itself joined the United States* in the declaration of this decision and this policy.

I further recall to your memory the instructions given in 1826 to your envoys to the Congress of Panama, Richard Anderson and John Sergeant, where it is clearly stated that the United States would have opposed, with their whole force, the interference of Continental Powers with that struggle for independence.

It is true, that this declaration to go even to war, to protect the independence of foreign states against foreign interference, was not only restricted to the Continent of America, but President Monroe declares in his message that the United States can have no concern in European struggles, being distant and separated from Europe by the great Atlantic Ocean.

But I beg leave to remark that this indifference to European concerns is again a matter, not of *principle* but of temporary *exigency*—the motives of which have, by the lapse of time, entirely disappeared—so much that the balance even turned to the opposite side.

President Monroe mentions *distance* as a motive of the above-stated distinction. Well, since the prodigious development of your Fulton's glorious invention, distance is blotted out of the dictionary—or rather replaced by the word *time*. Distance is no more calculated by *miles* but by *hours*. And being so, Europe is of course less distant from you than the greater part of the American Continent. But, let even the word distance be taken in its nominal sense, Europe is nearer to you than the greatest part of the American Continent, yea, even nearer than perhaps some parts of your own territory.

President Monroe's second motive is, that you are separated from Europe by the Atlantic. Now, at the present time, and in the present condition of navigation, the Atlantic is no separation, but rather a connecting benefit, the facilitating source of that commercial intercourse which brings the interests of Europe home to you, connecting you with it with every tie of moral as well as material interest.

It is chiefly in New York that I feel induced to speak so, because New York is by innumerable ties connected with Europe, more connected than several parts of Europe itself.

It is the agricultural interest of this great country which chiefly wants an outlet and a market. Now it is far more Europe than the American Continent to which you have to look in that respect. This very circumstance cannot allow you to remain indifferent to the fate of freedom on the European continent, because, be sure, gentlemen, and let me have spoken this chiefly to the gentlemen of trade, should Absolutism gain ground in Europe, it will, it must, make every possible obstacle to the commercial intercourse of republican America, because commercial intercourse is the most powerful *locomotive of principles;* and be sure the victory of Absolutism on the European Continent will in no quarter have more injurious national consequences, then in the vast extent of your agricultural and commercial interests.

Then, why not prevent it,—while yet there is a possibility to do so with none, or comparative small sacrifices, rather than to abide that fatal catastrophe, and to mourn the immense sacrifices it would then cost?

Even in political considerations now-a-days, you have stronger motives to feel interested in the fate of Europe, than even in the fate of the central or southern parts of America. Whatever may happen in the institutions of these parts, you are too powerful to see your own institutions affected by it. But let Europe become absolutistical,—as without the restoration of Hungary to its independence, and the freedom of Italy so strongly connected with Hungary, to be sure it will—and your children will see those words, which your National Government spoke in 1827, fulfilled on a larger scale than they were meant, that "*the absolutism of Europe will not be appeased until every vestige of human freedom had been obliterated even here.*" And oh! do not rely too fondly upon your power. It is great, to be sure. You have not to fear whatever single power on earth; but look to history. Ancient Rome has fallen, and mighty empires have vanished from earth. Let not the enemies of freedom grow too strong. Victorious over Europe, and then united, they would be too strong even for you! And be sure, they hate you with an infernal hatred. They must hate you even more than me. They consider you as their most dangerous opponents. Absolutism cannot tranquilly sleep while the republican principle has such a mighty representative as your country is.

Yes, gentlemen, it was the fear from the political reäction of absolutistic principles which induced your great statesmen—that principle which they professed for Central and Southern America, not to extend to Europe also, and by no means the publicly avowed feeble motives. Every manifestation of your public life out of those times, shows that I am right to say so. Europe's nations were, about 1823, in such a degraded situation that indeed you must have felt anxious not to come into any contact with that pestilential atmosphere of Europe, when, as Mr. Clay said in 1818, in his speech about the emancipation of South America, "Paris was transferred to St. Petersburg."

But scarcely has, within a year later, the Greek nation come in its contest to an important standing, which gave you hope that the spirit of freedom is waking again, and at once you abandoned your principle of political indifference for Europe. You know how your Clays and your Websters spoke, as if really they were speaking for my very case. You know how your citizens acted in behalf of that struggle for liberty, in that part of Europe which is more distant than Hungary; and again, when Poland fell, you know what spirit pervaded the United States.

So I have shown you how Washington's doctrine of perfect neutrality in your foreign relations has by-and-by changed into the declaration to oppose, with all your forces, absolutistical Europe, in interfering with the independence or republican institutions of Central or Southern America. I have shown you why this manly resolution was not extended then to Europe. I have shown you the further differences between your present convenience and that of the time of President Monroe—not less important than those between Monroe's and Washington's time. But one mighty difference I must still commemorate. That is, that your population has, since Monroe's time, nearly doubled, I believe; at least increased by millions. And what sort of men are these millions? Are they only native born Americans? No! European emigrants they are; men who, though citizens of the United States, are by the most sacred ties of relationship attached to Europe's fate. That is a consideration worthy of the reflection of your calmest and wisest men, who, after calm reflection, must agree with me, that in your present condition you are at least as much interested in the fate of Europe, as your fathers twenty-eight years ago declared themselves interested in the fate of Central and Southern America.

And really so it is. The unexampled, immense, prodigious sympathy for the cause of my country which I met with in the United States proves that it is so. Your generous interference with the Turkish captivity of the Governor of Hungary proves that it is so. And this development, rather than change in your foreign policy, is not even more an instinctive ebullition of public opinion, which is called by-and-by to impart a direction to your National Governmental policy; the direction is already imparted, and the opinion of the people is already an avowed principle of the policy of the Government.

I have as good, I have a most decisive authority, to rely upon in saying so. It is the Message of the President of the United States. His Excellency, Millard Fillmore, communicated to the Congress, a few days ago; there I read the paragraph—" The deep interest which we feel in the spread of liberal principles, and the establishment of free governments, and the sympathy with which we witness every struggle against oppression, *forbid that we should be indifferent to a cause in which the strong arm of a foreign power is invoked to stifle public sentiment and repress the spirit of freedom in any country.*" Now, gentlemen, here is the ground which I take for my earnest endeavors to benefit the cause of Hungary. I have only respectfully to ask, is a principle which the public opinion of the people of the United States so resolutely professes, and the Government of the United States, with the full sentiment of its responsibility, declares to your Congress to be the ruling principle of your National Government; is that principle meant to be serious ? Indeed, I confess that it would be the most impertinent outrage toward your great people, and your National Government, to entertain the offending opinion, that what the people of the United States, and its National Government, in such a solemn diplomatic manner, profess to be a ruling principle of your policy, should not be meant to be but a jcke about the most sacred interests of humanity. God forbid that I should feel the impertinent arrogance to think so; therefore I take the principle of your policy to be as I find it established, without any interference, and I come in the name of oppressed humanity to claim the natural, logical, unavoidable, practical consequences of your own freely chosen Government policy, which you have avowed to the whole world, the right to claim the realization of those expressions which your sovereign people of the United States have chosen out of your own accord, to raise in the bosom of my countrymen and of oppressed humanity.

You will excuse me, gentlemen, for having dwelt so long about that principle of non-interference with European measures, but I have found this rock thrown in my way when I spoke of what I humbly request from the United States. I have been charged to have the arrogance to change your existing policy, and as in one speech, I of course cannot exhaust the whole mighty complex of my mission, I choose for the present opportunity to develop my views about that fundamental principle of not caring about European concerns, and having shown, not theoretically, but practically, that it is a mistake to think that you had, at whatever time, such a policy, and having shown that should you ever have entertained such a policy, you had abandoned it. So much, at least, I hope to have achieved. My humble requests to your operative sympathy may still be opposed by I don't know what other motives; but that objection I will never more meet—not to interfere with European concerns—this objection is disposed of, and forever, I hope. It remains now to investigate, that having professed not to be indifferent to the cause of Hungary, such as to be indifferent to the cause of European freedom, is the cause of Hungary such as to have just claims to your active and operative assistance and support? It is, gentlemen—to prove this I do not intend to enter into an explanation of the particulars of our struggle, which I had the honor to direct, as the chosen Chief Magistrate of my native land—it is highly gratifying to me to see the cause of Hungary is—excepting some ridiculous misrepresentations of ill-will—correctly understood here. I will only state one fact, and that is that our endeavorings for independence were crushed down by the armed interference of a foreign despotic power—the principle of all evil on earth—Russia. And stating this fact I will not again intrude upon you with my own views, but recall to your memory the doctrines established by your own statesmen.

Firstly: Again I return to your great Washington. He says in one of his letters to La Fayette, "My policies are plain and simple; I think every nation has a right to establish that form of government under which it conceives it can live most happy, and that no governments ought to interfere with the internal concerns of another." Here I take my ground—I take my ground upon a principle of Washington—a *principle*, and no doctrine of temporary policy, calculated for the first twenty years of your infancy. Russia has interfered with the internal concerns of Hungary, and by doing so has violated the policies of the United States, established as a lasting principle by Washington himself. It *is* a lasting principle—I would invoke in my support the opinion of every statesman of the United States, of every party, of every time. But to save time, I come from the first President of the United States at once to the last, and recall to your memory this word of the present Annual Message of his Excellency President Fillmore: "Let every people choose for itself, and make and alter its political institutions to suit its own condition and convenience." Here again I take my ground upon the principle established by Washington—making the basis of your own existence, and professed and acknowledged by your very present Government, only to show that I am aware of the policy and political opinion of your present Government also. I beg leave to quote your present Secretary of State, Mr. Webster's statement, who, in his speech on the Greek question, speaks so: "The law of nations maintains that in extreme cases, resistance is lawful, and that one nation has no right to interfere in the affairs of another." Well, that precisely is the ground upon which we Hungarians stand. But I may perhaps meet the objection. I am sorry to say I have met it already. "Well, we own that it has been violated by Russia in the case of Hungary, but after all what is Hungary to us? Let every people take care of itself, what is that to us?" So some speak; it is the old doctrine of private egotism, "every one for himself and God for all." I will answer the objection not by my own humble views but again by the words of Mr. Webster, who, in his alluded-to speech on the Greek question, having professed the sovereign right of every nation to dispose of its own concerns, to be a law of nations—thus is going on: "But it may be asked what is all that to us? The question is easily answered. We are one of the nations, and we as a nation have precisely the same interest in international law as a private individual has in the laws of his country."

You see, gentlemen, I had again a good authority to quote. The principle which your honorable Secretary of State professes is a principle of eternal truth. No man can disavow it—no political party can disavow it. Thus I am in the happy condition to address my humble prayers, in that respect, not to a party, but to the whole people of the United States, which I will go on to do so long as I have no reason to contemplate one party opposite or indifferent to my country's cause, because else of course I would have to address those who are friends, and not those who are either indifferent or antagonistic. But it may be from some quarters avowed: "Well, we acknowledge the justice of that principle of every nation's sovereign right—we acknowledge it to be a law of nations that no foreign power has a right to interfere in the affairs of another, and we are determined to respect this common law of mankind; but if others do not respect that law it is not our business to meddle with them." Let me answer by an analysis. "Every nation has the same interest in the international career, as a private individual has in the laws of his country." That is an acknowledged principle of the United States. Consequently every nation is, in respect to international law, precisely in the same condition as a private individual is in respect to the laws of his country. Well, where is the condition of a private individual in respect to the laws of his country? Is it only that he has himself not to violate the law? or is it that so far as is in his power he should also prevent others to violate the law? Suppose you see that a wicked man is about to rob—to murder your neighbor, or to burn his house, will you wrap yourself in your own virtuous lawfulness, and say, "I don't rob—don't murder—don't burn; but what others do is not my business. I am not my brother's keeper. I sympathize with him; but I am not obliged to help him that he may not be robbed, murdered, or burnt." What honest man of the world would answer so? None of you. None of the people of the United States, I am sure. That would be the damned maxim of the Pharisees of old, who thanked God that they were not as others were. Our Saviour was not content to go himself treading in the hall of the temple, but he had driven out those who were treading there. Now, what the duty of an individual is in respect to the laws of his country, the same duty has a nation, in respect to international law. This duty has no other limit, but only the power to fulfil it. Of course, it cannot be expected that the Republic of St. Marino, or the Prince of Morocco, should stop the Czar of Russia in his ambitious annoyance. It was ridiculous when the Prince of Modena refused to recognize the government of Louis Philippe—but "to whom much is given, will much be expected from him," says the Lord. And every condition has not only its rights, but also its own desires, and any which is in the condition to be a power on earth has the duty to consider himself as a part of the executive power of mankind, called to maintain the law of nations. Woe, a thousand-fold woe to humanity, should there nobody on earth be to maintain the laws of humanity. Woe, a thousand-fold woe to humanity, should even those who are as mighty as they are free, not feel interested in the maintenance of the laws of mankind—because they are laws—but only in so far as some scanty money interests would desire it. Woe to humanity, if every despot of the world may dare to trample down the laws of humanity, and no free nation arises to make respected those laws. People of the United States, humanity expects that your glorious republic will prove to the world, that republics are founded on virtue—it expects to see you the guardians of the laws of humanity. Well, I will come to the last possible objection. I may be told, " You are right in your principles, your cause is just, and you have our sympathy ; but after all we cannot go to war for your country ; we cannot furnish you with armies and fleets ; we cannot fight your battle for you." There is the rub. Who can exactly tell what would have been the issue of your own struggl for independence, though your country was in a far happier geograph ical position than we poor Hungarians, should France have give such an answer to your forefathers in 1778 and 1781, instead of sending to your aid a fleet of thirty-eight men of war, and auxiliary troops, and 24,000 muskets, and a loan of nineteen millions. And what is far more than all this, does it not show that France resolved with all its power to espouse the cause of your independence ? But, perhaps, I will be told that France did this not out of love of freedom, but out of hatred against England. Well, let it be ; but let me also ask, shall the cause of olden times—hatred—be more efficient in the destinies of mankind than love of freedom, principles of justice, and laws of humanity ? Perhaps I will be told that Europe is so far from America. But let me ask is America in the days of steam navigation more distant from Europe to-day than France was from America seventy-three years ago ? However, I most solemnly declare that it is not my intention to rely literally upon this example. It is not my wish to entangle the United States in war, or to engage your great people to send out armies and fleets to restore Hungary to its sovereign independence. Not at all, gentlemen ; I most solemnly declare that I never entertained such expectations, such hopes, and here I come to the practical point.

The principle of evil in Europe is the enervating spirit of Russian absolutism. It is upon this rests the daring boldness of every petty tyrant to trample upon oppressed nations, and to crush down liberty. To this Moloch of ambition has fallen a victim my poor native land. It is this with which Montalembert threatens the French republicans. It is Russian intervention in Hungary which governed French intervention in Rome, and gave the temerity to German tyrants to crush down all the endeavors for freedom and unity in Germany. The despots of the European continent are leagued against the freedom of the world. That is a matter of fact. The second matter of fact is that the European continent is on the eve of a new revolution. It is not necessary to be initiated in the secret preparations of the European democracy to be aware of that approaching contingency. It is pointed out by the French Constitution itself, prescribing a new Presidential election for the next spring. Now, suppose that the ambition of Louis Napoleon, encouraged by Russian secret aid, awaits this time, (which I scarcely believe,) and suppose that there will be a peaceful solution, such as would make contented the friends of Republican France, of course the first act of the new French President must be, at least, to recall the French troops from Rome. Nobody can doubt that a revolution will follow, if not precede, this recall in Italy. Or if there is no peaceful solution in France, but a revolution, then every man knows that whenever the heart of France boils up, the pulsation is felt throughout Europe, and oppressed nations once more rise, and Russia again interferes. Now I humbly ask, with the view of these circumstances before my eyes, can it be convenient to such a great power as this Republic, to await the very outbreak and then only to discuss and decide what direction you will be willing to take in your foreign policy? It may come again, as under the last President, at a late hour, agents to see how matters stood in Hungary. Russian interference and treason achieved what the sacrilegious Hapsburg dynasty failed to achieve. You know the old words, "while Rome debated, Byzantium fell." So I respectfully entreat the people of the United States, in time, to express its will as to what course it wishes to be pursued by its National Government in the case of the approaching events I have mentioned. And I most confidently hope that there is only one course possible, consistent with the above recorded principles. If you acknowledge the right of every nation to alter its institutions and government—if you acknowledge the interference of foreign powers in that sovereign right to be a violation of the law of nations, as you really do—if you are forbidden to remain indifferent to this violation of international law, as your President openly professes that you are, then there is no other course possible than not to interfere in that sovereign right of nations, but also not to admit whatever other powers to interfere. But you will, perhaps, object me that is so much as to go to war. I answer, no—that is so much as to prevent war. What is wanted to that effect? It is wanted, that being aware of the precarious condition of Europe, your National Government should so soon as possible send instructions to your Minister at London, to declare to the English Government that the United States, acknowledging the sovereign right of every nation to dispose of its own domestic concerns, have resolved not to interfere, but also not let to interfere whatever foreign power with this sovereign right, in order to repress the spirit of freedom in any country. Consequently, to invite the Cabinet of St. James to unite with the United States in this policy, and to declare that the United States are resolved to act conjointly with England in that decision in the case of that approaching crisis on the European continent, which is impossible not to foresee. If the citizens of the United States, instead of honoring me with the offers of their hospitality, would be pleased to express this their will, by passing convenient resolutions, and ratifying them to their National Government—if the people by all constitutional means—if the independent press would hasten to express the public opinion in a similar sense—if in consequence of this, the National Government would instruct its Minister in England accordingly, and by a convenient communication to the Congress, give so as it is wont to do, publicity to this his step, I am entirely sure that you would find the people of Great Britain heartily joining this direction of policy,—nobody in the world could feel especially offended by it, and no existing relation would be broken or injured, and still the interference of Russia in the restoration of Hungary to its independence (formally declared in 1849) prevented—Russian arrogance and preponderance checked, and the oppressed nations of Europe soon become free. There may be some over-anxious men who perhaps would say, "But if such a declaration of your Government will not be respected, and Russia still does interfere, then you would be obliged by this previous declaration to go to war, and you don't desire to have a war." That objection seemed to me like as if somebody would say, "If the vault of Heaven breaks down what will we do?" My answer is, "But it will not break down," even so I answer—but your declaration will be respected—Russia will not interfere—you will have no occasion for war, you will have prevented war. Be sure Russia would twice, thrice consider to provoke against itself, besides the roused fury of nations—besides the legions of Republican France, also the English Leopard and the star surrounded Eagle of America. Please to consider the fact that you, united to England, have made already such a declaration, not to admit any interference of the European absolutistical powers, into the affairs of the formerly Spanish Colonies of America, and has this declaration brought you to a war? Quite the contrary; it has prevented war—so it would be in our case also.

Let me therefore most humbly entreat you, gentlemen—let me entreat you on this occasion by the means of publicity—the people of the United States to be pleased to give such practical direction to its generous sympathy for Hungary, as to arrange meetings and pass such resolutions here and there, and in every possible place of this great Union, as I took the liberty to mention above. Why not do so? I beg leave to reiterate what I had the honor to say yesterday to a Committee of Baltimore. Suppose there should in Cuba a revolution occur, a revolution from the inhabitants of Cuba themselves, and whatever European power would send down a fleet to support Spain against this revolution, would you admit this foreign intervention in a foreign country? I am confident there is not one in the United States who would not oppose this intervention. Then what is the difference between this supposed case and the case of Hungary? Is there a difference in principle? No. Then what? The difference is that Cuba is at six days' distance from New York, and the port of Hungary (Fiume) at eighteen days' distance. That is all: and who would affirm that the policy of such a great, free and glorious nation as the United States shall be regulated by hours and not by principles. Allow me to remark that there is an immense truth in that which the French legation in the United States expressed to your Government, in an able note of 27th October past which I beg leave to quote: " America is closely connected with Europe, being only separated from the latter by a distance scarcely exceeding eight days' journey, by one of the most important of general interests—the interest of commerce. The nations of America and Europe are at this day so dependent upon one another, tha the effects of any event, prosperous or otherwise, happening on on side of the Atlantic, are immediately felt on the other side. The result of this community of interests, commercial, political and moral, between Europe and America—of this frequency and rapidity of intercourse between them, is that it becomes as difficult to point out the geographical degree where American policy shall terminate and European policy begin, as it is to trace out the line where American commerce begins and European commerce terminates. Where may be said to begin or terminate the ideas which are in the ascendant in Europe and in America." The second measure which I beg leave to mention has reference to commercial interest. There has, in latter times, a doctrine stolen into the code of international law which is even as contrary to the commercial interests of nations as to their independence. The pettiest despot of the world has the faculty to exclude your commerce from whatever port it pleases to do so. He has only to arrange a blockade, and your commerce is shut out; or if down-trodden Venice, bleeding Lombardy, or my down-oppressed but resolute Hungary, rises to shake off the Austrian tyrant's yoke, as surely they will, that tyrant believes to have the right from the very moment to exclude your commerce with the risen nations.

Now, this is an absurdity—a tyrannical invention of tyrants violating your interest—your own sovereign independence. The United States have not always regarded things from this point of view. I find in a note of Mr. Everett, Minister of the United States in Spain, dated, " Madrid, Jan. 20, 1826," these words: " In the war between Spain and the Spanish American colonies the United States have freely granted to both parties the hospitalities of their ports and territory, and have allowed the agents of both to procure within their jurisdiction, in the way of lawful trade, any supplies which suited their convenience." Now, gentlemen, this is the principle which humanity expects, for your own and for mankind's benefit to see maintained by you, and not yonder fatal course, which admits to tyrants to draw from your country whatever supply of oppression against their nations, but forbids to nations to buy the means of defence. That was not the principle of your Washington; when he speaks of harmony, of friendly intercourse and of peace, he always takes care to speak of nations and not of governments—still less of tyrants who subdue nations by foreign arms. The sacred word of nation, with all its natural rights, should, at least, of your political dictionary, not to be blotted out; and yet I am sorry to see that the word nation is replaced by the word government. Gentlemen, I humbly wish that public opinion of the people of the United States, conscious of its own rights, should highly and resolutely declare that the people of the United States will carry on trade and continue its commercial intercourse with whatever nation, be that nation in revolution against its oppressors or not; and that the people of the United States express, with confidence from its Government, to provide for the protection of your trade. I am confident that your National Government, seeing public opinion so pronounced, will judge it convenient to augment your naval forces in the Mediterranean; and to look for some such station for it which would not force the Navy of Republican America to such abrogations toward tyrants, which cannot be consistent with Republican principles or Republican dignity, only because the king so-so, be he even the cursed King of Naples, grants you the favor of an anchoring-place for the naval forces of your Republic. I believe your glorious country should everywhere freely unfurl the star-spangled banner of liberty with all its congenial principles, and not make itself dependent in whatever respect or the glorious smiles of the Kings Bombaste Compagne.

The third object of my humble wishes, gentlemen, is the recognition of the independence of Hungary. Your glorious Declaration of Independence proclaims the right of every nation to assume among the powers of the earth the separate and equal station to which the laws of nature and nature's God entitle them. The political existence of your glorious republic is founded upon this principle, upon this right. My nation stands upon the same ground, and there is a striking resemblance between your cause and that of my country. On the 4th July, 1776, John Adams spoke such in your Congress, " Sink or swim, live or die, survive or perish, I am for this declaration. It is true in the beginning we aimed not at independence, but ' there's a divinity which shapes our ends.' " These whole words were present to my mind on the 14th of April, 1849, when I moved the Declaration of Independence in the National Assembly of Hungary. Our condition was the same, and if there be any difference I dare say it is in favor of ourselves. Your country was before this declaration not a self-consisting, independent state. Hungary was. Through the lapse of a thousand years, through every vicissitude of this long period, while nations vanished and empires fell, the self-consisting independence of Hungary was never disputed but recognized by all powers of the earth, sanctioned by treaties made with the Hapsburg Dynasty, when this dynasty, by the free will of my nation, and by a bilateral part was invested with the kingly crown of Hungary. Even more, this independence of king was acknowledged to make a part of the international law of Europe, and was guaranteed not only by the foreign European governments, such as Great Britain, but also by several of those, when yet constitutional states, which belonged formerly to the German, and, after its dissolution, to the Austrian Empire. This independent condition of Hungary is clearly defined in one of our fundamental laws of 1791, in these words: "Hungary is a free and independent kingdom, having its own self consistent existence and constitution, and not subject to any other nation or country in the world." This, therefore, was our ancient right. We were not dependent from, nor a part of, the Austrian Empire, as your country was dependent from England. It was clearly defined that we were to Austria nothing but good neighborhood, and the only tie between us and Austria was, that we elected, to be our kings, the same dynasty which were also the sovereigns of Austria, and occupied the same line of hereditary succession of our kings; but by accepting this our forefathers, with the consent of the king, again declared that though she accepts the dynasty to be our hereditary kings, all the other franchises, rights and laws of the nation shall remain in full power and intact; and our country shall be governed like other dominions of that dynasty, but according to our constitutionally established authorities. We would not belong to the Austrian Empire, because that empire did not exist while Hungary did already nearly two years exist, and exist some two hundred and eighty years under the government of that Hapsburgian dynasty. The Austrian Empire, as you know, was only established in 1806, when the Rhenish Confederacy of Napoleon struck the death-blow to the German Empire, of which Francis II. of Austria, was not hereditary, but elected Emperor. That Hungary had belonged to the German Empire, that is a thing which no man in the world ever imagined yet. It is only now when the Hapsburgian tyrant professes the intention to melt Hungary into the German Confederation; but you know this intention to be in so striking opposition to the European public law, that England and France solemnly protested against this intention which is not carried out even to-day. The German Empire having died, its late Emperor Francis, also King of Hungary, has established the Austrian Empire in 1806, but even in that fundamental charter of the new established Austrian Empire, he solemnly declared that Hungary and its annexed provinces are not intended, and will not make a part of the Austrian Empire. Subsequently we entered with this empire into the German Confederation of 1805, but Hungary, as well as Lombardy and Venice, not making part of the Austrian Empire, remained again separated, and were not entered into the confederacy. The laws which I succeeded to carry in 1848, did, of course, nothing alter in that old chartered condition of Hungary. We transformed the peasantry into freeholders, free proprietors, abolished feudal incumbrances. We replaced the political privileges of aristocracy by the common liberty of the whole people; gave political representation to the people for the legislature; transformed our municipal corporations into democratic corporations; introduced equality in rights and duties, and before the law, for the whole people, abolished the immunity of taxation of the nobility, secured equal religious liberty to all, secured liberty of the press and of association, provided for public gratuitous instruction for the whole people, of every confession and of whatever tongue; but not injuring, in any way, the rights of the King. We replaced our own aristocratical constitution by a democratic constitution founded upon nearly universal suffrage of the whole people—of whatever religion, of whatever tongue. All these were, as you see, internal reforms which did in no way interfere with our allegiance to the King, and were carried lawfully in peaceful legislation, with the sanction of the King.

Besides this, there was one other thing which was carried. We were formerly governed by a Board of Council, which had the express duty to govern according to sure laws, and be responsible for doing so; but we saw by long experience that this responsibility is an empty sound, because a corporation cannot really be responsible; and here was the reason why the absolutistical tendency of the dynasty succeeded to encroach upon our liberty. So we replaced the Board of Council by Ministers; the empty responsibility of a Board by the individual responsibility of men—and the King consented to it. I myself was named by him Minister of the Treasury. That is all. But precisely here was the rub. The tyrant could not bear the idea that I would not give to his ambitionary disposal the life-sweat of my people; he was not contented with $1,500,000 loans which we generously appropriated to him yearly. He would have his hands in our pockets, and he could not bear the idea that he shall never more be at liberty to dispose without any control of our brave army, and to crush the spirit of freedom in the world. Therefore, he resorted to the most outrageous conspiracy, and attacked us by arms, and by a false report of a victory which never was won, issued a proclamation declaring that Hungary shall not more exist—that its Independence, its Constitution, its very existence is abolished, and it shall be melted, like a farm or fold, into the Austrian Empire. To this we answered, "Thou shalt not exist, tyrant, but we will;" and we banished him, and issued the Declaration of our Independence. So you see, gentlemen, that there is a very great difference between yours and ours—it is in our favor. There is another similar difference; you declared your independence when it was yet very doubtful if you would be successful. We declared ours when we, in legitimate defence, were already victorious; when we had beaten our enemies, and so proved, before our declaration, that we had strength and power enough to become one of the independent powers on earth. One thing more; our Declaration of Independence was not only voted unanimously in our Congress, but every county, every municipality, has solemnly declared its consent and adherence to it; so it became not the supposed, but by the whole realm positively, and sanctioned by

he fundamental laws of Hungary. And so it is even now. There happened since nothing contrary to this declaration on the part of the nation. No contrary law, no declaration issued. Only one thing happened—a foreign power, Russia, came with his armed bondsmen, and, aided by treason, overthrew us for a while. Now, I put the question, before God and humanity, to you, free, sovereign people of America, can this violation of international law abolish the legitimate character of our Declaration of Independence ? If not, then, here I take my ground, because I am in this very Declaration of Independence, entrusted with the charge of Governor of my fatherland. I have sworn, before God and my nation, to endeavor to maintain and secure this act of independence. And so may God the Almighty help me as I will—I will, until my nation is again in the condition to dispose of its government, which I confidently trust—yea more, I know, will be a Republican. And then I retire to the humble condition of my former private life, equalling in one thing, at least, your Washington, not in merits, but in honesty—that is the only ambition of my life. Amen. So my third humble wish is that the people of the United States would be pleased, by all constitutional means of its wonted public life, to declare that, acknowledging the legitimate character of the Declaration of Independence of Hungary, it is anxious to greet Hungary among the independent powers of the earth, and invite the Government of the United States to recognize this independence at the earliest convenient time. That is all. Let me see the principle announced ; the rest may well be left to the wisdom of your Government, with some confidence in my own respectful discretion also. And so, gentlemen, I have respectfully stated what are my humble requests to the sovereign people of this country, in its public and political capacity. It is that the people of the United States may be pleased, by all constitutional means, to declare—
First that, feeling interested in the maintenance of the laws of nations acknowledging the sovereign right of every people to dispose of its own domestic concerns to be one of these laws, and the interference with this sovereign right to be a violation of these laws of nations, the people of the United States—resolved to respect and make respected these public laws—declares the Russian past intervention in Hungary to be a violation of these laws, which, if reiterated, would be a new revolution, and would not be regarded indifferently by the people of the United States—that you, therefore, invite your Government to act accordingly, and so invite Great Britain to unite with the United States in this policy.

Second, that the people of the United States is resolved to maintain its right of commercial intercourse with the nations of Europe, whether they be in a state of revolution against their Governments or not—and that with the view of approaching scenes on the Continent of Europe, the people invites the Government to take appropriate measures for the protection of the trade of the people on the

Mediterranean, and third, that the people of the United States pronounce its opinion in respect to the question of independence of Hungary, so as I had the honor to state. I hope nobody can reproach me to have done by this anything inconsistent with the high regards which I owe to the United States, or not appropriate to my capacity. I would regard it as a very judicious and beneficial thing, if those generous men who sympathize with the cause of Hungary, would form committees through the different parts of the United States, with the purpose to occasion appropriate meetings, to pass such resolutions as I had the honor humbly to suggest. So much for the generous people of the United States, in its public and political capacity. And if that sympathy which I have the honor to meet with in the United States is really intended to become beneficial to the cause of my poor native land, then there is one humble wish more which I anxiously entertain. But this is a private business; it is a respectful appeal to the generous feelings of individuals. Gentlemen, I would rather starve than rely, for myself and family, on foreign aid; but, for my country's freedom, I would not be ashamed to go a begging from door to door. Gentlemen, I mean financial aid; money to assist the cause of freedom and independence of Hungary. I took the advice of some kind friends, if it be lawful to express such an humble request, because I feel the honorable duty neither to offend nor to evade your laws. I am told it is lawful. There are two means to see this, my humble wish, accomplished. The first is from spontaneous subscription, to put the offerings of kind friends at my disposal, for the benefit of my country's cause. The second is a loan. As to this loan, that is a business of a more private nature, which, to be carried on in an appropriate way, requires private consultation in a more close circle. So here I only mention that if there are such generous men who are willing to enter into the idea, provided it will be arranged in an acceptable way, I would most humbly entreat them to enter into a private communication about the subject with me; and secondly, I express my conviction that even this matter of loan could be efficiently promoted by the other measure of free, gratuitous subscriptions, which would afford me the means necessary for the practical initiation of the loan itself. Now, as to these subscriptions. The idea was brought home to my mind in a plain but very generous letter which I had the honor to receive, and which I beg to read. It is as follows:—

CINCINNATI, Ohio, Friday, Nov. 14, 1851.

M. LOUIS KOSSUTH, Governor of Hungary—SIR: I have authorized the office of the Ohio Life Insurance and Trust Company, in New York, to hand you drafts on me for one thousand dollars.

Respectfully yours, W. SMEAD.

I beg leave here publicly to return my most humble thanks to the gentleman for his ample aid, and the delicate manner in which he offered it; and it came to my mind that where one single individual is ready to make such sacrifices to my country's cause, there may perhaps be many who would give their small share to it, if they were only apprised that it will be thankfully accepted, however small it may be.

And it came to my mind then that drops of millions make an ocean, and the United States number many millions of inhabitants, all attached with warm feelings to the principles of liberty, agglomerated by single dollars, is even so many millions of dollars, as if it were one single draft, to me yet more precious, because it would practically show the sympathy of the people at large. I will consider it highly beneficial should I be so happy to see that generous men would form Committees throughout the United States, to raise out of the free offerings of the people some material aid to assist the second course of freedom and independence of Hungary. It is a delicate matter, gentlemen, for me to speak so. It is, perhaps, one of the greatest sacrifices to my country that I do so. But I love my country. And readily will I undergo even this torturing humiliation for her sake. Would I were so happy as your Washington was, when for your glorious country's sake, in the hours of your need, he also called for money in France. Sir, I have done. Conscious of no personal merit, I came to your shores a poor, persecuted exile, but you poured upon me the triumph of a welcome such as the world has never yet seen, and why? Because you took me for the representative of that principle of liberty which God has destined to be the common benefit of humanity; and it is a glorious sight to see a mighty, free, powerful people, come forth to greet with such a welcome the principle of freedom, even in a poor, persecuted, penniless exile. Be blessed for it. Your generous deed will be recorded through all posterity; and, as even now, millions of Europe's oppressed victims will raise their thanksgiving to God for the ray of hope which you by this, your act, have thrown on the dark night of their fate; even so, through all posterity, oppressed men look to your memory as a token of God that there is hope for freedom on earth, because there is a people like you to feel its worth and to support its cause.

SPEECH TO THE PRESS AT NEW YORK.

GENTLEMEN: Rising respectfully to return my most warm thanks for the honor of the toast, and the high benefit of the sympathy manifested by this solemn demonstration, it is with mingled feelings of joy and fear that I address you, gentlemen!

I address you with joy, because, conscious of the immensity of the power which you wield, it is natural to feel some awe in addressing those in whose hands the success or the failure of our hopes is placed; still I equally know that, in your hands, gentlemen, the independent Republican Press is a weapon, but a weapon to defend truth and justice, and not to offend; it is no screen to hide, no snuffers to extinguish the light, but a torch lit at the fire of immortality a spark of which is glistening in every man's soul, to prove its divine origin; a torch which you wield loftily and high to spread light with it to the most lonely regions of humanity.

And as the cause of my country is the cause of justice and truth; as it has in no respect to fear light, but rather wants nothing but light to see secured to it the support and protection of every friend of freedom, of every noble-minded man, these are the reasons why I address you with joy, gentlemen.

The more with joy, because, though it is sorrowful to see that ill-willed misrepresentations or secret Austrian intrigues, distorting plain, open history to a tissue of falsehood and lies, know how to find their way even to a small, insignificant part of the American press, still I am proud and happy to see that the immense majority of the American press not only proved inaccessible to these venomous intrigues, but conscious of the noble vocation of an Independent Press, and yielding to the generous inclination of Freemen, of protecting truth and justice against the dark plots of tyranny, has, without any interference on my part, come forth to protect the sacred cause of Hungary.

The Independent Press of this great Republic has in this very case also proved to the world that even against the mischievous pow er of calumnies the most efficient protection is the Freedom of the Press, and not preventive measures, condemning human intellect to eternal minority.

I address you, gentlemen, the more with joy, because, through you I have the invaluable benefit to address the whole university of the great, glorious and free people of the United States.

That is a great word, gentlemen, and yet is literally true.

While eighty years ago immortal Franklin's own press was almost the only one in the Colonies; now there are over three thousand newspapers in the United States, having a circulation of five millions of copies, and amounting in their yearly circulation to the prodigious number of nearly four and a half hundred millions; every grown man in the Union reads on the average two newspapers a week, and one hundred and five copies a year; nearly eighteen copies fall, in the proportion to the population, to every human being in the Union, man, woman, and child.

I am told that the journals of New York State alone exceed in number those of all the rest of the world beyond your great Union, and the circulation of the newspapers of this City alone nearly exceeds those of the whole Empire of Great Britain.

But there is yet one particularly remarkable fact which I cannot forbear to mention, gentlemen.

I boldly declare that beyond the United States there exists scarcely a practical Freedom of the Press: at least in Europe, not except, perhaps, Norway, of whose condition in that respect I am not quite aware. You know, gentlemen, how the press is fettered throughout the European Continent, even for the present, in France itself, whose great nation, by a strange fate, sees under a nominal Republican but centralized Government, all the glorious fruits of their great and victorious Revolutions wasting between the blasting fingers of centralized administrative and legislative omnipotence. You know how the Independent Press of France is murdered by imprisonment of their Editors and by fees: you know how the present Government of France feels unable to bear the force of public opinion—so much that in the French Republic the very legitimate shout of

"Vive la Republique"

has almost become a crime. This very circumstance is sufficient to prove that in that glorious land, where the warm and noble heart of the French nation throbs with self-confidence and noble pride, a new Revolution is an unavoidable necessity. It is a mournful view which the great French nation now presents, but it is also an efficient warning against the propensities of centralization, inconsistent with freedom, because inconsistent with self-government, and it is also a source of hope for the European continent, because we know that things in France cannot endure thus as they are; we know that to become a true Republic is a necessity for France, and thus we know also that whoever be the man, who in the approaching crisis will be honored by the confidence of the French nation, he will, he must be faithful to that great principle of Fraternity towards the other nations, which being announced by the French Constitution to the world, raised such encouraging, but bitterly disappointed expectations through Europe's oppressed Continent.

But it is chiefly, almost only Great Britain in Europe which boasts to have a free press, and to be sure during my brief stay in England, I joyfully saw that really there is a freedom to print, almost an unlimited one, so far that I saw printed advertisements spread at every corner, and signed by the publishers, stating that Queen Victoria is no lawful Queen—that she ought to be sent to the Tower, and all those who rule ought to be hanged. Men laughed, and nobody cared about the foolish extravagancy.

And yet I dare say, and I hope the generous people of Great Britain will not feel offended at my stating the fact, that there is no practical freedom of the press.

The freedom of the press, to be a practical one, must be a common benefit to all—else it is no freedom, but a privilege. It is wanting two ingredients—freedom of printing and freedom of reading. Now there is no freedom of reading there, because there is no possibility for the people at large to do so; because the circulation of newspapers, the indispensable moral food of human intellect, is by a heavy taxation, checked. The press is a source of public revenue, and by the incumbrance of stamp and paper duties, made almost inaccessible to the poor. Hence it is that the newspapers in the United States are only one tenth, and in some cases one twentieth the price of English or French papers, and hence, again, is the immense difference in their circulation. In the United States several of the daily papers every morning reach from thirty to forty thousand readers, whereas *The London Times* is considered to be a monster power, because it has a circulation of from twenty-five to thirty thousand copies, of which, I was told during my stay in England, that the good, generous sense of the people has abated some six thousand copies, in consequence of its foul hostility to the just and sacred cause of Hungary.

Such being the condition of your press, gentlemen, it must of course be a high source of joyful gratification to me to have the honor to address you, gentlemen; because in addressing you, I really address the whole people of the United States—not only a whole people, but a whole intelligent people, gentlemen.

That is the highest praise which can upon a people be bestowed, and yet is no praise—it is the acknowledgment of a real fact. The very immensity of the circulation of your journals proves it to be so—because this immense circulation is not only due to that constitutional right of yours to speak and print freely your opinions; it is not only due to the cheap price which makes your press a common benefit to all, and not a privilege to the rich—but it is chiefly due to the universality of public instruction which enables every citizen to read. It is a glorious thing to know that in this flourishing young city alone, where streets of splendid buildings proudly stand, where a few years ago the river spread its waves or the plough tilled, nearly one hundred thousand children receive public education annually.

Do you know, gentlemen, where I consider the most glorious monument of your country?—if it be so as I have read it once—it is that fact, that when in the steps of your wandering squatters your engineers go on to draw geometrical lines, even in the territories where the sound of a human step never yet has mixed with the murmurs by which virginal nature is adoring the Lord; in every place marked to become a township, on every sixteenth square you place a modest wooden pole, with the glorious mark,

"POPULAR EDUCATION STOCK."

This is your proudest monument.

However, be this really the case or not, in every case, in my opinion, it is not your geographical situation, not your material power, not the bold, enterprising spirit of your people which I consider to be the chief guarantee of your country's future, but the universality of education; because an intelligent people never can consent not to be free. You will be always willing to be free and you are great and powerful enough to be so good as your will.

My humble prayers to benefit my country's cause, I must so address to the public opinion of the whole intelligent people of the United States. You are the mighty engineers of this sovereign power, upon which rest my country's hopes—it must be, therefore, highly gratifying to me, to see not isolated men, but the powerful complete of the great word "PRESS," granting me this important manifestation of generous sentiments and of sympathy. Still I address you with fear, gentlemen, because you are aware that since my arrival here, I had the great honor and valuable benefit to see my whole time agreeably occupied by the reception of the most noble manifestations of public sympathy, so much that it became entirely impossible for me to be thus prepared to address you, gentlemen, in a language which I but very imperfectly speak—as the great importance of this occasion would have required, and my high regards for yourselves had pointed out as a duty to me.

However, I hope you will take this very circumstance for a motive of excuse. You will generously consider that whenever and wherever I publicly speak, it is always chiefly spoken to the press; and lowering your expectations to the humility of my abilities, and to the level of the principal difficulties of my situation, you will feel inclined to some kind indulgence for me, were it only out of broth erly generosity for one of your professional colleagues, as I profess to be one.

Yes, gentlemen, it is a proud recollection of my life that I commenced my public career in the humble capacity of a journalist. And in that respect, I may, perhaps, be somewhat entitled to your brotherly indulgence, as you, in the happy condition which the institutions of your country insures to you, can have not even an idea of the tortures of a journalist who has to write with fettered hands, and who is more than fettered by an Austrian arbitrary preventive Censorship. You have no idea what a torture it is to sit down to your writing-desk, the breast full of the necessity of the moment, the heart full of the righteous feelings, the mind full of convictions and of principles—and all this warmed by the lively fire of a patriot's heart—and to see before your eyes the scissors of the Censor ready to fall upon your head, like the sword of Damocles, lopping your ideas, maiming your arguments, murdering your thoughts; and his pencil before your eyes, ready to blot out, with a single draft, the work of your laborious days and of your sleepless nights; and to know that the people will judge you, not by what you have felt, thought, or written, but by what the Censor wills; to know that the ground upon which you stand is not a ground known to you, because limited by rules, but an unknown slippery ground, the limits of which lie but within the arbitrary pleasure of your Censor—doomed by profession to be stupid, and a coward, and a fool;—to know all this, and yet not to curse your destiny—not to deny that you know how to read and to write, but to go on, day by day, in the torturing work of Sysiphus. Oh! it is the greatest sacrifice which an intelligent man can make to fatherland and humanity.

And this is the present condition of the Press, not in Hungary only, but in all countries cursed by Austrian rule. Our past revolution gave freedom to the Press, not only to my fatherland, but by indirect influence also to Vienna, Prague, Lemberg; in a word, to the whole empire of Austria. This very circumstance must be sufficient to insure your sympathy to my country's cause; as on the contrary, the very circumstance that the victory of the Hapsburgian dynasty, achieved by treason and Russian arms, was a watchword to oppress the Press in Hungary, in Austria, in Italy, in Germany—nay, throughout the European Continent. The contemplation that the freedom of the Press on the European Continent is inconsistent with the preponderance of Russia, and the very existence of the Austrian dynasty, this sworn enemy of freedom and of every liberal thought—this very circumstance must be sufficient to insure your generous support, to sweep away those tyrants and to raise liberty where now foul oppression proudly rules.

Gentlemen, a considerable time ago there appeared in certain New York papers a systematic compound of the most foul calumnies, falsehood and misrepresentations about the Hungarian cause, going so far as, with unexampled effrontery, to state that we struggled for oppression, while it was the cursed Austrian dynasty which stood forth for liberty. Now *there* is a degree of effrontery, the temerity of which becomes astonishing even to me, who, having seen the unexampled treachery of the house of Austria, became familiar with the old Roman maxim, "*nil admirari*," through my tempest-tossed life. We may be misrepresented, scorned, jeered, charged with faults; our martyrs, the blood of whom cries for revenge, may be laughed at as fools; and even heroes, commanding the veneration of history, may be represented as Don Quixotes, of tragi-comedy;—all this I could, if not bear, at least conceive. I have seen strange specimens of the aberrations of the human mind; but that, in the midst of the most mournful sufferings, not even the honor of an unfortunate nation should be sacred to some men, who enjoy the benefit of free institutions and profess to be Republicans—that is too much! it is a sorrowful page in mankind's history.

You cannot, of course, expect to see me, on this occasion, entering into a special refutation of this astonishing compound of calumnies. I will reserve it for my pen, so soon as I can have a free day for it. It will be very easy work, because all artificial compounds of misrepresentations must fall into dust before the dispassionate, plain statement of facts, the greatest part of which, I thankfull have to acknowledge, are already not unknown to you.

Permit me rather to make some humble remark upon the question of "nationalities" which plays such an important,and, I dare say, such a mischievous part in the destinies of Europe. I say mischievous, because no word ever was so much misrepresented or mistaken as the word "nationality:" so that it would be indeed a great benefit to humanity, could I succeed to contribute something to the rectification of this idea, the misrepresentation of which became the most mischievous instrument in the hands of absolutism against the spirit of liberty.

Let me ask you, gentlemen, are you, the people of the United States, a nation or not? Have you a *National* Government or not? Have you? You answer yes; and yet you, the people of the United States, are not all of one blood, and speak not one language. Millions of you speak English, others French, others German, others Italian, others Spanish, others Danish, and even several Indian dialects—and yet you are a nation!

And your Government, even the Government of your single States; nay, the municipal governments of your different cities, are not legislating and governing and administering in all and every language spoken in your Union, in the respective States and in the respective cities themselves—and yet you *have* a National Government!

Now, suppose that one part of the people of the United States, struck by a curse like that with which the builders of Babel were once struck, should at once rise and say—" The Union in which we live is an oppression to us. Our laws, our institutions, our State and City Governments, our very freedom, is an oppression to us! What is Union to us? what rights? what laws? what freedom? what history? what geography? what community of interests? They are all nothing. Language—that is all. Let us divide the Union; divide the States; divide the very cities. Let us divide the whole territory, by, and according to languages, and then let the people of every language live distinct, and form each a separate state. Because every nation has a right to a national life, and to us the language is the nation—nothing else; and your Union, your rights, your laws, and your freedom itself, though common to us, is an oppression to us, because language is the only basis upon which States must be founded. Everything else is tyranny."

What would you say of such reasoning? What would become of your great Union? What of your Constitution—this glorious legacy of your greatest men—those immortal stars on mankind's moral canopy? What would become of your country itself, whence the rising spirit of freedom spreads its mighty wings, and rising hope clears up the future of humanity? What would become of this grand, mighty complex of your Republic, should it ever be attacked in its consistency by the furious hands of the fanaticism of language? Where now she wanders and walks among the rising temples of human happiness, she soon would tread upon the ruins of liberty, mourning over the fragility of human hopes.

Happy art thou, free nation of America, that thou hast founded thy house upon the only solid basis of a nation's liberty! Liberty! A principle steady like the world, eternal like the truth, and universal for every climate, for every time, like Providence. Thou hast no tyrants among thee to throw the apple of Eros in thy Union. Thou hast no tyrants among thee to raise the fury of hatred in thy national family—hatred of nations, that curse of humanity, that venomous instrument of Despotism.

What a glorious sight it is to see the oppressed of so different countries, different in language, history, and habits, wandering to thy shores, and becoming members of thy great nation, regenerated by the principle of common liberty!

Would I could do the same! but I can't, because I love my native land, inexpressibly, boundless, fervently. I love it more than life, more than happiness. I love it more in its gloomy sufferings than I would in its proudest, happiest days.

What makes a nation? Is it the language only? Then there is no great, no powerful nation on earth, because there is no moderately large country in the world, whose population is counted by millions, where you would not find several languages spoken.

No! it is not language only which makes a nation. Community of interests, community of history, communities of rights and duties, but chiefly community of institutions of a population, which, though perhaps different in tongue, and belonging to different races, is bound together by its daily intercourse in their towns, the centres of their homely commerce and homely industry, the very mountain ranges, and systems of rivers and streams, the soil, the dust of which is mingled with the ashes of those ancestors who bled on the same field, for the same interest—the common inheritance of glory and of woe, the community of laws, tie of institutions, tie of common freedom or common oppression—all this enters into the definition of a nation. That this is true—that this is instinctively felt by the common sense of the people, nowhere is more apparently shown than at this very moment in my native land. Hungary was declared by Francis Joseph of Austria no more to exist as a Nation, no more as a State. It was and is put under martial law; strangers rule, in a foreign tongue, where our fathers lived and our brothers bled. To be a Hungarian became almost a crime in our own native land. Now, to justify before the world the extinction of Hungary, the partition of its territory, and again the centralization of the dissected limbs into the common body of servitude, the treacherous dynasty was anxious to show that the Hungarians are in a minority in their own native land. They hoped that intimidation and terrorism would induce even the Hungarians—Magyars, as we are in our own language termed—to abnegate their language and birth. They ordered a census of nationalities to be made. They performed it with the iron rule of martial law; they employed terrorism in the highest degree, so much that thousands of women and men, who professed to be Magyars, preferred not to know, nay, not to have perhaps heard any other language than the Magyar, notwithstanding all their protestations, were put down to be Sclaves, Serbs, Germans, or Wallachians, because their names had not quite a Hungarian sound. And still what was the issue of this malignant plot? Out of the twelve millions of inhabitants of Hungary proper, the Magyars turned out to be more than eight millions, some two millions more than we know the case really is. The people instinctively felt that the tyrant had the design to destroy, under the pretext of language, the very existence of the nation formed by the compound of all those ingredients which I have mentioned above, and with that common good sense which every nation possesses, met the tyrannic plot as if it answered, "We want to be a nation, and if the tyrant takes language only for the mark of our nationality, then we are all Hungarians." And mark well, gentlemen! this happened not under my governorship, but even under the rule of Austrian Martial Law. The Cabinet of Vienna became furious; it thought of a new census, but prudent men told them that a new census would give the whole twelve millions as Magyars, and thus no new census was taken. So true is my assertion that it is not language alone which makes a nation, an assertion which of course your own great Republic proves to the world.

But on the European Continent there unhappily grew up a school which bound the idea of language only to the idea of language, and joined political pretensions to it. There are some who advocate the theory that existing countries must cease, and the territories of the world be anew divided by languages and nations, separated by tongues.

You are aware that this idea, if it were not impracticable, would be but a curse to humanity—a death-blow to civilization and progress, and throw back mankind by centuries—it were an eternal source of strife and war, because there is a holy, almost religious tie, by which man's heart to his home is bound, and no man ever would consent to abandon his native land only because his neighbors speak another language than he himself; and, by this reason, claims for him that sacred spot where the ashes of his fathers lie—where his own cradle stood—where he dreamed the happy dreams of youth, and where nature itself bears a mark of his manhood's laborious toil. The idea were worse than the old migration of nations was—despotism only would rise out of the strife of mankind's fanaticism.

And really it is very curious. Nobody of the advocates of this mischievous theory is willing to yield to it for himself—but others he desires to yield to it. Every Frenchman becomes furious when his Alsace is claimed to Germany by the right of language—or the borders of his Pyrenees to Spain—but there are some among the very men who feel revolted at this idea who claim for Germany that it should yield up large territory because one part of the inhabitants speak a different tongue, and would claim from Hungary to divide its territory which God himself has limited by its range of mountains and the system of streams, as also by all the links of a community of more than a thousand years, to cut off our right hand, Transylvania, and to give it up to the neighboring Wallachia, to cut out, like Shylock, one pound of our very breast—the Banat—and the rich country between the Danube and Theiss—to augment by it Turkish Serbia and so forth. It is the new ambition of conquest, but an easy conquest, not by arms but by language.

So much I know, at least, that this absurd idea cannot, and will not, be advocated by any man here in the United States, which did not open its hospitable shores to humanity, and greet the flocking millions of emigrants with the right of a citizen, in order that the Union may be cut to pieces, and even your single states divided into new-framed independent countries by and according to language.

And do you know, gentlemen, whence this absurd theory sprung up on the European Continent? It was the idea of Panslavismus —that is, the idea that the mighty stock of Sclavonic races is called to rule the world, as once the Roman did. It was a Russian plot— it was the infernal idea, to make out of national feelings a tool to Russian preponderance over the world.

Perhaps you are not aware of the historical origin of this plot. It was after the third division of Poland, this most immoral act or tyranny, that the chance of fate brought the Prince Czartorisky to the court of Catharine of Russia. He subsequently became Minister of Alexander the Czar. It was in this quality that, with the noble aim to benefit his down-trodden fatherland, he claimed from the young Czar the restoration of Poland, suggesting for equivalent the idea of Russian preponderance over all nations of the old Sclavonic race. I believe his intention was sincere; I believe he thought not to misconsider those natural borders, which, besides the affinity of language, God himself has between the nations drawn. But he forgot that the spirits which he raises, he will not be able to master more, and that uncalled fanaticism will sundry fantastical shapes force into his frame, by which the frame itself must burst in pieces soon. He forgot that Russian preponderance cannot be propitious to liberty; he forgot that it can even not be favorable to the development of the Sclave nationality, because Sclavonic nations would by this idea be degraded into individuals of Russianism—all absorbed by Russia, that is, absorbed by despotism.

Russia got hold of the sensible idea very readily. May be that young Alexander had in the first moment noble inclinations; he was young, and the warm heart of youth is susceptible to noble instincts. It is not common in history, such Francis Joseph of Austria—so young and yet such a Nero as he is. But few years of power were sufficient to extinguish every spark of noble sentiment—if there was one in Alexander's young heart. Upon the throne of the Romanow's, is the man soon absorbed by the Autocrat. The air of the traditional policies of St. Petersburg, is not that air where the plant of regeneration can grow, and the sensible idea became soon a weapon of horror, oppression, and Russian preponderance. Russia availed herself of the idea of Panslavism to break Turkey down, and make an obedient satellite of Austria. Turkey withstands yet, but Austria has fallen into the snare. Russia sent out its agents, its moneys, its venomous secret diplomacy through the world; it spoke to the Sclave nations of the hatred against foreign dominion—of independence of religion connected with nationality under its own supremacy; but chiefly it spoke to them of Panslavism under the protectorate of the Czar. The millions of its own large empire also, all oppressed —all in servitude—all a tool to his ambition; he flattered them with the idea to become the rulers of the world, in order that they might not think of liberty; he knew that man's breast cannot harbor two passions at once. He gave them ambition and excluded the spirit of liberty. This ambition got hold of all the Sclave nations through Europe; so became Panslavism the source of a movement, not of nationality, but of the dominion of languages. That word "language" replaced every other sentiment, and so it became the curse to the development of liberty.

Only one part of the Sclavonic races saw the matter clear, and withstood the current of this infernal Russian plot. They were the Polish Democrats—the only ones who understood that to fight for liberty is to fight for nationality. Therefore they fought in our ranks, and were willing to flock in thousands of thousands to aid us in our struggle; but I could not arm them, so I could not accept them. We ourselves, we had a hundred-fold more hands ready to fight than arms—and nobody was in the world to help us with arms.

There is the same origin and real nature of the question of nationalities in Europe.

Now let me see what was the condition of Hungary under these circumstances.

Eight hundred and fifty years ago, when the first King of Hungary, St. Stephen, becoming Christian himself, converted the Hungarian nation to Christianity, it was the Roman Catholic clergy of Germany whom he invited to assist him in his pious work. They did, but it was natural that the pious assistance happened also to be accompanied by some worldly designs. Hungary offered a wide field to the ambition of foreigners. And they persuaded the King to adopt a curious principle, which he laid down in his political testament; that is, that it is not good, when the people of a country is but of one extraction and speaks but one tongue. There was yet adopted another rule; that is, to advise the language of the Church —Latin—for the diplomatic language of the Government, Legislature, law and all public proceedings. The Hungarian, scarcely yet believing Christian, spoke not the Latin of course. This is the origin of that fatality that Democracy did not develop for centuries in Hungary. The public proceedings having been carried on in Latin, the laws given in Latin, the people were excluded from the public life. Public instruction being carried on in Latin, the great mass of the people, being agriculturists, did not partake in it, and the few who, out of the ranks of the people, partook in it, became, by the very instruction, severed and alienated from the people's interests. This dead Latin language, introduced into the public life of a living nation, was the most mischievous barrier against liberty. The first blow to it was stricken by the Reformation. The Protestant Church, introducing the national language into the Divine services, became a medium to the development of the spirit of liberty. So were our ancient struggles for religious liberty always connected with the maintenance of political rights. But still, Latin public life went on so far as to 1780. At that time, Joseph of Hapsburg, aiming at centralization, replaced the Latin by the German tongue. This raised the national spirit of Hungary; and our forefathers, seeing that the dead Latin language excluded the people from the public concerns, could be propitious to liberty, and anxious to oppose the design of the Viennese Cabinet of Germanizing Hungary, and so melting it into the common absolutism of the Austrian dynasty—I say, anxious to oppose the design by a cheerful public life of the people itself, begun in the year 1790, passed laws in the direction that by-and-by step by step, the Latin language should be replaced in the public proceedings of the Legislature and of the Government by a living language, familiar to the people itself. And Hungary being Hungary, what was more natural than that, being in the necessity to choose one language, they chose the Hungarian language in and for Hungary, the more because that was the language spoken in Hungary, not only by a comparative majority of the people, but almost by an absolute majority; that is, those who spoke Hungarian were not only more than those who spoke whatever one of the other languages, but, if not more, at least equal to all those who spoke several other languages together.

Be so kind to mark well, gentlemen, no other language was oppressed—the Hungarian language was upon nobody enforced—wherever another language was in use even in public life; for instance, of whatever church—whatever popular school—whatever community—it was not replaced by the Hungarian language. It was only the dead Latin which by-and-by became eliminated from the diplomatic public life, and replaced by the living Hungarian in Hungary.

In Hungary, gentlemen, be pleased to mark it. never was this measure extended into the municipal public life of Croatia and Sclavonia, which, though belonging for 800 years to Hungary, still were not Hungary, but a distinct nation, with distinct municipal public life.

They themselves, Croatians and Sclavonians, repeatedly urged it in the common Parliament to afford them opportunity to learn the Hungarian language, that having the right they might also enjoy the benefit of being employed to common governmental offices of Hungary. This opportunity was afforded to them, but nobody was forced to make use of it if he desired not to do so; but with their own municipal and public life, as also with the domestic, social, religious life, of whatever other people in Hungary itself, the Hungarian language did never interfere, but replaced only the Latin language, which no people spoke, which to no living people belonged, and which therefore was contrary to liberty, because it excluded the people from any share in the public life. Willing to give freedom to the people, we eliminated that Latin tongue, which was an obstacle to its future. We did what every other nation in the world did, clearing by it the way to the people's common universal liberty.

Your country is a happy one even in that respect; being a young nation, you did not find in your way the Latin tongue when you established this Republic; so you did not want a law to eliminate it from your public life. You have a living diplomatic language which is spoken in your own Congress, in your State Legislatures, and by which your Government rules. That language is not the native language of your whole people—scarcely of that of a majority; and yet no man in the Union takes it for an oppression that Legislature and Government is not carried on in every possible language that is spoken in the United States; and yet are found in your common law, inherited from England, some Latin expressions, the affidavits, &c.; and having found it in law, you felt the necessity to eliminate it by law, as you really did.

And one thing I have to mention yet. This replacing of the Latin language by the Hungarian was not a work of our revolution, it was done before step by step, by-and-by from 1791. When we carried in 1848 our democratic reforms, and gave political, social, civil and full religious freedom to the whole people, without distinction of religion or tongue, considering that unhappy excitement of the question of languages prevailing through Europe in consequence of the Russian plot, which I developed, we extended our cares to the equal protection of every tongue and nationality, affording to all equal right, to all aid out of the public funds, for the moral, religious and scientific development in churches and in schools. Nay, our revolution extended this regard even to the political development of every tongue, sanctioning the free use of every tongue, in the municipalities and communal corporations, as well as the administration of justice itself. The promulgation of the laws in every tongue, the right to petition and to claim justice in whatever tongue, the duty of the Government to answer accordingly—all this was granted, and thus, far more done in that respect also than whatever other nation ever accorded to the claims of tongues; by far more than the United States ever did, though there is no country in the world where so many different languages are spoken as here.

It is, therefore, the most calumnious misrepresentation to say that the Hungarians struggled for the dominion of their own race. No; we struggled for civil, political, social and religious freedom, common to all, against Austrian despotism. We struggled for the great principle of self-government against centralization; and, because centralization, absolutism. Yes, centralization is absolutism; it is inconsistent with constitutional rights. Austria has given the very proof of it. The House of Austria had never the slightest intention to grant constitutional life to the nations of Europe. I will prove it on another occasion. It hates Constitutions as hell hates the salvation of human souls. But the friends of the Hapsburg say it has granted a Constitution—in March, 1849. Well, where is that constitution now? It was not only never executed, but it was three months ago formally withdrawn. Even the word Ministry is blotted out from the dictionary of the Austrian Government. Schwarzenburg is again House, Court, and State Chancellor, as Metternich was; only Metternich ruled not with the iron rule of martial law over the whole Empire of Austria: Schwarzenburg does. Metternich encroached upon the constitutional rights of Hungary, Transylvania, Croatia, and Sclavonia. Schwarzenburg has abolished them, and the young Nero, Francis Joseph, melted all nations together in a common bondage, where the promised equality of nationalities is carried out most literally, to be sure, because they are all equally oppressed, and all are equally ruled by absolutistical principles in the German language. And why was that illusory Constitution withdrawn? Because it was a lie from the beginning; because it was an impossibility. And why so? Because it was founded upon the principle of centralization, and centralized thirteen different nations, which now groan under Austrian rule; and yet, to have a constitutional life, is more than an impossibility. It is an absurdity, it is an oppression augmented by deceit.

I cannot exhaust this vast topic in one speech, so I go to the end. I only state clearly my own and my nation's ruling principle, even in respect to the claims of the nationalities of languages; and that is—we will have Republican institutions, founded on universal suffrage, and so the majority of the sovereign people shall rule in every respect, in the village, in the city, in the country, in the Congress and Government—in all and everything. What to the public concerns of the village, of the city, of the country, of the Congress belongs—self-government everywhere—and universal suffrage and the rule of the majority everywhere. That is our principle, for which we live and are ready to die. This is the cause for which I humbly request the protecting aid of the people of the United States, and chiefly your aid and protection, gentlemen,—you, the mighty engineers of the public opinion of your glorious land!

Let me entreat you, gentlemen, to accord this protection to the cause of my down-trodden land; it is the cause of oppressed humanity on the European Continent. It is the cause of Germany, bleeding under the scourge of some thirty petty tyrants, all leaning upon that league of despots, the basis of which is Petersburg. It is the cause of fair but unfortunate Italy, which, in so many respects, is dear to my heart. We have a common enemy; so we are brothers in arms for freedom and independence. I know how Italy stands, and I dare confidently declare there is no hope for Italy but in that great Republican party, at the head of which Mazzini stands. I has nothing to do with Communistical schemes or the French doctrines of Socialism. But it wills Italy independent, free and Republican. Whither could Italy look for freedom and independence, if not to that party which Mazzini leads? To the King of Naples, perhaps Let me be silent about that execrated man. Or to the dynasty of Sardinia and Piedmont? It professes to be constitutional, and it captures those poor Hungarian soldiers, who seek an asylum in Piedmont; it captures and delivers them to Austria to be shot—and they are shot, increasing the number of those 3,742 martyrs whom Radetsky murdered on the scaffold during three short years. The house of Savoy became the blood-hound of Austria to spill Hungarian blood.

Gentlemen, the generous sympathy of the public opinion of the United States—God be blessed for it!—is strongly aroused to the wrongs and sufferings of Hungary. My humble task in that respect is done. Now I look for your generous aid to keep that generous sympathy alive, that it may not subside like the passing emotion of the heart.

I look for your generous aid to urge the formation of societies to collect funds and to create a loan.

I look for your generous aid to urge the public opinion of the sovereign people of the United States to pronounce in favor of the humble propositions which I have had the honor to express at the Corporation Banquet of the City of New York, until the resolutions of the people succeed to impress the favorite decision to the policy of the United States.

In that respect I beg leave one single remark to make. In speaking of the principle of non-admission of any interference in any country's domestic concerns, I took the liberty to express my humble wish to see Great Britain invited to unite in this protective policy. The reason is, because I take the present French Government for one of the oppressors—it has interfered, and continues to interfere in Rome. But the French nation, I take for one of the oppressed. The French nation will do the same as Hungary, Italy and Germany. The alliance of the French nation is insured by its necessary principles, if the Republic becomes a reality. The decisive question is, what the neutral powers will do—and these are Great Britain and the United States.

Let me hope, gentlemen, that however low I may have fallen in your expectations by this humble address, which, though sketched down, was still without eloquence, nor by want of time elaborate; still, following the generous impulse of your republican hearts, and considering not the immerit of my humble self, but merit of the cause which I plead, you will accord me that protective aid of the free, independent Press, upon which rest, for the greater part, the hopes of my nation and those of oppressed humanity. And if you generously accord me that protective aid, I will yet also see fulfilled, in my own country's cause, those noble words which you, Sir, (to the Chairman,) from that height where the genius of poetry soars, have told your people, which so likes to listen to the noble inspirations of its Bryant,

> "Truth crushed to earth shall rise again;
> The eternal years of God are hers;
> But Error, wounded, writhes in pain,
> And dies among—

Let me add, Sir, *with*
———his worshippers."

SPEECH TO THE BAR OF NEW YORK.

GENTLEMEN—Highly as I value the opportunity to meet the gentlemen of the Bar, I would have felt very much embarrassed to have to answer the address of that corporation before such a numerous and distinguished assembly, had you, Sir, not relieved my well-founded anxiety by an anticipated just appreciation of the difficulties I am surrounded with, and which, of course, make it entirely impossible for me to answer any expectation of all, and especially such expectations as such an intelligent meeting would be entitled to entertain. But you, Sir, have paved my way; let me hope, that in acknowledging the difficulties of my position, you were the interpreter of this distinguished assembly's equanimity and indulgence, which I respectfully beg, may not be refused to me when I end—having been promised before I began. Gentlemen of the Bar, you have the noble task to be the first interpreters of the law; to make it subservient to justice; to maintain its eternal principles against the encroachments of facts; and to restore those principles to life, whenever they become obliterated by misunderstanding or by violence. When darkness is cast upon the light of truth, then we are told by an old Roman:

"Veniet de plebe togata
Qui juris nodas et legum epigrammata solvat."

Let me in that respect, briefly state my opinion about the system of Codification, as opposite to customary law.

You have a great authority for codification—Livingston, and really it may be presumptuous to state an opinion contrary to his— still I confess I am no friend of codification. I am no friend of it, because I am a friend of free, unarrested progress. And a code arrests progress. It is an iron hand, which hinders the circulation of intelligence, and fetters its development, which freely must go on toward boundless perfection—the destiny of humanity. You know what a thick shadow was cast over centuries, upon the field of justice, by the code of Justinian; and how, even yet, whole enlightened nations are laboring within its iron grasp. My opinion is, that law must hold pace in its development with the development of institutions and intelligence ; but, until this, law is and must be an object of continual progress. Justice is immortal, eternal, and immutable, like God himself. And the progress in the development of law is only then a progress, when it is directed towards those immortal principles of justice which are eternal like God himself; and whenever prejudice or error succeeds in establishing whatever doctrine in customary law which is contrary to the eternal principles of justice, it is one of your noblest duties, gentlemen, to avail yourselves of the privilege of not having a written code to fetter justice within the bonds of error and prejudice ; it is one of your noblest duties to apply principles, to show that an unjust custom is a corrupt practice, an abuse ; and by showing this, to originate that change, or rather development in the unwritten, customary law, which is necessary to make it protect justice, instead of opposing and violating it. If this be your noble vocation in respect to the private laws of your country, let me entreat you, gentlemen, to extend it to that public law which, regulating the mutual duties of nations towards each other, rules the destinies of humanity. You know that upon this field, where rests no code but that of nature and of nature's God, which your forefathers invoked when they raised the colonies of England to the noble rank of a free nation and an independent power on earth—you know that in that eternal code there are not written pettifogging subtleties, but only everlasting principles : everlasting, like those by which the world is ruled by God. You know that when artificial cunning of ambitious oppressors succeeds to distort those principles into practice contrary to them, and when passive indifference or thoughtlessness submits to that above, as weakness must submit, it is the noble destiny—let me say duty—of enlightened nations, alike powerful as free, to restore those eternal principles to practical value, that justice, right, and truth may sway, where injustice, oppression and error prevailed. Raise high with manly hands the blazing torch of truth upon the dark field of arbitrary prejudice. Become the champions of principles, and your people will become the regenerators of international public law. It will. A tempest-tossed life has somewhat sharpened the eyes of my soul ; and had it even not done so, still I would dare say, I know how to read your people's heart. It is so easy to read it, because it is open, like nature, and unpolluted like a virgin's heart. May others shut their ears to the cry of oppressed humanity because they regard duties but through the glass of petty interests. Your people have that instinct of justice and generosity which is the stamp of mankind's heavenly origin; and it is conscious of your country's power; it is jealous of its own dignity ; it knows that it has the power to restore the law of nations to the principles of justice and right ; and knowing itself to have the power, it is willing to be as good as its power is. Let the cause of my country, this eternal object of my feelings and my thoughts, of my sorrows and my hopes, become the opportunity to the restoration of true and just international law. Mankind is come to the eleventh hour in its destinies. One hour of delay more, and its fate may be sealed, and nothing left to the generous inclinations of your people—so tender-hearted, so noble and so kind—than to mourn over murdered nations, its beloved brethren in humanity.

I had the honor, on a former occasion, these humble wishes to state; each of them connected with one principle of the law of nations, which you are called to enlighten, and your people to defend. The first was that the United States may be pleased to protect the sovereign right of nations to dispose of their own domestic concerns against the encroaching interference of foreign powers. A gentleman who came to honor me with the invitation of Cincinnati—that rising wonder of the West—has, yesterday, with that sublime eloquence which speaks volumes in one word, qualified that interference to be a piracy. The word is true—like truth itself. It spreads light upon the subject. It convinces the mind, and warms the heart. I felt, when I heard the word, a sort of moral power, which almost made me forget that I am but a powerless exile. I felt but to be a man, a member of humanity; and I almost cried out, "Pirate! Where is he? Let us go and hunt him down, that common enemy of humanity." There is such a moving power in a word of truth. That word has relieved me of many speeches. I want no more to discuss about the principle in that respect. There can be no doubt about what is lawful, what is a duty, against piracy. I have but to make a few remarks about two objections which I am told I will have to contend with. The first is, that it is a leading principle of the United States not to interfere with European nations; and that, therefore, you will not do it. I suppose that you were pleased to become acquainted with what I had the honor to say on a certain occasion in that respect—stating pragmatically that the United States had never entertained or confessed such a principle; and that, had it even done so, the United States had abandoned it, and were obliged to abandon it, because it could have been no principle, but a matter of temporary policy, the exigencies of which have entirely changed. I stated the mighty difference between neutrality and non-interference. So I will only briefly remark that precisely the same difference exists between alliance and interference. Every independent power has the right to form alliances, but has not the duty to do so. It can remain neutral if it pleases to remain so. Neither alliances nor neutrality are matter of principles, but simply of policy; and in that respect a power has the right not to consider anything but its own interest. By forming alliances, or by abstaining from them and remaining neutral, you may, perhaps, contravene the interests of every other people, but you offend not their rights. It is quite so as, for instance, you may have chosen to dine this evening at the Tripler Hall, and not in some hotel; or you can choose not to dine at any hotel at all, and remain neutral towards all. You of course will not very much have forwarded their interests by your neutrality, or the interests of the hotel proprietors, by entangling yourself into a treaty of decisive alliance with Mr. ——. However, you have violated no law—you have offended no right either by your neutrality or by your alliance. I beg to be excused for the vulgarity of this comparison, but I want to be exactly understood, that it is not a cunning subtlety which I intend to start when I speak of an essential difference between neutrality and non-interference: so I may be permitted to make use of a popular simile, which conveys more clearly to the mind what I mean than scientific oratory would do in a foreign tongue, where I am often at a loss to find out the appropriate word. So alliance and its opposite, neutrality—may hurt interest, but do not violate law; whereas, with interference, the contrary. Interference with the sovereign right of nations to resist oppression, to alter their institutions, their government, is a violation of the law of nations, a violation of the laws of nature and of nature's God— therefore non-interference is a duty common to every power, to every nation, and placed under the safeguard of every power, of every nation. He who violates that law is like a pirate; every power or earth has the duty to chase him down—the pirate, that curse of humanity. Well, there is not a single man in the United States who would hesitate to avow that a pirate must be chased down, and no man would more readily avow it than the gentlemen of trade. Your naval forces are—they must be—instructed to put down piracy where they meet it; for this purpose you know no geographical line—no difference of longitude and latitude—no difference of European and American waters. You have sent your Decatur for that purpose to the Mediterranean, who answered the Dey of Algiers that if "he claims powder he will have it with the balls," and no man in the United States imagined them to oppose your government for having done so. Nobody thought to advertise that it is the ruling principle of the United States not to meddle with European or African concerns; rather, if your government would have neglected so to do, I am sure, precisely, the gentlemen of trade would have been the foremost to claim from your government to beat and chase down piracy in the Mediterranean sea.

Now, in the name of all which is agreeable to God and sacred to man, if every man is ready thus to unite in the outcry against a rover, who, at the danger of his own life, boards some frail ship, murders some poor sailors, or takes some bales of cotton—is there no hope to see a similar universal outcry against those great pirates who board, not some small cutters, but the beloved home of nations —who murder, not some few sailors, but nations—who shed blood, not by drops, but by torrents—who rob not some hundred weight of merchandise, but the freedom, independence, welfare, and the very existence of nations? Oh God Almighty! Father of Humanity! Spare—oh spare that degradation to thy son—mankind; that in his destinies some bales of cotton should more weigh than those laws! Thou, Thyself, hast given to men more weight than the bloody scars of oppressed humanity; more weight than Christian brotherly love; more weight than the sufferings of down-trodden millions. Almighty God! what a pitiful sight! A miserable pickpocket, a drunken highway robber, chased by the whole of humanity to the gallows, and those who pickpocket the life-sweat of nations, rob them of their welfare, of their liberty, and murder them by thousands—these execrable criminals raise proudly their brow, trample upon humanity, and degrade humanity's laws before their high reverential name, and term them "most sacred majesties." But may God be blessed, there is hope for humanity; because there is a powerful, free mighty people here on the virgin soil of America, ready to protect the laws of nature and of nature's God, against the execrated piracy of the accursed pirates and their associates. Neutrality your people may have been taught by your wisest and best men; but none of them have ever taught your people to be indifferent to the violation of the eternal laws of nations, which are yours also; they have never been taught to remain indifferent at the mournful sight of oppressed humanity. But again and again I am told, "The United States, as a power, are not indifferent; it sympathizes deeply with those who are oppressed; and they will respect the laws of nations; but they have no interest to make them respected by others towards others." Interest! and always interest! Oh how cupidity succeeded to misrepresent the word. Is there any interest which could outweigh the interest of justice and right? Interest! but I answer by the very words of one of the most distinguished of your profession, gentlemen, the present Honorable Secretary of State—"The United States, as a nation, have precisely the same interest, (yes, interest is his word) in international law as a private individual has in the laws of his country." He was a member of the bar who advanced that principle of eternal justice against the mere fact of policy—now he is in the position to carry out that principle which he has advanced. I confidently trust he will be as good as his word. And I confidently trust that his honorable colleagues, the gentlemen of the bar, will remember their calling to be, to maintain the actual principles of justice against the encroachments of accidental policy—that they will endeavor to make policy subservient to justice, and not justice to the wavering claims of policy, and that they will support their high situated brother in the profession to carry out the principle which he advanced. Carry out—but how? I had the honor to state it at the banquet of the City of New-York, by declaring that the United States will not permit any foreign power to interfere with the sovereign right of nations to dispose of their own domestic concerns; that the United States consider themselves to have the duty not to permit any violation of the laws of nations, and that they invite Great Britain to unite with them to safeguard and to guarantee these laws. I cannot claim the honor to be the first to speak to you thus; no, the idea is not my invention. It is an American one. It is your own. I have heard the same principles advanced by your Consul at Southampton, Mr. Croskey. I have heard the same irresistible eloquence of truth developed in England by Mr. Walker. Nay, more—I have here in my hands two letters from Richard Rush, of Pennsylvania, to William Henry Prescott, of South Carolina, published in last March, nine months ago, where I find these words. (Here Governor Kossuth read an extract from a pamphlet containing an avowal of the same principles.) There are in this little book, views, truths, and principles worthy of the consideration of every citizen of the United States—worthy of the consideration of the United States as of Great Britain also. But, of course, I cannot by long quotations, misuse your indulgence. I beg leave only to draw your attention to it. But I may be answered—" Well, if we (the United States) make such a declaration of non-admission of the interference of Russia in Hungary, (because that is the practical meaning of the word, I will not deny,) and Russia will not respect our declaration; then we might have to go to war." And there is the rub. Well, I am not the man to decline the consequences of my principles. I will not steal into your sympathy by slippery evasion. Yes, gentlemen, I confess, should Russia not respect such a declaration of your country, then you are obliged, literally obliged to go to war, or else be prepared to be degraded before mankind from your dignity. Yes—I confess that would be the case. But you are powerful enough to defy any power on earth in a just cause, as your Washington said—so may God help me, as it is true, that never was there yet a more just cause. There was enough of war on the earth for ambition, or egotistical interests, even for womanly whims—to give to humanity the glorious example of a great people going even to war, not for egotistical interest, but for justice, for the law of nations, for the law of nature and of nature's God—and it will be no great mischief after all. It will be the noblest, the greatest glory which a nation yet has earned, nobler and greater than any nation yet has earned; and its greatest benefit will be, that it will be the last war, because it will make the laws of nations to become a reality, which nobody will dare violate, seeing them put under the safeguard of all humanity. It will be the last war, because it will make nations contented—contented because free. And what still must be foremostly considered, you have nothing to fear by that war for your own country—for your own security. If it were otherwise, I never would have pronounced that wish. But I am certain that there is not a single citizen of the United States who would not agree with me that there is no plausible issue of that

supposed war which could affect the security of your own country.
I think, gentlemen, it is time to get rid of the horror to "review
former opinions," as Mr. Rush says. I believe it is time to establish
that will, and I believe the people of the United States are called to
establish it. That policy must be made subservient to justice, international law, and the everlasting principle of right. There is an
axiom in jurisprudence, which I hope you will not contradict: "Laws
were a vain word if nobody were to execute them." Unhappy mankind! that was the condition of thy common laws until now—every
despot ready to violate them, but no power on earth to defend them.
People of the United States! here I bow before thee; and claim out
of the bottom of my national declaration: Raise thy young gigantic
arm, and be the executive power of nature and of nature's God;
which laws thou hast invoked when thou hast proclaimed thy independence. Protect them; defend them ever—if thou hast to go to
war for it! That will be a holier war than ever yet was, and the
blessing of God will be with thee.

And yet if the question of war is to be considered, not from the
view of right, duty, and law—which still, in my opinion, is a decisive
one—but from the view of mere policy, then I believe that you must
not shrink back from the mere word "war." There is no harm in
the mere empty word; three little letters, very innocent—that's all!
But you must consider if there really is any probability that your
declaration would not be respected, and you really had to go to war.
And here I most decidedly, most solemnly declare, that there is not
the slightest probability, nay, not even any possibility to it. You
must not take the Muscovite cabinet to be a blind fool. Oh! no!
they are not. Morality I deny to them, but skill not at all. Oh!
they are but very skilful! I know it too well. But precisely because they are skilful, be sure that, advised by England and yourself, the Czar will finally remain at home, when Hungary will send
the Hapsburgs home. There is no power in Europe which has more
vulnerable points than Russia; there is none affected with more elements of interior weakness than despotic Russia; there is no power
which has more to fear from a war, when, besides his neighboring
necessary enemies, the United States and England, or even only the
United States, also would be enlisted against him. He is not a fool
to risk such a war. I have stated in another place, how comparatively weak that supposed big giant is in military, financial, political
and social respects. Here I beg leave only to state how it came that
Russia, though comparatively so weak, has dared to interfere in Hungary. This is very easily explained. The last revolution in France
broke out in February, 1848. The republican principle raised its
head. Did the Czar interfere? No. Is he, perhaps, in love with
the word republic? He hates it, and would feel an infinite delight
to sweep away every republican—together with you, gentlemen—
and even the word "republic" from the earth. He knows very well

that in the long run his despotism cannot subsist on the same continent where a mighty republic exists, and still he did not interfere. He did not interfere in 1830 against Louis Philippe, for the so-called legitimate Bourbons. He did not interfere in 1848 for monarchy against the republican principle. Why? He dared not. He was prudently afraid. He got in a fury, and his armies moved towards South and West; but a calm night's sleep brought reflection home, and his armies moved again back. But he resorted to another power, in which he is more dangerous than in arms—to that power before which also poor Hungary fell—the power of secret diplomacy. He sent masculine and feminine diplomatists to Paris; and by the very means by which he—after 1830—succeeded to make out of the Citizen King, a satellite of the Holy Alliance, he also succeeded to make out of the revolution of 1848 a mock republic. But the pulsations of the great French heart vibrated throughout the continent. Every tyrant trembled. Every throne quaked. Germany cared not about his petty tyranny. The confederation of princes was blown asunder like void chaff. The German nation took its own destiny into its own hands, and from St. Paul's Church at Frankfort threatened to become one. The power of his father-in-law in Berlin stood not more steady upon its feet than a drunken fellow. The Emperor of Austria fled from his palace, after having waved out of his own window, the flag of freedom by his own hand, a few weeks before. And only think, gentlemen, in Vienna, in very Vienna, a Parliament met to give a constitution to the Austrian empire; a constitution also to Gallicia—Polish Gallicia, linked by blood, history and nature, and immediate neighborhood to that part of Poland which he himself ruled, and of whose western frontier another Polish province, Posen, stood in full revolutionary flames. You can imagine how the Czar raged, how he wished to unite all mankind in one head, so as he could cut it off with a single blow; and still he did nowhere interfere. Why? He was prudently afraid! so he took for motto, "I would, but I can't." However, the French republic became very innocent to him—almost an ally in some respects, really an ally in some respects, as in unfortunate Rome we have seen. The gentlemen at Frankfort proved also to be very innocent. The hopes of Germany failed—his father-in-law shot down, his people in Vienna, Prague, Lemberg, were shot down—the Austrian mock Parliament sent from Vienna to Kremsen, and from Kremsen home. Only Hungary stood firm, steady, victorious—the Czar had nothing more to fear from all revolutionary Europe—nothing from Germany—nothing from France; he had nothing to fear from the United States, because he knew that your government then was not willing to meddle with European matters—so he had free hands in Hungary. But one thing still he did not know, and that was—what will England—what will Turkey say, if he interferes—and that consideration alone was sufficient to check his inclinations to interfere. So anxious was he to feel the pulse of England and Turkey, that he sent first a small army—some ten thousand men—to help the Austrians in Transylvania; and sent them in such a manner as to have, in case of need, for excuse, that he was called to do so, not by Austria only, but by that part of the people also, which, deceived by foul delusion, stood by Austria! Oh, it was an infernal plot! Of course we beat down and drove out his 10,000 men, together with all the Austrians—but the Czar had gained his play. He got assured that he would have no foreign power opposing him when he dared to violate the law of nations by an armed interference in Hungary. So he interfered. It is a sorrowful matter for me to think upon; it is dreadful even to remember what torture I felt when I saw vanish like a dream, all my hopes that there is yet justice on earth, and respect for the laws of "nature, and of nature's God." When I saw myself with my nation, the handful of brave forsaken, alone, to fight that immense battle for humanity; when I saw Russian diplomacy stealing, like secret poison, into our ranks, introducing treason into them; then I saw a world of cares and sorrows put upon shoulders, a heavier weight than that which the fabulous Atlas of old had to bear. But let me not look back— it is all in vain, the past is past. Forward is my word, and I will go forward with unabated energy, because I know that there is yet a God in heaven, and there is a people like you on earth, and there is a power of decided will also here in this bleeding, aching heart. It is my motto still that "there is no difficulty to him who wills." But so much is a fact, so much is sure, that the Czar dared not interfere until he was assured that he would meet no foreign power to oppose his sacrilegious act. Show him, free people of America— show him in a manly declaration, that he will meet your power if he dares once more trample on the laws of nations—accompany this your declaration with an augmentation of your Mediterranean fleets, and be sure he will not. Still, you will have no war, and Austria falls almost without a battle, like a tottering house without foundation, raised upon the sand, and Hungary—my poor Hungary—will be free,—and Europe's oppressed Continent free to dispose of its domestic concerns. So much, gentlemen, for the first wish—the first principle which I had the honor to advance at the banquet of the City of New York. I could never have a more pleasant opportunity in a like manner to develop two other principles—one of which is to see restored in international law the true eternal, everlasting principles of an assured national intercourse commercial between nations, and to see it predicated by the power of your country. And the third is my humble wish to see recognized the legitimate character of the Declaration of Independence of Hungary. I would try, gentlemen, to develop these two principles in a like manner as I did the first, relying on the indulgence you have shown me. I cannot, gentlemen, I am so worn out that, perhaps in every hundred, ninety-nine men would be in bed instead of addressing such an assembly as this.

therefore I must reserve it for another occasion. I know that whenever I speak, there is also the mighty engine, the Press, who makes me also speak to you and to the people of the United States. This is my consolation for not being able to answer your expectation, if you have had some. Therefore let me end, and without any appeal to your sympathy—you have the source in your own generous hearts. This your meeting is a substantial proof of it. Be thanked for it; and let me say that the only gound upon which rests the hope of my native land is the ground of eternal principles—justice, right and law. You have devoted your lives to extend justice, right and law against the violence of tyrannous acts. Gentlemen of the Bar, I place these principles in your protecting care, and I trust they will find mighty advocates in you.

SPEECH BEFORE THE LADIES OF NEW YORK.

I WOULD I were able to answer that call. I would I were able conveniently to fill the place which your kindness has assigned to me; but really I am in despair. I do not know how many times I have spoken within the last fourteen days in New York. Permit me to make some few remarks which are suggested to my mind by what has been stated. You were pleased to say that Austria was blind to let me escape. Be assured that it was not the merit of Austria. Austria would have been very glad to bury me, if not in the cold grave of death, at least in the equally cold grave of moral inactivity. But the Emperor of Turkey took courage at the interference of America; and notwithstanding all the reclamations of Austria, I am free—restored to life, because restored to duty and activity. If Austria would not have murdered down the very existence of my nation, it is true I should have vanished out of the memory of man. It is a curious fate which I have. Perhaps there never was a man in the world who was so fond of tranquillity as I am; and perhaps no man so fond of doing as much good as possible without being known, or even noticed as being in the world. Thus, longing for tranquillity, it was my destiny never to have a single moment in my life to see it fulfilled. But my guiding star was, and will be, "Duty," and the pleasure and delight of the heart must wait, even forever, if necessary, when duty calls. Ladies, worn out as I am, still I am glad, very glad indeed, that it is the ladies of New York who have condescended to listen to my farewell. This my farewell, cannot, will not be eloquent. When in the midst of a busy day, the watchful care of a guardian angel throws some flowers of joy in the thorny way of man, he gathers them up with thanks, a cheerful thrill quivers through his heart, like the melody of an Æolian harp; but the earnest duties of life soon claim his attention and his cares. The melodious thrill dies away, and on he must go, and on he goes, joyless, cheerless, and cold, every fibre of his heart bent to the earnest dutie ' the day. But when the hard work of the day is done, and the stress of mind for a moment subsides, then the heart again claims its right, and the tender fingers of our memory gather up again the violets of joy which the guardian angel threw in our way, and we look at them with so much joy, we cherish them as the favorite gifts of life—we are so glad—as glad as the child on Christmas eve. These are the happiest moments of man's life. But when we are not noisy, not eloquent, we are silent, almost mute, like nature on a midsummer's night, reposing from the burning heat of the day. Ladies, that is my condition now. It is a hard day's work which I have to do here. I am delivering my farewell address ; and every compassionate smile, every warm grasp of the hand, every token of kindness which I have received (and I have received so many) every flower of consolation which the ladies of New York have thrown on my thorny way, rushes with double force to my memory. I feel so happy in this memory—there is a solemn tranquillity about my mind ; but in such a moment I would rather be silent than speak, I scarcely can speak. You know, ladies, that it is not the deepest feelings which are the loudest. And besides, I have to say farewell to New York. This is a sorrowful word. What immense hopes are linked in my memory in this word New York—hopes of resurrection for my down-trodden fatherland—hopes of liberation for oppressed nations on the European continent! Will the expectations which the mighty outburst of New York's young and generous heart foreshadowed, be realized ? Will these hopes be fulfilled, or will the ray of consolation which New York cast on the dark night of my fatherland—will it pass away like an electric flash ? Oh, could I cast one single glance into the book of futurity! No, God forgive me this impious wish. It is He who hid the future from man, and what He does is well done. It were not good for man to know his destiny. The energy of his sense of duty would falter or subside, if we were assured of the failure or success of our aims. It is because we do not know the future that we retain our energy of duty. So will I go on my work, with the full energy of my humble abilities, without despair, but with hope. It is Eastern blood which runs in my veins ; and I come from the East. I have, accordingly, somewhat of Eastern fatalism in my disposition, but it is the fatalism of a Christian, who trusts with unwavering faith in the boundless goodness of a Divine Providence.

But among all these different feelings and thoughts that come upon me in the hour of my farewell, one thing is almost indispensable to me, and that is, the assurance that the sympathy I have met with here will not pass away like the cheers which a warbling girl receives on the stage—that it will be preserved as a principle, and that when the emotion subsides, the calmness of reflection will but strengthen it, because it is a principle. This consolation I wanted, and this consolation I have, because, ladies, I place it in your hands. I bestow on your motherly and sisterly cares, the hopes of Europe's oppressed nations,—the hopes of civil, political, social, and religious liberty. Oh, let me entreat you, with the brief and stammering words of a warm heart, overwhelmed with emotions and with sorrowful cares—let me entreat you, ladies, to be watchful of the sympathy of your people, like the mother over the cradle of her beloved child. It is worthy of your watchful care, because it is the cradle of regenerated humanity. Especially in regard to my poor fatherland, I have particular claims on the fairer and better half of humanity, which you are. The first of these claims is, that there is not, perhaps, on the face of the earth a nation which in its institutions has shown more chivalric regard for ladies than the Hungarians. It is a praiseworthy trait of the Oriental character. You know that it was the Moorish race, in Spain, who were the founders of the chivalric era in Europe, so full of personal virtue, so full of noble deeds, so devoted to the service of ladies, and heroism, and to the protection of the oppressed. You are told that the ladies of the East are almost degraded to less than a human condition, being secluded from all social life, and pent up within the harem's walls. And so it is. But you must not judge the East by the measure of European civilization. They have their own civilization, quite different from ours in views, inclinations, affections, and thoughts. Eastern mankind is traditional—the very soil retains the stamp of traditional antiquity. When you walk upon that old soil, with the Old Testament in your hand, and read the prophets and patriarchs on the very spot where they lived and walked, you are astonished to find that nature is as it was five thousand years ago, and that the cedars still grow on her boundary, under the shadow of which the patriarchs were protected. You see the well just as Jacob saw it when Rachel gave drink to him and his camels. Everything—the aspect of nature, the habits, the customs, the social life of the people—is measured, not by centuries, but by thousands of years. The women of the East live as they lived in the time of the patriarchs, and they feel happy. Let them remain so. Who can wish them more on earth than happiness? Nothing is more ridiculous than to pity those who feel happy. But such is the fact that there is almost a religious regard paid to women in the East. No man dares to injure or offend a woman there. He who would do so would be despised by all like a dog. That respect goes so far, that the lord does not dare raise the carpet of his harem's door, still less enter it, where a pair of slippers before the threshold tells him that a lady is in the room. Respect and reverence for women is the characteristic of the Orient. The Magyars are of Eastern stock, cast in Europe. We found all the blessings of civilization in your ladies; but we conserved for them the regard and reverence of our Oriental character. Nay, more than that, we carried these views into our institutions and into our laws. With us, the widow remains the head of the family, as the father was. As long as she lives, she is the mistress of the property of her deceased husband. The chivalrous spirit of the nation supposes she will provide, with motherly care, for the wants of her children, and she remains in possession so long as she bears her deceased husband's name. The old Constitution of Hungary, which we reformed upon a democratic basis—it having been aristocratic—under that instrument the widow of a lord had the right to send her Representative to the Parliament, and in the county elections of public functionaries widows had a right to vote alike with the men. Perhaps this chivalric character of my nation, so full of regard toward the fair sex, may somewhat commend my mission to the ladies of America. Our second particular claim is, that the source of all the misfortune which now weighs so heavily upon my bleeding fatherland, is in two ladies—Catharine of Russia, and Sophia of Hapsburg, the ambitious mother of the young Nero, Francis Joseph. You know that one hundred and fifty years ago, Charles the Twelfth, of Sweden, the bravest of the brave, foreseeing the growth of Russia, and fearing that it would oppress and overwhelm civilization, ventured with a handful of men to overthrow the rising power of Russia. After immortal deeds, and almost fabulous victories, one loss made him a refugee upon Turkish soil, like myself. But, happier than myself, he succeeded in persuading Turkey of the necessity of checking Russia, in her overweening ambition, and in curtailing her growth. On went Mehemet Balzordsi with his Turks, and met Peter the Czar, and pent him up in a corner, where there was no possibility of escape. There Mehemet held him with iron grasp till hunger came to his aid. But nature claimed her rights, and in a council of war it was decided to surrender to Mehemet. Then Catharine, who was present in the camp, appeared in person before the Grand Vizier to sue for mercy. She was fair, and she was rich with jewels of nameless value. She went to the Grand Vizier's tent. She came back without any jewels, but she brought mercy, and Russia was saved. From that celebrated day dates the downfall of Turkey, and that of Russia's growth. Out of this source flowed the stream of Russian preponderance over the European continent; and down-trodden liberty, and the nameless sufferings of Poland and of my poor native land, are the dreadful fruits of Catharine's success on that day, cursed in the records of humanity.

The second lady who will be cursed through all posterity, in her memory, is Sophia, the mother of the present usurper of Hungary—she who had the ambitious dream to raise the limited power of a child upon the ruins of liberty, and on the neck of down-trodden nations. It was her ambition—the evil genius of the house of Hapsburg in the present day—which brought desolation upon us. I need only mention one fact to characterize what kind of a heart was in that cursed woman. On the anniversary of the day of Arad, where our martyrs bled, she came to the Court with a bracelet of rubies gathered together in so many roses as were numbered by the heads of the brave Hungarians who fell there, and declared it a gift which she joyfully presented to the company as a memento which she wears on her very arm to cherish its eternal memory, that she might not forget the pleasure she derived from the killing of those men who died at Arad. This very fact can give you a true knowledge of the character of that woman. And this is the second claim to the ladies' sympathy for oppressed humanity and my poor fatherland. I wish the free women of free America will help my down-fallen land to get out of that iron grasp, or to get out of those bloody fangs, and become independent and free. Our third particular claim is the behavior of our ladies during the last war. It is no wanton praise— it is a fact what I say—that, in my hard task to lead on the struggle and to govern Hungary, I had no more powerful auxilliaries, and no more faithful executors of the will of the nation, than the women of Hungary. You know that in ancient Rome, after the battle of Canæ, which was won by Hannibal, the victor was afraid to come down to the very walls of Rome. The Senate called on the people spontaneously to sacrifice all their wealth on the altar of their fatherland, and the ladies were the first to do it. Every jewel, every ornament, was brought forth, so much so that the tribune judged it necessary to pass a law prohibiting the ladies of Rome to wear jewelry or any silk dresses, in order that it might not appear the ladies of Rome had not, by their own choice, have done so. Now, we wanted in Hungary no such law. The women of Hungary brought all that they had. You would have been astonished to see how, in the most wealthy houses of Hungary, if you were invited to dinner, you would be forced to eat soup with iron spoons; and when the wounded and the sick—and many of them we had, because we fought hard—when the wounded and sick were not so well provided as it would have been our duty and our pleasure to do, I ordered the ministry and the respective public functionaries to take care of them. But the poor wounded went on suffering, and the ministry went on slowly to provide for them. When I saw this, one single word was spoken to the ladies of Hungary, and in a few hours there was provision made for hundreds of thousands of sick. And I never met a single mother who would have withheld her son from sharing in the battle; but I have met many who ordered and commanded their children to fight for their fatherland. I saw many and many brides who urged on the bridegrooms to delay their day of happiness till they would come back victorious from the battles of their fatherland. Thus acted the ladies of Hungary. That country deserves to live; that country deserves to have a future left yet, which the women, as much as the men, love and cherish.

But I have a stronger motive than all these to claim your protecting sympathy for my country's cause. It is her nameless woe, nameless sufferings. In the name of that ocean of bloody tears which the sacrilegious hand of the tyrant wrung from the eyes of the childless mothers, of the brides who beheld the hangman's sword between them and their wedding-day—in the name of all those mothers, wives, brides, daughters, and sisters, who, by thousands of thousands, weep over the graves of Magyars so dear to their hearts, and weep the bloody tears of a patriot (as they all are) over the face of their beloved native land—in the name of all those torturing stripes with which the flogging hand of Austrian tyrants dared to outrage humanity in the womankind of my native land—in the name of that daily curse against Austria with which even the prayers of our women are mixed—in the name of the nameless sufferings of my own dear wife—the faithful companion of my life—of her, who for months and for months was hunted by my country's tyrants, like a noble deer, not having, for months, a moment's rest to repose her wearied head in safety, and no hope, no support, no protection but at the humble threshold of the hardworking people, as noble and generous as they are poor—in the name of my poor little children, who so young are scarcely conscious of their life, had already to learn what an Austrian prison is—in the name of all this, and what is still worse, in the name of down-trodden liberty, I claim, ladies of New York, your protecting sympathy for my country's cause. Nobody can do more for it than you. The heart of man is as soft as wax in your tender hands. Mould it, ladies; mould it into the form of generous compassion for my country's wrongs, inspire it with the noble feelings of your own hearts, inspire it with the consciousness of your country's power, dignity and might. You are the framers of man's character. Whatever be the fate of man, one stamp he always bears on his brow—that which the mother's hand impressed upon the soul of the child. The smile of your lips can make a hero out of a coward—and a generous man out of the egotist; one word from you inspires the youth to noble resolutions; the lustre of your eyes is the fairest reward for the toils of life. You can even blow up the feeble spark of energy in the breast of broken age, that once more it may blaze up in a noble, a generous deed before it dies. All this power you have. Use it, ladies, use it in behalf of your country's glory, and for the benefit of oppressed humanity, and when you meet a cold calculator, who thinks by arithmetic when he is called to feel the wrongs of oppressed nations, convert him, ladies. Your smiles are commands, and the truth which pours forth instinctively from your hearts, is mightier than the logic articulated by any scholar. The Peri, excluded from Paradise, brought many generous gifts to heaven in order to regain it. She brought the dying sigh of a patriot; the kiss of a faithful girl imprinted on the lips of her bridegroom distorted by the venom of the plague. She brought many other fair gifts; but the doors of Paradise opened before her only when she brought with her the first prayer of a man converted to charity and brotherly love for his oppressed brethren and humanity. I have many tokens received of this brotherly love; and at the very moment of my entering this hall, I was informed of a circumstance which I consider so important as to beg permission to make in respect to it one single remark. I am told that one of the newspapers, with friendly and generous intention toward that cause which I have the honor to plead before you, has pointed out as the success of my standing here, that there is a committee established out of such men whose very share in that committee gives importance to it, and who are about to raise money for the purpose of revolutionizing Europe.—My axiom is that of the Irish poet, "Who would be free, themselves must strike the blow." All that I claim is fair play; and that is the aim for which I claim the United States to become the executive power of the laws of Nature and of Nature's God. That is the aim for which I claim your generous public and private aid and support. The revolutions in Europe will be made by the nations of Europe; but that they shall have fair play is what the nations of Europe expect from the peotection of the United States of America. Remember the power which you have, and which I have endeavored to point out in a few brief words. Remember this, and form associations; establish ladies' committees to raise substantial aid for Hungary. Who could, who would, refuse, when the melody of your voice is pleading the cause of my bleeding, my oppressed native land.

Now, ladies, I am worn out very much, so I am done. One word only remains to be said—a word of deep sorrow, the word, "Farewell, New York!" New York! that word will forever make thrill every string of my heart. I am like a wandering bird. I am worse than a wandering bird. He may return to his summer home. I have no home on earth! Here, at New York, I felt almost at home. But "Forward" is my call, and I must part. I part with the hope that the sympathy which I have met here is the trumpet sound of resurrection to my native land; I part with the hope that, having found here a short, transitory home, will bring me yet back to my own beloved home, that my ashes may yet mix with the dust of my native soil. Ladies, remember Hungary, and—farewell!

SPEECH IN WASHINGTON.

SIR,—As once Cyneas, the Epirote, stood among the senators of Rome, who, with an earnest word of self-conscious majesty, controlled the condition of the world and arrested the mighty kings in their ambitious march, thus full of admiration and of reverence, I stand before you, Legislators of the new capitol—that glorious hall of your people's collective majesty. The capitol of old yet stands, but the spirit has departed from it and come over to yours, purified by the air of liberty. The old stands a mournful monument of the fragility of human things—yours as a sanctuary of eternal rights. The old beamed with the red lustre of conquest, now darkened by oppression's gloomy night—yours beams with freedom's bright ray. The old absorbed the world by its own centralized glory—yours protects your own nation against absorption, even by itself. The old was awful with irrestricted power—yours is glorious with having restricted it. At the view of the old, nations trembled—at the view of yours humanity hopes. To the old, misfortune was only introduced with fettered hands to kneel at the triumphant conqueror's heels—to yours, the triumph of introduction is granted to unfortunate exiles, invited to the honor of a seat, and where kings and Cæsars never be hailed, for their powers, might, and wealth, there the persecuted chief of a downtrodden nation is welcomed as your great Republic's guest, precisely because he is persecuted, helpless, and poor. In the old, the terrible væ victis was the rule—in yours, protection to the oppressed, malediction to ambitious oppressors, and consolation to the vanquished in a just cause. And while out of the old a conquered world was ruled, you in yours provide for the common confederative interests of a territory larger than the conquered world of the old. There sat men boasting their will to be sovereign of the world—here sit men whose glory is to acknowledge the laws of Nature and of Nature's God, and to do that their sovereign, the people, wills.

Sir, there is history in these parallels. History of past ages, and history of future centuries, may be often recorded in a few words. The small particulars to which the passions of living men cling with fervent zeal—as if the fragile figure of men could arrest the rotation of destiny's wheel; these particulars die away. It is the issue which makes history, and that issue is always logical. There is a necessity of consequences wherever the necessity of position exists. Principles are the Alpha, they must finish with Omega, and they will. Thus history may be told often in a few words. Before yet the heroic struggle of Greece first engaged your country's sympathy for the fate of Freedom in Europe, then so far distant, and now so near, Chateaubriand happened to be in Athens, and he heard from a minaret raised upon the Propylæan ruins, a Turkish priest in Arabic language announcing the lapse of hours to the Christians of Minerva's town. What immense history in the small fact of a Turkish Imaum crying out, "Pray, man, the hour is running fast, and the judgment draws near." Sir, there is equally a history of future ages written in the honor bestowed by you to my humble self. The first Governor of independent Hungary, driven from his native land by Russian violence, an exile on Turkish soil protected by a Mohammedan Sultan against the blood-thirst of Christian tyrants, cast back a prisoner to far Asia by diplomacy, rescued from his Asiatic prison by America, crossing the Atlantic, charged with the hopes of Europe's oppressed nations, pleading, a poor exile, before the people of this great Republic, his down-trodden country's wrongs, and its intimate connection with the fate of the European continent, and with the boldness of a just cause, claiming the principles of the Christian religion to be raised to a law of nations; and to see not only the boldness of the poor exile forgiven, but to see him consoled by the sympathy of millions, encouraged by individuals, meetings, cities and states, supported by operative aid, and greeted by Congress and by the Government as the nation's guest, honored out of generosity, with that honor which only one man before him received—and that man received then out of gratitude—with honors such as no potentate can ever receive, and this banquet here, and the toast which I have to thank for—oh, indeed, Sir, there is a history of future ages in all these facts.

Sir, though I have the noble pride of my principles, and though I have the inspiration of a just cause, still I have also the conscience of my personal humility. Never will I forget what is due from me to the sovereign source of my public capacity. This I owe to my nation's dignity, and, therefore, respectfully thanking this highly distinguished assembly, in my country's name, I have the boldness to say, that Hungary well deserves your sympathy—that Hungary has a claim to protection, because it has a claim to justice. But as to myself, permit me humbly to express that I am well aware not to have in all these honors any personal share. Now, I know that even that which might seem to be personal in your toast, is only an acknowledgment of a historical fact; very instructively connected with a principle valuable and dear to every republican heart .n the United States of America. Sir, you were pleased to mention in your toast that I am unconquered by misfortune and unseduced by ambition. Now, it is a providential fact, that misfortune has the privilege to ennoble man's mind and to strengthen man's character. There is a sort of natural instinct of human dignity in the heart of man, which steels his very nerves not to bend beneath the heavy blows of a great adversity. The palm-tree grows best beneath a ponderous weight— even so the character of man. There is no merit in it—it is a law of psychology. The petty pangs of small daily cares have often bent the character of men, but great misfortunes seldom. There is less danger in this than in great good luck; and as to ambition, I, indeed, never was able to understand how anybody can more love ambition than liberty. But I am glad to state a historical fact as a principal demonstration of that influence which institutions exercise upon the character of nations. We Hungarians are very fond of the principle of municipal self-government; and we have a natural horror against the principle of centralization. That fond attachment to municipal self-government, without which there is no provincial freedom possible, is a fundamental feature of our national character. We brought it with us from far Asia, a thousand years ago, and we conserved it throughout the vicissitudes of ten centuries.

No nation has perhaps so much struggled and suffered from the civilized Christian world as ours. We do not complain of this lot. It may be heavy but it is not inglorious. Where the cradle of our Saviour stood, and where his divine doctrine was founded, there another faith now rules, and the whole of Europe's armed pilgrimage could not avert this fate from that sacred spot, nor stop the rushing waves of Islamism absorbing the Christian Empire of Constantine. We stopped those rushing waves. The breast of my nation proved a breakwater to them. We guarded Christendom, that Luthers or Calvins might reform it. It was a dangerous time, and the dangers of the time often placed the confidence of all my nation into one man's hand, and their confidence gave power into his hands to become ambitious. But there was not a single instance in history where a man honored by his people's confidence had deceived his people by becoming ambitious. The man out of whom Russian diplomacy succeeded in making the murderer of his nation's confidence—he never had it, but was rather regarded always with distrust. But he gained some victories when victories were the moment's chief necessity. At the head of an army, circumstances placed him in the capacity to ruin his country. But he never had the people's confidence. So, even he is no contradiction to the historical truth, that no Hungarian whom his nation honored with its confidence, was ever seduced by ambition to become dangerous to his country's liberty. That is a remarkable fact, and yet it is not accidental. It is the logical consequence of the influence of institutions upon the national character. Our nation, through all its history, was educated in the school of municipal self-government, and in such a country, ambition having no field, has also no place in man's character.

The truth of this doctrine becomes yet more illustrated by a quite contrary historical fact in France. Whatever have been the changes of government in that great country—and many they have been, to be sure; we have seen a Convention, a Directorate of Consuls, and one Consul, and an Emperor, and the restoration—the fundamental tone of the Constitution of France was power always centralized, Omnipotence always vested somewhere; and remarkably, indeed, France has never yet raised the single man to the seat of power who has not sacrificed his country's freedom to his personal ambition. It is sorrowful, indeed; but it is natural. It is in the garden of centralization where the venomous plant of ambition thrives. I dare confidently affirm, that in your great country there exists not a single man through whose brains has ever passed the thought that he would wish to raise the seat of his ambition upon the ruins of your country's liberty. If he could, such a wish is impossible in the United States. Institutions react upon the character of nations. He who sows the wind will reap the storm. History is the revelation of Providence. The Almighty rules by eternal laws, not only the material but the moral world; and every law is a principle, and every principle is a law. Men, as well as nations, are endowed with free will to choose a principle, but that once chosen, the consequences must be abided. With self-government is freedom, and with freedom is justice and patriotism. With centralization is ambition, and with ambition dwells despotism. Happy your great country, Sir, for being so warmly addicted to that great principle of self-government. Upon this foundation your fathers raised a home to freedom more glorious than the world has ever seen. Upon this foundation you have developed it to a living wonder of the world. Happy your great country, Sir, that it was selected by the blessing of the Lord, to prove the glorious practicability of a federative Union of many sovereign States, all conserving their State rights and their self-government, and yet united in one. Every star beaming with its own lustre, but all together one constellation on mankind's canopy.

Upon this foundation your country has grown to a prodigious power in a surprisingly brief period. You have attracted power in that. Your fundamental principles have conquered more in seventy-five years than Rome by arms in centuries. Your principles will conquer the world. By the glorious example of your freedom, welfare, and security, mankind is about to become conscious of its aim. The lesson you give to humanity will not be lost, and the respect of the State rights in the Federal Government of America and in its several States, will become an instructive example for universal toleration, forbearance, and justice, to the future States and Republics of Europe. Upon this basis will be got rid of the mysterious question of language, and nationalities raised by the cunning despotisms in Europe to murder Liberty, and the smaller States will find security in the principles of federative union, while they will conserve their national freedom by the principles of sovereign self-government; and while larger States abdicating the principles of centralization, will cease to be a blood-field to sanguinary usurpation, and a tool to the ambition of wicked men, municipal institutions will insure the development of local particular elements—Freedom, formerly an abstract political theory, will become the household benefit to municipalities, and out of the welfare and contentment of all parts will flow happiness, peace, and security for the whole. That is my confident hope. There will at once subside the fluctuations of Germany's fate. It will become the heart of Europe, not by melting North Germany into a Southern frame, or the South into a Northern; not by absorbing historical peculiarities, by centralized omnipotence; not by mixing in one State, but by federating several sovereign States into a Union like yours, upon a similar basis, will take place the national regeneration of the Sclavonic States, and not upon the sacrilegious idea of Panslavism, equivalent to the omnipotence of the Czar.

Upon a similar basis will we see fair Italy independent and free. Not Unity, but Union, will and must become the watchword of national bodies, severed into desecrated limbs by provisional rivalries, out of which a flock of despots and common servitude arose. To be sure, it will be a noble joy to this your great Republic, to feel that the moral influence of your glorious example has operated in producing this glorious development in mankind's destiny; and I have not the slightest doubt of the efficacy of your example's influence. But there is one thing indispensable to it, without which there is no hope for this happy issue. This indispensable thing is, that the oppressed nations of Europe become the masters of their future, free to regulate their own domestic concerns, and to secure this nothing is wanted but to have that fair play to all, and for all, which you, Sir, in your toast were pleased to pronounce as a right of my nation, alike sanctioned by the law of nations as by the dictates of eternal justice. Without this fair play there is no hope for Europe—no hope of seeing your principle spread. Yours is a happy country, gentlemen. You had more than fair play. You had active, operative aid from Europe in your struggle for independence, which, once achieved, you so wisely used as to become a prodigy of freedom and welfare, and a Book of Life to nations. But we, in Europe—we, unhappily, have no such fair play with us, against every palpitation of Liberty. All despots are united in a common league, and you may be sure despots will never yield to the moral influence of your great example. They hate the very existence of this example. It is the sorrow of their thoughts and the incubus of their dreams. To stop its moral influence abroad, and to check its spreading development at home, is what they wish, instead of yielding to its influence. We will have no fair play. The Cossack already rules, by Louis Napoleon's usurpation, to the very borders of the Atlantic Ocean.

One of your great statesmen—now to my sorrow bound to the sick bed of advanced age—alas, that I am deprived of the advice which his wisdom could have imparted to me—your great statesman told me thirty years ago that Paris was transferred to St. Petersburg. What would he now say, when St. Petersburg is transferred to Paris, and Europe is but an appendix to Russia? Alas! Europe can no longer secure to Europe fair play. Albion only remains. But even Albion casts a sorrowful glance over the waves. Still we will stand our place, sink or swim, live or die. You know the word. It is your own. We will follow it. It will be a bloody path to tread. Despots have conspired against the world. Terror spreads over Europe, and anticipating persecution rules from Paris to Pesth. There is a gloomy silence, like the silence of nature before the terrors of a hurricane. It is a sensible silence, only disturbed by the thousand-fold rattling of muskets by which Napoleon murders the people which gave him a home when he was an exile, and by the groans of new martyrs in Sicily, Milan, Vienna and Pesth. The very sympathy which I met in England, and was expected to meet here, throws my sisters into the dungeons of Austria. Well, God's will be done. The heart may break but duty will be done. We will stand in our place, though to us in Europe there be no fair play. But so much I hope, that no just man on earth can charge me with unbecoming arrogance, when here, on this soil of freedom, I kneel down and raise my prayer to God—" Almighty Father of Humanity, will Thy merciful arm not raise a power on earth to protect the law of nations, when there are so many to violate it?" It is a prayer and nothing else. What would remain to the oppressed if they were not permitted to pray? The rest is in the hand of God.

Gentlemen, I know where I stand. No honor, no encouraging generosity, will make me ever forget where I stand and what is due from me to you. Here my duty is silently to await what you in your wisdom will be pleased to pronounce about that which public opinion knows to be my prayer and my aim, and be it your will to pronounce, or be it your will not to take notice of it, I will understand your will, and bow before it with devotion, love, and gratitude to your generous people, to your glorious land. But one single word, even here, I may be permitted to say, only such a word as may secure me from being misunderstood. I came to the noble-minded people of the United States to claim its generous operative sympathy for the impending struggle of oppressed freedom on the European Continent, and I freely interpreted the hopes and wishes which these oppressed nations entertain, but as to your great Republic, as a State, as a power on earth, I stand before the Statesmen, Senators and Legislators of that Republic, only to ascertain from their wisdom and experience what is their judgment upon a question of national law and international right. I hoped, and now hope, that they will by the foreboding events on the other great continent, feel induced to pronounce in time their vote about that law and those rights, and I hoped and hope that in pronouncing their vote, it will be in the broad principles of international justice, and consonant with their republican institutions and their democratic life.

That is all I know and Europe knows—the immense weight of such a pronunciation from such a place. But never had I the impious wish to try to entangle this great Republic into difficulties inconsistent with its own welfare, its own security, its own interest. I rather repeatedly and earnestly declared that a war on this account by your country is utterly impossible, and a mere phantom. I always declared that the United States remained masters of their actions, and under every circumstance will act as they judge consistent with the supreme duties to themselves. But I said and say that such a declaring of just principles would insure to the nations of Europe fair play in their struggle for freedom and independence, because the declaration of such a power as your Republic will be respected even where it is not liked; and Europe's oppressed nations will feel cheered in resolution, and doubled in strength, to maintain the decision of their American brethren on their own behalf with their own lives. There is an immense power in the idea to be right, when this idea is sanctioned by a nation like yours, and when the foreboding future will become present, there is an immense field for private benevolence, and sympathy upon the basis of the broad principles of international justice pronounced in the sanctuary of your people's collective majority. So much to guard me against misunderstanding.

Sir, I must fervently thank you for the acknowledgment that my country has proved worthy to be free. Yes, gentlemen, I feel proud of my nation's character, heroism, love of freedom and vitality, and I bow with reverential awe before the decree of Providence which placed my country in a position that, without its restoration to independence, there is no possibility for freedom and the independence of nations on the European continent. Even what now in France is about to pass, proves the truth of this. Every disappointed hope with which Europe looked towards France, is a degree more added to the importance of Hungary to the world. Upon our plains were fought the decisive battles for Christendom. There will be fought the decisive battle for the independence of nations, for state rights, for international law, and for democratic liberty. We will live free or die like men; but should my people be doomed to die, it will be the first whose death will not be recorded as a suicide, but as a martyrdom for the world; and future ages will mourn over the sad fate of the Magyar race, doomed to perish, not because in the nineteenth century there was nobody to protect the laws of nature and of nature's God. But I look to the future with confidence and with hope Adversities manifold of a tempest-tossed life, could, of course, not fail to impart a mark of cheerfulness upon my heart, which, if not a source of joy, is at least a guarantee against sanguine illusions. I, for myself, would not want the hope of success for doing what is right to me. The sense of duty would suffice. Therefore, when I hope, it has nothing in common with that desperate instinct of a drowning man, who, half sunk, is still grasping at a straw for help. No; when I hope, there is motive for the hope.

I have a steady faith in principles. I dare say that experience taught me the logic of events, in connection with principles. I have fathomed the entire bottom of this mystery, and was, I perceive, right in my calculations there, about once in my life, I supposed a principle to exist in a certain quarter, where, indeed, no principle proves to exist. It was a horrible mistake, and resulted in a horrible issue. The present condition of Europe is a very consequence of it; but precisely this condition of Europe proves, I did not wantonly suppose a principle to exist there, where I found none would have existed. The consequences could not have failed to arrive as I have contemplated them well. There is a providence in every fact. Without this mistake, the principles of American republicanism would, for a long time yet, find a sterile soil on that continent, where it was considered wisdom to belong to the French school. Now, matters stand thus: That either the Continent of Europe has no future at all, or this future is American Republicanism. And who could believe that three hundred millions of that Continent, which is the mother of civilization, are not to have any future at all? Such a doubt would be almost blasphemy against Providence. But there is a Providence, indeed—a just, a bountiful Providence—I trust, with the piety of my religion in it; I dare say my very humble self was a continual instrument of it. How could I be else in such a condition as I was—born not conspicuous by any prominent abilities? Having nothing in me more than an iron will which nothing can bend, and the consciousness of being right, how could I, under the most arduous circumstances, accomplish many a thing which my sense of honest duty prompted me to understand?

Oh, there is, indeed, a Providence which rules, even in my being here, when four months ago I was yet a prisoner of the league of European despots, in far Asia, and the sympathy which your glorious people honor me with, and the high benefit of the welcome of your Congress, and the honor to be your guest—to be the guest of your great Republic—I, the poor, humble, unpretending exile—is there not a very intelligible manifestation of Providence in it?—the more when I remember that the name of your humble, but thankful guest, is, by the furious rage of the Austrian tyrant, to the gallows nailed. Your generosity is great, and loud your patriotism of republican principles against despotism. I firmly trust to those principles;

and relying upon this very fact of your generosity, I may be permitted to say that that respectable organ of the free press may be mistaken, which announced that I considered my coming hither to be a failure. I confidently trust that the nations of Europe have a future. I am aware that the future is contradicted. Bayonets may support, but afford no chair to sit upon. I trust to the future of my native land, because I know that is worthy to have it; and it is necessary to the destinies of humanity. I trust to the principles of republicanism, whatever be my personal fate. So much I know, that my country will remember you and your glorious land with everlasting gratitude.